CRIMINAL COPYRIGHT

Since the birth of criminal copyright in the nineteenth century, the copyright system has blurred the distinction between civil and criminal infringements. Today, in many jurisdictions, infringement of copyrighted materials can result in punitive fines and even incarceration. In this illuminating book, Eldar Haber analyzes the circumstances, justifications, and ramifications of the criminalization process and tells the story of how a legal right in the private enforcement realm has become over-criminalized. He traces the origins of criminal copyright legislation and follows the movement of copyright criminalization and enforcement on local and global scales. This important work should be read by anyone concerned with the future of copyright and intellectual property in the digital era.

Eldar Haber is a Senior Lecturer at the Faculty of Law, University of Haifa, and a faculty associate at the Berkman-Klein Center for Internet & Society at Harvard University. He teaches and writes about copyright, criminal law, surveillance, privacy and data protection, and civil rights and liberties in the digital age. He has published on all these matters in many flagship law reviews and leading law & technology journals. He has won several academic awards, prizes and grants, and his work is frequently cited in many scholarly articles, book chapters, books, Federal Courts, as well as the media.

Criminal Copyright

ELDAR HABER

Faculty of Law, University of Haifa

CAMBRIDGE
UNIVERSITY PRESS

University Printing House, Cambridge CB2 8BS, United Kingdom

One Liberty Plaza, 20th Floor, New York, NY 10006, USA

477 Williamstown Road, Port Melbourne, VIC 3207, Australia

314–321, 3rd Floor, Plot 3, Splendor Forum, Jasola District Centre, New Delhi – 110025, India

79 Anson Road, #06–04/06, Singapore 079906

Cambridge University Press is part of the University of Cambridge.

It furthers the University's mission by disseminating knowledge in the pursuit of education, learning, and research at the highest international levels of excellence.

www.cambridge.org
Information on this title: www.cambridge.org/9781108416511
DOI: 10.1017/9781108241342

First published 2018

Printed and bound in Great Britain by Clays Ltd, Elcograf S.p.A.

A catalogue record for this publication is available from the British Library.

Library of Congress Cataloging-in-Publication Data
NAMES: Haber, Eldar, 1981– author.
TITLE: Criminal copyright / Eldar Haber, University of Haifa.
DESCRIPTION: Cambridge [UK] ; New York, NY : Cambridge University Press, 2018. | Includes index.
IDENTIFIERS: LCCN 2018003697 | ISBN 9781108416511 (hardback) | ISBN 9781108403917 (pbk.)
SUBJECTS: LCSH: Copyright infringement. | Copyright infringement–Great Britain. | Copyright infringement–United States.
CLASSIFICATION: LCC K1485 .H33 2018 | DDC 345.41/02662–dc23
LC record available at https://lccn.loc.gov/2018003697

ISBN 978-1-108-41651-1 Hardback
ISBN 978-1-108-40391-7 Paperback

For my father, Avi Haber

Contents

Figures

Tables

Preface

Copyright law has always intrigued me, especially when it interacts with digital technology. When almost every work of art can be digitally accessed for free worldwide, how can we ensure that a sufficient incentive will remain to create these works of art? While copyright law was born in the private realm, at one moment in history, several policymakers have opined that criminal law should also come under its enforcement. The digital age has made criminal enforcement even more attractive, as it was extremely difficult for many rights holders to fight against infringers. These so-called copyright wars are now at their peak and will most likely continue to be fought in years to come. What will become of criminal copyright eventually? No one knows for sure. Technology will most likely play a key role in shaping it. But the only way properly to evaluate whether criminal copyright is both just and optimal for rights holders and society is to examine it thoroughly.

This book sets out to tell the story of criminal copyright and to provide such an analysis. To this end it asks several questions: When did criminal copyright make its debut, and why? What are the reasons and justifications behind the movement of copyright criminalization? What is the scope of criminal copyright enforcement, and does it keep up with the rapid pace of criminal copyright legislation? How does criminal copyright align with theories of criminal law and copyright law? And, if criminal law is not the answer to the copyright infringement puzzle in the digital age, what is? These and many other matters will be explored in depth throughout this book.

My book aims to do more than merely contribute to academic research on copyright criminalization. It offers a framework for policymakers and stakeholders to examine whether criminal law is appropriate when copyright legislation is crafted. It further warns against copyright criminalization movements, and largely supports criminalization in rare instances, and then only as an *ultima ratio* – a last resort. It calls for a recalibration of current criminal copyright provisions and an examination of other – non-criminal – measures to address the challenges of copyright infringements in the digital age. The copyright wars are not likely to end soon, but I hope that this book will help to reduce the casualties of current and future battles.

Acknowledgments

This book is the result of intensive research on copyright criminalization, which began as I was nearing the end of writing my LL.M. thesis and continued throughout my work on my doctoral dissertation on this topic and in the years that followed. Throughout this period, I learned a great deal from all my academic endeavors, including, but not limited to, domestic and international colloquiums, workshops, and conferences. I cannot adequately express my gratitude for every intellectual encounter I have had throughout my life, each of which has contributed to my research skills. Specifically, in the context of writing this book, I am extremely grateful to Amit Ashkenazi, Barton Beebe, Yochai Benkler, Asaf Ekshtein, Niva Elkin-Koren, Orit Fishman-Afori, Olga Frishman, Khalid Ghanayim, Asaf Harduf, Alon Harel, Miriam Marcowitz-Bitton, Peter S. Menell, Heesob Nam, Kyung-sin (K. S.) Park, Guy Pessach, Ariel Porat, and Shai Stern. I also wish to thank Michele Manspeizer, Joshua Pens, and Murray Rosovsky for their helpful suggestions, comments, and editorial work, as well as Ori Gorali for research assistance in the final stages of the writing.

Above all, I am deeply indebted to my Ph.D. advisor and mentor, Professor Michael Birnhack, for his insightful guidance, suggestions, and comments, but mainly for his mentoring. This research would not have been the same without Michael's painstaking supervision of my work on my LL.M. thesis and doctoral dissertation. He made me the scholar I am today, and for that I am forever grateful.

I am also deeply indebted to the Zvi-Meitar Center for Advanced Legal Studies and the Law faculty at Tel Aviv University for their generous support of many aspects of the research I conducted, presented throughout this book. The same applies to the Law faculty at the University of Haifa, my home institution, for enabling me to complete my scholarly research on this important topic.

Last, but definitely not least, I am infinitely grateful to Hadar, my wife, for her enormous encouragement in overcoming the difficulties I encountered along the way – and to my parents, who support me always.

It is to my father, Avi Haber, that I dedicate this book, with much appreciation and love.

Introduction

Diego Gómez, a conservation biology student at the University of Quindío in Colombia, decided one day that another researcher's master's thesis could greatly benefit other researchers. Without the author's permission he shared it online with a study group, thereby violating Colombian copyright law. Aside from facing potential civil litigation, Mr. Gómez faced criminal charges. If convicted, he could spend eight years in prison simply for sharing an academic work without permission.[1]

After almost three years of court proceedings in Colombia, Mr. Gómez was eventually acquitted.[2] While ending well for Mr. Gómez, his story sheds light on the potential criminal aspects of copyright law. Individuals in modern society could potentially face substantial prison time for infringing copyright, sometimes even without gaining any direct financial benefit from their actions. In other words, in legal jurisdictions where criminal copyright exists, policymakers made a statement: on meeting a certain criterion, enforcement of copyright infringements should enter the public realm – and more specifically – the criminal law realm. By this approach, under certain circumstances the state is tasked to protect its citizens from copyright infringements.

Whether or not Diego Gómez's actions should be lawful is debatable. On the one hand, sharing content, specifically academic research, could greatly benefit society and enrich individuals' knowledge and perhaps should therefore be permitted by the law. On the other hand, much like almost any copyrighted work, academic research also necessitates incentives (monetary or otherwise) in the form of intellectual property (IP) rights. Beyond potential economic incentives, sharing one's colleagues' master's theses could greatly harm those individuals, especially if they are

---

[1] *See* Kerry Grens, *Student Could Be Jailed for Online Post*, THE SCIENTIST (Aug. 1, 2014), www.the-scientist.com/?articles.view/articleNo/40666/title/Student-Could-Be-Jailed-for-Online-Post.

[2] *See* Kerry Grens, *Grad Student Acquitted in Thesis-Sharing Case*, THE SCIENTIST (May 25, 2017), www.the-scientist.com/?articles.view/articleNo/49514/title/Grad-Student-Acquitted-in-Thesis-Sharing-Case.

aspiring academics. But even if Mr. Gómez should be held accountable for his alleged wrongdoing – without delving into theories that could help determine if criminal law should apply in his case – one feels intuitively that he should not have been treated as a criminal to begin with.

The case of Diego Gómez clearly illustrates how the use of criminal copyright could be absurd. It does not, however, imply that copyright law must remain only civil or even administrative in nature. There are instances where private enforcement is rather limited, and public enforcement should be considered instead. For instance, the operators of online mega platforms that knowingly host and perhaps even encourage individuals to infringe copyright might deserve interference on the state level or even the international level, especially when private enforcement could not prevail. Indeed, in recent years we have witnessed large-scale international operations against the founders and operators of platforms that enabled copyright infringements. Famous examples include Kim Dotcom, founder of the file-hosting service Megaupload, the founders of The Pirate Bay, and Kickass Torrents' alleged owner Artem Vaulin. But even if these cases change our attitude to criminal copyright, it should take more than intuition to decide whether criminal law is the panacea for the copyright infringement puzzle in the digital era.

To understand the digital challenges to copyright protection and the potential use of criminal law as a panacea for infringements, we must first understand copyright law's origins, which trace back to long before the invention of digital technology. Initially, modern copyright law was a matter of civil law. Only in 1862 in the United Kingdom, and in 1897 in the United States, was copyright first criminalized. This was the birth of *criminal copyright*. However, in its infancy, criminal copyright was rather narrow and limited. From its emergence to the 1970s, in both the United Kingdom and the United States, criminal copyright made rare legislative appearances; its scope was limited and was usually applied to specific types of works with relatively light criminal sanctions. However, in the 1970s criminal copyright gained a more dominant role in copyright law. While policymakers extended its scope to additional types of works and raised criminal penalties higher, criminal copyright was only applied to commercial infringement. More recently criminal copyright has become more dominant than ever before: many policymakers have expanded it repeatedly and extensively to cover most types of works and actions and have instituted monetary and nonmonetary sanctions. In some jurisdictions criminal copyright now also covers infringements without commercial gain. In other words, individuals could potentially serve time simply for downloading protected content.

The expansion of criminal copyright to cover most types of works and acts of infringement could potentially mark a paradigm shift in copyright law toward a criminal-oriented legal right, and raises further important questions about the protection of IP in the digital era. What is the scope of the expanding global copyright criminalization trend, and what implications could it carry for end users? What is the scope of criminal enforcement, and is it in line with the wide-ranging criminal copyright legislation? Is criminal copyright justified by copyright and criminalization theories? What are the potential ramifications for day-to-day activities in the online environment and vis-à-vis the development of technology and civil rights and liberties? And what does the future hold for criminal copyright infringement?

Criminal Copyright tells the story of how a legal right deriving from a private commercial interest slowly integrated into the penal system of various jurisdictions by diverse means. It is a story of legislation, regulation, market forces, politics, technology, and society. It is also a story of human behavior and whether it can be shaped by the various modalities that regulate it. The potential paradigm shift to public enforcement of copyright law, more specifically to criminal copyright, must be further explored to understand its historical origins, politics, theoretical background, and justifications; criminal copyright could have huge ramifications for the legal system, technological developments, and society. On a broader, normative scale, telling the story of criminal copyright may further illustrate an important facet of the interface between criminal law and technology.

It is not, however, a story (to date) wholly untold. IP criminalization has been widely researched and explored in the academic literature. Simply to illustrate the academic scope of this matter, some scholars have compared the criminalization process in different types of IP. For example, Irina Manta made an important contribution to the discussion on IP criminalization. She argued that criminal law sanctions the violation of only some forms of IP, such as copyright and trademark, but fails to criminalize patent infringement.[3] Some scholars focused on economic justifications and ramifications: for example, Andrea Wechsler, who discussed the state of economic research in criminal enforcement of IP law;[4] Steven Penney, who explored the impact of digitization on the economics of copyright enforcement and recommends restrained expansion of criminal copyright law;[5] and Jonathan Masur

---

[3] Irina D. Manta, *The Puzzle of Criminal Sanctions for Intellectual Property Infringement*, 24 Harv. J.L. & Tech. 469 (2011). *See also* Grace Pyun, *The 2008 Pro-IP Act: The Inadequacy of the Property Paradigm in Criminal Intellectual Property Law and Its Effect on Prosecutorial Boundaries*, 19 DePaul J. Art Tech. & Intell. Prop. L. 355 (2009); Ronald D. Coenen Jr., Jonathan H. Greenberg & Patrick K. Reisinger, *Intellectual Property Crimes*, 48 Am. Crim. L. Rev. 849 (2011).

[4] Andrea Wechsler, *Criminal Enforcement of Intellectual Property Law: An Economic Approach*, in Criminal Enforcement: A Blessing or a Curse for Intellectual Property? 128 (Christophe Geiger ed., 2012); Robin Andrews, *Copyright Infringement and the Internet: An Economic Analysis of Crime*, 11 B.U. J. Sci. & Tech. L. 256 (2005).

[5] Steven Penney, *Crime, Copyright, and the Digital Age*, in What is a Crime? Criminal Conduct in Contemporary Society 61 (Law Comm'n of Canada ed., 2004); Geraldine Szott Moohr, *Defining Overcriminalization Through Cost-Benefit Analysis: The Example of Criminal Copyright Laws*, 54 Am. U. L. Rev. 783 (2005).

and Christopher Buccafusco, who offered an economic analysis of criminal copyright (and IP) infringement.[6]

In scholarship on criminal copyright specifically, Trotter Hardy proposed an important theory to explain the public attitude, which is based on the *harm principle* in criminal law, and concludes that the public's acceptance of criminal copyright depends on its admission of a "pure" property-like view of infringements.[7] Geraldine Moohr examined criminal copyright through both the *harm principle* and *wrongfulness*.[8] Diane L. Kilpatrick-Lee, in a notable input to the criminal copyright discussion, argued that the basis for criminalizing conduct is twofold: the conduct is morally wrong and a harm is associated with it.[9]

Other scholars have discussed the effects of criminalization on copyright policy and its justifications. For instance, Geraldine Moohr reviewed criminal law theory and copyright principles, suggesting that the result of criminalization of personal use of copyrighted works is inconsistent with copyright policy.[10] Lydia Pallas-Loren discussed the American constitutional compatibility of criminal legislation in copyright and seeks the proper constitutional balance.[11] Eric Goldman analyzed the ramifications of the potential paradigm shift in American criminal copyright legislation through the No Electronic Theft (NET) Act, and offered insights on copyright criminalization.[12]

Much more important scholarship exists on this and related topics, which is set forth throughout this book. The purpose here is to provide, for the first time, a more inclusive analysis of criminal copyright. The book will further develop these and other arguments that have been raised in the literature, while also revealing many untold aspects of copyright criminalization. For a better understanding of the copyright criminalization process, it will analyze the circumstances, ramifications, and justifications of the criminalization process of copyright law. This book will also examine the criminalization process in different countries and from distinct aspects: historical, practical, legal-political, and theoretical.

Chapter 1 outlines distinctions between criminal and civil law on the one hand and public and private enforcement on the other. This discussion serves as an

---

[6] *See* Jonathan S. Masur & Christopher Buccafusco, *Innovation and Incarceration: An Economic Analysis of Criminal Intellectual Property Law*, 87 S. CAL. L. REV. 276, 295–96 (2014).

[7] I. Trotter Hardy, *Criminal Copyright Infringement*, 11 WM. & MARY BILL RTS. J. 305 (2002).

[8] Geraldine S. Moohr, *The Crime of Copyright Infringement and Inquiry Based on Morality, Harm, and Criminal Theory*, 83 B.U. L. REV. 731 (2003).

[9] *See* Diane L. Kilpatrick-Lee, *Criminal Copyright Law: Preventing a Clear Danger to the U.S. Economy or Clearly Preventing the Original Purpose of Copyright Law?*, 14 BALT. INTELL. PROP. L.J. 87 (2005).

[10] Moohr, *supra* note 8.

[11] Lydia Pallas-Loren, *Digitization, Commodification, Criminalization: The Evolution of Criminal Copyright Infringement and the Importance of the Willfulness Requirement*, 77 WASH. U. L.Q. 835 (1999).

[12] Eric Goldman, *A Road to No Warez: The No Electronic Theft Act and Criminal Copyright Infringement*, 82 OR. L. REV. 369 (2003).

introduction to understanding copyright criminalization. To place criminal copyright in its broader context, the chapter proceeds with a discussion of international efforts to criminalize copyright infringements. It reviews, inter alia, the TRIPS Agreement, the Anti-Counterfeiting Trade Agreement (ACTA), and the Trans-Pacific Partnership (TPP), all of which require enhanced criminal IP enforcement. This chapter also extensively reviews the informal pressure to criminalize copyright law in foreign countries through the United States Trade Representative (USTR) "Special 301 Report," issued annually since 1989.

The purpose of this chapter is to lay the foundation for the core argument of the book: that copyright law is in the midst of a criminalization process that could result in a paradigm shift from civil to *criminal copyright*. It will acquaint the reader with the international context for criminal copyright and proper tools to evaluate the movement toward public enforcement models as exemplified by the case studies of the United Kingdom and the United States.

Chapter 2 provides an analysis of the criminalization process in the United Kingdom. Chosen mainly for its past imperial influence over copyright legislation in numerous overseas territories, the United Kingdom serves as an important case study in criminal copyright. Chapter 2 reviews copyright criminalization since its inception in 1862 and well into the twenty-first century. This chapter will show that since 1862, when the United Kingdom introduced criminal copyright for the first time, its scope and sanctions have repeatedly increased. While at first the United Kingdom reserved criminal copyright for unauthorized usage of painting, drawing, or photographs, since 1982 criminal copyright has been repeatedly and widely extended to include additional types of works, new acts of infringement, and higher monetary and nonmonetary sanctions.

Within the historical review, this chapter outlines potential technological and social influences on legislation, and strives to highlight the perceived motives behind such legislative acts. The proclaimed reasons were: (1) a rise in copyright infringements and infringers, due mostly to technological developments, which are not deterred by civil sanctions; (2) national interests; (3) international movement promoting criminal copyright; and (4) political forces.

Chapter 3 analyzes the criminalization process in the United States. This country was chosen for its key role and influence on the formation of contemporary international IP treaties, its global enforcement of IP, and its economic and cultural influence on domestic legislation in several countries. Recognizing various movements that led to copyright criminalization in the United States (including, but not limited to, technological developments), this chapter divides the criminalization process into two separate phases: the *low-tech phase*, at the end of the nineteenth century, and the *high-tech phase*. The latter is further divided into two sub-phases: an *analog phase*, from the beginning of the 1970s until 1992, and a *digital phase*, which began in 1992.

This chapter identifies and analyzes every Congressional Act relating to criminal copyright since its inception in 1897. It shows that during the low-tech phase and the high-tech analog phase criminal copyright mainly targeted large-scale infringers, while the onset of the high-tech digital phase – which still prevails – marked a legislative shift to small-scale infringers. Much like Chapter 2's historical analysis of the United Kingdom, this legislative overview reveals some of the reasons behind the criminalization process: (1) a rise in copyright infringements and infringers, mostly due to technological developments that remained undeterred by civil sanctions; (2) national interests; (3) international movement toward criminal copyright; and (4) political forces.

Chapter 4 examines the hypothesis that copyright is undergoing a paradigm shift toward criminal-oriented law. Essentially, this chapter questions whether the increase in criminal provisions in copyright law leads to the changed perception of the law from a civil-focused to a criminal-oriented law. As our perception of criminal copyright also depends on practice – not solely on legislation – this chapter moves on to review enforcement and practical use of the legislative increase of criminal copyright. I present statistics on filings and prosecution of criminal copyright cases following the initial enactment of criminal copyright in the United Kingdom and the United States to assess whether litigation parallels legislation.

After establishing that the ongoing legislative process of copyright criminalization is not being enforced, or at least not to the extent expected, considering the marked expansion of criminal legislation, I search for possible explanations for what I term the *criminal copyright gap* – namely, the gap between the scope of criminal copyright liability/penalties and the infrequency of prosecution/punishment.[13] Finally, this chapter summarizes the discussion and returns to the questions it has examined: (1) is criminal copyright undergoing a paradigm shift? and (2) what are the possible reasons for and implications of the criminal copyright gap?

Chapter 5 searches for viable explanations for – and examines what led to – the copyright criminalization process, focusing on and classifying internal reasons. It conceptualizes the internal reasoning for copyright criminalization as an important piece of a broader movement of *copyright expansion*. Under this conceptualization I argue that, within copyright law, criminalization is one piece of an ongoing expansion of copyright holders' rights that have gradually increased over the years, especially in recent decades.

First, I briefly review the movement of copyright expansion to give a general background (apart from copyright criminalization) and then locate criminal copyright within the expansion movement. Next, I explore three major reasons for copyright expansion, which are linked to copyright criminalization – the foremost being the negative financial impact on rights holders, which is attributed mainly to the potential (if not actual) increase of copyright infringements. I then explore

---

[13] This chapter builds upon a previous work dealing with the criminal copyright gap in the United States. *See* Eldar Haber, *The Criminal Copyright Gap*, 18 STAN. TECH. L. REV. 247 (2015).

various reasons for this: namely, technological developments combined with globalization, accessibility, and a social norm that favors infringement (without a moral standard that opposes it). I locate criminal copyright within this movement, and argue that the actual and potential harm of copyright infringement has resulted in legislative and non-legislative responses, while criminal copyright is both a preemptive and a reactive measure of copyright infringement.

Second, I discuss the potential shift toward a pure property paradigm, i.e., the transformation of copyright law from a limited set of exclusive rights granted for purposes of market regulation, to a property regime. Under this argument, copyright criminalization is directly linked to copyright's (assumed) paradigmatic change into a property regime by transforming the current (low) protection of copyright into a regime resembling tangible property, inter alia, through criminal sanctions.

Third, I explore rights holders' increasing and effective political influence over legislatures, resulting in criminal legislation. This third reason for copyright expansion is not based on political means only, which rights holders obviously use to advance criminal copyright, but also serves as an important explanation of the process in itself, as public choice theory implies.

Chapter 6 continues to explore the criminalization of copyright law, and adds external, non-copyright explanations to the picture. It examines whether copyright criminalization is also affected by external reasons linked to other global criminalization processes, and if so, to what extent. In this analysis, the chapter locates criminal copyright in three main legal frameworks: first, an *IP framework*, which places copyright criminalization in a broader IP legal framework; second, a *technological framework*, which views copyright criminalization as part of various legal fields now criminalized due to similar technological developments; and third, a *legal framework*, which locates copyright criminalization in the wider context of general criminalization of the law, and covers both the IP and the technological frameworks. I argue that criminal copyright, with its internal dynamic toward criminalization, is at the same time part of other external frameworks that sometimes affect each other, and all of which are part of the general criminalization legal framework. Thus, criminal copyright is a part of both IP and technological frameworks, which in turn are all part of general criminalization movements.

Chapter 7 explores both criminal and copyright law theories to determine whether copyright criminalization complements them. This chapter provides a descriptive analysis of current theories of both criminal and copyright laws. I examine the main theoretical frameworks of criminalization as discussed in the criminalization literature, beginning with single-element approaches, namely the harm principle and/or wrongfulness requirement. After concluding that single-element approaches are insufficient in providing an adequate criminalization theory, I proceed to evaluate multiple-element approaches to criminalization as suggested by Feinberg and further developed by Simester and von Hirsch. Then I review criminalization theories (formulated by Schonsheck and Husak) that are based primarily on *principled* approaches to criminalization. By isolating the main elements that are relevant to copyright criminalization, I suggest an integrated approach to criminalization and prepare the ground for a normative evaluation, which is conducted in Chapter 8. Arguing that any criminalization theory should adapt to criminalized law theories, the chapter goes on to explore the main theories of copyright law. I briefly review copyright's main theoretical frameworks: the *incentive/utilitarian* theory, the *personality* theory, the *labor-desert* theory, and the *users' rights* theory.

Chapter 8 suggests a heuristic for policymakers under the various criminalization approaches, and chiefly evaluates whether copyright criminalization is vindicated. To assess whether copyright criminalization is justified from the perspective of criminal law, this chapter examines copyright criminalization through an integrated approach. I examine it on four consecutive measures: (1) harm and wrongfulness (examined separately or combined); (2) substantial public interest; (3) efficiency of criminalization; and (4) the consequences of criminalization. Satisfaction of the four measures could support criminalizing copyright infringements. However, as this theory integrates different approaches to criminal law, each policymaker should separate the theory's measures and apply only those that accord with its legal system's view of criminal law. Criminal law theories are only one prong of the analysis. A second prong requires that we examine criminal copyright under the main copyright law theories and distinguish infringements for commercial advantage or financial gain from those not for commercial advantage or financial gain, while also separating small-scale from large-scale infringements.

The first measure of the integrated approach examines whether copyright infringement is harmful or wrongful, or both. I argue that copyright infringement can cause various players both financial and social harm, and can therefore potentially satisfy the harm principle requirement. Nevertheless, infringements for commercial advantage or financial gain are not necessarily harmful in the same sense as infringements without such advantage or gain. Accordingly, not every act meets the harm principle requirement. Examining the wrongfulness of copyright infringements – *mala prohibita* conduct (wrong because prohibited) and not *mala in se* conduct (wrong in itself) – leads to the conclusion that infringement could be wrong to some extent, but not necessarily wrong for every type of infringement. Not every act of infringement meets the wrongfulness requirements. Thus, some types of copyright infringements will pass the first measure of evaluation. But it is highly doubtful that all types of infringement will pass all the measures, which indicates that not all types of infringement are justifiably criminalized.

The second measure examines whether the state (or society) has a substantial interest in the statute's objective. This step identifies the interest, determines its legitimacy, and decides whether that interest is substantial. I argue that criminal copyright meets this requirement upon concluding that the state's interest – to protect the creation and dissemination of copyrighted works for both authors' and the public's welfare – is both legitimate and substantial.

The third measure tests whether criminal law will directly advance the substantial interest, and whether it is more efficient than other measures (e.g., civil or administrative law). Under the third measure, policymakers must assess and identify alternatives to criminal law and examine whether they are more efficient. Here I use two different forms of evaluation: an *ex-ante* evaluation, based on an economic analysis of crime, and an *ex-post* evaluation, based on evidence from implementing criminal copyright in the past and evaluating whether the results of such an imposition agree with the efficiency stage requirements. I argue that criminal law can advance the state's interest in some types of infringements (e.g., some large-scale infringements with financial gain), but that criminal law is not necessarily the optimal enforcement mechanism to curtail other forms of infringements (e.g., small-scale infringements without commercial advantage or financial gain).

Finally, the fourth measure examines the consequences of criminalization. This requires that the legislature examine the consequences of imposing criminal law using cost-benefit analysis. Under the fourth measure, criminal copyright is not always justified as the potential drawbacks for some activities support non-criminalization as they outweigh the potential benefits.

Examining criminal copyright through the integrated approach reveals that copyright criminalization is not always justified. Importantly, each legal system's approach to both criminal and copyright law will yield different outcomes. To illustrate, a *natural-right* philosophy of copyright will justify criminalization more than an *incentive/utilitarian* or *users' rights* approach. Moreover, scrutinizing the various types of copyright infringements under the *incentive/utilitarian* approach might lead to different outcomes, depending on the type of infringement. Accordingly, this chapter concludes that copyright criminalization requires careful implementation, and only when the integrated approach supports it.

Chapter 9 discusses criminal copyright in the broader context of the law and technology paradigm. It revisits the main challenges to law enforcement caused by digital technology and distributed networks. It evaluates the future of copyright protection under a rapidly changing technological era that enables faster, cheaper, and wider dissemination of protected works, along with new emerging technologies and social networks that make enforcement and detectability nearly impossible and implausible. This chapter evaluates the potential benefits of public enforcement; it asks whether administrative law should be deployed to challenge infringements, and if so, when.

The purpose of this chapter is to discuss the challenges to the protection of copyright in a rapidly changing digital era and to take a brief look at the future of criminal copyright in this era. While it cautions against the use of criminal copyright as ineffective and unjust in dealing with the many types of infringements online, it offers optimistic suggestions on how to better protect works in the future. Ultimately, Chapter 9 serves as a call to policymakers and stakeholders to reconsider their current criminal copyright laws, recalibrate them, and adhere to other forms of protection that could greatly benefit all of us.

The final chapter summarizes the main arguments of the book, while holding that copyright is undergoing a global criminalization process. Yet, as Chapter 4 shows, the ongoing increase in criminal copyright legislation is rarely applied in practice, resulting in a *criminal copyright gap* between the scope of criminal copyright liability and actual penalties, and infrequent prosecution and punishment. Furthermore, the motivation for criminal copyright is not always known and should therefore be analyzed thoroughly to uncover the broader meaning of the process – a task that my book undertakes. Examining copyright criminalization through criminal and copyright law perspectives leads to the conclusion that copyright criminalization is too broad and not always justified, and that the process has negative ramifications for copyright law, the legal system at large, and society's interests. By this evaluation, I conclude that *criminal copyright* should be revisited and revised to align it with both criminal law and copyright law theories. I propose that policymakers limit criminal copyright to instances supported by the fields of criminal and copyright law alike. Finally, this last chapter warns against over-criminalization of daily activities of end users online, which would endanger the development of new technologies, the improvement of existing ones, and the rights and liberties of individuals in democratic societies.

1

Criminal Copyright Overview

INTRODUCTION

While copyright law could contain both administrative and criminal procedures, infringement of a copyrighted work is primarily treated as a civil wrong since it affects private commercial interests. Emerging in the eighteenth century, modern copyright was initially a matter of civil law and did not contain criminal sanctions. Copyright was first criminalized in 1862 in the United Kingdom. This was the birth of *criminal copyright*. Ever since various countries first introduced criminal copyright there has been a substantial increase in criminal copyright legislation, leading to a criminalization of copyright law, i.e., the expansion of civil copyright laws to criminal laws. The infancy of criminal copyright is long over.

The criminalization process in copyright law is intriguing. What started as minor adjustments to copyright protection via criminal law has expanded tremendously to cover most types of infringements that carry high monetary and non-monetary sanctions. Understanding the depth of this process which occurred in many jurisdictions first requires background from two aspects. The first aspect is that of the key differences between civil and criminal copyright. This chapter provides an overview of the differences between private and public enforcement – mainly criminal vs. civil law – in an outline that will assist in the further evaluation of the reasons for enacting criminal copyright law, as discussed throughout this book.

The second aspect is contextual. Prior to examining two leading test cases of copyright criminalization in local jurisdictions in Chapters 2 and 3, it is crucial to locate criminal copyright in the international context. Accordingly, the second part of this chapter provides a glimpse of criminal copyright in a global context. This glimpse will mainly focus on international treaties and IP conventions that regulate criminal copyright. Naturally, however, the global evaluation of criminal copyright is rather limited here, as a state-by-state scrutiny of criminal copyright is beyond the scope of this – or any book. The intention is therefore more modest: to locate the potential existence of criminal copyright within a global framework for copyright protection. And, as this chapter further shows, this framework, at least on the formal international level, is rather limited in scope. On the informal level, however, criminal copyright seems to play a more dominant role, as reflected in the United States 301 special reports.

I CRIMINAL VS. CIVIL LAW

Analyzing the implementation of criminal provisions into copyright law requires scrutiny of the basic elements and fundamental distinctions between public and private enforcement. Within this dichotomy, it is crucial to understand the main differences between criminal and civil law, which will assist in understanding the meaning of any criminalization process. These fundamental distinctions, which are mostly obvious and discussed at length in academic literature, are important, as they can aid in understanding the legislators' and rights holders' motives in enacting criminal copyright law.

Prior to such general outlining of the criminal-civil debate, a caveat is due: since criminal and civil law systems are different globally, i.e., every legal system could encompass various distinctions between criminal and civil law and could justify imposing criminal sanctions on different grounds,[1] this part merely highlights general features. With that in mind, the general view is that civil, administrative, and criminal law all aim to shape human conduct to benefit society by preventing citizens from doing what is considered bad for society or by compelling them to do what is good for society.[2]

Another caveat for this chapter's analysis is equally due: there is a substantive difference between public and private enforcement which extends far beyond the criminal/civil dichotomy. The potential choice of public enforcement – not bound to the criminal realm – could be proven as a potential solution to copyright infringement,[3] as further discussed and evaluated in Chapter 9. However, as policy-makers thus far usually opt for either criminal or civil law to protect copyright (and administrative law is rarely invoked), it would be more accurate at this point to focus on the general key-distinctions between criminal and civil law.[4] These key-

---

[1] Some legal systems will focus on the notion of potential or actual *harm* to individuals and to society, and/or whether the conduct is inherently immoral and should be criminalized due to its *wrongful nature*. Another legal approach primarily emphasizes the protection of social values, suggesting that criminalizing behavior should mostly rely on identifying an important *protected social interest/value*. For more on the different approaches to criminal law, see Chapter 7.

[2] See WAYNE R. LaFAVE, CRIMINAL LAW 15 (4th ed. 2003).

[3] See Peter S. Menell, *This American Copyright Life: Reflections on Re-equilibrating Copyright for the Internet Age*, 61 J. COPYRIGHT SOC'Y U.S.A. 235, 329 (2013).

[4] As mentioned, these distinctions are generalized and sometimes differ among various legal systems. Comparing general differences between criminal and civil law, for the purpose of this

distinctions are roughly divided into five categories: goals, penalties, procedure, evidence and mental state.

Goals. Criminal law's aim is to protect the public and third-party interests against harm, risks, and/or morally wrong behavior.[5] Society sanctions wrongful acts, because they violate a collective, not merely an individual, interest. On the one hand, sanctions can apply in cases where no direct injury occurs.[6] On the other hand, in civil law, sanctions usually apply to actual harm caused by the wrongdoer to another.[7] Another notable distinction between civil and criminal law is society's moral condemnation of criminal behavior.[8] While society seeks to discourage a breach of a contract, or for this matter an infringement of copyright, these actions do not necessarily carry moral blameworthiness sufficient to merit the condemnation implicit in criminal conviction.[9]

Penalties. Criminal sanctions can include monetary fines that are usually paid to the state, but also punishments, which can curtail the criminal's freedom via, e.g., imprisonment or even capital punishments, and also impose a stigma associated with conviction.[10] In contrast, civil law, such as tort law, mainly aims to restore the loss to the victim at the expense of the injurer, either by mandating a return to the *status quo ante* or by mandating compensation for damage.[11]

Procedure. Criminal and civil law follow different procedures depending on the legal system and specific legislation. Generally speaking, the main procedural difference between the two is the identity of the entity initiating the procedure: In criminal law, the state brings criminal proceedings, while in civil law, the injured

---

book, serves to highlight part of the major consequences of criminalizing a conduct, and the various motivations of legislators and rights holders to enact criminal copyright laws.

[5] Roger Bowles, Michael Faure & Nuno Garoupa, *The Scope of Criminal Law and Criminal Sanctions: An Economic View and Policy Implications*, 35 J.L. & Soc. 389, 391 (2008). Specifically, criminal copyright sanctions are usually "warranted to punish and deter the most egregious violators: repeat and large-scale offenders, organized crime groups, and those whose criminal conduct threatens public health and safety." See U.S. Dep't of Justice, Prosecuting Intellectual Property Crimes 5–6 (3d ed. 2006) [hereinafter Prosecuting IP Crimes], *available at* www.justice.gov/criminal/cybercrime/docs/ipma2006.pdf. *See also* Diane L. Kilpatrick-Lee, *Criminal Copyright Law: Preventing a Clear Danger to the U.S. Economy or Clearly Preventing the Original Purpose of Copyright Law?*, 14 Balt. Intell. Prop. L.J. 87, 95 (2005).

[6] Kenneth Mann, *Punitive Civil Sanctions: The Middle Ground between Civil and Criminal Law*, 101 Yale L.J. 1795, 1806 (1992). I further discuss and analyze "harmfulness" and "wrongfulness" in the context of criminal legislation in Chapters 7 and 8.

[7] *Id.* at 1796. However, civil law can also contain punitive sanctions, which exceed mere compensation. See, e.g., *id.* at 1797–98 (exemplifying punitive civil damages). Regarding copyright law, see, e.g., Kilpatrick-Lee, *supra* note 5, at 95.

[8] *See* LaFave, *supra* note 2, at 15; Paul H. Robinson, *The Criminal-Civil Distinction and the Utility of Desert*, 76 B.U. L. Rev. 201, 205–06 (1996).

[9] Robinson, *supra* note 8, at 206; Mann, *supra* note 6, at 1805.

[10] *See* Bowles, Faure & Garoupa, *supra* note 5, at 392; Mann, *supra* note 6, at 1809.

[11] Robinson, *supra* note 8, at 207; Mann, *supra* note 6, at 1809.

party usually initiates the proceedings.[12] Thus, criminal law relies mostly on public enforcement tempered by prosecutorial discretion.[13] In addition, under specific circumstances and dependent on the charges, some jurisdictions provide a defense attorney for the defendant, whereas in civil law each party is responsible for her own legal representation and legal fees.[14] Another procedural difference between criminal and civil law could be varying lengths of statute of limitations for initiating suits. For example, in the United States, a civil copyright action can be initiated only within three years after the alleged infringement accrued, whereas a criminal copyright proceeding must be commenced within five years after the cause of action.[15]

Evidence. Criminal and civil law differ in their evidentiary rules. For example, criminal procedure is generally more intrusive into individual privacy and corporate domain, and has more compulsory measures over those under investigation than does civil procedure.[16] In addition, criminal law usually has stronger procedural protections, which are designed to avoid false convictions,[17] and requires a higher threshold of proof: while criminal law conviction usually requires proof beyond a reasonable doubt, the burden of proof in civil law is preponderance of evidence or balance of probabilities.[18]

Mental State. A criminal conviction requires proving the mental state of the wrongdoer, i.e., *mens rea* or subjective liability, meaning that, not withholding exceptions,[19] a person will be held criminal liable only for her intended actions.[20]

---

[12] See, for example, in the United States copyright system, 17 U.S.C. § 501(b), which states that the legal or beneficial owner of an exclusive right under a copyright is entitled to institute an action for any infringement of that particular right committed while he or she is its owner (subject to the requirements set in 17 U.S.C. § 411). However, note that the State has standing to bring a civil copyright action in some cases. *See* United States v. Brown, 400 F. Supp. 656 (S.D. Miss. 1975); MELVILLE B. NIMMER & DAVID NIMMER, NIMMER ON COPYRIGHT § 15–6 (2012) [hereinafter NIMMER ON COPYRIGHT].

[13] John C. Coffee, *Paradigms Lost: The Blurring of the Criminal and Civil Law Models – And What Can Be Done about It*, 101 YALE L.J. 1875, 1878 (1992).

[14] *See, e.g.*, in the United States, Gideon v. Wainwright, 372 U.S. 335 (1963).

[15] 17 U.S.C. § 507; Brian T. Yeh, *Intellectual Property Rights Violations: Federal Civil Remedies and Criminal Penalties Related to Copyrights, Trademarks, and Patents*, CRS REPORT FOR CONGRESS 4 (2008).

[16] Mann, *supra* note 6, at 1810.

[17] Wouter P.J. Wils, *Is Criminalization of EU Competition Law the Answer?*, in CRIMINALIZATION OF COMPETITION LAW ENFORCEMENT – ECONOMIC AND LEGAL IMPLICATIONS FOR THE EU MEMBER STATES 60, 62 (Katalin J. Cseres, Maarten-Pieter Schinkel & Floris O. W. Vogelaar eds., 2006).

[18] For example, in the United States, see *In re* Winship, 397 U.S. 358, 368 (1970). For more on civil law's burden of proof, see Neil Orloff & Jery Stedinger, *Framework for Evaluating the Preponderance-of-the-Evidence Standard*, 131 U. PA. L. REV. 1159, 1159 (1983).

[19] Criminal law does not always require actual intent, e.g., negligence and recklessness. *See* Bowles, Faure & Garoupa, *supra* note 5, at 392, 399.

[20] *See* KATARINA SVATIKOVA, ECONOMIC CRITERIA FOR CRIMINALIZATION: OPTIMIZING ENFORCEMENT IN CASE OF ENVIRONMENTAL VIOLATIONS 73 (2012).

Criminal law puts a greater emphasis on subjective awareness as compared to the notion of objective liability and reasonableness in civil law, while the mental element of wrongdoing is only rarely invoked.[21] For example, Unites States copyright law limits criminal charges to willful infringement as opposed to civil copyright litigation that does not.[22]

In general, criminal copyright infringement prosecution differs from civil lawsuits mainly in two ways: a *mens rea* requirement of willfulness and a requirement that the infringement exceed a minimum set value.[23] With that are many possible distinctions, depending on a specific branch of a civil law matter and on the jurisdiction in question. For example, Unites States copyright law possesses unique characteristics: both civil and criminal proceedings require proof that a valid copyright exists and that one or more of the owner's exclusive rights were infringed upon.[24] In both instances, the burden of proof lays with the plaintiff or prosecutor.[25] However, American criminal copyright prosecution requires less formal requirements than civil copyright litigation. On the one hand, in a civil action, registration or preregistration of a domestic work is a necessary requirement to sue for copyright infringement of domestic work and to claim attorney's fees and statutory damages.[26]

---

[21] Coffee, *supra* note 13, at 1878. There are several civil laws that encompass mental element of wrongdoing, e.g., negligence in torts. However, as a general argument and under some exceptions, criminal law requires higher mental element of wrongdoing.

[22] *See* 17 U.S.C. § 506(a)(1); Mann, *supra* note 6, at 1805–06. However, in copyright law, innocence could sometimes reduce statutory damages. *See, e.g.,* in the United States, 17 U.S.C. § 504(c)(2). For more on statutory damages, see Pamela Samuelson & Tara Wheatland, *Statutory Damages in Copyright Law: A Remedy in Need of Reform,* 51 WM. & MARY L. REV. 439 (2009); R. Anthony Reese, *Innocent Infringement in U.S. Copyright Law: A History,* 30 COLUM. J.L. & ARTS 133 (2006).

[23] Aaron M. Bailey, *A Nation of Felons: Napster, the Net Act, and the Criminal Prosecution of File-Sharing,* 50 AM. U. L. REV. 473, 476 (2000).

[24] 17 U.S.C. § 106.

[25] *Id.* §§ 501(a), 506(a).

[26] Attorney's fees and statutory damages cannot be claimed unless the work was registered prior to infringement or within three months of publication. *Registration* in the United States is codified at 17 U.S.C. §§ 408–412. After reviewing the application to register a copyright, if eligible for copyright protection, the Copyright Office grants registration which could be used as a presumptive evidence that the copyright is valid (17 U.S.C. § 410(c)) and recover statutory damages and attorneys' fees in such an action. However, registration is not required for civil or criminal cases involving foreign works, as 17 U.S.C. § 411 only applies to a "United States work" (with the exception of an action brought for a violation of the rights of Attribution and Integrity of a visual art author, set in 17 U.S.C. § 106A(a)). *See* PROSECUTING IP CRIMES, *supra* note 5, at 22. *Preregistration* is codified as 17 U.S.C. § 408(f). The United States Copyright Office defines preregistration as "a service intended for works that have had a history of prerelease infringement. It focuses on the infringement of movies, recorded music, and other copyrighted materials before copyright owners have had the opportunity to market fully their products." To apply for preregistration, the work must be either a motion picture, a sound recording, a musical composition, a literary work being prepared for publication in book form, a computer program (including a videogame), or an advertising/marketing photograph. In addition, the work must be unpublished and in the process of being prepared for commercial distribution (in either physical or digital format, e.g., film copies, CDs, or computer programs to be sold

On the other hand, criminal prosecution does not require registration or preregistration of a work.[27]

In addition, the scope of criminal copyright is usually narrower than civil copyright. In the United States, for example, civil law protects all of the copyright owner's exclusive rights; yet criminal law primarily focuses on distribution and reproduction.[28] Moreover, while civil copyright requires only proving an infringement, criminal copyright sometimes additionally requires the prosecution to prove that it was not an isolated instance.[29]

To sum up, civil law and criminal law vary across many issues, and the choice of legal framework could lead to a different enforcement scheme. In the field of copyright, using criminal law instead of, or along with, civil law can benefit rights holders on multiple levels, which partially explains their campaign for criminalizing copyright, as discussed in Chapter 5. The main benefits are: (1) expanding copyright protection and enforcement means; (2) achieving higher levels of deterrence; (3) reducing civil enforcement and litigation costs – shifting them from the civil

---

online). Preregistration was created in response to the increase in prerelease infringement, in order to provide rights holders a basis for a civil infringement action, although it does not enjoy the same legal protections as registered works. *See generally,* Aaron B. Rabinowitz, *Criminal Prosecution for Copyright Infringement of Unregistered Works: A Bite at an Unripe Apple?,* 49 Santa Clara L. Rev. 793, 794, 798 (2009). Although registration and preregistration are necessary requirements in order to sue for copyright infringement of a domestic work, copyright protection is generally not subject to any formalities. This is due to Article 5(2) of the Berne Convention for the Protection of Literary and Artistic Works, Sept. 9, 1886, as last revised July 24, 1971, 25 U.S.T. 1341, 828 U.N.T.S. 221.

[27] *See* 17 U.S.C. § 411. Note, however, that until 2008, it was unclear whether criminal copyright litigation required preregistration or registration, as the law previously stated that "No action for infringement of the copyright in any work shall be instituted until registration of the copyright claim has been made in accordance with this title." In 2008, Congress clarified that § 411(a) (2006) applies only to civil litigation. *See* Prioritizing Resources and Organization for Intellectual Property Act of 2008, Pub. L. No. 110–403, § 101(a)(2), 122 Stat. 4256 (2008) (codified as amended at 17 U.S.C. § 411(a)). For an example of § 411 uncertainty prior to 2008, see, e.g., Michael Coblenz, *Intellectual Property Crimes,* 9 Alb. L.J. Sci. & Tech. 235, 246 (1999); United States v. Backer, 134 F.2d 533 (2d Cir. 1943) (stating that the term "action" includes a criminal as well as a civil action). On the other hand, see Prosecuting IP Crimes, *supra* note 5, at 22–23. Note that the prima facie from a copyright registration certificate applies equally to civil and criminal actions, as set in § 410(c), which states that "In *any* judicial proceedings the certificate of a registration made before or within five years after first publication of the work shall constitute prima facie evidence of the validity of the copyright and of the facts stated in the certificate" [emphasis added – E. H.]. *See* Nimmer on Copyright, *supra* note 12, at § 15-5. Also, for criticism on criminal prosecutions for infringement of unregistered or preregistered works, see generally, Rabinowitz, *supra* note 26.

[28] *See* Prosecuting IP Crimes, *supra* note 5, at 3.

[29] For example, in the United States, a criminal infringer is currently defined as "any person who infringes a copyright willfully either for purposes of commercial advantage or private financial gain, or by the reproduction or distribution, including by electronic means, during any 180-day period, of one or more copies or phonorecords of one or more copyrighted works, which have a total retail value of more than $1,000." (17 U.S.C. § 506). *See also* Mary J. Saunders, *Criminal Copyright Infringement and the Copyright Felony Act,* 71 Denv. U. L. Rev. 671, 690–91 (1994).

complainant to the criminal justice system and ultimately to taxpayers; (4) reducing litigation time (as criminal cases are usually decided faster than civil dockets); and (5) improving rights holders' reputation, while reducing the possibility of alienating their existing and potential customers.

II INTERNATIONAL COPYRIGHT CRIMINALIZATION

Copyright criminalization occurs worldwide. Simply to exemplify beyond the United States and the United Kingdom, which will be further explored in Chapters 2 and 3, criminal copyright exists in Australia, Brazil, Canada, China, Colombia, France, Germany, India, Israel, Japan, the Republic of Korea, Malaysia, Mexico, Nigeria, the Philippines, Russia, Switzerland, Turkey, Vietnam, among many other jurisdictions.[30] The scope of criminalization, however, could fairly differ between them.

While copyright law is territorial by nature, i.e., each country determines its domestic laws, the growth of international trade and cultural exchanges formed a need to protect copyright globally.[31] As domestic regulation of IP infringement alone could result in "pirated" forms of protected works and in revenue loss, many countries have entered into bilateral and multilateral agreements, including international treaties and IP conventions.[32]

Nevertheless, up until the end of the twentieth century, international treaties and copyright conventions, i.e., the Berne Convention for the Protection of Literary and Artistic Works; the Universal Copyright Convention; and the WIPO Copyright Treaty (WCT), refrained from addressing criminal sanctions.[33] As academic

[30] *See, e.g., Copyright Laws and Regulations 2018*, ICLG, https://iclg.com/practice-areas/copyright-laws-and-regulations#general-chapters (last visited Dec. 1, 2017); Nadine Courmandias, *The Criminalisation of Copyright Infringement in Japan and What This Tells Us about Japan and the Japanese*, 17 ASIA PAC. L. REV. 167 (2009) (reviewing criminal copyright in Japan); Cheng Lim Saw, *The Case for Criminalising Primary Infringements of Copyright– Perspectives from Singapore*, 18 INT'L J.L. INFO. TECH. 95 (2009) (reviewing copyright offenses in Singapore); Asa Jansson & Mary L. Riley, *The White Collar Crime of Intellectual Property Infringement: Criminal Liability in China*, 10 I.C.C.L.R. 47 (1999) (discussing criminal IP provisions in China).

[31] *See* Daniel J. Gervais, *The Internationalization of Intellectual Property: New Challenges from the Very Old and the Very New*, 12 FORDHAM INTELL. PROP. MEDIA & ENT. L.J. 929, 935 (2002).

[32] *See, e.g.*, art. 1717–18 of the North American Free Trade Agreement (NAFTA), which requires "criminal procedures and penalties" to be applied to "copyright piracy on a commercial scale," and "the adoption of effective border control measures to interdict pirated goods" (*North American Free Trade Agreement*, Dec. 17, 1992, Can.-Mex.-U.S., art. 1717–1718, 32 I.L.M. 289 [1993]); PAUL GOLDSTEIN, INTERNATIONAL COPYRIGHT: PRINCIPLES, LAW, AND PRACTICE 52 (2001).

[33] Berne Convention for the Protection of Literary and Artistic Works (1971 Paris text), 24 July 1971, 1161 U.N.T.S. 3; Universal Copyright Convention, Sept. 6, 1952, 6 U.S.T. 2731, T.I.A.S. No. 3324, 216 U.N.T.S. 132, as revised at Paris on July 24, 1971; WIPO Copyright Treaty, Dec. 20, 1996, 36 I.L.M. 65 (1997). Some of these conventions addressed rights enforcement,

literature does not directly refer to the logic of this absence, it seems that until the 1970s, criminalization was rare and has mostly grown since the emergence of the internet. Thus, the first multinational appearance of criminal copyright in the 1994 TRIPS agreement came as no surprise.

A *Agreement on Trade-Related Aspects of Intellectual Property Rights (TRIPS)*

The Agreement on Trade-Related Aspects of Intellectual Property Rights (TRIPS) is a multilateral agreement signed on April 15, 1994,[34] which established minimum standards for the protection and enforcement of IP rights for all members of the World Trade Organization (WTO).[35] The declared objective of the TRIPS agreement is that protecting and enforcing IP rights should contribute to promoting technological innovation and to the transfer and dissemination of technology. In addition, protecting and enforcing IP rights should enrich the mutual advantage of producers and users of technological knowledge in a manner conducive to social and economic welfare and balance rights and obligations.[36]

The TRIPS agreement obligates members to provide for criminal procedures and penalties,[37] which should apply at least in cases of willful commercial copyright

---

but not criminal measures (Articles 13(3) and 15 of the Berne Convention for the Protection of Literary and Artistic Works and Articles 9 and 10 of the Paris Convention for the Protection of Industrial Property). *See also* Henning Grosse Ruse-Khan, *From TRIPS to ACTA: Towards a New "Gold Standard" in* CRIMINAL IP ENFORCEMENT?, MAX PLANCK INSTITUTE FOR INTELLECTUAL PROPERTY COMPETITION TAX LAW RESEARCH PAPER SERIES 2 (2010). In addition, international treaties and conventions on neighboring rights and other forms of IP, also refrained from addressing criminal sanctions. *See* International Convention for the Protection of Performers, Producers of Phonograms and Broadcasting Organizations, Oct. 26, 1961, 496 U.N.T.S. 43; Paris Convention for the Protection of Industrial Property, 20 March 1883, as last revised at Stockholm, 14 July 1967, Art 28, 21 UST 1583, 828 U.N.T.S. 305; Convention for the Protection of Producers of Phonograms Against Unauthorized Duplication of Their Phonograms art. 5, Oct. 29, 1971, 866 U.N.T.S. 72 (This convention could be considered to hold a criminal provision, whereas article 3 provides that each contracting state may implement the Convention by means of penal sanctions); WIPO Performances and Phonograms Treaty, Dec. 20, 1996, 2186 U.N.T.S. 245.

[34] Agreement on Trade-Related Aspects of Intellectual Property Rights, Apr. 15, 1994, Marrakesh Agreement Establishing the World Trade Organization, Annex 1C, 1869 U.N.T.S. 299, 33 I.L.M. 1197 (1994) [hereinafter TRIPS].

[35] For a general review of the TRIPS Agreement negotiations, see Peter K. Yu, *The objectives and principles of the TRIPS Agreement*, 46 HOUS. L. REV. 979 (2009).

[36] *See* TRIPS, art. 7. *See Overview: the TRIPS Agreement*, WTO, www.wto.org/english/tratop_e/trips_e/intel2_e.htm (last visited Dec. 1, 2017).

[37] *See* TRIPS, art. 41.1. However, during the Uruguay Round of Negotiations of TRIPS agreement, the magnitude level of criminal sanctions in intellectual property was inherently different between negotiating states. While some countries, e.g., Japan, proposed a broad criminal statute for intellectual property infringement, other countries, e.g., India, suggested a very narrow criminal section, including only infringements that have harmed the interests of

"piracy."[38] Commercial means "engaged in buying and selling, or pertaining to, or bearing on, buying and selling."[39] Punishment for criminal offenses include imprisonment, monetary fines, or both, sufficient to provide a deterrent consistent with the level of penalties applied to crimes of a corresponding gravity.[40] In addition, TRIPS requires that in appropriate cases, available criminal remedies should also include seizure, forfeiture, and destruction of infringing goods and of dominant materials and mechanisms used in the commission of the offense. Lastly, TRIPS does not obligate, but suggests to, its members to provide for criminal procedures and penalties to be applied in other cases of infringement of IP rights, i.e., apart from trademark counterfeiting and copyright "piracy," in particular when infringements are committed willfully and commercially.[41]

TRIPS also obligates its members to enforce IP rights, although with some limitations; and various articles mandate that member countries provide judicial authorities with sufficient powers.[42] For example, Article 42 obligates the implementation of civil judicial procedures enforcing any intellectual property right covered by TRIPS[43]; Article 44 requires that judicial authorities have the power to issue an injunction blocking imported, pirated goods from entering into national commerce

---

society or that pose a threat to society, and not merely those of a private party. *See* Adam Ainee, *What is 'Commercial Scale'? A Critical Analysis of the WTO Decision in WT/DS362/R*, 33 E.I.P.R. 342, 346 (2011); Christophe Geiger, *The Anti-Counterfeiting Trade Agreement and Criminal Enforcement of Intellectual Property: What Consequences for the European Union?*, MAX PLANCK INSTITUTE FOR INTELLECTUAL PROPERTY & COMPETITION LAW RESEARCH PAPER No. 12–04, at 3 (2012); Enforcement of Trade-Related Intellectual Property Rights: Proposal by Japan, *Negotiating Group on Trade-Related Aspects of Intellectual Property Rights, including Trade in Counterfeit Goods*, GATT Doc MTN.GNG/NG11/W/43 (1989); Negotiating Group on Trade-Related Aspects of Intellectual Property Rights including Trade in Counterfeit Goods, Meeting of Negotiating Group of September 11–13, 1989, GATT Doc MTN.GNG/NG11/15 (1989); Enforcement of Intellectual Property Rights: Submission from Hong Kong, *Negotiating Group on Trade-Related Aspects of Intellectual Property Rights, including Trade in Counterfeit Goods*, GATT Doc MTN.GNG/NG11/W/54 (1989). Also, see generally Timothy P. Trainer, *Intellectual Property Enforcement: A Reality Gap (Insufficient Assistance, Ineffective Implementation)?*, 8 J. MARSHALL REV. INTELL. PROP. L. 47 (2008).

[38] *See* TRIPS, art. 61. The term "Piracy" is defined as "any goods which are copies made without the consent of the rights holder or person duly authorized by the right holder in the country of production and which are made directly or indirectly from an article where the making of that copy would have constituted an infringement of a copyright or a related right under the law of the country of importation." *See* TRIPS, art. 51, n.14. I further discuss the possible meanings of the usage of "piracy" relating to intellectual property infringements in Chapter 5. However, note that the meaning of commercial scale is vague and can be interpreted differently in different jurisdictions. For a thorough analysis of the meaning of commercial scale, see Ainee, *supra* note 37.

[39] Daniel Gervais, *China – Measures Affecting the Protection and Enforcement of Intellectual Property Rights*, 103 AM. J. INT'L L. 549, 552 (2009).

[40] *See* TRIPS, art. 61.

[41] *Id.*

[42] *Id.* art. 41.

[43] *Id.* art. 42. Under this requirement, countries are obliged to allocate resources and change their spending priorities according to external interests. *See* Michael Birnhack, *Trading Copyright:*

immediately after customs clearance[44]; Article 45 provides that judicial authorities
can mandate the infringer to compensate the rights holder for any injuries suffered,
including legal expenses[45]; Article 46 requires members states to provide judicial
authorities the authorization to order the disposal of both goods that infringed
intellectual property rights and materials used to create these goods[46]; Articles
51–60 allow rights holders to work with national customs authorities to temporarily
cease imported goods from being released into national commercial channels, upon
a showing by the rights holders that the goods are "pirated" or counterfeit.[47]

B *The Council of Europe Convention on Cybercrime*

The Council of Europe Convention on Cybercrime ("Cybercrime Convention")[48]
is a multinational agreement that regulates criminal conduct over the internet. This
agreement was opened for signature in November 2001, and came into force on July
2004. Although mainly composed of European Union (EU) members, other non-
EU countries such as Australia, Canada, Israel, Japan, and the United States have
signed and ratified the Convention as well.[49]

While the Cybercrime Convention covers other criminal activities, it does have
specific articles that relate to copyright infringement. Article 10 obliges member
countries to criminalize the infringement of copyright and related rights, as defined
under their domestic law.[50] With that, the Convention also provides limited exceptions for a member country to impose criminal liability – which only arise when
"other effective remedies are available and that such reservation does not derogate
from the Party's international obligations set forth in the international instruments
referred to in paragraphs 1 and 2 of this article."[51] It seems that any member can
enact the "limited circumstances" exception to avoid enacting criminal copyright if
it can argue that other effective remedies are available, and therefore criminal

Global Pressure on Local Culture, in THE DEVELOPMENT AGENDA: GLOBAL INTELLECTUAL
 PROPERTY AND DEVELOPING COUNTRIES 363, 366 (Neil Netanel ed., 2008).

[44] TRIPS, art. 44.
[45] *Id.* art. 45.
[46] *Id.* art. 46.
[47] *Id.* art. 51–60; Agarwal, *supra* note 89, at 796.
[48] Council of Europe, *European Treaty Series* no. 185.
[49] For a full list of member states, see *id.*
[50] Pursuant to the obligations it has undertaken under the Paris Act of 24 July 1971 revising the
 Bern Convention for the Protection of Literary and Artistic Works, TRIPS, the WCT, the
 International Convention for the Protection of Performers, Producers of Phonograms and
 Broadcasting Organisations (Rome Convention), and the WIPO Performances and Phonograms Treaty, with the exception of any moral rights conferred by such conventions, where
 such acts are committed willfully, on a commercial scale and by means of a computer system.
 See European Treaty Series no. 185, Article 10; JONATHAN CLOUGH, PRINCIPLES OF CYBER-
 CRIME 225 (2010).
[51] Council of Europe, *European Treaty Series* no. 185, Article 10.

copyright is unnecessary. Nevertheless, the Cybercrime Convention is another part of the international copyright criminalization movement that potentially influences domestic criminal copyright legislation in many countries, especially in the EU.

C *The Anti-Counterfeiting Trade Agreement (ACTA)*

In 2005, Japan suggested a plural-lateral anti-counterfeiting trade agreement to the *Group of Eight* (G8).[52] Two years later, not long after the adoption of WIPO's Development Agenda, the United States, the EU, and Japan announced their plans to negotiate a plural-lateral Anti-Counterfeiting Trade Agreement (ACTA) outside of the World Intellectual Property Organization (WIPO) and the World Trade Organization (WTO) as a means to establish more stringent standards for enforcing copyright protection than those found in TRIPS.[53] After eleven rounds of deliberations and public criticism,[54] ACTA's final version was approved and signed by the majority of its deliberators thus far.[55]

ACTA intended to complement the TRIPS Agreement by providing effective and appropriate means for enforcing IP rights through enhanced international cooperation and more effective international enforcement.[56] The Agreement's announced

---

[52] *See* Tove Iren S. Gerhardsen, *Japan Proposes New IP Enforcement Treaty*, INTELL. PROP. WATCH (Nov. 15, 2005), www.ip-watch.org/weblog/2005/11/15/japan-proposes-new-ip-enforce ment-treaty; Peter K. Yu, *Six Secret (and now Open) Fears of ACTA*, 64 SMU L. REV. 101, 106 (2011).

[53] Anti-Counterfeiting Trade Agreement, Oct. 1, 2011, 50 I.L.M. 243 [hereinafter ACTA]. *See* Susan K. Sell, *TRIPS was never enough: Vertical Forum Shifting, FTAs, ACTA, and TPP*, 18 J. INTELL. PROP. L. 447, 455 (2011); Margot E. Kaminski, *An Overview and the Evolution of the Anti-Counterfeiting Trade Agreement*, 21 ALB. L.J. SCI. & TECH. 385, 386 (2011). *See also* Emily Ayoob, *The Anti-Counterfeiting Trade Agreement*, 28 CARDOZO ARTS & ENT. L.J. 175, 182–83 (2010); Miriam Bitton, *Rethinking the Anti-Counterfeiting Trade Agreement's Criminal Copyright Enforcement Measures*, 102 J. CRIM. L. & CRIMINOLOGY 67, 102 (2012).

[54] For criticism on ACTA, see Gwen Hinze, *Preliminary Analysis of the Officially Released ACTA Text*, ELECTRONIC FRONTIER FOUND (Apr. 22, 2010), www.eff/org/deeplinks/2010/04/eff-analy sis-officially-released-acta-text.

[55] For a thorough review of deliberation rounds, Peter K. Yu, *ACTA and Its Complex Politics*, 3 WIPO J. 1 (2011); Bitton, *supra* note 53. However, ACTA is highly controversial and problematic and was often criticized as adversely affecting civil rights. For more on ACTA's criticism, see, e.g., Yu, *supra* note 52.

[56] *See* ACTA § 1. ACTA also notes that it desires to combat the proliferation of counterfeit and pirated goods, as well as of services that distribute infringing material, through enhanced international cooperation and more effective international enforcement; to ensure that measures and procedures to enforce intellectual property rights do not themselves become barriers to legitimate trade; to address the problem of infringement of intellectual property rights, including infringement taking place in the digital environment, in particular with respect to copyright or related rights, in a manner that balances the rights and interests of the relevant rights holders, service providers, and users; to promote cooperation between service providers and rights holders to address relevant infringements in the digital environment; and that it will operate in a manner mutually supportive of international enforcement work and cooperation conducted within relevant international organizations.

reasoning for enforcing IP rights is that the proliferation of counterfeit and pirated goods, as well as of services that distribute infringing materials, undermines legitimate trade and sustainable development of the global economy, causes rights holders and legitimate businesses significant financial losses, and, in some cases, provides a new source of revenue for organized crime, as well as posing risks to the public.[57]

ACTA addresses criminal copyright in the criminal enforcement chapter.[58] First, it obliges members to provide for criminal procedures and penalties for copyright "piracy" on a commercial scale,[59] and to treat it as an unlawful activity that is subject to criminal penalties. ACTA allow its members to comply with its obligation relating to import and export of pirated copyright goods, by providing for distribution, sale (or offer for sale) of such goods on a commercial scale as unlawful activities subject to criminal penalties.[60] Second, ACTA obliges its members to create criminal procedures and penalties for willful import and domestic use,[61] in the course of trade and on a commercial scale, of labels or packaging.[62] Third, ACTA requires members to implement criminal procedures and penalties for unauthorized copying of cinematographic works from a performance in a motion picture exhibition facility generally open to the public.[63] Fourth, ACTA calls for the creation of new penalties for aiding and abetting IP infringements.[64] Fifth, ACTA obliges its members to adopt necessary measures, consistent with its legal principles, to establish a liability (perhaps criminal) for specified offenses.[65] Regarding criminal penalties, ACTA also requires its members to provide penalties for criminal offenses that include imprisonment – as well as "sufficiently high" monetary fines.[66]

---

[57] *Id.*

[58] *Id.* § 4. For more on ACTA's criminal provisions, see Ryan Rufo, *Below the Surface of the ACTA: The Dangers that Justify New Criminal Sanctions Against Intellectual Property Infringement*, 39 *AIPLA Q.J.* 511, 513–14 (2011).

[59] ACTA's definition of acts carried out on a commercial scale include "at least those carried out as commercial activities for direct or indirect economic or commercial advantage." *See* ACTA § 23(1).

[60] *Id.* § 23(1).

[61] "A Party may comply with its obligation relating to importation of labels or packaging through its measures concerning distribution." *See id.* § 23(2).

[62] "A Party may comply with its obligations under this paragraph by providing for criminal procedures and penalties to be applied to attempts to commit a trademark offence." *See id.* § 23(2) (which categories labels and packaging as "to which a mark has been applied without authorization which is identical to, or cannot be distinguished from, a trademark registered in its territory and which are intended to be used in the course of trade on goods or in relation to services which are identical to goods or services for which such trademark is registered.").

[63] *Id.* § 23.3.

[64] *Id.* § 23.4 ("[w]ith respect to the offences specified in this Article for which a Party provides criminal procedures and penalties, that Party shall ensure that criminal liability for aiding and abetting is available under its law.").

[65] ACTA notes that "such liability shall be without prejudice to the criminal liability of the natural persons who have committed the criminal offences." *See id.* § 23.5.

[66] The reason, in the words of the agreement is to "provide a deterrent to future acts of infringement, consistently with the level of penalties applied for crimes of a corresponding gravity." *See id.* § 24.

ACTA also obliges its members to grant competent authorities the ability to: (1) seize suspected pirated copyright goods, any related materials, and implements used in the commission of the offense; (2) document relevant evidence and the assets derived from, or obtained directly or indirectly through, the alleged infringing activity[67]; (3) seize and destroy all pirated copyright goods[68]; (4) order the forfeiture or destruction of materials and implements predominantly used in the creation of pirated copyright goods, or at least used in serious offenses, of the assets derived from, or obtained directly or indirectly through, the infringing activity[69]; (5) provide judicial authorities with the power to order the seizure of assets, the value of which corresponds to that of the assets derived from, or obtained directly or indirectly through, the allegedly infringing activity; (6) order the forfeiture of assets, the value of which corresponds to that of the assets derived from, or obtained directly or indirectly through, the infringing activity[70]; and (7) extend criminal (and civil) enforcement to infringing acts in the digital environment, including expeditious remedies to prevent infringement and provide remedies – with the goal of deterring further infringements.[71]

Does ACTA surpass TRIPS criminal provisions? ACTA generally strengthens criminal enforcement through various methods[72]: enforcement is broadened to include "piracy" of copyright-related rights, whereas TRIPS was applied only to trademark counterfeiting and copyright "piracy."[73] The definition of acts carried out on a 'commercial scale' are less flexible than TRIPS: ACTA added trademark labeling and packaging, recording movies in theaters, and aiding and abetting criminal offenses.[74] Finally, ACTA broadens seizure, forfeiture, and destruction of defendant assets provisions, and inserts *ex officio* enforcement.[75]

---

[67] *Id.* § 25.1.

[68] *Id.* § 25.3. Also, ACTA requires that if the goods are not destroyed, the authorities shall ensure that, but for exceptional circumstances, such goods shall be disposed of outside the channels of commerce in such a manner as to avoid causing any harm to the right holder, and that the forfeiture or destruction of such goods shall occur without compensation to the infringer.

[69] The forfeiture or destruction will occur without compensation to the infringer. *See id.* § 25.4.

[70] *Id.* § 25.5. In addition, ACTA obliges its members to provide that its competent authorities may act upon their own initiative begin investigation or legal action with respect to the criminal offenses for which it provided criminal procedures and penalties. *See id.* § 26.

[71] *Id.* § 27.1.

[72] *See* Bitton, *supra* note 53, at 105–09.

[73] ACTA § 23.1; TRIPS, *supra* note 34, art. 61. In addition, the definition of "commercial scale" in ACTA is as acts "carried out as commercial activities for direct or indirect economic or commercial advantage." *See* Bitton, *supra* note 53, at 105.

[74] ACTA § 23.1 Bitton, *supra* note 53, at 108.

[75] Kaminski, *supra* note 53, at 409–10; Bitton, *supra* note 53, at 108.

D *The Trans-Pacific Partnership (TPP)*

The Trans-Pacific Partnership (TPP)[76] was signed on February 4, 2016, between the United States and eleven trading partners in the Asia-Pacific region.[77] In terms of intellectual property enforcement, the TPP obliges member parties to ensure that effective enforcement measures are available under their law, including expeditious remedies to prevent infringements and remedies that constitute a deterrent to future infringements.[78] Enforcement procedures must be "fair and equitable," and shall not be unnecessarily complicated or costly, or entail unreasonable time-limits or unwarranted delays.[79]

As for criminal IP provision, the TPP, much like TRIPS, obliges that parties to the agreement will provide criminal procedures and penalties to be applied at least in cases of willful copyright piracy on a commercial scale.[80] The difference between the two agreements in this respect lies mainly within the definition of commercial scale. The TPP clearly states that "a commercial scale" includes at least: (a) acts carried out for commercial advantage or financial gain; and (b) significant acts, not carried out for commercial advantage or financial gain, that have a substantial prejudicial impact on the interests of the copyright or related rights holder in relation to the marketplace.[81] Thus, the TPP potentially greatly expands the requirements of TRIPS.

The TPP specifically recognizes the need to address the unauthorized copying of a cinematographic work from a performance in a movie theatre that causes significant harm to a right holder, and oblige its parties at a minimum, to adopt or maintain appropriate criminal procedures and penalties. Unlike TRIPS, the TPP also requires criminalization for the aiding and abetting of copyright infringement.[82] Also, it should be noted that the TPP requires parties to provide for criminal procedures and penalties to be applied if any person is found to have engaged willfully and for the purposes of commercial advantage or financial gain for some activities.[83]

---

[76] Trans-Pacific Partnership Agreement, Feb. 4, 2016, *available at* https://ustr.gov/trade-agree ments/free-trade-agreements/trans-pacific-partnership/tpp-full-text.

[77] For an analysis of the TPP, see, e.g., Peter K. Yu, *The Investment-Related Aspects of Intellectual Property Rights*, 66 Am. U. L. Rev. 829 (2017); Sara K. Morgan, *The International Reach of Criminal Copyright Infringement Laws – Can the Founders of The Pirate Bay Be Held Criminally Responsible in the United States for Copyright Infringement Abroad?*, 49 Vand. J. Trasnat'l. L. 553, 571–74 (2016).

[78] TPP, *supra* note 76, art. 18.71, ¶ 1.

[79] *Id.*, art. 18.71, ¶ 3.

[80] *Id.*, art. 18.77, ¶ 1.

[81] *Id.*

[82] *Id.*, art. 18.77, ¶¶ 4, 5.

[83] *Id.*, art. 18.68.

In terms of criminal sanctions, to name a few,[84] parties shall provide "penalties that include sentences of imprisonment as well as monetary fines sufficiently high to provide a deterrent to future acts of infringement, consistent with the level of penalties applied for crimes of a corresponding gravity"[85]; "its judicial authorities have the authority, in determining penalties, to account for the seriousness of the circumstances, which may include circumstances that involve threats to, or effects on, health or safety;" and "its judicial or other competent authorities have the authority to order the seizure of suspected counterfeit trademark goods or pirated copyright goods, any related materials and implements used in the commission of the alleged offence, documentary evidence relevant to the alleged offence and assets derived from, or obtained through the alleged infringing activity."[86]

E *Criminal Copyright in the European Union (EU)*

Currently, there is no single EU copyright act. Instead, the EU has enacted several directives that address copyright – none of which demands criminal copyright. The EU unsuccessfully attempted to insert criminal copyright provisions into two other directives: the Information Society Directive[87] and the Enforcement Directive.[88]

In 2004, the Commission of the European Communities published two "green papers" associating IP infringements with organized crime and proposing enforcement of IP substantive law by each member state.[89] Originally, the proposed directive included criminal penalties, including imprisonment, for an intentional infringement and for commercial IP infringements.[90] However, the final version dealt solely with civil enforcement measures, leaving criminal legislation to the

---

[84] *See id.*, art. 18.77, ¶¶ 6, 7.

[85] *Id.*, art. 18.77, ¶ 6.

[86] *Id.*

[87] Directive 2001/29/EC of the European Parliament and of the Council of 22 May 2001 on the Harmonisation of Certain Aspects of Copyright and Related Rights in the Information Society, 2001 O.J. (L 167).

[88] For a general review on EU copyright law, see Mireille Van Eechoud et al., Harmonizing European Copyright Law: The Challenges of Better Law making (2009).

[89] *See Commission Green Paper on Combating Counterfeiting and Piracy in the Single Market*, COM (1998) 569 final (Oct. 15, 1998), *available at* http://europa.eu/documents/comm/green_papers/pdf/com98_569_en.pdf (last visited Dec. 1, 2017); *Commission Follow-up to the Green Paper on Combating Counterfeiting and Piracy in the Single Market*, COM (2000) 789 final (Nov. 20, 2000), *available at* http://europa.eu/legislation_summaries/fight_against_fraud/fight_against_counterfeiting/l26057_en.htm (last visited Dec. 1, 2017); Directive 2004/48/EC, of the European Parliament and of the Council of 29 April 2004 on the Enforcement of Intellectual Property Rights, 2004 O.J. (L 195) [hereinafter Enforcement Directive]. *See generally*, Benjamin Farrand, *'Piracy. It's a Crime.' – The Criminalisation Process of Digital Copyright Infringement, in* Net Neutrality and other challenges for the future of the Internet 137, 140–41 (Agustí Cerrillo-i-Martínez et al. eds., 2011); Neeraj Agarwal, *Evaluating IPRED2: The Wrong Answer to Counterfeiting and Piracy*, 27 Wis. Int'l L.J. 790 (2010).

[90] *See* Proposal for a Directive of the European Parliament and of the Council on Measures and Procedures to Ensure the Enforcement of Intellectual Property Rights, COM/2003/46, art. 20.

choice of its members.[91] Although in the year 2004, there was no new introduction of any criminal provisions, to some extent, it represents a change in criminal copyright in Europe.[92]

In 2005, the European Commission proposed a directive on criminal measures aimed to ensure the enforcement of IP rights.[93] The European Council stated that: "[A] sufficiently dissuasive set of penalties applicable throughout the Community is needed to make the provisions laid down in that Directive complete," and that:

> Certain criminal provisions need to be harmonised so that counterfeiting and piracy in the internal market can be combated effectively. The Community legislature has the power to take the criminal-law measures that are necessary to guarantee the full effectiveness of the rules it lays down on the protection of intellectual property.[94]

However, after several Member States raised concerns regarding the scope of criminal procedures and penalties, which were broader than international treaties' requirements, the Commission decided to withdraw the proposal.[95] Thus, as the EU has refrained from obligating the implementation of criminal copyright directly, each Member State is free to enact its own domestic legislation.

It would be interesting to follow the development of IP enforcement in the EU in years to come. In 2014, the European Commission adopted a Communication on an Action Plan aiming at renewing the consensus on the enforcement of IP rights, and mainly commercial scale infringements.[96] Subsequently, it would be interesting to follow the new proposal for a Directive on copyright in the Digital Single Market, which currently does not include criminal copyright provisions.[97]

F *Informal Copyright Criminalization in the Global Context*

Although criminal copyright is included in a variety of international agreements, e.g., TRIPS, ACTA and TPP, and might continue to do so soon,[98] it is still relatively

---

[91] *See* Enforcement Directive, *supra* note 89, art. 3(b)-(c) and art. 28.

[92] *See* Farrand, *supra* note 89, at 141.

[93] Amended Proposal for a Directive of the European Parliament and Council on Criminal Measures Aimed at Ensuring the Enforcement of Intellectual Property Rights, COM/2006/0168 final COD 2005/0127.

[94] *See id.*; Farrand, *supra* note 89, at 148.

[95] OJEU, 18 September 2010, 2010/C 252/9; Farrand, *supra* note 89, at 148.

[96] *See* Communication from the Commission to the European Parliament, the Council and the European Economic and Social Committee 'Towards a renewed consensus on the enforcement of Intellectual Property Rights: An EU Action Plan' – COM (2014) 392 final.

[97] *See* Proposal for a Directive of the European Parliament and of the Council on copyright in the Digital Single Market – COM (2016) 593.

[98] For instance, during the writing of this book, another proposed free trade agreement was negotiated among the ten member states of the Association of Southeast Asian Nations and Australia, China, India, Japan, South Korea and New Zealand. This agreement, currently named the Regional Comprehensive Economic Partnership (RCEP), could potentially impact

low in comparison to legislation in the two chosen test cases of the United Kingdom and the United States, as will be shown in the next two chapters. Unlike the attempt to create a unified global civil copyright system, harmonizing criminal and enforcement provisions in domestic copyright laws could be precarious and even unjust, as each domestic criminal system is distinct since criminal law is based on moral and cultural norms of that specific society.[99] Thus, each legislature's perception of what is unlawful behavior, and thus a criminal offense, as well as the various gradients within unlawful behavior, is distinct to each society.

In addition, cultural differences could also lead to disparate criminal sanctions and procedures. For example, some countries impose the death penalty for certain offenses, while others abstain from imposing such sanctions. This reasoning led to compromises in the criminal copyright provisions found in TRIPS.[100] Thus, when implementing any international agreement, members should retain considerable flexibility in applying criminal penalties in their national law. Accordingly, it is highly unlikely that a global criminalization process could exist – at least to the extent that criminal copyright will be fully harmonized worldwide. With that said, international agreements can set a global bar for criminal copyright and advance copyright criminalization to a great extent.

Pressure to enact and amend criminal copyright legislation is not limited to international agreements, and countries can affect domestic measures that influence domestic legislation in foreign countries. Take, for example, the United States influence *via* the United States Trade Representative (USTR) "Special 301 Report." Beginning in 1989, the USTR issues an annual report on the state of intellectual property rights protection and enforcement in American trading partners around world.[101] Special 301 Report, mainly places countries on three lists: Priority Foreign Country (PFC), Priority Watch List (PWL), and a Watch List (WL) – which have implications for US trade sanctions. Hence, classification in any of the lists can cause political pressure on a foreign country due to fear of trade sanctions and thus promote amendments to contemporary legislation or the enactment of new legislation.[102]

---

intellectual enforcement, and criminal copyright within. Currently, the RCEP mostly reaffirms the existing rights and obligations under the TRIPS Agreement, but it also calls for criminal procedures and penalties for unauthorized cam-cording in cinemas. *See* Peter K. Yu, *The RCEP and Trans-Pacific Intellectual Property Norms*, 50 VAND. J. TRASNAT'L. L. 673, 714–16 (2017).

[99] Geiger, *supra* note 37, at 3.

[100] *Id.*

[101] The report is pursuant to Section 182 of the Trade Act of 1974, Pub. L. 93–618, 88 Stat. 2041 (1975), as amended by the Omnibus Trade and Competitiveness Act of 1988, Pub. L. 100–418, 102 Stat. 1107 (1988), and the Uruguay Round Agreements Act of 1994, Pub. L. 103–465, 108 Stat. 4939 (1994), amending 19 U.S.C. § 2411(d)(3). *See, e.g.*, USTR, 2012 *Special 301 Report* (2012), www.ustr.gov/sites/default/files/2012%20Special%20301%20Report_0.pdf.

[102] For more on the political process of the USTR Special 301 Reports, see generally, Birnhack, *supra* note 43.

Reviewing Special 301 Reports (1989–2017)[103] reveals that in the beginning (1989–92), the United States did not consider criminal copyright legislation and enforcement an important measure that other countries should address, thus these reports did not include information on criminal copyright. However, in 1993, the USTR announced that they will conduct an "out-of-cycle" review on Cyprus (labeled WL), since it sought "the lifting of the suspension of criminal penalties for copyright violations."[104] While in 1994 lack of criminal copyright was still not sufficient to negatively brand a country, the USTR placed Panama in a "special mention" category,[105] partially because computer software infringement was "not adequately protected by criminal penalties."[106] Hence, the United States began to use political pressure to criminalize copyright even prior to obligations set in international agreements (e.g., TRIPS).

Since TRIPS, usually with respect to each country's TRIPS implementation obligations (with some exceptions), the Special 301 Reports addressed criminal copyright legislation and enforcement to a great extent, demanding many countries amend their copyright laws and increase criminal enforcement. Between the years 1995–2000, the USTR expanded its criminal copyright requirements to Italy,[107] Russia,[108]

---

[103] The Knowledge Ecology International (KEI) maintains a collection of all the Special 301 reports since 1989. *See The USTR Special 301 Reports, 1989 to 2017,* KNOWLEDGE ECOLOGY INTERNATIONAL, www.keionline.org/ustr/special301 (last visited Dec. 1, 2017).

[104] USTR, *1993 Special 301 Report* 5 (1993), http://keionline.org/sites/default/files/ustr_special301_1993.pdf.

[105] The "special mention" category was designed to "draw attention to areas or concern," while the USTR expected that "these countries will respond to these concerns so that the Administration will not have to take additional steps." Panama was placed on the "special mention" category along with Brazil, Canada, Germany, Honduras, Israel, Paraguay, Russia and Singapore. *See* USTR, *1994 Special 301 Report* (1994), http://keionline.org/sites/default/files/ustr_special301_1994.pdf.

[106] *Id.* at 15.

[107] The USTR added Italy to the WL in 1995, partially because of an "inadequacy of criminal [copyright – E. H.] penalties." In 1998, Italy was elevated to the PWL, because of a failure "to enact effective anti-piracy legislation that includes TRIPS-consistent penalties sufficient to provide a deterrent to piracy and counterfeiting." The USTR noted that they are extremely concerned "because Italy currently has some of the lowest criminal penalties in Europe and one of the highest rates of piracy." *See* USTR, *1995 Special 301 Report* (1995), at 8, http://keionline.org/sites/default/files/ustr_special301_1995.pdf; USTR, *1998 Special 301 Report* (1998), at 13, http://keionline.org/sites/default/files/ustr_special301_1998.pdf; USTR, *1999 Special 301 Report* (1999), www.keionline.org/ustr/1999special301.

[108] The USTR added Russia to the WL in 1996, because of Russia's failure to combat "extensive piracy of U.S. video cassettes, films, music, recordings, books, and computer software." In 1997, Russia was elevated to the PWL. Regarding criminal copyright, the USTR welcomed the new Russian criminal code which "significantly increases criminal penalties for copyright and trademark infringements," but noted that "there are shortcomings in this law that need to be addressed." *See* USTR, *1996 Special 301 Report* (1996), at 15, http://keionline.org/sites/default/

Ireland,[109] Argentina,[110] Ukraine,[111] Peru,[112] Israel,[113] Belarus, Spain, and Brazil.[114] Since 2000, when developing countries were required to implement TRIPS, the USTR greatly increased the number of countries that were put on notice and were required to legislate stricter criminal copyright provisions or to enhance criminal copyright enforcement. For example, since 2000, the following countries (at least once) lacked sufficient criminal copyright provisions and were so included: Algeria, Argentina, Armenia, Azerbaijan, Barbados, Belarus, Belize, Bolivia, Brazil, Brunei Darussalam, Bulgaria, Canada, Chile, China, Colombia, Costa Rica, Croatia, Czech Republic, Dominican Republic, Ecuador, Egypt, Finland, Greece, Guatemala, Hungary, India, Indonesia, Ireland, Israel, Italy, Jamaica, Kazakhstan, Kuwait, Latvia, Lebanon, Malaysia, Mexico, Moldova, Pakistan, Paraguay, Peru, Philippines, Poland, Romania, Russia, Saudi Arabia, Spain, Switzerland, Taiwan, Tajikistan, Thailand, Trinidad and Tobago, Turkey, Turkmenistan, Uruguay, Uzbekistan, Venezuela and Vietnam.[115] Between 2000 and 2017, perceived inadequate criminal copyright legislation lowered many countries from WL to PWL, and even to PFC. Accordingly, the Special 301 Reports became more focused on criminal

---

files/ustr_special301_1996.pdf; USTR, *1997 Special 301 Report* (1997), www.keionline.org/ustr/1997special301.

[109] The USTR added Ireland to the WL in 1997, as it did not fully amend its copyright law to comply with the TRIPS Agreement, and among other things, has "very low criminal penalties which fail to deter piracy, all of which have contributed to high levels of piracy in Ireland." *See* USTR, *1997 Special 301 Report* (1997), www.keionline.org/ustr/1997special301.

[110] In 1998, noting on Argentina, which was already on the PWL, the USTR stated that it is concerned with an amendment to the proposed bill to criminalize software "piracy," which allows for "unlimited reproduction of software by public educational entities, a provision that is clearly incompatible with international agreements." *See* USTR, *1998 Special 301 Report* (1998), at 10, http://keionline.org/sites/default/files/ustr_special301_1998.pdf.

[111] In 1998, the USTR added the Ukraine to the WL, partially because it "does not provide adequate criminal penalties, including prison terms, for piracy, and apparently, no criminal penalties for copyright infringements involving sound recordings, performers, or broadcasters." It later elevated to the PWL and to PFC in 2013, but currently is back to PWL. *See generally, The USTR Special 301 Reports*, *supra* note 103.

[112] In 1999, Peru was elevated to the PWL, as its administrative and criminal avenues for enforcement has inadequacies. *See* USTR, *1999 Special 301 Report* (1999), www.keionline .org/ustr/1999special301.

[113] Israel was added to the PWL in 1998, and remained on that list partially because the Government of Israel did not adopt an "Action Plan" which includes passage of the new copyright bill and stepped up efforts to combat piracy. That action plan should have included, inter alia, the implementation of tough criminal penalties. *See id.*

[114] In 1999, The USTR partially justified the inclusion of Belarus and Spain on the WL, as either they lack criminal penalties for commercial-scale copyright infringement or that the current criminal penalties are insufficient to prove a real deterrent for "piracy." Regarding Brazil, which was already on the WL, the USTR noted that it is concerned "with proposed legal reforms that could reduce criminal penalties for intellectual property crimes and remove police authority to engage in ex officio searches and seizures on their own initiative." *See id.*

[115] *See generally, The USTR Special 301 Reports, 1989 to 2017, supra* note 103.

copyright (and IP) legislation and enforcement, referring to criminal copyright in the evaluation of most countries mentioned in the report.

*

The importance of the probable unilateral effect on copyright criminalization is vast. Political power can shape copyright criminalization not only in domestic legislation, as will be shown throughout this book using examples of United Kingdom and United States criminalization. It can also, in the form of domestic processes in a separate foreign regime measuring foreign states' legislation and enforcement, have repercussions on the criminalization of others' domestic legislation and enforcement. Hence, the Special 301 Reports mark a substantial rise in the importance of criminal copyright legislation and enforcement worldwide and a likely shift toward a criminal copyright regime. If at first, in 1989, criminal copyright was not perceived as an international problem by the USTR, the 2000 report and onwards indicates that this reality had changed dramatically and again emphasizes the important role of politics in copyright criminalization – which I further discuss in Chapter 5.

CONCLUSION

Criminal copyright is mostly domestic in nature. While international agreements address criminal copyright to some extent, these are fairly limited in shaping domestic criminal copyright, at least at a formal level. At an informal level, however, the political pressure to legislate criminal copyright should not be overlooked or underestimated. The example of the Special 301 Reports shows that a pressure to include criminal copyright in domestic legislation exists and that this pressure could be even higher than that of a formal agreement.

This chapter has shown that criminal copyright is almost absent from the international framework. While it exists to some extent, it is usually rather limited and vague, and aside for minimum requirements, it usually leaves states to legislate at their own discretion. But the international aspects of criminal copyright are not equivalent to those of local jurisdictions. As the next two chapters show, copyright law is in the midst of an ongoing criminalization process around the world. To illustrate this argument, Chapters 2 and 3 will present two leading examples of copyright criminalization: first, the United Kingdom, due to its past imperial influence over copyright legislation in overseas territories; second, the United States, due to its key role and influence over the formation of contemporary IP international treaties on domestic legislation in several countries, its global IP enforcement, and its economic and cultural global influence.

2

Copyright Criminalization in the United Kingdom

INTRODUCTION

The 1709 Statute of Anne, the first modern copyright act to be passed in Great Britain, initially only applied throughout Britain, i.e., in England, Wales, and Scotland.[1] In 1800, the kingdoms of Great Britain and Ireland formed the "United Kingdom of Great Britain and Ireland,"[2] extending the Statute of Anne throughout the United Kingdom and to "any Part of the British Dominions from Europe."[3]

Initially, copyright protection in the United Kingdom was divided between imperial and local, colonial legislation. The imperial scope of copyright law in the United Kingdom began in 1814, when the owner of a copyrighted book first published in Britain was able to bring action against any person, in any part of the United Kingdom.[4] By 1842, books published in the United Kingdom by a British resident were entitled to copyright protection throughout the British dominions.[5] Thus, imperial legislation was limited at that time, leaving colonies to pass local copyright legislation, which was excluded from the imperial copyright regime.[6]

---

[1] Wales became part of the Kingdom of England in 1535, prior to the enactment of the Statute of Anne. *See* Lionel Bently, *The "Extraordinary Multiplicity" of Intellectual Property Laws in the British Colonies in the Nineteenth Century*, 12 THEORETICAL INQ. L. 161, 171–72 (2011).

[2] The Union with Ireland Act 1800, 39 & 40 Geo. III, c. 67 (Gr. Brit.); The Act of Union (Ireland) 1800, 40 Geo. III, c. 38 (Ireland).

[3] The Act applied to Ireland, Gibraltar, Minorca and possibly Malta (ceded by the French in 1800, but was officially only British from 1814), i.e., other British dominions and colonies were not subjected to copyright in books (until Copyright Act, 1814, 54 Geo. III, c.56 (U.K.); Copyright Act 1801, 41 Geo. III, c. 107, § 1 (U.K.)). Bently, *supra* note 1, at 171–72.

[4] Act to Amend Several Acts for the Encouragement of Learning 1814, 54 Geo. III, c. 156 (U.K.); Bently, *supra* note 1, at 172–73.

[5] *See* Literary Copyright Act 1842, 5 & 6 Vict., c. 45 (U.K.); Bently, *supra* note 1, at 173.

[6] *See, e.g.*, Act for the Protection of Copy Rights 1832, 2 Will. IV, c. 53 (Lower Can.); Act for Securing Copy Rights 1839, 2 Vict., c. 36 (Nova Scotia); Bently, *supra* note 1, at 176; MICHAEL D. BIRNHACK, COLONIAL COPYRIGHT: INTELLECTUAL PROPERTY IN MANDATE PALESTINE (2012) (describing colonial legislation, while focusing on Mandate Palestine (1917–48)).

Focusing on copyright criminalization in the United Kingdom is essential for understanding the roots of criminal copyright. As evident from its imperial background, the United Kingdom had tremendous influence over copyright legislation in territories that were part of the British Empire and are now independent countries.[7] More closely, the United Kingdom was also the first state in modern society that gave birth to criminal copyright. As further described in this chapter, the birth of criminal copyright occurred in 1862 under the Fine Arts Copyright Act while Parliament provided copyright protection for paintings, drawings, and photographs.[8] As this chapter further shows, copyright criminalization did not stop at its infancy. It expanded rapidly and extensively throughout the centuries, and it is now broader than ever in the United Kingdom.

The objective of this chapter is to describe, review, and summarize the legislative history of criminal copyright in the United Kingdom. While normative evaluations of legislation are limited in this chapter, it will highlight four important aspects of the first layer of the normative evaluation of the criminalization process that continues throughout the book: First, I highlight important characteristics that directly rise from legislation and legislative materials; second, argue that copyright law undergoes a criminalization process, expanding from a civil law to both civil and criminal ones; third, examine whether copyright law is in the midst of a transformation from a civil-based law to a criminal-based law, and whether it marks a paradigm shift or is part of other trends, such as the ongoing shift from targeting large-scale infringers to focusing on end-users' actions; and fourth, assess the direct perceived explanations for criminal copyright legislation, as evident from legislative materials and is developed further in Chapters 5–6, which search for the deeper causes of criminal copyright.

I CRIMINAL COPYRIGHT IN THE UNITED KINGDOM

For more than 150 years – from 1709, when Great Britain passed the first modern copyright, until 1862, when Great Britain introduced criminal copyright for the first time for unauthorized usage of painting, drawing, or photographs – copyright statutes did not include criminal offenses.[9] For the next 120 years, criminal copyright made only three legislative appearances, in 1906, 1911, and 1956, and their penalties

---

[7] For a comprehensive analysis of British copyright law over the period from 1760 through 1911, see Lionel Bently & Brad Sherman, The Making of Modern Intellectual Property Law: The British Experience, 1760–1911 (1999).

[8] *See* Part II.A.

[9] Copyright Act 1709, 8 Ann., c. 19 (Gr. Brit.). Although the Statute of Anne was not the first British statute to deal with copyright, it was the first that Parliament adopted. The Statute was applied only in Britain, and was extended only in 1801, following the union of the two Kingdoms of Great Britain and Ireland. *See generally*, Bently, *supra* note 1, at 171–72; Kevin Garnett et al., Copinger and Skone James on Copyright 13 (16th ed. 2011) [hereinafter Copinger].

were relatively moderate. However, beginning in 1982 and concluding in 2017, for a 35-year period, criminal copyright has extended repeatedly and extensively. In this part, I review the addition of criminal provisions to British copyright law, since it made its first appearance in the Fine Arts Copyright Act of 1862.[10]

While the review of United Kingdom criminalization process is confided to copyright law, it is worth mentioning that neighboring rights, e.g., performers' rights, were also criminalized during this period. United Kingdom first recognized performers' rights, to some extent, in 1925, under the Dramatic and Musical Performers' Protection Act, which provided a criminal fine in respect of the making of recordings of dramatic and musical performances and dealing with such recordings without written consent.[11] This Act was enacted in an attempt to deter a growing practice of making recordings of radio broadcasters of performances for further reproduction and sale, and raised concerns regarding the effect on artists' reputations of the poor quality of such recordings. In 1956, although performers were not protected, the 1956 Act amended the 1925 Act, extending performers' rights into the realm of motion pictures. Between 1958 and 1972, the Dramatic and Musical Performers' Protection Act of 1925 was amended three times: first, in 1958, consolidating and amending the Dramatic and Musical Performers' Protection Act, 1925, and the provisions of the Copyright Act, 1956[12]; second, in 1963, extending the scope of protection set in the 1958 Act.[13] The scope was extended from those who perform dramatic and musical works to "any actors, singers, musicians, dancers or other persons who act, sing, deliver, declaim, play in or otherwise perform literary, dramatic, musical or artistic works." Finally, in 1972, raising the maximum fines set in the 1925 Act, and imprisonment length. Upon conviction on indictment for making a recording of a performance or for dealing with a recording of a performance, the infringer is liable to a two years imprisonment.[14]

Back to direct criminal copyright acts in the United Kingdom, for each legislative act I point to the year the act was enacted, the formal reasons for including criminal copyright (when known), parties who lobbied to advance criminal copyright in the legislation (when known), elements of criminal copyright provisions, and possible ramifications of the act on the ongoing criminalization process.[15]

---

[10] *See* Fine Arts Copyright Act.

[11] Dramatic and Musical Performers' Protection Act 1925, 15 & 16 Geo. V, c. 46. (U.K.).

[12] The Dramatic and Musical Performers Protection Act 1958, 6 & 7 Eliz. 2, c. 44 (U.K.).

[13] Performer's Protection Act 1963, c. 53 (U.K.).

[14] For more on this matter, see COPINGER, *supra* note 9, at 47, 1251; Musical Performers' Prot. Ass'n v. British Int'l Pictures, Ltd., (1930) 46 T.L.R. 485 (K.B.) (holding that the Act of 1925 did not intend to give the performers any right of property in their works); Walter L. Pforzheimer, *Copyright Protection for the Performing Artist in His Interpretative Rendition*, 1 COPYRIGHT L. SYMP. 14 (1939).

[15] It is important to note that until 1911, copyright protection was regulated in numerous acts, each regulating another aspect of copyrighted works trading. For example, the 1814 Act applied only to books; the 1862 Act applied only to paintings, drawings, and photographs. *See* Act to Amend

A *Fine Arts Copyright Act of 1862*

In 1862, Parliament introduced the Fine Arts Copyright Act to provide copyright protection for paintings, drawings, and photographs.[16] The Society for the Encouragement of the Arts, Manufactures and Commerce lobbied for its enactment and argued that current laws concerning copyright of artistic works should be revised and expanded.[17] The Court's interpretation of the Act was that it imposed criminal sanctions, through national, rather than, imperial legislation, while allowing for the first time copyright protection for artists of paintings, drawings, and photographs in the United Kingdom.[18] The Act included a criminal offense for the unauthorized usage of a copyrighted painting, drawing, or photograph, and was liable to a fine not exceeding ten pounds or double the full price of the work, in addition to its forfeiture.[19]

Thus, while 1862 marks the birth of criminal copyright in the United Kingdom, criminalization was not extensive: The Fine Arts Copyright Act limited criminal copyright to certain types of works and set relatively low criminal sanctions, while excluding imprisonment. Still, as I further discuss in this chapter, the 1862 Act demonstrates the first glimpse of the potential power of the copyright-related industries in copyright criminalization. Furthermore, as history teaches us, the 1862 Act was a harbinger of criminal copyright not merely in the United Kingdom, but worldwide.

B *Musical Copyright Act of 1906*

The first imprisonment provision for criminal copyright infringement was introduced in the Musical Copyright Act of 1906,[20] which amended the Musical Copyright Act of 1902.[21] The 1906 Act was directed against "pirated" copies of musical works and was enacted due to a growing practice of illegal sales of music

---

Several Acts for the Encouragement of Learning; Fine Arts Copyright Act 1862, 25 & 26 Vict., c. 68 (U.K.).

[16] Fine Arts Copyright Act. *See generally,* Ronan Deazley, *Commentary on Fine Arts Copyright Act 1862, in* PRIMARY SOURCES ON COPYRIGHT (1450–1900) (2008) (Lionel Bently & Martin Kretschmer eds., 2008), http://copy.law.cam.ac.uk/cam/tools/request/showRecord?id=commen tary_uk_1862 (commentating on the 1862 Act).

[17] *See generally,* Deazley, *supra* note 16.

[18] *See In re* Prince Ex parte Graves (1868) L.R. 3 Ch. 642 (CA); COPINGER, *supra* note 9, at 1249 (referring to Ex parte Graves, In re prince (1868) L.R. 3 Ch. 642); Isabella Alexander, *Criminalising Copyright: A Story of Publishers, Pirates, and Pieces of Eight,* 66 CAMBRIDGE L.J. 625, 631 n.33 (2007); Bently, *supra* note 1, at 178.

[19] Fine Arts Copyright Act §§ 6–8.

[20] Musical Copyright Act of 1906, 6 Edw. VII, c. 36 (U.K.).

[21] Musical Copyright Act of 1902, 2 Edw. VII, c. 15 (U.K.).

sheets at very low prices.[22] The Act provided that printing, reproducing, selling, exposing, offering, or possessing for the purpose of selling "pirated" copies of musical works, or possessing plates for the purpose of printing or reproducing pirated copies of musical works, was punishable by a fine up to five pounds.[23] Second-time or subsequent offenders could be sentenced to a maximum of two months in prison or fined up to ten pounds.[24]

Thus, in 1906, Parliament extended the scope of criminal copyright to musical works and extended the types of punishments infringers could receive: criminal copyright now included imprisonment. Moreover, the reason behind the criminal copyright insertion in 1906, was based on the possible deterrent effect of the criminal law, hoping that it was sufficient to deter infringers. As further showed, deterrence played, and still plays, an important role in many of the United Kingdom's criminal copyright legislation.

C *Copyright Act 1911*

Parliament enacted the 1911 Copyright Act, which also contained criminal copyright sanctions, in an Act to establish unified copyright law in the British Empire.[25] While it was not linked to any particular industry or lobbying specifically, it is evident that authors and publishers in the United Kingdom pressured for a copyright reform because of a growing practice of infringement of English language works.[26] The 1911 Act had an imperial, hence global, dimension, as it introduced and shaped copyright law into protectorates and also mandates after World War I,[27] but it was applied mostly to crown colonies and self-governing dominions. British colonies were bound by its terms but were able to make local variations if they considered them necessary – subject to London's approval.[28] The 1911 Act was also implemented, although not mandated, in the self-governing dominions; dominions that

---

[22] *See* COPINGER, *supra* note 9, at 1250; HL Deb 14 March 1902 vol. 105 cc4–8 (U.K.) ("I rise to call attention to the serious loss inflicted upon copyright holders of music by the illegal sale in the streets and elsewhere of copyright music by hawkers, and to the impracticability of their obtaining redress under the existing law.").

[23] Musical Copyright Act of 1906 § 3. The term "pirated" was originally used, and referred to "any copies of any musical work written, printed, or otherwise reproduced without the consent lawfully given by the owner of the copyright in such musical work." The expression "plates" includes any stereotype or other plates, stones, matrices, transfers, or negatives used or intended to be used for printing or making copies of any musical work.

[24] Musical Copyright Act of 1906 § 1(1).

[25] Copyright Act, 1911, 1 & 2 Geo. V, c. 46 (U.K.). For an overview of copyright law in the British colonies during the nineteenth and the beginning of the twentieth centuries, see Bently, *supra* note 1.

[26] *See* Uma Suthersanen, *The First Global Copyright Act*, *in* A SHIFTING EMPIRE: 100 YEARS OF THE COPYRIGHT ACT 1911 1, 28 (Uma Suthersanen & Ysolde Gendreau eds., 2013).

[27] *See*, *e.g.*, Copyright Act, 1911 (Extension to Palestine) Order, 1924, 114 Official Gazette 643 (Palestine).

[28] Bently, *supra* note 1, at 190.

wished to implement the legislation required London's approval.[29] Thus, criminal copyright sanctions were not limited to the United Kingdom and had a global impact on copyright law.

Under the 1911 Act, Parliament introduced new criminal provisions that were dependent upon the category of infringement: for example, provisions were for commercial (or commercial-like) activities,[30] but not for non-commercial direct activities.[31] The Act criminalized knowingly infringing a copyright, by either selling or hiring, exhibiting in public, distributing or importing for sale or hire – and was punishable by a fine up to 40 shillings for every copy, but not to exceed fifty pounds for the entire transaction.[32] A second or subsequent offense was punishable by imprisonment, with or without hard labor, with a maximum sentence of two months. An additional criminal provision was knowingly copying, making, or possessing any plate for the purpose of making an infringing copy of a copyrighted work or knowingly causing a public, for-profit performance without consent. This offense was also punishable by fine (which was not to exceed fifty pounds), and in case of a second or subsequent offense, imprisonment with or without hard labor, for a term not exceeding two months.[33]

The 1911 Act was of crucial importance due to its then-imperial, now-global, scope; its criminal sanctioning of all types of infringements; and for focusing on commercial infringement. Sanctions included fines, imprisonment, or hard labor. Since this Act, however, criminal copyright took a rest for a relatively long period. With minor changes in the 1956 Act regarding criminal copyright, major changes came only seventy-one years later in 1982. Since then, as further described, criminal copyright took a turn.

D Copyright Act 1956

Prior to delving into the rapid changes that occurred in the United Kingdom in since the 1980s, it is important to note that criminal copyright was affected also by the copyright revision of 1956. The 1956 Act was enacted due to a perceived inadequacy of the 1911 Act – particularly due to advanced technological and societal changes.[34] It repealed the 1911 Act, and other copyright legislation; it also contained criminal legislation, but its geographic scope was more limited than before. The

---

[29] *See, e.g.,* Copyright Act, 1912 (Cth) (Austl.); Act Respecting Copyright, 1912 (Newfoundland); Copyright Act, 1913 (N.Z.); Patents, Designs, Trade Marks and Copyright Act, No. 9 of 1916, § 143 (S. Africa); Bently, *supra* note 1, at 191.
[30] Most criminal copyright infringements dealt with commercial activities, with one exception set in the distribution of infringing copies.
[31] Copyright Act, 1911, 1 & 2 Geo. V, c. 46, § 11 (U.K.).
[32] *Id.* § 11(1). Criminal distribution of infringing copies was not only limited to purposes of trade, but rather also applied on distribution to an extent as to "affect prejudicially the owner of the copyright." *Id.* § 11(1)(c).
[33] *Id.* § 11(2).
[34] Copyright Act, 1956, 4 & 5 Eliz. II, c. 74 (U.K.). *See* JOHN FEATHER, PUBLISHING, PIRACY AND POLITICS: AN HISTORICAL STUDY OF COPYRIGHT IN BRITAIN 7 (1994) (reviewing copyright legislation in the United Kingdom).

Gregory Committee was involved in its legislation,[35] but industry representatives were not directly linked to its enactment. However, interested parties played an important role in the 1956 Act provisions as they lobbied for the conversion of the Gregory Committee recommendations into the 1956 Act.[36] More specifically, Parliament expanded the criminal scope of public performance to literary, dramatic, or musical copyrighted work. Hence, criminalization applied not only to secondary commercial (or commercial-like) infringements,[37] but rather also tied to direct activities.[38]

E Copyright Act 1956 (Amendment) Act 1982 and Copyright (Amendment) Act 1983

In 1982 and 1983, Parliament introduced two amendments in response to concerns of "piracy" of sound recordings and cinematograph films.[39] The Copyright Act 1956 (Amendment) Act of 1982 criminalized the possession or trading of an infringing copy of a sound recording or a cinematograph film.[40] The Copyright (Amendment) Act of 1983 introduced a fine of up to the statutory maximum, or up to two years imprisonment, or both, for the offense of making for sale, hire, import, and distribution of infringing copies of cinematograph films or sound recordings.[41]

The year 1982 marks a change in United Kingdom copyright criminalization. Although prior to 1982, technology played a (limited) role in copyright legislation, it was not directly linked to criminalization justifications. The 1982 and 1983 amendments were a direct response to technological developments that made infringing faster, easier, and cheaper than ever before. Hence, criminalization was a responsive measure to technology. However, the 1982 and 1983 amendments, much like the 1911 Act, only criminalized commercial (or commercial-like) activities and still did not address non-commercial activities.

---

[35] BOARD OF TRADE, REPORT OF THE COPYRIGHT COMMITTEE, 1952, Cmnd. 8662 (U.K.).
[36] Lionel Bently, R. v. The Author: From Death Penalty to Community Service, 32 COLUM. J.L. & ARTS 1, 34–35 (2008).
[37] With one exception set in the distribution of infringing copies for purposes to such an extent as to affect prejudicially the owner of the copyright. Copyright Act 1956, § 21(2)(b).
[38] Copyright Act 1956, 4 & 5 Eliz. II, c. 74, § 21 (U.K.) (repeal the Copyright Act 1911, 1 & 2 Geo. V. c. 46 (U.K.) (except sections 15, 34 and 37); The Fine Arts Copyright Act, 1862, 25 & 26 Vict., c. 68 (U.K.); The Musical (Summary Proceedings) Copyright Act, 1902, 2 Edw. VII, c. 15 (U.K.); The Musical Copyright Act, 1906, 6 Edw. VII, c. 36 (U.K.); The Copyright Order Confirmation (Mechanical Instruments: Royalties) Act 1928, 18 & 19 Geo. V, c. 3 (U.K.); The Ceylon Independence Act 1947, 11 & 12 Geo. 6, c. 7 (U.K.). See COPINGER, supra note 9, at 47.
[39] See HL Deb 04 May 1982 vol. 429 cc1050–1 (U.K.) ("This Bill in its amended form will, hopefully, cure the mischief of the piracy of sound recordings and cinematograph films which is now assuming alarming proportions"); Bently, supra note 36, at 11.
[40] See Copyright Act 1956 (Amendment) Act 1982, c. 35 (U.K.).
[41] See Copyright (Amendment) Act 1983, c. 42 (U.K.). The statutory maximum was set in the Criminal Justice Act 1982, c. 48 (U.K.).

F *Copyright (Computer Software) Amendment Act 1985*

In 1985, Parliament introduced the Copyright (Computer Software) Amendment Act.[42] The Act was a result of the software industry's concerns that the contemporary civil remedies were ineffective for deterring the frequently, easily-"pirated" computer software – causing an estimated annual loss of £150 million.[43] Accordingly, F.A.S.T. (Federation Against Software Theft) lobbied for the first proposed private members' bill advocating the strengthening of copyright law with respect to computer software, including augmenting criminal provisions.[44] Parliament added computer programs to the classification of literary works, while raising the maximum criminal penalty applicable to computer program infringement – equal to those previously set for sound recordings and cinematograph film infringements.[45]

Much like the 1982 and 1983 amendments, the 1985 Act was enacted because of technological changes and rights holders' perceived need for deterrence. Criminal copyright in 1985 was a responsive measure to digital technology, but much like the 1982 and 1983 amendments, the 1985 Act addressed commercial (or commercial-like) activities,[46] and not non-commercial, direct activities.

G *Copyright, Designs and Patents Act 1988*

In 1988, Parliament repealed the 1956 Act, by enacting the Copyright, Designs and Patents Act (CDPA).[47] Copyright expansion under the CDPA was a direct attempt to "stamp out piracy" and counterfeiting,[48] and was lobbied for by various interest groups and organizations, e.g., F.A.S.T.[49]

---

[42] Copyright (Computer Software) Amendment Act 1985, c. 41 (U.K.).

[43] *See* David I. Bainbridge, *Copyright (Computer Software) Amendment Act (1985)*, 49 MOD. L. REV. 214, 214 (1986).

[44] *Id.*

[45] *See* Copyright (Computer Software) Amendment Act 1985 § 1(1) ("The Copyright Act 1956 shall apply in relation to a computer program (including one made before the commencement of this Act) as it applies in relation to a literary work and shall so apply whether or not copyright would subsist in that program apart from this Act," and § 3: "[w]here an infringing copy of a computer program consists of a disc, tape or chip or of any other device which embodies signals serving for the impartation of the program or part of it, sections 21 to 21B of the Copyright Act 1956 (offences and search warrants) shall apply in relation to that copy as they apply in relation to an infringing copy of a sound recording or cinematograph film."). Bainbridge, *supra* note 43, at 220.

[46] *See supra* note 37.

[47] Copyright, Designs and Patents Act 1988, c. 48 (U.K.) [hereinafter CDPA].

[48] *See* Michael Hart, *Infringement and Remedies under the Copyright, Designs and Patents Act 1988*, 11 E.I.P.R. 113 (1989).

[49] *See* Federation Against Software Theft, *Submission to the Inquiry by the All-Party Parliamentary Group: Has Gowers Helped or Hindered Enforcement of IP Rights?* (2008), www.allpartyipgroup.org.uk/pdfs/FAST%20Response%20to%20All%20Party%20IP%20inquiry.pdf.

The official reason for enacting the CDPA was the need to:[50]

> [R]estate the law of copyright, with amendments; to make fresh provision as to the rights of performers and others in performances; to confer a design right in original designs; to amend the Registered Designs Act 1949; to make provision with respect to patent agents and trade mark agents; to confer patents and designs jurisdiction on certain county courts; to amend the law of patents; to make provision with respect to devices designed to circumvent copy-protection of works in electronic form; to make fresh provision penalizing the fraudulent reception of transmissions; to make the fraudulent application or use of a trade mark an offence; to make provision for the benefit of the Hospital for Sick Children, Great Ormond Street, London; to enable financial assistance to be given to certain international bodies; and for connected purposes.

The CDPA extensively expanded criminal copyright liability and penalties, in order to increase deterrence of sound recordings, films, and computer programs infringement.[51]

The expansion took various forms. First, the Act expanded the criminal copyright offense to include the possession of an infringing copy of a copyright work in the course of business, with a view to committing an infringing act.[52] Second, the CDPA introduced a provision of making or possessing an article specifically designed or adapted for making copies of a particular copyright work.[53] Third, the CDPA fixed an anomaly that existed prior to its enactment – which criminalized the public performance of a literary, dramatic, or musical work without consent – adding public playing or showing of films or sound recordings.[54] Fourth, the Act loosened the *mens rea* requirement, by changing the test of relevant knowledge from "actual knowledge" to "a reason to believe" that the subject case is an infringing copy of a copyright work.[55] Finally, the CDPA exposed directors and officers of companies to personal criminal liability under certain circumstances.[56]

Essentially, the CDPA extended the scope of criminal penalties for trading or infringing copies to cover all types of copyright works.[57] Under the Act, the penalty for these actions was imprisonment for a term not exceeding six months and/or a fine not exceeding the statutory maximum. For a conviction of an indictable

---

[50] *See* CDPA.
[51] *See* COPINGER, *supra* note 9, at 1252.
[52] CDPA § 107(1)(c).
[53] *Id.* § 107(2).
[54] *See* Hart, *supra* note 48, at 117; CDPA § 107(3).
[55] *See* Hart, *supra* note 48, at 117; CDPA § 107(e).
[56] *See* Hart, *supra* note 48, at 117; CDPA § 110.
[57] CDPA § 107(4). However, in the course of business, possessing an infringing copy – or selling, hiring, or exhibiting an infringing copy – are only summary offenses. *See* Hart, *supra* note 48, at 118.

offense, the penalties were set to a fine and/or imprisonment for a term not exceeding two years.[58]

The CDPA also introduced criminal liability for commercially making, trading, or using illicit recordings.[59] Section 198 introduced an offense for making for sale or hire, importing into the United Kingdom otherwise than for private and domestic use or possessing in the course of a business, an illicit recording, without sufficient consent. Moreover, Section 198 set an offense for showing or playing a performance, without sufficient consent, in public broadcast or in a cable program service.[60]

A summary conviction for making, dealing with, or using illicit recordings brought imprisonment for a term not exceeding six months and/or a fine not exceeding the statutory maximum. An offender convicted of an indictable offense for making, dealing with, or using illicit recordings, can be fined and/or imprisoned for a term not exceeding two years. Any person guilty of any other offense under Section 198, will be liable for a summary conviction and a fine not exceeding level five on the standard scale or imprisonment for a term not exceeding six months, or both.[61]

In other words, copyright criminalization continued in 1988, when Parliament expanded the types of copyright infringing activities and the scope of criminal infringement. Mainly, the CDPA expanded the provisions of the 1982 and 1983 amendments, which only applied to sound recording and films, to all other works. In addition, the CDPA marks perhaps the most extensive responsive measure to the perceived problem of "piracy," which was linked to technological developments. Expanded criminal copyright under this Act marks the perceived linkage of "piracy" to criminal copyright as a possible deterrent.

H *Copyright, etc. and Trade Marks (Offences and Enforcement) Act 2002*

In 2002, Parliament enacted the Copyright, etc. and Trade Marks (Offences and Enforcement) Act.[62] Lobbied for by various interest groups, such as the Alliance Against Counterfeiting and Piracy,[63] the private bill was proposed as a means to

---

[58] See CDPA § 107(4)(b). In addition, the CDPA also changed criminal procedures to some extent. While under the 1956 Act, ordering delivery-up of the infringing copy or an article specifically designed or adapted for making infringing copies only applied to infringing copies or plates in the person's actual possession, the 1988 Act extended this to items within the person's possession, custody or control. In addition, the 1988 Act extended the power to obtain search warrants that deal with criminal offenses to cover all copyright works. See CDPA §§ 109, 113(4); Hart, *supra* note 48, at 118.

[59] CDPA § 198; Note that this section has been restructured into The Performances (Moral Rights, etc.) Regulations, 2006, S.I. 2006/18 (U.K.).

[60] CDPA §§ 198(1)–(2).

[61] *Id.* §§ 198(5)(a)–(b), 198(6).

[62] Copyright, etc. and Trade Marks (Offences and Enforcement) Act 2002, c. 25 (U.K.).

[63] See *Alliance Success in Private Members' Ballot – Vincent Cable*, ALLIANCE FOR INTELLECTUAL PROPERTY (Aug. 10, 2001), www.allianceagainstiptheft.co.uk/news/10_aug_01.htm.

harmonize the copyright and trademark regimes. These groups had perceived that the offenses under the CDPA were insufficient to serve as a deterrent and had brought organized crime into the field.[64] Regarding criminal copyright, the Act increased the penalty for making or trading infringing articles and for making, trading, or using illicit recordings, from a two-year maximum tariff to ten years.[65]

The possibility of a ten-year imprisonment term marks a huge step in criminal copyright penalties in the United Kingdom. In addition, unlike most criminal copyright acts in the United Kingdom, the 2002 criminalization was attributed to an assumed linkage between copyright and other criminal activities. Notably, however, the 2002 amendment did not apply to online infringement, thus creating a gap between physical and digital infringement of copyrighted works.

I Copyright and Related Rights Regulations 2003

In 2003, the Secretary of State exercised her power to issue specific regulations to amend the Copyright Designs and Patents Act of 1988. The Secretary passed the 2003 Regulations in part to implement the European Copyright in the Information Society Directive, which followed the EU's implementation of the WIPO Copyright Treaty (WCT).[66] The criminal provisions were a result of a broad interpretation of Article 8 of the Information Society Directive that required the implementation of "appropriate sanctions and remedies."[67]

Regarding criminal copyright, the regulations included two new criminal offenses. The first was knowingly infringing upon a copyrighted work by communicating it to the public in the course of a business or to such an extent as to prejudicially affect the copyright owner.[68] This offender was liable on summary conviction to imprisonment for a term not exceeding three months or a fine not exceeding the statutory maximum, or both. A person guilty and convicted of indictment is liable to a fine or imprisonment for a term not exceeding two years, or both.[69]

---

[64] See COPINGER, *supra* note 9, at 1253. Before the 2002 Act, criminal copyright offenses carried a maximum sentence of two years' imprisonment, while criminal trademarks carried a maximum sentence of ten years' imprisonment for equivalent offenses.

[65] See Copyright, etc. and Trade Marks (Offences and Enforcement) Act 2002 § 1(2).

[66] The Copyright and Related Rights Regulations, 2003, S.I. 2003/2498 (U.K.); WIPO Copyright Treaty, Dec. 20, 1996, 36 I.L.M. 65 (1997) [hereinafter WCT]. The Copyright and Related Rights Regulations of 2003 applies most of the provisions set in the Directive 2001/29/EC of the European Parliament and of the Council of 22 May 2001 on the Harmonisation of Certain Aspects of Copyright and Related Rights in the Information Society, art. 6., 2001 O.J. (L 167).

[67] Directive 2001/29/EC ("Member States shall provide appropriate sanctions and remedies in respect of infringements of the rights and obligations set out in this Directive and shall take all the measures necessary to ensure that those sanctions and remedies are applied. The sanctions thus provided or shall be effective, proportionate and dissuasive.").

[68] See The Copyright and Related Rights Regulations § 26(1)(a) (inserting § 107(2A)).

[69] Id. § 26(1)(b) (inserting § 107(4A)).

The second new offense set criminal liability for making, dealing with, or using illicit recordings. The Regulations added an offense of knowingly infringing upon the making available right, in making, dealing with, or using illicit recordings in the course of a business or to such an extent as to negatively affect the copyright owner.[70] A person guilty of such offense is liable on summary conviction and maximum imprisonment of three months and/or a fine not exceeding the statutory maximum and for conviction on indictment to a fine and/or imprisonment for a term not exceeding two years.[71]

In addition, the 2003 Regulations amended Section 296 of the CDPA, by introducing a criminal offense for knowingly engaging in an activity related to devices and services designed to circumvent technological measures.[72] These offenses are liable on summary conviction, to imprisonment for a term not exceeding three months, and/or to a fine not exceeding the statutory maximum; and on conviction on indictment to a fine and/or imprisonment for a term not exceeding two years.[73]

Criminal copyright provisions in the 2003 Regulations are a part of EU, and consequently (at that time) the United Kingdom, expansion of copyright law. Parliament, inter alia, introduced new rights of communication to the public's and performers' rights to reproduce; provided anti-circumvention provisions; and redefined exceptions to copyright infringements.[74] Thus, technological changes, and especially the internet, are partially responsible for copyright expansion in the United Kingdom, which also included criminal sanctions. The year 2003, not only marks a rise in criminal copyright by expanding the scope of possible criminal copyright offenses, it also criminalizes para-copyright through the criminalization of anti-circumvention activities. These criminal copyright provisions are yet another step-up in criminalization, while digital technology plays an important part in the process. Still, at that time, the gap between physical and digital infringement remained.

J *Digital Economy Act 2010*

In 2010, Parliament enacted the Digital Economy Act (DEA),[75] which was a result of Digital Britain White Paper recommendations to adapt to developments and usage of digital technologies by industry and consumers.[76] Although industry

---

[70] *Id.* § 26(3)(a) (inserting § 198(1A)). In addition, the 2003 Act broadened § 198(2)(b), from "broadcast or included in a cable programme service" to "communicated to the public."

[71] *Id.* § 26(3)(b) (§ 198(5A)).

[72] *Id.* § 24 (§ 296ZB(1) (U.K.)).

[73] *Id.* § 24 (§ 296ZB(4) (U.K.)).

[74] *Id.*

[75] Digital Economy Act 2010, c. 24, § 42 (U.K.).

[76] *See generally*, Dep't for Business Innovation and Skills, Digital Britain Final Report (2009).

representatives are not officially linked to the lobbying efforts of this Act, several media reports indicate that the music and film industry lobbied the DEA intensively.[77] Regarding criminal copyright, the Gowers Review of Intellectual Property[78] recommended amending Section 107 of the CDPA to match the criminal penalties for online copyright infringement to physical infringements.[79] Along with various other amendments made in the CDPA,[80] Parliament implemented recommendations of the Gowers Review and increased criminal penalties for infringing articles or illicit recordings.[81] Criminal liability for making or trading with infringing articles and for making, trading or using illicit recordings penalties were increased from the statutory maximum to £50,000.[82] At least for criminal fines, the DEA increased fine now applied for both physical and digital infringements (but not imprisonment).

Seemingly, the DEA criminal provisions are relatively less important than other provisions of the Act. Mainly, the DEA expanded the sanctions for copyright infringement in the form of a *three strikes/graduated response* policy, which provides for the termination of subscriptions and accounts of repeat infringers in appropriate circumstances.[83] Although mainly considered administrative, this measure could also be classified as criminal-like, as it possess many similar characteristics and by targeting end users with no financial gain, is an important step in the United Kingdom's responsive measures against copyright infringements.[84]

---

[77] *See, e.g.,* Jane Merrick, *The Net Closes in on Internet Piracy,* THE INDEPENDENT (Aug. 16, 2009), www.independent.co.uk/arts-entertainment/music/news/the-net-closes-in-on-internet-piracy-1772820.html.

[78] In 2005, the Chancellor of the Exchequer asked Andrew Gowers, former editor of the Financial Times, to lead an independent review into intellectual property rights in the United Kingdom. Andrew Gowers presented the "Gowers Review of intellectual property" to the Government in December 2006. *See* ANDREW GOWERS, GOWERS REVIEW OF INTELLECTUAL PROPERTY (2006), webarchive.nationalarchives.gov.uk/+/http:/www.hm-treasury.gov.uk/d/pbr06_gowers_report_755.pdf (last visited Dec. 1, 2017).

[79] Digital Economy Act, (Explanatory Notes), *available at* www.legislation.gov.uk/ukpga/2010/24/pdfs/ukpgaen_20100024_en.pdf.

[80] The Digital Economy Act of 2010 enhanced enforcement measures mainly via a *three strikes/graduated response* policy (Digital Economy Act 2010 §§ 124A–124N). For more information on United Kingdom's three strikes policy, see Eldar Haber, *The French Revolution 2.0: Copyright and the Three Strikes Policy,* 2 HARV. J. SPORTS & ENT. L. 297 (2011).

[81] For more information regarding the Digital Economy Act, see generally Monica Horten, *Copyright at a Policy Cross-Roads – Online Enforcement, the Telecoms Package and the Digital Economy Act, in* NET NEUTRALITY AND OTHER CHALLENGES FOR THE FUTURE OF THE INTERNET 157 (Agustí Cerrillo-i-Martínez et al. eds., 2011).

[82] At that time, the statutory maximum was £5,000 in England and Wales and £10,000 in Scotland. *See* Digital Economy Act 2010 § 42.

[83] *Id.* §§ 124A–124N.

[84] For the characterization of the three strikes policy as a possible criminal copyright offense, see Haber, *supra* note 80.

K *Copyright, Designs and Patents Act 1988 (Amendment) Regulations 2010*

In 2010, the Secretary of State exercised his power to issue regulations to amend the Copyright, Designs and Patents Act of 1988.[85] The Copyright, Designs and Patents Act 1988 (Amendment) Regulations 2010, were designed to re-implement Article 8 (2) of the EU Rental and Lending Directive.[86] Regarding criminal copyright, the regulations decreased (from six to three months) imprisonment for some of the offenses under Section 107 of the CDPA.[87] Although this decrease marks a potential de-criminalization movement, it was legislated due to a conflict with other United Kingdom legislation: under the 2010 Regulations, an offense under Section 107(3) of the CDPA,[88] also fits those circumstances that the copyright exemptions would have previously applied.[89] Since the European Communities Act of 1972 forbids legislation of an offense involving the imposition on summary conviction of a sentence of imprisonment of more than three months,[90] Parliament amended Section 107(3) and (slightly) de-criminalized copyright law in the United Kingdom.

*

---

[85] The Copyright, Designs and Patents Act 1988 (Amendment) Regulations, 2010, S.I. 2010/2694 (U.K.).

[86] Directive 2006/115/EC of the European Parliament and of the Council of 12 December 2006 on Rental Right and Lending Right and on Certain Rights Related to Copyright in the Field of Intellectual Property, 2006, O.J. (L 376). The re-implementation of article 8(2) of the 2006/115/ EC Directive was made by "removing exceptions to rights conferred on performers and owners of copyright sound recordings for use of their recordings," and "repealing a mechanism introduced in 2003 whereby some licensing terms for these rights must be notified to the Secretary of State and may be further referred to the Copyright Tribunal for a determination on their reasonableness." See Explanatory MEMORANDUM TO THE COPYRIGHT, DESIGNS AND PATENTS ACT 1988 (AMENDMENT) REGULATIONS 2010 (2010) [hereinafter EXPLANATORY MEMO-RANDUM], *available at* www.legislation.gov.uk/uksi/2010/2694/pdfs/uksiem_20102694_en.pdf.

[87] The Copyright, Designs and Patents Act 1988 (Amendment) Regulations 2010 § 5. These offenses include: possession without the license of the copyright owner in the course of a business with a view to committing any act infringing the copyright; in the course of a business – sells or lets for hire, or offers or exposes for sale or hire, or exhibits in public; where copyright is infringed, otherwise than by reception of a communication to the public – by the public performance of a literary, dramatic, or musical work, or by the playing or showing in public of a sound recording or film.

[88] CDPA, *supra* note 47, § 107(3) stats:

> Where copyright is infringed (otherwise than by reception of a communication to the public)
>
> (a) by the public performance of a literary, dramatic, or musical work, or
> (b) by the playing or showing in public of a sound recording or film, any person who caused the work to be so performed, played, or shown is guilty of an offence if he knew or had reason to believe that copyright would be infringed.

[89] *See* EXPLANATORY MEMORANDUM, *supra* note 86.

[90] European Communities Act 1972, c. 68, § 1(1)(d) of Sch. 2 (U.K.).

It should be noted that in 2015, the Secretary of State, in exercise of her powers, made a few changes that also effected the fines set under the CDPA.[91] Since then, the criminal sections, once set on a fine not exceeding £50,000, were substituted to "a fine." This move, while it highly impacts the criminalization of copyright, also applies to many other criminal offences, and could be attributed mainly to general criminalization movements, as further discussed in Chapter 6.

L *Digital Economy Act 2017*

In 2017, Parliament enacted yet another Digital Economy Act, which in the context of criminal copyright was a result of the perceived need to harmonize the penalties for online and physical copyright infringement.[92] The Act amended sections 107 and 198 of the CDPA by expanding the criminal liability for making or dealing with infringing articles and for making, dealing with, or using illicit recordings. The 2017 amendment made two crucial changes regarding criminal copyright protection. First, it expanded the *mens rea* to apply to individuals who know or have reason to believe that they are infringing copyright in the work, and either intend to make a monetary gain for themselves or others; or who know or have reason to believe that their actions will cause loss to the owner of the right or expose the owner to a risk of loss.[93] Second, and perhaps most dramatically, the Act increased the maximum sentence for online copyright infringement from two to ten years.[94] Under this amendment, Parliament finally harmonized the non-monetary sanctions for online and physical copyright infringement.

II EVALUATING COPYRIGHT CRIMINALIZATION IN THE UNITED KINGDOM

Since 1862, when United Kingdom introduced criminal copyright for the first time,[95] its scope and sanctions have repeatedly increased. At first, the United Kingdom reserved criminal copyright for unauthorized usage of painting, drawing, or photographs. Until 1982, criminal copyright made only three legislative appearances, in 1906, 1911, and 1956, and their penalties were relatively low. Since 1982,

---

[91] The Legal Aid, Sentencing and Punishment of Offenders Act 2012 (Fines on Summary Conviction) Regulations 2015 (S.I. 2015/664), reg. 1(1), Sch. 4 para. 17(2)(b) (U.K.).

[92] *See Changes to Penalties for Online Copyright Infringement*, UK-IPO, Newport (2015), www.gov .uk/government/uploads/system/uploads/attachment_data/file/517528/Government_Consultation_ Response_Criminal_Sanctions_-_Accessi. . .pdf. For criticism on the initial proposal that eventually led to the enactment of the Digital Economy Act 2017, see Felipe Romero-Moreno & James GH Griffin, *The UK's Criminal Copyright Proposals in an Era of Technological Precision*, 7 Eur. J.L. & Tech. 1 (2016).

[93] Digital Economy Act 2017, c. 30, § 32 (U.K.).

[94] *Id.*

[95] Fine Arts Copyright Act 1862, 25 & 26 Vict., c. 68 (U.K.).

criminal copyright has been repeatedly and extensively extended: Parliament has expanded criminal copyright to include additional types of works, new actions, and has raised monetary and nonmonetary sanctions.

Criminal copyright in the United Kingdom has dramatically increased since it was first introduced. The rise of criminalization since 1982, as shown throughout legislative overview, was mainly due to the following causes: (1) industry concerns that civil remedies were ineffective for deterring "piracy and counterfeiting"[96] (particularly the Musical Copyright Act of 1906, the Copyright [Computer Software] Amendment Act 1985, and the Copyright, Designs and Patents Act 1988); (2) governmental concerns over organized crime (particularly the Copyright, etc. and Trade Marks [Offences and Enforcement] Act 2002); (3) adapting copyright law to technological developments and usage of digital technologies by industry and consumers (particularly the 1982 and 1983 Amendments, the Copyright [Computer Software] Amendment Act 1985, the Digital Economy Act 2010, and the Digital Economy Act 2017); and (4) broad interpretations of requirements set in EU Directives (particularly the Copyright and Related Rights Regulations 2003 and the Copyright, Designs and Patents Act 1988 [Amendment] Regulations 2010). In addition, the legislative overview reveals that in many instances, industry-related groups were involved in the criminal copyright legislation process, i.e., politics played an important role in copyright criminalization (particularly the Fine Arts Copyright Act of 1862, the Copyright Act of 1956, the Copyright [Computer Software] Amendment Act 1985, the Copyright, Designs and Patents Act 1988, and the Digital Economy Act 2010). These motivations and reasons are best summarized in Table 1.

In sum, the reasons for the criminalization process in the United Kingdom could be divided into four main groups: (1) a rise in copyright infringements and infringers, due mostly to technological developments, which are not deterred by civil sanctions; (2) national interests; (3) international movement promoting criminal copyright; and (4) political powers. These, along with other possible reasons are further discussed in Chapters 5 and 6 and evaluated in Chapters 8 and 9.

CONCLUSION

Copyright Criminalization in the United Kingdom tells an interesting story. When copyright was first introduced in the Statute of Anne, it was absent of any criminal provisions. When Great Britain gave birth to criminal copyright in 1862, it was still rather limited. The rise in criminal copyright legislation took time. The main growth in copyright criminalization could be traced to the early 1980s, along with a burst in technological developments. It seems that Parliament has not ceased its

[96] The reference to copyright infringement within property terminology, e.g., "piracy," is an important element in copyright criminalization, and is further analyzed and discussed in Chapter 5.

TABLE 1 *Characteristics of Copyright Criminalization in the United Kingdom*

Reasons	United Kingdom Legislation
Deterrence due to copyright infringement	• Musical Copyright Act of 1906 • Copyright (Computer Software) Amendment Act 1985 • Copyright, Designs and Patents Act 1988 • Digital Economy Act 2010 • Digital Economy Act 2017
Government concerns of organized crime and to protect public interests	• Copyright, etc. and Trade Marks (Offences and Enforcement) Act 2002
Technology	• 1982 and 1983 Amendments • Copyright (Computer Software) Amendment Act 1985 • Copyright, Designs and Patents Act 1988 • Copyright and Related Rights Regulations 2003 • Digital Economy Act 2010 • Digital Economy Act 2017
Broad interpretation of international requirements	• Copyright and Related Rights Regulations 2003 • Copyright, Designs and Patents Act 1988 (Amendment) Regulations 2010)
Known lobbying efforts (politics)	• Fine Arts Copyright Act of 1862 • Copyright Act of 1956 • Copyright (Computer Software) Amendment Act 1985 • Copyright, Designs and Patents Act 1988 • Digital Economy Act 2010

criminalization as evident from the recent amendments to the CDPA under the Digital Economy Act of 2017.

It is evident from the test case of the United Kingdom that copyright law no longer remains an exclusive matter of civil liability and that criminal copyright legislation continually rises. In a broader context, the United Kingdom's examination is insufficient to assess whether copyright law is in the midst of a criminal paradigm shift, i.e., if copyright law will turn into a criminal-oriented law or not. To do so, the next chapter will examine the criminalization process from an American perspective, using a similar methodology used on the British experience. Upon this examination, the potential paradigm shift to criminal copyright will be examined through actual enforcement of both test cases in Chapter 4.

3

Copyright Criminalization in the United States

INTRODUCTION

This chapter focuses on the second chosen test case of copyright criminalization: that of the United States. Much like the choice of the United Kingdom in chapter II, the choice of the United States is not arbitrary. The American case study is important due to the United States' key-role and influence on the formation of contemporary IP international treaties,[1] domestic legislation in several countries,[2] global enforcement of IP,[3] and the US' economic and cultural global influence.[4] The review of the Unites States focuses on two phases: (1) the *low-tech phase*, which took place at the end of the nineteenth century; and (2) the *high-tech phase*, which itself encompasses two sub-phases – the *analog phase*, beginning in the early 1970s and lasting until 1992, and the *digital phase*, beginning at the onset of 1992, which still continues. We see that during the low-tech phase and the analog high-tech phase, criminal copyright mainly targeted large-scale infringers, whereas the digital high-tech phase (which we are still in) has marked a legislative shift to small-scale infringers.

---

[1] See, e.g., Pamela Samuelson, *The U.S. Digital Agenda at the World Intellectual Property Organization*, 37 VA. J. INT'L L. 369 (1997); Graeme B. Dinwoodie, *Essay: The Integration of International and Domestic Intellectual Property Lawmaking*, 23 COLUM.-VLA J.L. & ARTS 307 (2000).

[2] See, e.g., Mike Masnick, *Latest Wikileaks Release Shows How US Completely Drove Canadian Copyright Reform Efforts*, TECHDIRT (Apr. 29, 2011), http://bit.ly/jCXg9w.

[3] The United States has a global influence through the USTR, exercising its power under section 301 of the U.S. Trade Act of 1974 (Pub. L. 93–618, 88 Stat. 1978). For more on the political process of the USTR's Special 301 Reports, see generally, Michael Birnhack, *Trading Copyright: Global Pressure on Local Culture, in* THE DEVELOPMENT AGENDA: GLOBAL INTELLECTUAL PROPERTY AND DEVELOPING COUNTRIES 363 (Neil Netanel ed., 2008).

[4] See, e.g., Daniele Conversi, *The Limits of Cultural Globalisation?*, 3 J. CRITICAL GLOBALISATION STUD. 36 (2010); S. REP. NO. 104–315, at 7 (1996).

The objective of this chapter is to describe, review, and summarize the legislative history of copyright criminalization in the United States. Much like the examination of copyright criminalization in the United Kingdom, normative evaluation of legislation is limited in this chapter. However, I shall lay out four important aspects of the first layer of normative evaluation of the criminalization process: the first, highlighting important characteristics that arise from legislation and legislative materials; the second, arguing that copyright law is undergoing a criminalization process, expanding from a civil law to both civil and criminal laws; the third, exploring whether copyright law is in the midst of a transformation from a civil-based to a criminal-based law, and whether this marks a paradigm shift or is part of other trends (such as the ongoing shift from targeting large-scale infringers to focusing on end-users' actions); and the fourth, assessing explanations for criminal copyright legislation in search of deeper causes (developed further in Chapters 5 and 6).

I CRIMINAL COPYRIGHT IN THE UNITED STATES

American copyright law grants rights holders exclusive rights, subject to several limitations and exceptions, to their work. If a person violates any exclusive right, she has infringed upon the copyright.[5] Currently, American copyright law provides both civil and criminal legislative venues. The first federal copyright statute was enacted in 1790[6]; while it was amended over time, it only afforded civil remedies. Criminal provisions were included more than a century later,[7] and even then, infringement was considered a private, economic wrong that should usually be handled through civil remedies.[8]

The introduction of criminal law into copyright occurred in two stages, which I term the *low-tech* and the *high-tech* phases.[9] The *low-tech phase* took place at the end of the nineteenth century, adding criminal procedures for profitable

---

[5] 17 U.S.C. § 501(a).

[6] *See* Act for the Encouragement of Learning, Act of May 31, ch. 15, 1 Stat. 124 (1790). Under the 1790 Copyright Act, civil remedies included injunctions, destruction of infringing copies, and damages.

[7] Although the 1790 Act did not contain a criminal provision *per-se*, it contained a criminal-like provision which addressed unauthorized copying ("recording the title") of a copyrighted map, chart, or book resulted in a civil fine of fifty cents for every sheet which was found in possession, and one half of the penalties being paid to the United States. *See id.* § 2. *See also* James Lincoln Young, *Criminal Copyright Infringement and a Step Beyond*, 30 COPYRIGHT L. SYMP. 157, 158 (1983); Lori A. Morea, *The Future of Music in a Digital Age: The Ongoing Conflict Between Copyright Law and Peer-to-Peer Technology*, 28 CAMPBELL L. REV. 195, 209–10 (2006).

[8] *See* Steven Penney, *Crime, Copyright, and the Digital Age*, in WHAT IS A CRIME? CRIMINAL CONDUCT IN CONTEMPORARY SOCIETY 61, 61 (Law Comm'n of Canada ed., 2004); Alan N. Young, *Catching Copyright Criminals: R. v. Miles of Music Ltd.*, 5 I.P.J. 257, 257 (1990); ANDREW A. KEYES & CLAUDE BRUNET, COPYRIGHT IN CANADA: PROPOSALS FOR A REVISION OF THE LAW 185 (1977); Cal Becker, *Criminal Enforcement of Intellectual Property Rights*, 19 C.I.P.R. 183, 183 (2003).

[9] *See infra* Parts II. A–B.

commercial-based infringements. The *high-tech phase* includes two sub-phases: an *analog phase* beginning in the early 1970s and lasting until 1992, mostly extending copyright protection to sound recordings and restructuring criminal rationales in copyright, such as the *mens rea* requirement; and a *digital phase*, beginning in 1992 and addressing criminal aspects of copyright-related activities on the internet. During the low-tech phase and the analog high-tech phase, criminal copyright mainly targeted large-scale infringers, whereas the digital high-tech phase mainly targets relatively small-scale infringers. We are still within the digital phase.[10]

My discussion on each legislative act, points to the year the act was enacted; when known, the formal reasons for including criminal copyright clauses; when known, the parties that lobbied for the legislation; elements of the criminal copyright provisions; and ramifications on the ongoing criminalization process. Prior to analyzing each specific legislative act, it is important to note that many scholars, including myself,[11] have addressed the process of copyright criminalization in the United States throughout the years.[12] This chapter mainly seeks to provide a more detailed scrutiny of each legislative act that would aid in the normative evaluations set in this book.

[10] Further attempts to add additional criminal copyright layers followed, though not all were successful. See for example the Stop Online Piracy Act (SOPA) (to promote prosperity, creativity, entrepreneurship, and innovation by combating the theft of U.S. property, and for other purpose), H.R. 3261, 112th Cong. (2011). The bill would have imposed criminal penalties for public performances by means of digital networks with a retail value of more than $1,000 and felony penalties if the retail value is more than $2,500, while under current copyright law, infringing public performances rights are subject to lower criminal penalties than reproductions or distributions rights. However, the bill was withdrawn. *See also* the 2010 Joint Strategic Plan on Intellectual Property Enforcement as an indicator of governmental efforts to "combat intellectual property theft": Victoria Espinel, *Releasing the Joint Strategic Plan to Combat Intellectual Property Theft* (June 22, 2010, 11:15 AM), www.whitehouse.gov/blog/2010/06/22/releasing-joint-strategic-plan-combat-intellectual-property-theft; Todd Wasserman, *SOPA Is Dead: Smith Pulls Bill*, MASHABLE (Jan. 20, 2012), http://mashable.com/2012/01/20/sopa-is-dead-smith-pulls-bill.

[11] Part of the analysis in this Chapter previously appeared in Eldar Haber, *The Criminal Copyright Gap*, 18 STAN. TECH. L. REV. 247, 250–68 (2015).

[12] The legislative history of American criminalization deserved much academic attention, mostly as a descriptive matter. *See, e.g.*, Mary J. Saunders, *Criminal Copyright Infringement and the Copyright Felony Act*, 71 DENV. U. L. REV. 671 (1994); I. Trotter Hardy, *Prosecuting White Collar Crime: Criminal Copyright Infringement*, 11 WM. & MARY BILL RTS. J. 305, 315–23 (2002); Karen J. Bernstein, *Net Zero: The Evisceration of the Sentencing Guidelines under the No Electronic Theft Act*, 27 NEW ENG. J. ON CRIM. & CIV. CONFINEMENT 57, 67–69 (2001); Lydia Pallas-Loren, *Digitization, Commodification, Criminalization: The Evolution of Criminal Copyright Infringement and the Importance of the Willfulness Requirement*, 77 WASH. U. L.Q. 835, 840–50 (1999); Grace Pyun, *The 2008 Pro-IP Act: The Inadequacy of the Property Paradigm in Criminal Intellectual Property Law and Its Effect on Prosecutorial Boundaries*, 19 DEPAUL J. ART TECH. & INTELL. PROP. L. 355, 358–61 (2009); Ting Ting Wu, *The New Criminal Copyright Sanctions: A Toothless Tiger?*, 39 IDEA 527, 542–45 (1999); Irina D. Manta, *The Puzzle of Criminal Sanctions for Intellectual Property Infringement*, 24 HARV. J.L. & TECH. 469, 481–85 (2011); Miriam Bitton, *Rethinking the Anti-Counterfeiting Trade Agreement's Criminal Copyright Enforcement Measures*, 102 J. CRIM. L. & CRIMINOLOGY 67, 84–89 (2012).

A *Criminalization: Low-Tech Phase*

Even after the United States introduced criminal copyright for the first time in 1897, in practice, copyright infringement was almost entirely a civil wrong, while criminal prosecutions were rare and reserved for profitable, large-scale commercial-based infringements.[13] Thus, even after Congress criminalized part of copyright law, it did so with caution and reserved criminal sanctions for very limited actions.[14] Below, I review the low-tech phase of *criminal copyright* in the United States, which occurred between 1897 and 1909.

1 Musical Public Performance Right Act of 1897

In 1897, Congress passed three acts related to copyright law. The Musical Public Performance Act of 1897 (hereinafter, The Music Act) introduced criminal penalties for the first time,[15] mainly due to pressure by the music industry due to music copyright owner concerns that civil remedies would not deter unlawful performances of music,[16] as unlicensed performances throughout the country were difficult to monitor.[17] For instance, as described in hearings before Congress, owners of copyrighted plays argued "the performances are usually given at points remote from the location or headquarters of the dramatic author or producer, and by irresponsible persons, who jump their companies nightly from town to town."[18]

The Music Act addressed a public performance right for musical compositions, prescribing civil damages of $100 for the first infringement and $50 for subsequent infringements.[19] But the Act did not stop there. Introducing criminal penalties for

---

[13] Saunders, *supra* note 12, at 673; Carol Noonan & Jeffery Raskin, *Intellectual Property Crimes*, 38 Am. Crim. L. Rev. 971, 990 (2001).

[14] *See* Dowling v. United States, 473 U.S. 207, 221 (1985) ("Not only has Congress chiefly relied on an array of civil remedies to provide copyright holders protection against infringement, see 17 U.S.C. §§ 502–505, but in exercising its power to render criminal certain forms of copyright infringement, it has acted with exceeding caution.").

[15] The second Act (Act of February 19, 1897, 54th Cong., 2d Sess., 29 Stat. 545 (1897)) established the position of Register of Copyrights. The third Act (Act of March 3, 1897, 54th Cong., 2d Sess., 29 Stat. 694 (1897)) amended the provisions on affixation of a false notice of copyright, so that the previous penalty of $100 was applied also to anyone who knowingly issued, sold, or imported articles bearing a false notice of copyright. *See* Dorothy Schrader, *Music Licensing Copyright Proposals: An Overview of H.R. 789 and S. 28*, CRS Report for Congress 2 (1998); William F. Patry, Patry on Copyright 284–85 (2009).

[16] The public performance right for dramatic works did not contain criminal penalties, as it was considered easier to enforce, less frequent, and occur on a more circumscribed basis than music performances. *See* Schrader, *supra* note 15, at 4.

[17] *See id.* at 2–3; Hardy, *supra* note 12, at 315.

[18] *See Revision of Copyright Laws: Hearings before the Joint Comm. on Patents*, 60th Cong. 24 (1908) (statement of Ligon Johnson), *reprinted in* 5 Legislative History of the 1909 Copyright Act 24 (E. Fulton Brylawski & Abe Goldman eds., 1976); Hardy, *supra* note 12, at 315.

[19] Musical Public Performance Right Act of Jan. 6, 1897, ch. 4, 29 Stat. 481 (1897). For the origins of the Musical Public Performance Right Act of 1897, see Zvi Rosen, *The Twilight of the Opera*

the first time, the Act included a liability provision of willful, unlawful performance or representation of a dramatic or musical composition for profit.[20] The Act prescribed a misdemeanor[21] sanction of maximum imprisonment of one year.[22]

Thus, the first criminal copyright legislation in the United States was mainly due to industry's concerns that civil remedies were ineffective for deterring copyright infringements. While 1897 marks the birth of criminal copyright in the United States, the criminal provisions were reserved for willful and profitable infringements, limited in scope and did not apply to all copyright works.

2 Copyright Act of 1909

As part of copyright law's general revision in 1909, which repealed previous copyright legislation,[23] Congress continued with criminalization of copyright law. The 1909 Act was driven by industry representatives with a vested interest in copyright law.[24] Congress extended criminal provisions to all copyrighted works – rather than just public performances, representations, or infringements of copyrighted dramatic or musical compositions – with the exception of sound recordings.[25] In addition, it broadened liability's

---

Pirates: a Prehistory of the Exclusive Right of Public Performance for Musical Compositions, 24 CARDOZO ARTS & ENT. L.J. 1157 (2007). A public performance right in dramatic works was introduced in 1856 (Act of August 18, 1856, 11 Stat. 138 (1856)).

[20] *See* Musical Public Performance Right Act of Jan. 6, 1897, ch. 4, 29 Stat. 481–82 (1897). Criminal infringement was differentiated from civil infringement when it was pursued for purposes of commercial exploitation. In addition, the 1897 Act requirement of criminal intent, i.e., mens rea, is therefore a showing that the conduct was "willful" and for profit. *See* Saunders, *supra* note 12, at 673; Note, *The Criminalization of Copyright Infringement in the Digital Era*, 112 HARV. L. REV. 1705, 1706–07 (1999). Note that Congress choose to criminalize unauthorized performances of music and plays and not older pedigree in United States copyright law, e.g., books, maps and charts. *See* Hardy, *supra* note 12, at 315. Also, note that other forms of copyright infringement, i.e., the unauthorized reproduction or distribution of a copyrighted work, were still resolved through civil litigation. *See* Lanier Saperstein, *Copyrights, Criminal Sanctions and Economic Rents: Applying the Rent Seeking Model to the Criminal Law Formulation Process*, 87 J. CRIM. L. & CRIMINOLOGY 1470, 1474 (1997) (citing Saunders, *supra* note 12, at 673).

[21] Criminal acts in the United States fall into two categories: felonies and misdemeanors. Misdemeanors carry sentences of one year or less, while felonies may result in prison sentences of more than one year. For more on the sentencing classification of offenses in the United States, see 18 U.S.C. § 3559.

[22] Musical Public Performance Right Act § 4966 (stating that "If the unlawful performance and representation be willful and for profit, such person or persons shall be guilty of a misdemeanor and upon conviction be imprisoned for a period not exceeding one year."). *See also* PATRY, *supra* note 15, at § 1:41.

[23] *See* Copyright Act of 1909, ch. 320, 33 Stat. 1075–82 (1909).

[24] *See* Saperstein, *supra* note 20, at 1474. For more on the 1909 Act's background, see generally, Jessica Litman, *Copyright, Compromise and Legislative History*, 72 CORNELL L. REV. 857, 884–86 (1987); JESSICA LITMAN, DIGITAL COPYRIGHT 38–40 (2d ed. 2006).

[25] *See* Copyright Act of 1909 § 5. Although copyright protection for sound recordings was considered during the 1909 revision, it was eventually rejected. *See* Saunders, *supra* note 12, at 673.

scope to include any person who willfully aids or abets infringement. The 1909 Act provided misdemeanor penalties for a willful and for-profit infringement of all types of copyrighted works, while keeping the Musical Public Performance Right Act of 1897 *mens rea* requirement[26] of up to one-year imprisonment, and inserted a fine between $100 and $1,000 (or both).[27] In addition, in order to address concerns regarding making innocent infringers, e.g., schoolchildren, as accessories to criminal infringements, Congress reserved the "aiding and abetting" offense to cases of knowing and willful infringement, while adopting a "for-profit" limitation.[28]

Thus, since 1909, criminal copyright is no longer reserved to specific types of works and the scope of criminal copyright has been expanded. However, it remained only a misdemeanor, reserved for willful and for-profit infringements. Nonetheless, 1909 marks the first comprehensive lobbying effort to criminalize copyright; hence, politics became an important reason for the rise in criminal copyright.

*

After 1909, copyright criminalization was on hold for a relatively long period. Between 1909 and 1971, despite various bills that proposed revising the Copyright

---

[26] *See supra* note 20.

[27] Copyright Act of 1909 § 28:

> Any person who willfully and for profit shall infringe any copyright secured by this Act, or who shall knowingly and willfully aid or abet such infringement, shall be deemed guilty of a misdemeanor, and upon conviction thereof shall be punished by imprisonment for not exceeding one year or by a fine of not less than one hundred dollars nor more than one thousand dollars) or both, in the discretion of the court: *Provided, however,* That nothing in this Act shall be so construed as to prevent the performance of religious or secular works, such as oratorios, cantatas, masses, or octavo choruses by public schools, church choirs, or vocal societies, rented, borrowed, or obtained from some public library, public school, church choir, school choir, or vocal society, provided the performance is given for charitable or educational purposes and not for profit.

> *Id.* § 29:

> Any person who, with fraudulent intent, shall insert or impress any notice of copyright required by this Act, or words of the same purport, in or upon any uncopyrighted article, or with fraudulent intent shall remove or alter the copyright notice upon any article duly copyright shall be guilty of a misdemeanor, punishable by a fine of not less than one hundred dollars and not more than one thousand dollars. Any person who shall knowingly issue or sell any article bearing a notice of United States copyright which has not been copyrighted in this country, or who shall knowingly import any article bearing such notice or words of the same purport, which has not been copyrighted in this country, shall be liable to a fine of one hundred dollars.

[28] *See* Schrader, *supra* note 15, at 3. However, as interpreted later by Unites States courts, the profit requirement need only be for the purpose of profit, while not actual profit has to be attained. *See* United States v. Cross, 816 F.2d 297, 301 (7th Cir. 1987) (stating that a conviction does not require that a defendant actually realize either a commercial advantage or private financial gain, while it is only necessary that the activity be for the purpose of financial gain or benefit, citing United States v. Moore, 757 F.2d 1228 (9th Cir. 1979), and arguing that it is irrelevant whether there was an exchange for value so long as there existed the hope of some pecuniary gain); Hardy, *supra* note 12, at 316.

Act – particularly adding criminal sanctions – criminal copyright remained unchanged.[29] Until the high-tech phase, even though criminal copyright existed, it only provided relatively light sanctions, as it was classified as a misdemeanor (maximum $1,000 fine, maximum one-year imprisonment, or both).[30] In practice, law enforcement agencies did not place a high priority on criminal copyright and there were relatively few state prosecutions.[31]

Within the broader context of copyright enforcement, the low-tech criminalization phase marks an attempt to use criminal sanctions to protect mainly against infringement of the public performance right. At that time, copyright enforcement played a modest role in the copyright regime.[32] To a large extent, copyright enforcement was manageable due to the high costs of infringement and the relatively high visibility of infringers.[33] However, along with the technological advances, the copyright industry began to face another problem: unauthorized copying, commonly referred to as "piracy." In the mid-1950s, Congress reacted to the new enforcement problem by initiating a comprehensive copyright reform to address the new enforcement measures needed to better protect content owners. This reform took more than 20 years, mainly due to various controversies,[34] which partially explains why Congress was silent on criminal copyright for such a long period.

B *Criminalization: Analog High-Tech Phase*

The high-tech criminalization phase marks a shift in criminal copyright perception and was seemingly triggered by a growth in the record industry and an increase in "piracy," counterfeiting, and bootlegging of music recordings.[35] Both the record companies and motion picture industries lobbied Congress to strengthen copyright

---

[29] For a summary of such proposals, see Robert S. Gawthrop, *An Inquiry into Criminal Copyright Infringement, reprinted in* 20 COPYRIGHT L. SYMP. 154, 156–57 (1972). For examples of criminal copyright proposed provisions between 1909 and 1971, see H.R. 12549, 71st Cong., 3d Sess. (1931); S. 5687, 71st Cong., 3d Sess., introduced Jan 5, 1931; H.R. 10364, 72nd Cong., 1st Sess., introduced Mar. 10, 1932; S. 3043, 76th Cong., 3d Sess., introduced Jan 8, 1940.

[30] *See* Penney, *supra* note 8, at 62.

[31] *Id.* at 62–63; Kent Walker, *Federal Remedies for the Theft of Intellectual Property*, 16 HASTINGS COMM. & ENT. L.J. 681 (1994); Note, *supra* note 20, at 1710.

[32] Peter S. Menell, *This American Copyright Life: Reflections on Re-Equilibrating Copyright for the Internet Age*, 62 J. COPYRIGHT SOC'Y U.S.A. 201, 210–14 (2014).

[33] *Id.*

[34] For the full legislative history of the 1976 Copyright Act, see GEORGE S. GROSSMAN, OMNIBUS COPYRIGHT REVISION LEGISLATIVE HISTORY (2001); Peter S. Menell, *In Search of Copyright's Lost Ark: Interpreting the Right to Distribute in the Internet Age*, 59 J. COPYRIGHT SOC'Y U.S.A. 1 (2011).

[35] Penney, *supra* note 8, at 63; Charles H. McCaghy & S. Serge Denisoff, *Pirates and Politics: An Analysis of Interest Group Conflict, in* DEVIANCE, CONFLICT, AND CRIMINALITY 297, 301–03 (S. Serge Denisoff & Charles H. McCaghy eds., 1973).

protection and enforcement,[36] which resulted in the beginning of the high-tech criminalization phase, reintroducing criminal copyright legislation in the United States. For the purposes of the discussion here, I differentiate between two distinct stages of the high-tech criminalization phase – analog and digital – as they each possess several, different characteristics.

1 Sound Recording Act of 1971

In 1971, the United States Congress awarded copyright protection to sound recordings,[37] while also reintroducing criminal copyright. The 1971 Act was partially a result of the record and motion picture industries' lobbying efforts, and criminalization was due to Congress' estimate that the exclusion of willful, for-profit recordings from the 1909 Copyright Act criminal provisions had led to record and tape "piracy" exceeding $100 million annually.[38] The Act aimed to reduce rights holders' loss of revenue – which also decreased tax revenues,[39] and criminalized willful, for-profit infringement of sound recordings.

Criminal copyright in 1971 marks the beginning of the high-tech criminalization phase, and its justifications will continue to play an important role in copyright criminalization: copyright infringements, which are linked to technological developments, cause criminalization as a responsive measure.

2 Copyright Act Amendments of 1974

In 1974, Congress increased penalties for unauthorized copying of sound recordings.[40] The amendments to the Copyright Act in 1974, lobbied for (inter alia) by the record industry,[41] were legislated due to Congress' perception that ordinary penalties

---

[36] *See* Penney, *supra* note 8, at 61; Saunders, *supra* note 12, at 674–75.

[37] Sound Recording Act of 1971, Pub. L. No. 92–140, 85 Stat. 391 (1971). United States Courts protected sound recordings even prior to legislation. *See* Capitol Records, Inc. v. Spies, 264 N.E.2d 874 (Ill. App. Ct. 1970) (holding that prevention of record piracy under state law was precluded by federal preemption doctrines); Robert P. Merges, *One Hundred Years of Solicitude: Intellectual Property Law, 1900–2000*, 88 CALIF. L. REV. 2187, 2197 (2000).

[38] *See* Saunders, *supra* note 12, at 674 (citing H.R. REP. No. 487, 92d Cong., 1st Sess. 2 (1971)); Bitton, *supra* note 12, at 85.

[39] *See* H.R. REP. No. 487, 92d Cong., 1st Sess. 2 (1971) at 2 ("[t]he pirating of records and tapes is not only depriving legitimate manufacturers of substantial income, but of equal importance is denying performing artists and musicians of royalties and contributions to pension and welfare funds and Federal and State governments are losing tax revenues.").

[40] Act of Dec. 31, 1974, Pub. L. No. 93–573, 88 Stat. 1873 (1974); Dowling v. United States, 473 U.S. 207 (1985); Note, *supra* note 20, at 1708 (1999).

[41] Jessica Wang, *A Brave New Step: Why the Music Industry Should Follow the Hulu Model*, 51 IDEA 511, 518 (2011).

failed to deter unauthorized copying of sound recordings (record "piracy"),[42] and attempted to reduce infringers' economic incentives.[43]

The Act provided that willful and for-profit infringement of copyrighted sound recordings – or knowingly and willfully aiding or abetting this type of infringement - is subject to a maximum fine of $25,000 and/or a maximum imprisonment of one year. In addition, under the Act, subsequent offenses were subject to a fine up to $50,000 and/or imprisonment of up to two years,[44] making subsequent offenses a felony.[45] However, Congress rejected a proposal to increase imprisonment to three years for a first offense and seven years for a subsequent offense, since it perceived record "piracy" to be primarily an economic offense.[46]

The 1974 amendments continued on the same path toward criminalization as did the Sound Recording Act of 1971, i.e., increased technological advances meant increased infringement and thus necessitated criminalization. However, Congress took deterrence one-step further, and in certain circumstances, copyright infringement of sound recordings was a felony.

3 Copyright Act of 1976

In 1976, as part of the new Copyright Act, Congress further criminalized copyright law.[47] The 1976 Copyright Act was legislated after the introduction of advanced technologies that generated new industries as well as unique reproduction and dissemination methods of copyrighted works. The Act, and accordingly copyright criminalization, was largely lobbied for by the entertainment industries, arguing that technological advances led to financial losses.[48]

---

[42] See H.R. Rep. No. 93–1581, at 4 (1974), *reprinted in* 1974 U.S.C.C.A.N. 6849, 6852 ("record piracy is so profitable that ordinary penalties fail to deter prospective offenders."). The usage of "piracy" in relation to copyright and other IP infringements will be discussed further in Chapters 5 and 6.

[43] See Young, *supra* note 7, at 162.

[44] The 1974 Act inserted a new subsection (b) to § 104, stating that:

> Any person who willfully and for profit shall infringe any copyright provided by section 1(f) of this title [i.e., the exclusive right to reproduce and distribute to the public by sale or other transfer of ownership, or by rental, lease, or lending, reproductions of the copyrighted work if it be a sound recording – E. H.], or who should knowingly and willfully aid or abet such infringement, shall be fined not more than $25,000 or imprisoned not more than one year, or both, for the first offense and shall be fined not more than $50,000 or imprisoned not more than two years, or both, for any subsequent offense.

[45] See Young, *supra* note 7, at 163.

[46] See H.R. Rep. No. 93–1581, *supra* note 42; Dowling v. United States, 473 U.S. 207 (1985); Note, *supra* note 20, at 1708.

[47] Copyright Act of 1976, Pub. L. No. 94–553, 90 Stat. 2541 (1976).

[48] Copyright law was prone to revision prior to 1976, however due to conflicting sectional interests, the law was revised only in 1976. See Saperstein, *supra* note 20, at 1475–76; H.R. Rep. No. 1476, 94th Cong., at 47 (1976), *reprinted in* 1976 U.S.C.C.A.N. 5659; *Copyright Law*

Under the Act, Congress loosened the *mens rea* requirement for criminal copyright infringement by replacing the "for profit" requirement with "for purposes of commercial advantage or private financial gain."[49] In addition, the act increased criminal sanctions for copyright infringement.[50] First, it added a misdemeanor conviction of a criminal infringement, except those of sound recordings and motion pictures, subject to a $10,000 fine and/or up to a one-year imprisonment.[51] Second, infringement of sound recordings or motion pictures carried a maximum fine up to $25,000.[52] Third, convicted repeat infringers of sound recordings or motion pictures could face a $50,000 fine and/or imprisonment for no more than two years.[53] Finally, upon conviction of criminal copyright infringement, the Act provided for the mandatory forfeiture, destruction, or disposition of all infringing copies or phonorecords and all implements, devices, or equipment used in the manufacturing of pirated copies or phonorecords.[54] Seemingly, the 1976 Act also de-criminalized copyright as it

---

Revision: Hearings on S. 1006 Before the Subcomm. on Patents, Trademarks and Copyrights of the Senate Comm. on the Judiciary, 89th Cong. 66 (1965); Mills Music, Inc. v. Snyder, 469 U.S. 153, 159–61 (1985) (noting that the 1976 Copyright Act was the culmination of twenty years of congressional hearings); *See also* Saunders, *supra* note 12, at 674–75; Bitton, *supra* note 12, at 86; L. RAY PATTERSON & STANLEY W. LINDBERG, THE NATURE OF COPYRIGHT: A LAW OF USERS' RIGHTS 90 (1991); Barbara Ringer, *First Thoughts on the Copyright Act of 1976,* 22 N.Y.L. SCH. L. REV. 477, 479 (1977); Julien H. Collins, *When in Doubt, Do without: Licensing Public Performances by Nonprofit Camping or Volunteer Service Organizations under Federal Copyright Law,* 75 WASH. U. L.Q. 1277, 1288 (1997).

[49] 17 U.S.C. § 506(a) (1978). The 1976 Act clarified that a desire of financial gain is sufficient to qualify for criminal copyright infringement, and that the actual receipt of financial benefit is irrelevant. *See* Bernstein, *supra* note 12, at 68; United States v. Cross, 816 F.2d 297, 301 (7th Cir. 1987) (holding that a conviction under 17 U.S.C. § 506(a) does not require that a defendant actually realize either a commercial advantage or private financial gain. It is only necessary that the activity be for the purpose of financial gain or benefit, while citing United States v. Moore, 604 F.2d 1228, 1235 (9th Cir.1979) (noting that it is irrelevant whether there was an exchange for value so long as existed a hope of some pecuniary gain)); Saperstein, *supra* note 20, at 1478; Saunders, *supra* note 12, at 674. However, some United States Courts rejected the defense that the defendant did not actually receive a benefit. *See* United States v. Taxe, 380 F. Supp. 1010, 1018 (C.D. Cal. 1974) (rejecting the defense of lack of realization of profit); Note, *supra* note 20, at 1708. Moreover, other scholars argue that the 1976 Act only changed the wording of the *mens rea* standard for criminal culpability, not actually altering or "loosening" the proof requirement. *See, e.g.,* Young, *supra* note 7, at 167; Pallas-Loren, *supra* note 12, at 841.

[50] The increase of criminal copyright infringement fines could be linked, among other things, to the prevailing inflation the United States economy at that time. For this argument, see Young, *supra* note 7, at 170.

[51] 17 U.S.C. § 506(a) (1978). Note that minimum fines are absent from the United States Copyright Act as Congress wished to create conformity with the general pattern of U.S. Criminal Code (18 U.S.C.). *See House Comm. On the Judiciary, Copyright Law Revision,* H.R. REP. NO. 1476, 94th Cong., 2d Sess. 163 (1976).

[52] 17 U.S.C. § 506(a) (1978).

[53] *Id.* § 506(a).

[54] *See id.* § 506(b); Saunders, *supra* note 12, at 675; Saperstein, *supra* note 20, at 1478. In a civil infringement, under 17 U.S.C. § 503(b), the destruction of infringing copies is obligatory, while in a criminal infringement, the destruction is mandatory. *See* Young, *supra* note 7, at 175.

eliminated the offense of aiding and abetting infringement.[55] However, it seems that
Congress did so because the U.S. Criminal Code already governed aiding and
abetting,[56] and thus the Act did not actually de-criminalize copyright law.

As such, the 1976 Act was legislated mostly due to technological developments,
which presumably caused financial losses to rights holders, and due to their political
influence on legislation. In a broader context of copyright enforcement, the 1976 Act
marked a change of perception: both civil damages and criminal sanctions were
proven insufficient to deal with the new enforcement problems, caused mainly by
technological advances.[57] Aside from changes in civil copyright, the 1976 Act is an
important step up in criminal copyright in which Congress expanded the type of
works and actions and increased criminal sanctions.

4 Piracy and Counterfeiting Amendments Act of 1982

In 1982, Congress introduced the Piracy and Counterfeiting Amendments Act.[58]
Again, legislation was due to the entertainment industries' lobbying efforts that
pushed for stronger copyright protection and enforcement.[59] The entertainment
industries argued that new copying technologies, i.e., audiotape and videocassette
recorders, enabled "piracy" at unprecedented rates.[60]

Under the Act, Congress enacted felony penalties for first time copyright offenders,[61] while removing criminal sanctions from the Copyright Act and placing them
in the U.S. Criminal Code.[62] Felony penalties were imposed on the "mass piracy" of
sound recordings and audiovisual works. Mass piracy was defined as the reproduction or distribution of at least 1,000 phonorecords or infringing copies of one or more

---

[55] *See* Saunders, *supra* note 12, at 674.
[56] 18 U.S.C. § 2 (1976) ("aiders, abettors, and other accessories before the fact of any offense
defined as criminal by federal law are treated as principals in the commission of the offense.").
See Young, *supra* note 7, at 169.
[57] *See generally*, Menell, *supra* note 32.
[58] Piracy and Counterfeiting Amendments Act of 1982, Pub. L. No. 97–180, 96 Stat. 91 (1982).
[59] The lobbying was conducted by the Recording Industry Association of America, Inc. (RIAA)
and the Motion Picture Association of America, Inc. (MPAA). The RIAA and the MPAA
organized an effort to increase film and record infringements penalties, as they claimed that
they spent more than $1 million a year on investigations and piracy battles, but the problem
remained epidemic. They also estimated that by 1979 all forms of record and film counterfeiting and piracy deprived the industries of more than $650 million each year. *See Hearing on
Reform of Federal Criminal Laws Before the Senate Comm. on the Judiciary*, 96th Cong., 1st
Sess. 10694–10697 (1979) (Joint statement of the Motion Picture Association of America, Inc.,
and Recording Industry Association of America, Inc.); *See* Saunders, *supra* note 12, at 675;
Dowling v. United States, 473 U.S. 207 at 224 (1985); Pallas-Loren, *supra* note 12, at 842;
Penney, *supra* note 8, at 63.
[60] *See* S. REP. No. 97–274, at 4 (1982), *reprinted in* 1982 U.S.C.C.A.N. 127 at 130; Note, *supra* note
20, at 1710; Penney, *supra* note 8, at 63.
[61] Prior to this Act, only a subsequent offense of copyright infringement that exceeded a one-year
imprisonment term was considered an offense. Saunders, *supra* note 12, at 674.
[62] Copyright penalties shifted to 18 U.S.C. § 2319 (1982). *See* Hardy, *supra* note 12, at 317.

sound recordings over a 180-day period and for the reproduction or distribution of at least 65 copies of audiovisual works.[63] Congress raised sanctions from a maximum fine of $10,000 to a maximum fine of $250,000 and/or up to five years in prison. Moreover, offenders making infringing copies (from 100 to 999) of sound recordings or (seven to 64) audiovisual works over a six-month period were subject to a maximum fine of $250,000 and/or two years imprisonment.[64] The *mens rea* element remained unchanged, requiring proof of commercial advantage or private financial gain. However, even after the 1982 amendments, the Copyright Act still considered most criminal offenses to be misdemeanors,[65] subject to a fine up to $25,000, and/or imprisonment for not more than one year.[66]

Thus, under the 1982 Act, Congress focused on sound recordings and audiovisual works, and criminalized copyright infringement to a high extent. Felony penalties were imposed for the first time on first-time offenders and extended sanctions to include a $250,000 fine (the highest fine imposed at the time) and maximum imprisonment of five years. The 1982 Act marks another step in the entertainment industry's lobbying efforts, which linked the justification of criminal copyright to technological developments that cause copyright infringement.

5 Sentencing Reform Act of 1984

Due to concern over lack of deterrence, Congress passed the 1984 Sentencing Reform Act, which led to the creation of the Federal Sentencing Guidelines.[67] Its main goal was to create uniformity in federal sentencing.[68] The 1984 Reform originated, inter alia, from academic criticism of the indeterminate sentencing model and the lobbying of special interest groups (that are not directly linked to copyright protection).[69] Along with criminal copyright, Congress revised the entire

---

[63] 18 U.S.C. § 2319(b)(1)(A)–(B) (1982).

[64] Copyright infringements which do not fall into these categories remained the same, i.e., classified as misdemeanors and carrying fines of up to $25,000, one-year imprisonment, or both. *See* Penney, *supra* note 8, at 63.

[65] Except "mass piracy" of sound recordings and audiovisual works and a subsequent offense of willful and for profit copyright infringement in sound recordings.

[66] 18 U.S.C. § 2319(b) (3) (1988); Saperstein, *supra* note 20, at 1480.

[67] Sentencing Reform Act of 1984, Pub. L. No. 98–473, 98 Stat. 1987 (1984). *See* Lisa M. Seghetti & Alison M. Smith, *Federal Sentencing Guidelines: Background, Legal Analysis, and Policy Options*, CRS REPORT FOR CONGRESS 13 (2007).

[68] Orrin G. Hatch, *The Role of Congress in Sentencing: The United States Sentencing Commission, Mandatory Minimum Sentences, and the Search for a Certain and Effective Sentencing System*, 28 WAKE FOREST L. REV. 185, 187 (1993); William J. Wilkins, Jr. et al., *The Sentencing Reform Act of 1984: A Bold Approach to the Unwarranted Sentencing Disparity Problem*, 2 CRIM. L.F. 355, 364–65 (1991). *See generally*, Seghetti & Smith, *supra* note 67, at 13.

[69] For a full analysis of the different entities that played a role in the Sentencing Reform Act of 1984, see Erik S. Siebert, Comment, *The Process is the Problem: Lessons Learned from United States Drug Sentencing Reform*, 44 U. RICH. L. REV. 867, 880–902 (2010).

Federal Criminal Code as well as the federal sentencing system.[70] In the realm of copyright law, the Sentencing Reform Act lowered the threshold of infringing copies to one copy for a sound recording or seven to 65 copies of motion pictures.[71] In addition, the Act raised the maximum prison sentence to five years for the infringement of one thousand sound recordings or motion pictures.[72]

Although the 1984 Act is not directly linked to criminal copyright, it reflected Congress' recognition of the importance in deterring copyright infringement as seen in the decrease in the number of infringing copies of sound recording and motion pictures under this Act (along with the increase in the maximum prison sentence for some infringements).

6 Anti-Drug Abuse Act of 1988

In 1988, Congress introduced an amendment to the Money Laundering Control Act,[73] primarily enacted as a response to drug-related crimes and ills.[74] The amendment added copyright infringement under unlawful money laundering activities. However, Congress' specific intention in doing so is unclear from congressional discussions.

The 1988 amendment prohibited the monetary transactions of funds that were knowingly derived through unlawful activity.[75] While the original 1986 Act did not list copyright infringement as a specific, unlawful money laundering activity, the 1988 amendments targeted a broad range of illicit activities, including copyright infringement.[76] The classification of criminal copyright as a specified unlawful activity may seem insignificant, but its importance lies in the relatively high sanctions that could now be imposed: In sentencing, a convicted infringer is liable to a $500,000 fine or a fine equaling twice the value of the work involved in the transaction (whichever is greater), imprisonment up to 20 years, or both.[77]

*

---

[70] Seghetti & Smith, *supra* note 67, at 11.

[71] Sentencing Reform Act of 1984, Pub. L. No. 98–473, 98 Stat. 1987 (1984).

[72] *See* 18 U.S.C. § 2319(b)(1) (1984); Bernstein, *supra* note 12, at 68–69.

[73] In 1986, Congress enacted the Money Laundering Control Act as part of the Anti-Drug Abuse Act. *See* Money Laundering Control Act of 1986, Pub. L. No. 99–570, 100 Stat. 3207–22 (1986).

[74] *See generally*, Christopher D. Sullivan, *"User-Accountability" Provisions in the Anti-Drug Abuse Act of 1988: Assaulting Civil Liberties in the War on Drugs*, 40 HASTING L.J. 1223 (1989).

[75] *See* Anna Driggers, *Money Laundering*, 48 AM. CRIM. L. REV. 929, 930 (2011).

[76] Anti-Drug Abuse Act of 1988, Pub. L. No. 100–690, § 6466, 102 Stat. 4181 (1988) (codified as amended at 18 U.S.C. § 1956). For more information regarding the broad range of activities targeted by this Act, see James D. Harmon, Jr., *United States Money Laundering Laws: International Implications*, 9 N.Y.L. SCH. J. INT'L & COMP. L. 1, 10–12 (1988); More on money laundering and copyright infringement, see Ronald D. Coenen Jr., Jonathan H. Greenberg & Patrick K. Reisinger, *Intellectual Property Crimes*, 48 AM. CRIM. L. 849, 884 (2011).

[77] In addition to a civil penalty of not more than $10,000 or the value of the funds involved in the transaction, whichever is greater. *See* 18 U.S.C. § 1956 (1988).

In sum, during the *analog high-tech phase* (1971–1988), Congress broadly criminalized copyright law. This phase represents the impact of (mostly) analog technology
on copyright protection and the impact of digital technology on copyright. As is
clear from the legislative overview, the growth of various industries, which accumulated political power during this phase, used their influence to lobby for criminal
copyright legislation. However, as we see below, during the *digital high-tech phase*,
the growth of various industries and their political clout to amend and introduce
criminal legislation during the analog phase was merely the beginning.

C *Criminalization: Digital High-Tech Phase*

The digital criminalization sub-phase marks an increase in Congress' involvement
in copyright criminalization, both in enacted legislation and proposed bills.[78]
Moreover, the digital sub-phase reflects a crucial change of Congress' approach
toward copyright infringers: Unlike the *low-tech* phase and the *analog phase*, the
digital phase marks a legislative change from targeting large-scale to small-scale
infringers.

1 Copyright Felony Act of 1992

In 1992, Congress introduced the Copyright Felony Act.[79] Analog phase amendments, which increased the types of works that fell into the category of unauthorized
duplication of copyrighted works, did not cover computer software. Hence, copyright lobbyists were soon joined by software and video game industries lobbying for
legislative change.[80] For example, the Software Publishers Association argued that
the increase in home computers software "piracy," cost the industry $2.4 billion in
1990.[81] Software and video game industries, too, argued that advanced technological
developments and lack of deterrence, i.e., civil law alone, could not deter large-scale

---

[78] To demonstrate the scope of proposed criminal copyright bills in the digital criminalization
second phase, see, e.g., Intellectual Property Protection Act of 2002, H.R. 5057, 107th Cong.
(2002); Author, Consumer, and Computer Owner Protection and Security (ACCOPS) Act of
2003, H.R. 2752, 108th Cong. (2003); Artists' Rights and Theft Protection Act of 2003, S. 1932,
108th Cong. (2003); Piracy Deterrence and Education Act of 2004, H.R. 4077, 108th Cong. §§
108–110 (2004); Intellectual Property Enhanced Criminal Enforcement Act of 2007, H.R. 3155,
110th Cong. § 5 (2007); The Stop Online Piracy Act of 2011, H.R. 3261, 112th Cong. (2011).

[79] Copyright Felony Act of 1992, Pub. L. No. 102–561, 106 Stat. 4233 (1992).

[80] *Id.*; *Criminal Sanctions for Violations of Software Copyright: Hearing on S. 893 before the
Subcomm. on Intellectual Prop. and Judicial Admin. of the H. Comm. on the Judiciary*, 102d
Cong. (1992); Saperstein, *supra* note 20, at 1480.

[81] *See* Penney, *supra* note 8, at 63; Saunders, *supra* note 12, at 678–79; Pallas-Loren, *supra* note 12,
at 844; United States v. LaMacchia, 871 F. Supp. 535, 540 (D. Mass. 1994) [hereinafter
LaMacchia]; *Criminal Sanctions for Violations of Software Copyright*, *supra* note 80 ("we
estimate that revenue lost to software piracy in the U.S. was $2.4 billion in 1990, the last year for
which we have statistics.").

infringers and did not provide incentives for federal prosecutors.[82] They also cited the injury to public interests, rather than personal interests, i.e., protecting consumers, who were described as "victims of piracy,"[83] and to loss of employment and shrinking of the workforce caused by pirating.[84]

Under the 1992 Act, Congress imposed felony penalties for mass "piracy" of all types of copyrighted works,[85] including computer programs.[86] The Copyright Felony Act of 1992 lowered the threshold for felony penalties: making of at least ten infringing copies that are valued at more than $2,500 over a period of 180 days, increasing personal fines to $250,000 and organizational fines to $500,000 or in either case twice the value of the monetary gains.[87] Under the Act, first-time offenders could face five years of imprisonment and repeat offenders could face up to ten years.[88] It proscribed a misdemeanor sentence of up to one year for criminal copyright infringement, which does not account to mass "piracy" according to the law.[89]

The 1992 Act marks an additional step in copyright criminalization: prior to 1992, copyright infringements of most types of works were not considered a felony and proscribed relatively low criminal sanctions. However, since 1992, copyright

---

[82] *See Criminal Sanctions for Violations of Software Copyright, supra* note 80; Saperstein, *supra* note 20, at 1481.

[83] *See Criminal Sanctions for Violations of Software Copyright, supra* note 80, at 2.

[84] *See* H.R. REP. No. 102–997, 102d Cong. (1992), *reprinted in* 1992 U.S.C.C.A.N. 3569 ("The purpose of S. 893 is to harmonize the current felony provisions for copyright infringement and to provide an effective deterrence to the piracy of motion pictures, sound recordings, computer programs, and other original works of authorship. Piracy of copyrighted works costs U.S. industries millions of dollars a year, resulting in losses of jobs and diminution in the number of works created. Effective criminal penalties will aid in preventing such losses.").

[85] Except motion pictures and sound recordings that had required proof that the defendant had made at least one hundred copies. *See* Copyright Felony Act of 1992, Pub. L. No. 102–561, 106 Stat. 4233 (1992).

[86] The Senate proposed Bill 893 to impose criminal sanctions for willful violation of software copyright (S. 893, 102d Cong. (1991)). The bill was initiated by Senators Orrin Hatch and Dennis DeConcini, and at first was part of an omnibus crime package. Applying only to software, the proposed bill provided that reproduction or distribution of fifty or more copies infringing the copyright in one or more computer programs (including any tape, disk, or other medium embodying such programs) over a 180-day period would be punishable with up to a five-year prison term and a $250,000 fine, or a ten-year prison term if the offense is a second or subsequent offense. The reproduction of more than ten but less than fifty copies within that same period would be punishable by a fine of up to $250,000 and/or one year in prison. After a hearing by the Subcommittee on Intellectual Property and Judicial Administration, Representative Hughes suggested to expand the scope of the proposed bill, by an amendment to the Copyright Act, to apply felony provisions to willful infringement of all types of copyrighted works, and lowering the thresholds for imposing a felony liability. *See* Saunders, *supra* note 12, at 679; Saperstein, *supra* note 20, at 1481–82; H.R. REP. No. 102–997, *supra* note 84.

[87] Fines are set under 18 U.S.C. § 3571 (1992).

[88] *Id.* § 2319(b)(1)–(2). *See also* S. REP. No. 102–268 (1992); Penney, *supra* note 8, at 63; Note, *supra* note 20, at 1711.

[89] 18 U.S.C. § 2319(b)(3) (1994).

infringements for some types of actions and for all kinds of works were liable for a high fine of $250,000 (or twice the gains from the offense), and a possible ten-year imprisonment term.

2 The Anticounterfeiting Consumer Protection Act of 1996

In 1996, after lobbying by the International Anti-Counterfeiting Coalition,[90] Congress enacted the Anticounterfeiting Consumer Protection Act and further criminalized copyright infringement.[91] Senate protocols show that the Act was enacted to "provide additional tools to combat trademark and goods counterfeiting crimes that cost our Nation billions of dollars per year."[92] As discussed in Congress, counterfeiting of trademarked and copyrighted merchandise was associated with organized crime, deprived legitimate trademark and copyright holders substantial revenues and consumer goodwill, posed health and safety threats to consumers, eliminated jobs, and generally speaking was quickly becoming a multibillion-dollar drain on the economy.[93]

The Act made trafficking in counterfeit goods or services a RICO (Racketeer Influenced and Corrupt Organizations Act) offense,[94] through the additions of Section 2318 (trafficking in counterfeit labels for phonorecords, computer programs or computer program documentation or packaging and copies of motion pictures or other audiovisual works), Section 2319 (criminal infringement of a copyright) and Section 2319A (unauthorized fixation of and trafficking in sound recordings and music videos of live musical performances).[95] The insertion of criminal copyright into RICO made penalties for criminal organizations engaged in criminal copyright exceed penalties for repeat criminal offenders under the Copyright Act. An offender convicted under RICO is liable to an additional $250,000 fine and an additional

---

[90] *See Cracking Down on Trademark Counterfeiting: Testimony Before the Senate Committee on the Judiciary*, 104th Cong. (1995) (testimony of John S. Bliss, President, International Anti-Counterfeiting Coalition).

[91] Anticounterfeiting Consumer Protection Act of 1996, Pub. L. No. 104–153, 110 Stat. 1386 (1996).

[92] 141 Cong. Rec. S18594 (daily ed. Dec. 14, 1995) (statement of Sen. Leahy). Congress stated that "Existing Federal law is not adequate to protect consumers and American businesses from the crime of counterfeiting copyrighted and trademarked products." *See* S. Rep. No. 104–177 (1995).

[93] *See* S. Rep. No. 104–177 (1995), stating that "Organized crime is increasingly involved in this [counterfeiting copyrighted and trademarked products – E. H.] illegal business, reaping profits from the investment of legitimate companies which are plowed back into other activities traditionally associated with organized crime," and that "counterfeit products cost American businesses an estimated $200 billion each year." In addition, Senate reported that "[S]ome of these counterfeits threaten the health and safety of American citizens ... counterfeiting is a drain on the American economy, on the Federal treasury, and costs American jobs."

[94] 18 U.S.C. §1961(1)(B) (1996). In an effort to fight organized crime in the United States, RICO was enacted as title IX of the Organized Crime Control Act, Pub. L. 91–452, 84 Stat. 941 (1970).

[95] Anticounterfeiting Consumer Protection Act of 1996, Pub. L. No. 104–153, § 3, 110 Stat. 1386 (1996).

20-year imprisonment.[96] Moreover, the Act allows the prosecution of large-scale organizations, including the seizure and forfeiture of nonmonetary personal and tangible property of the infringers.[97]

In addition, the 1996 Act amended Section 2318 of the U.S. Criminal Code by extending the definition of trafficking in counterfeit labels to include computer programs, computer program documentation, and packaging applying prohibitions and penalties for labels affixed or designed to phonorecords, copies of a motion picture or other audiovisual work.[98]

The 1996 Act was yet another step in copyright criminalization and raised the stakes of criminal copyright: with its enactment, offenders could now face an additional fine of $250,000 and a supplementary, costly, 20-year imprisonment term. However, even after the 1996 Act, criminal copyright remained relatively limited in its scope and mainly targeted large-scale infringers who acted for a commercial advantage or had a profit motive. Thus, as technology continued to evolve, enabling individuals affordable and accessible reproduction and distribution, sometimes even with lower risk of detection, and even when infringement was not for profit, Congress sought to expand the scope of criminal copyright.

3 No Electronic Theft (NET) Act of 1997

Up until 1997, prosecution of copyright infringement depended on the commercial nature of the infringement, i.e., infringement was for commercial advantage or private financial gain. *United States v. LaMacchia*, a landmark case on this matter, proved the problematic nature of this requirement, particularly for online enforcement of copyright infringements, and ultimately, had enormous ramifications for criminal copyright legislation.[99]

In 1993–1994, David LaMacchia, a twenty-one-year-old student at the Massachusetts Institute of Technology (MIT), established an electronic bulletin board ("BBS") named Cynosure using MIT's computer network. Cynosure, which had two versions, was without commercial advantage and did not offer LaMacchia any private financial gain.[100] LaMacchia encouraged subscribers to upload popular software applications and computer games, which he transferred to a second

---

[96] 18 U.S.C. §§ 1963(a), 3571(b)(3) (1996). A criminal RICO violation is a separate offense from criminal copyright infringement. *See generally*, Julie L. Ross, *A Generation of Racketeers? Eliminating Civil RICO Liability for Copyright Infringement*, 13 VAND. J. ENT. & TECH. L. 55 (2010).

[97] Pyun, *supra* note 12, at 363–64.

[98] 18 U.S.C. § 2318 (1996).

[99] United States v. LaMacchia, 871 F. Supp. 535 (D. Mass. 1994).

[100] *See* Eric Goldman, *A Road to No Warez: The No Electronic Theft Act and Criminal Copyright Infringement*, 82 OR. L. REV. 369, 372 (2003).

encrypted address, and from which Cynosure users were able to download. In doing so, LaMacchia allegedly caused some rights holders to lose revenue.[101]

But since LaMacchia did not derive any financial benefits from his actions, he could not be prosecuted for criminal copyright infringement. Unable to charge LaMacchia with criminal copyright infringement, a federal grand jury charged him with conspiring with "persons unknown" to violate the Fraud by Wire statute. LaMacchia brought a motion to dismiss, arguing that the government had improperly resorted to using the Fraud by Wire statute as a copyright enforcement tool, referencing the Supreme Court decision in *Dowling v. United States*.[102] While criticizing LaMacchia's actions,[103] the Massachusetts District Court dismissed the case against LaMacchia holding that Congress never meant to use the Fraud by Wire statute to prosecute copyright infringement, noting that the legislature, not the court, is empowered to define crime and ordain its punishment.[104]

Following the LaMacchia case, Senator Leahy proposed the Criminal Copyright Improvement Act of 1995,[105] which sanctioned criminal infringement even for those lacking financial gain or commercial advantage. The Criminal Copyright Improvement Bill aimed to impose criminal liability on copyright infringement for non-financial gain or commercial advantage use,[106] and also amended Section 2319 of

---

[101] According to the indictment, LaMacchia's bulletin board system had as its object the facilitation "on an international scale" of the "illegal copying and distribution of copyrighted software" without payment of licensing fees and royalties to software manufacturers and vendors. The prosecutors alleged that LaMacchia's scheme caused losses of more than $1 million to software copyright holders. However, the prosecutor's loss estimate was unsupported. *See id.* at 372; Joseph F. Savage, Jr. & Kristina E. Barclay, *When the Heartland is "Outside the Heartland:" the New Guidelines for NET Act Sentencing*, 9 GEO. MASON L. REV. 373, 377 (2000).

[102] 473 U.S. 207 (1985). In *Dowling*, the Supreme Court held that a copyrighted musical composition impressed on a bootleg phonograph record is not property that is "stolen, converted, or taken by fraud" within the meaning of the National Stolen Property Act of 1934 (Pub. L. No. 73–246, 48 Stat. 794). *See, e.g.,* Elizabeth Blakey, *Criminal Copyright Infringement: Music Pirates don't Sing the Jailhouse Rock when they Steal from the King*, 7 LOY. ENT. L.J. 417 (1987). Prior to *Dowling*, United States Courts extended the protections of the National Stolen Property Act to copyrighted goods. *See, e.g.,* United States v. Drebin, 557 F.2d 1316, 1328 (9th Cir. 1977) (holding that copies of copyrighted motion pictures are considered goods or merchandise for purposes of the National Stolen Property Act); Coenen Jr., Greenberg & Reisinger, *supra* note 76, at 882–83.

[103] LaMacchia's behavior was described as "heedlessly irresponsible, and at worst as nihilistic self-indulgent, and lacking in any fundamental sense of values." *See LaMacchia*, 871 F. Supp. at 545.

[104] *Id.* at 545 (quoting United States v. Wiltberger, 18 U.S. 76 (1820)). The Court noted that it is Congress's prerogative to change the law if it wishes to criminalize such a behavior ("Criminal as well as civil penalties should probably attach to willful, multiple infringements of copyrighted software even absent a commercial motive on the part of the infringer. One can envision ways that the copyright law could be modified to permit such prosecution. But, it is the legislature, not the Court, which is to define a crime, and ordain its punishment."). *Id.*

[105] Criminal Copyright Improvement Act of 1995, S. 1122, 104th Cong. (1995).

[106] Mostly, the bill aimed to impose criminal liability on copyright infringement, by amending Section 506(a) of title 17, criminalizing acts of reproduction or distribution, including by

Title 18, which expanded the types of criminal copyright and increased the fine and imprisonment.[107] However, Congress never enacted the Bill after the Senate Judiciary Committee failed to act upon it.[108]

Outraged by LaMacchia's acquittal, the computer industry lobbied for criminalization of "computer theft" of copyrighted works and the elimination the profit requirement. According to lobbyists, the present situation endangered the computer industry, many of which were small businesses that depend on licensing agreements and royalties for survival.[109]

After failing to enact the Criminal Copyright Improvement Act of 1995, Congress introduced a similar statute entitled the No Electronic Theft (NET) Act,[110] which was signed by President Clinton on December 16, 1997, with a clear objective to close the "loophole" highlighted in *United States* v. *LaMacchia.*[111]

The NET Act addressed criminal copyright in various ways. First, it changed the definition of financial gain set in 17 U.S.C. §101, to include the receipt (or

transmission, or assisting others in such activities, of one or more copyrighted works, which have a total retail value of $5,000 or more.

[107] Under the new proposed section, a person who committed an offense under section 506(a)(2) of title 17, regarding reproduction or distribution, including by transmission, or assisting others in such reproduction or distribution of one or more copyrighted works, which have a total retail value of more than $10,000, could be imprisoned up to 5 years, and/or fined. Other infringers could face an imprisonment of up to one year, and/or a fine. In addition, in a second or subsequent felony offense, the bill proposed up to 10 years of imprisonment, and/or a fine. *See* Criminal Copyright Improvement Act of 1995, S. 1122, 104th Cong. § 2(d) (1995).

[108] Another version of the Act was proposed in 1997 in the United States Senate, but did not eventually pass. *See* Criminal Copyright Improvement Act of 1997, S. 1044, 105th Cong. (1997); Note, *supra* note 20, at 1715.

[109] *See* H.R. Rep. No. 105–339 (1996); *Copyright Piracy, and H.R. 2265, the No Electronic Theft (NET) Act: Hearings on H.R. 2265 Before the Subcomm. on Courts and Intellectual Prop. of the House Comm. on the Judiciary,* 105th Cong. (1997) (witnesses speaking before the committee included Greg Wrenn, Senior Corporate Counsel with Adobe System and Brad Smith of Microsoft, both speaking on behalf of the Business Software Alliance (BSA) and Sandra Sellers, Vice President of Intellectual Property Education and Enforcement for the Software Publishers Association); Michael Coblenz, *Intellectual Property Crimes,* 9 ALB. L.J. SCI. & TECH. 235, 2450–9 (1999).

[110] No Electronic Theft (NET) Act, Pub. L. No. 105–47, 111 Stat. 2678 (1997) (17 U.S.C. §§ 101, 506, 507; 18 U.S.C. §§ 2319, 2320; 28 U.S.C. § 1498 (1997)). The NET Act was not identical to the Criminal Copyright Improvement Act of 1995. For example, the Criminal Copyright Improvement Act of 1995 set a monetary threshold for non-commercially motivated criminal infringement at $5,000 and a felony threshold for a retail value in excess of $10,000, both, much higher than the No Electronic Theft (NET) Act provisions.

[111] The House Report, in the first draft of the NET Act (H.R. REP. NO. 105–339, at 3 (1997)), indicated:

The purpose of H.R. 2265, as amended, is to reverse the practical consequences of United States v. LaMacchia, 871 F. Supp. 535 (D. Mass. 1994) [hereinafter: LaMacchia], which held, inter alia, that electronic piracy of copyrighted works may not be prosecuted under the federal wire fraud statute; and that criminal sanctions available under Titles 17 and 18 of the U.S. Code for copyright infringement do not apply in instances in which a defendant does not realize a commercial advantage or private financial gain.

expectation of receipt) of anything of value, including other copyrighted works, by inserting the statement, that "'The term 'financial gain' includes receipt, or expectation of receipt, of anything of value, including the receipt of other copyrighted works.[112]"

Second, the NET Act amended 17 U.S.C. § 506(a), which regulates criminal infringements.[113] Under the new section, criminal infringement was defined as any person who willfully infringes a copyright,[114] either for purposes of commercial advantage or private financial gain, or by the reproduction or distribution, including by electronic means, during any 180-day period, of one or more copies or phonorecords of one or more copyrighted works, which have a total retail value of more than $1,000.[115]

Third, the NET Act expanded the statute of limitation on criminal proceedings set in 17 U.S.C. § 507(a) by two years, to be consistent with most other criminal statutes,[116] i.e., from three years to five years after the cause of action arose.

Fourth, the NET Act clarified that reproduction or distribution by electronic means was included in the felony provisions and clarified that the retail value of $2,500 is the total retail value.[117] Doing so, the NET Act clarified that reproduction and distribution of electronic copies via the internet can qualify for criminal sanctions.[118]

Fifth, the NET Act changed the punishment for criminal infringement. Under the Act, the sanction for infringements of more than $1,000 is imprisonment of up to one year and a fine and, for infringements of $2,500 or more imprisonment, of up to three years and a fine. In case of a second or subsequent offense, involving commercial advantages or private financial gain, punishment includes imprisonment of up to six years.[119]

---

[112] *See* No Electronic Theft (NET) Act § 2(a).

[113] *Id.* § 2(b).

[114] Although the NET Act states that evidence of making and distributing copyrighted works does not, by itself, establish willfulness (*id.* § 2(b); Goldman, *supra* note 100, at 373), the interpretation of the term "willfully" is still unclear. Many Courts interpreted the language of the term "willfully" in the Copyright Act as proving that the accused specifically intended to violate copyright law. Other Courts held that the term "willful" refers only to intent to copy, not intent to infringe. For example, see United States v. Moran, 757 F. Supp. 1046 (D. Neb. 1991) (citing United States v. Rose, 149 U.S.P.Q. (BNA) 820 (S.D.N.Y. 1966) and holding that "willfully" means that in order to be criminal the infringement must have been a "voluntary, intentional violation of a known legal duty); Saunders, *supra* note 12, at 688; Hardy, *supra* note 12, at 319–20.

[115] The punishment for this section is as provided under 18 U.S.C. § 2319 (1997).

[116] David Goldstone, Prosecuting Intellectual Property Crimes 64 (2001).

[117] By striking "with a retail value of more than $2,500" and inserting "which have a total retail value of more than $2,500." *See* No Electronic Theft (NET) Act § 2(d)(2)(A); Pallas-Loren, *supra* note 12, at 846.

[118] Copyright Piracy, and H.R. 2265, the No Electronic Theft (NET) Act, *supra* note 109, at 13.

[119] *See* No Electronic Theft (NET) Act § 2(d); Goldman, *supra* note 100, at 373–74.

Sixth, the NET Act enabled victims of copyright infringement to submit victim impact statements.[120] Under this provision, victims of copyright infringement can include information identifying the scope of injury and loss suffered, including an estimate of the economic impact of the offense on that victim. This information can be used as evidence in sentencing.[121]

Finally, the Act instructed the Sentencing Commission[122] to ensure that the applicable guideline range for a defendant convicted of a crime against IP is sufficiently stringent to deter such a crime, and to ensure that the guidelines provide for consideration of the retail value and quantity of the items with respect to which the crime against IP was committed.[123]

The NET Act marked a dramatic change in criminal copyright. Prior to the NET Act, copyright infringements for non-commercial purposes were not subject to criminal penalties. At least one scholar argued that the NET Act marked a paradigm shift in copyright law: particularly in that criminal copyright infringement is similar

---

[120] *See* No Electronic Theft (NET) Act § 3; 18 U.S.C. § 2319(d) (Supp. III 1997). Submitting a victim impact statement is a victim's right to introduce a statement, which describes the crime's impact upon them and upon their family, at the sentencing or disposition of a trial. Victims include both producers and sellers of legitimate works affected by the defendant's conduct. For more on victim impact statements, see, e.g., Phillip A. Talbert, *The Relevance of Victim Impact Statements to the Criminal Sentencing Decision*, 36 UCLA L. REV. 199 (1988); Kristin Henning, *What's Wrong with Victims' Rights in Juvenile Court?: Retributive Versus Rehabilitative Systems of Justice*, 97 CALIF. L. REV. 1107 (2009).

[121] Pallas-Loren, *supra* note 12, at 849.

[122] Under the authority of the Sentencing Reform Act of 1984, Pub. L. No. 98–473, 98 Stat. 1987 (1984); and of the Sentencing Act of 1987, Pub. L. No. 100–182, § 21, 101 Stat. 1271 (1987) (including the authority to amend the sentencing guidelines and policy statements).

[123] § 2(g) of the NET Act, instructed the United States Sentencing Commission to ensure that the applicable guideline range for a defendant convicted of a crime against IP is sufficiently stringent to deter such a crime and ensure that the guidelines provide for consideration of the retail value and quantity of the items with respect to which the crime against IP was committed. United States Congress implemented § 2(g) in 1999, by enacting the Digital Theft Deterrence and Copyright Damages Improvement Act of 1999, Pub. L. No. 106–160, 113 Stat. 1774 (1999). Mostly, under the amendments, Congress increased the base level offense from a Level 6 to a Level 8; directed courts to consider the value of the infringed-upon item in calculating the loss in all cases; provided a two-level upward adjustment for cases involving manufacture, importation, and uploading of infringing items and impose mandatory offense levels of 12 in such cases; provided a two-level upward adjustment based on use of special skill in cases involving circumvention of technical protection measures to protect copyrighted works; and it gave courts discretion in any case to apply an upward departure in a case where the ordinary calculation would substantially understate the seriousness of the offense. *See* United States Sentencing Commission, *Intellectual Property/Copyright Infringement: Group Breakout Session Two*, at 242 (2000), *available at* www.ussc.gov/Research_and_Statistics/Research_Projects/Economic_Crimes/20001012_Symposium/tGroupTwoDayTwo.pdf. For more information regarding the Digital Theft Deterrence and Copyright Damages Improvement Act, see Goldman, *supra* note 100, at 378–81; Coenen Jr., Greenberg & Reisinger, *supra* note 76, at 880–81.

to physical theft, and that the public should come to realize this.[124] Copyright scholarship discusses the perception of copyright as tangible property at length, and I analyze its implications vis-à-vis criminal copyright legislation in Chapters 5 and 6, as a possible explanation and justification of the criminalization process.

4 The Digital Millennium Copyright Act of 1998

In 1998, Congress enacted the Digital Millennium Copyright Act (DMCA),[125] which along with civil amendments to copyright statute, introduced new anti-circumvention rules that affect both civil and criminal law.[126] The DMCA was enacted partially to comply with two World Intellectual Property Organization (WIPO) treaties,[127] but

---

[124] See Goldman, *supra* note 100, at 370 (arguing that by enacting the NET Act, Congress adopted a paradigm that criminal copyright infringement is like physical-space theft, specifically shoplifting, while citing 143 CONG. REC. S12689, S12691 (daily ed. Nov. 13, 1997) (statement of Sen. Leahy): "[b]y passing this legislation, we send a strong message that we value intellectual property ... in the same way that we value the real and personal property of our citizens. Just as we will not tolerate the theft of software, CD's, books, or movie cassettes from a store, so will we not permit the stealing of intellectual property over the Internet."). *See also* 143 CONG. REC. H9883, H9885 (daily ed. Nov. 4, 1997) (statement of Rep. Goodlatte) ("Imagine the same situation occurring with tangible goods that could not be transmitted over the Internet, such as copying popular movies onto hundreds of blank tapes and passing them out on every street corner or copying personal software onto blank disks and freely distributing them throughout the world. Few would disagree that such activities are illegal and should be prosecuted. We should be no less vigilant when such activities occur on the Internet. We cannot allow the Internet to become the Home Shoplifting Network."); and 143 CONG. REC. E1527 (daily ed. July 25, 1997) ("the public must come to understand that intellectual property rights, while abstract and arcane, are no less deserving of protection than personal or real property rights.").

[125] Digital Millennium Copyright Act (DMCA), Pub. L. No. 105–304, 112 Stat. 2860 (1998) (codified as amended at 17 U.S.C. §§ 512, 1201–1205, 1301–1332 & 28 U.S.C. § 4001).

[126] For instance, the DMCA inserted limitations on liability, often referred to as "safe harbors," which shelter service providers from copyright infringement lawsuits. *See* 17 U.S.C. § 512 (1998). The first effort to regulate digital copying through United States copyright law was prior to the DMCA enactment, by the Audio Home Recording Act of 1992 (Pub. L. No. 102–563, 106 Stat. 4237 (1992)). However, this Audio Home Recording Act only established a technological solution to multi-generational digital copying while not generally prohibiting the circumvention of protective technology. *See* Stephen M. Kramarsky, *Copyright Enforcement in the Internet Age: The Law and Technology of Digital Rights Management*, 11 DEPAUL J. ART & ENT. L. 1, 17–22 (2001).

[127] *See* The Copyright and Related Rights Regulations, 2003, S.I. 2003/2498 (U.K.); WIPO Copyright Treaty, Dec. 20, 1996, 36 I.L.M. 65, arts. 11–12 (1997), and the WIPO Performances and Phonograms Treaty, 20 December 1996, 36 I.L.M. 76, arts. 18–19 (1997). As the United States signed and ratified these treaties, they were obliged to provide adequate legal protection and effective legal remedies against the circumvention of effective technological measures; to provide adequate and effective legal remedies against entities who remove or alter any electronic rights management information without authority or distribute works knowing that such information has been removed or altered without authority. *See* H.R. CONF. REP. NO. 105–796, at 63 (1998); Penney, *supra* note 8, at 85. It is still unclear whether the DMCA was necessary to implement the WCT, as American law already complied with most of the treaty, except the provision calling for protecting the integrity of rights management information. *See* Pamela Samuelson, *Big Media Beaten Back*, WIRED 64 (1997).

went beyond their requirements.[128] Similarly to most criminal copyright legislation, copyright industries, i.e., the Motion Picture Association of America (MPAA) and the Recording Industry Association of America (RIAA), lobbied for the enactment of the DMCA and most likely impacted the drafting of the anti-circumvention provisions.[129]

The DMCA included several prohibitions. It prohibited circumventing a technological measure that effectively controls access to a protected work.[130] With that, it provided limited exceptions to circumventions for academic institutions, nonprofit libraries, archives, law enforcement and other government activities,[131] as well as reverse engineering and encryption research exemptions to a list of activities;[132] and it prohibited trafficking in circumvention technology[133] and tampering with copyright management information.[134]

These provisions may be compensated by civil remedies, e.g., injunctions, actual damages, and statutory damages.[135] However, the DMCA even went further. It provided criminal sanctions, limited to entities acting willfully, and for purposes of commercial advantage or private financial gain.[136] Maximum criminal penalties for a first offense are $500,000 and/or five-year imprisonment and for subsequent offenses $1,000,000 and/or ten-year imprisonment. The DMCA sets an exception for criminal liability of a nonprofit library, archives, or educational institution,[137] and sets a statute of limitation of five years.[138]

---

[128] See Neil Netanel, *Recent Developments in Copyright Law*, 7 TEX. INTELL. PROP. J. 331, 332 (1999); Pamela Samuelson, *Intellectual Property and the Digital Economy: Why the Anti-Circumvention Regulations Need to be Revised*, 14 BERKELEY TECH. L.J. 519, 521 (1999).

[129] MATTHEW RIMMER, DIGITAL COPYRIGHT AND THE CONSUMER REVOLUTION 158 (2007).

[130] To circumvent a technological measure means to descramble a scrambled work, to decrypt an encrypted work, or otherwise to avoid, bypass, remove, deactivate, or impair a technological measure, without the authority of the copyright owner. See 17 U.S.C. § 1201(a)(3)(A) (1998). For criticism on the anti-circumvention rules in the DMCA, see, e.g., Samuelson, *supra* note 128. However, the DMCA also notes that the prohibition will not apply to persons who are users of a copyrighted work which is in a particular class of works, if such persons are, or are likely to be in the succeeding three-year period, adversely affected by virtue of such prohibition in their ability to make non-infringing uses of that particular class of works set by the Librarian of Congress regulations exemptions. In addition, libraries and educational institutions are permitted to circumvent protective measures prior to purchasing a work, and law enforcement and intelligence operations are also exempt from liability for the purpose of achieving the interoperability of computer programs, and encryption research. See *id.* § 1201. See also Penney, *supra* note 8, at 86.

[131] 17 U.S.C. § 1201(d)–(j) (1998).

[132] *Id.* 1201(f)–(g). In addition, based on rulemaking recommendations from the Register of Copyrights, the DMCA provides for the Librarian of Congress to adopt three-year renewable exemptions for particular classes of copyrighted works from the DMCA's prohibition on circumvention. See *id.* §1201(a)(1)(B)–(E).

[133] See *id.* §§ 1201(a)(2), 1201(b)(1).

[134] *Id.* § 1202; Penney, *supra* note 8, at 65.

[135] 17 U.S.C. § 1203 (1998).

[136] *Id.* § 1204(a).

[137] *Id.* § 1204(b).

[138] *Id.* § 1204(c).

The DMCA took criminal copyright a step further: it criminalized copyrighted-related activities, and not just copyright infringement itself. For example, sanctions for circumvention of a technological measure were even higher than fines for infringement. These anti-circumvention criminal rules, once again mark the crucial role of technological developments on criminal (para-) copyright legislation, designed to protect rights holders.

5 The Intellectual Property Protection and Courts Amendments Act of 2004

In 2004, Congress enacted the Intellectual Property Protection and Courts Amendments Act.[139] As indicated in the House Report, the 2004 Act was born out of a perceived need of software companies to deter counterfeiting of identification measures to verify computer software authenticity, e.g., holograms, micro-printing, and special ink.[140] As reported and lobbied for by the Microsoft representative in the Congressional hearing, counterfeiting-authenticating features to verify authenticity were highly profitable with a low risk of prosecution and significant punishment. The bundling of authentic labeling components with counterfeit software had become part of an intricate web of international organized crime.[141] In addition, as indicated in its House Report, preventing counterfeiting of labels, documentation, and packaging of copyrighted goods and phonorecords, will assist in preventing further revenue loss for rights holders (mainly in the software industry)[142]; it will lower fraudulent activities; and it will protect consumers from unknowingly purchasing counterfeited products.[143]

The 2004 Act expanded criminal provisions to combat the trafficking of counterfeit IP products. Specifically, the Act prohibited and criminalized knowingly and without the authorization of the copyright owner, trafficking in a counterfeit or illicit label affixed to copyrighted goods, such as a phonorecord, a copy of a

---

[139] Intellectual Property Protection and Courts Amendments Act, Pub. L. No. 108–482, 118 Stat. 3912 (2004) (amending 18 U.S.C. § 2318); John R. Grimm, Stephen F. Guzzi & Kathleen Elizabeth Rupp, *Intellectual Property Crimes*, 47 Am. Crim. L. Rev. 741, 766 (2010); Bitton, *supra* note 12, at 88.

[140] Although counterfeiting of identification features to verify authenticity occurs primarily in crimes involving software counterfeiting, there have been occurrences where it exists with other types of intellectual property. See H.R. Rep. No. 108–600 (2004).

[141] *Id. International copyright piracy: a growing problem with links to organized crime and terrorism: Hearing Before the Subcomm. on Courts, the Internet, and Intellectual Property*, 108th Cong. 41 (2003) (testimony of Rich LaMagna, a Senior Manager of Worldwide Anti-Piracy Investigations at Microsoft Corporation).

[142] For example, in November 2001 the United States Customs seized approximately $100 million in counterfeit software that was brought into the port of Long Beach, California. Moreover, an American software company estimated that over 500,000 of its legitimate authentication features have been stolen from authorized replicators. See H.R. Rep. No 108–600, at 4–5 (2004).

[143] *Id.* at 5.

computer program, motion picture (or other audiovisual work), literary work, or pictorial, graphic, or sculptural work, a work of visual art, or documentation or packaging, or counterfeit documentation or packaging.[144] Such an offense could be committed in the United States in addition to those facilitated through the use of the mail or a facility of interstate or foreign commerce.[145] Moreover, the Act provided for authorized forfeiture of equipment, devices, or materials used to manufacture, reproduce, or assemble counterfeit or illicit labels.[146] Under the Act's criminal sanctions, counterfeit documentation or packaging is subject to a fine or imprisonment for no more than five years, or both.[147]

The 2004 Act's criminalization is slightly different than most of the other *high-tech* phase legislation. It targeted the large-scale infringers acting for commercial advantages or with a profit motive, rather than end-users, in contrast to the NET Act, for example. Thus, the *high-tech* phase of criminal copyright is not limited to targeting small-scale infringers, and large-scale infringers still play a role in copyright criminalization.

6 The Family Entertainment and Copyright Act of 2005

In 2005, Congress enacted the Family Entertainment and Copyright Act.[148] Among other reasons,[149] the enactment was due to MPAA's claim that illicit "camcording" of motion pictures in motion picture exhibition facilities,[150] cost the movie industry an estimated $3.5 billion because of hard-goods "piracy."[151] The Act provides

[144] *See* Intellectual Property Protection and Courts Amendments Act, Pub. L. No. 108–482, § 102, 118 Stat. 3912 (2004), (codified as amended at 18 U.S.C. § 2318(a) (2004)). *See also* Grimm, Guzzi & Rupp, *supra* note 139, at 766.
[145] *See* 18 U.S.C. § 2318(c) (2004). Grimm, Guzzi & Rupp, *supra* note 139, at 766.
[146] 18 U.S.C. § 2318(d) (2004).
[147] *Id.* § 2318(a)(1)(B).
[148] Family Entertainment and Copyright Act of 2005, Pub. L. No. 109-9, 119 Stat. 218 (2005) (codified as amended at 18 U.S.C. § 2319B (2005)). The Family Entertainment and Copyright Act of 2005 is divided to Artist's Rights and Theft Prevention Act of 2005 and Family Home Movie Act of 2005.
[149] The Family Entertainment and Copyright Act purposes were to penalize camcorders motion pictures in movie theaters; to create civil and criminal penalties for those who willfully distribute pre-release works; to clarify the legal status of certain services and technologies that enable individuals to skip and mute content on certain works in the privacy of their own home; to reauthorizes the National Film Preservation Board and Foundation; and to correct a technical error in the "Sonny Bono Copyright Term Extension Act" that limited library and archive access to certain works during the last 20 years of term." *See* H.R. REP. NO. 109-33, at 2 (2005).
[150] The term motion picture exhibition facility means "[a] movie theater, screening room, or other venue that is being used primarily for the exhibition of a copyrighted motion picture, if such exhibition is open to the public or is made to an assembled group of viewers outside of a normal circle of a family and its social acquaintances." *See* 17 U.S.C. § 101; H.R. REP. NO. 109-33.
[151] *Id.* at 2.

prosecutors with resources to stem the "piracy" of commercially valuable motion pictures at its source.

The Act created a criminal penalty for the willful distribution of works being prepared for commercial distribution. Specifically, it prohibits any person from knowingly using or attempting to use an audiovisual recording device to transmit or make a copy of a motion picture or other audiovisual copyright protected work without the authorization of the copyright owner, from a performance of such work in a motion picture exhibition facility. Criminal sanctions for these actions include a fine and/or up to three years' imprisonment. A second or subsequent offender could face a fine and/or up to six years imprisonment.[152]

The 2005 Act continues the pattern that began in the high-tech phase – the use of criminal copyright to deter copyright infringements that were facilitated because of technological measures. Once again, the impact of political power over criminal copyright legislation is evident through lobbying efforts by industry groups.

7 The Prioritizing Resources and Organization for Intellectual Property Act of 2008

In 2008, following various propositions to amend the Copyright Act, Congress enacted the Prioritizing Resources and Organization for Intellectual Property Act of 2008 (PRO-IP Act).[153] Lobbied for by various interest groups,[154] its main purpose was to improve IP enforcement in the United States and abroad and enhance remedies for violations of IP laws.[155] The Act included Congress' official statement on the reasoning's of the PRO-IP Act. First, Congress found that counterfeiting and infringement results in billions of dollars yearly in lost revenue for American companies and even greater losses to the American economy in terms of reduced job growth, fewer exports, and decline in competitiveness.[156] Counterfeiting and

---

[152] *See* 18 U.S.C. § 2319B(a) (2005).

[153] Prioritizing Resources and Organization for Intellectual Property Act, Pub. L. No. 110–403, 122 Stat. 4256 (2008) ("PRO-IP Act"). For examples of various propositions to amend the copyright Act, see the Intellectual Property Protection Act of 2007, proposed to Congress by Attorney General Alberto Gonzales in May 2007: Letter from Richard A. Hertling, Principal Deputy Assistant Att'y Gen., U.S. Dep't of Justice, to Nancy Pelosi, Speaker, U.S. House of Representatives (May 14, 2007), www.justice.gov/olp/pdf/ip_protection_act_2007.pdf. Although the proposition only advanced to a committee referral, some provisions were inserted in the 2008 Act. *See* Pyun, *supra* note 12, at 372–73.

[154] Frank Ahrens, *House Bill to Create Anti-Piracy Czar Advances*, THE WASHINGTON POST (May 1, 2008), www.washingtonpost.com/wpdyn/content/article/2008/04/30/AR2008043003360.html; Eric Bangeman, *RIAA spent $2 million lobbying for tougher IP laws in 2007*, ARSTECHNICA (Apr. 21, 2008, 12:05 PM), http://arstechnica.com/tech-policy/2008/04/riaa-spent-2-million-lobbying-for-tougher-ip-laws-in-2007.

[155] *See* PRO-IP Act; H.R. REP. No. 110–617 (2007).

[156] The statement also indicated that: "The United States intellectual property industries have created millions of high-skill, high-paying United States jobs and pay billions of dollars in annual United States tax revenues;" and that "The United States intellectual property industries

infringement allegedly posed a serious threat to the long-term vitality of the American economy and the future competitiveness of American industry. Second, Congress found that there was a growing number of willful violations of existing federal criminal laws involving counterfeiting and infringement by offenders in the United States and, increasingly, by foreign-based individuals and entities. Finally, Congress determined that terrorists and organized crime utilize "piracy,"[157] counterfeiting, and infringement to fund some of their activities.[158]

The PRO-IP Act directly addressed criminal copyright by replacing the term "offense" with "felony," substantially reducing IP misdemeanors.[159] In addition, the Act mandated restitution by the convicted offender to the victim – as is the case with property offenses. It also mandates restitution across the board for all IP crimes including unauthorized recordings of motion pictures and uncovering trade secrets under the Economic Espionage Act.[160] It is highly important to note that the Act also granted the federal government power to seize and civilly forfeit property

continue to represent a major source of creativity and innovation, business start-ups, skilled job creation, exports, economic growth, and competitiveness." *See* PRO-IP Act § 503(1)–(2).

[157] Supposedly, "pirated" and counterfeited goods are sometimes linked with funding terror and large-scale organized crime groups. For example, the 1993 United States World Trade Center bombings was arguably financed, at least partially, by the sale of counterfeited T-shirts and sportswear. *See, e.g.,* Kathleen Millar, *Financing Terror: Profits from counterfeit goods pay for attacks,* U.S. Customs Today (Nov., 2002), www.cbp.gov/xp/CustomsToday/2002/November/ interpol.xml; Gregory F. Treverton et al., *Film Piracy, Organized Crime and Terrorism,* RAND Corp. (2009), www.rand.org/pubs/monographs/2009/RAND_MG742.pdf; Isabella Alexander, *Criminalising Copyright: A Story of Publishers, Pirates, and Pieces of Eight,* 66 Cambridge L.J. 625, 648 (2007); Ryan Rufo, *Below the Surface of the ACTA: The Dangers that Justify New Criminal Sanctions Against Intellectual Property Infringement,* 39 AIPLA Q.J. 511, 517–20 (2011). For more on the linkage between organized crime and IP crime in the United Kingdom, see Andrew Gowers, Gowers review of Intellectual Property 104 (2006), http://webarc hive.nationalarchives.gov.uk/+/http:/www.hm-treasury.gov.uk/d/pbr06_gowers_report_755.pdf (last visited Dec. 1, 2017).

[158] *See* PRO-IP Act § 503(1)–(6).

[159] *See id.* § 208; regarding criminal IP, the Act broadened penalties for bodily harm and death resulting in criminal trafficking of counterfeited goods by adding a provision designated to an offender who knowingly or recklessly causes or attempts to cause serious bodily injury from intentionally trafficking counterfeited goods could face a fine, or up to twenty years' imprisonment, or both. In addition, in cases of an offender which knowingly or recklessly causes or attempts to cause death from intentionally trafficking counterfeited goods, could face a fine, or up to a life sentence, or both; Pyun, *supra* note 12, at 376–77.

[160] PRO-IP Act §§ 201, 207. In addition, Title III creates an IP Enforcement Coordinator (IPEC) to oversee an interagency IP enforcement advisory committee; Title IV provides the DOJ with a grant to assist them in investigating IP crimes, provide specialized training, and to promote the sharing of information and analyses between federal and state agencies concerning investigations and prosecutions of criminal copyright infringement. In addition, Title IV adds more specialized personnel in the CHIP and CCIP units of the DOJ and U.S. Attorney's Office and requires that the FBI and Attorney General submit an annual report which includes statistics of investigations, arrests, prosecutions, and imposed penalties; Title V mandates a study conducted by the GAO to "help determine how the Federal Government could better protect the intellectual property of manufacturers." *See* Pyun, *supra* note 12, at 377–79.

allegedly tainted by copyright crime.[161] While administrative in nature, I note this important shift from private to public law, and relates directly to criminal copyright as it applies, inter alia, to forfeiture of criminally infringing articles and permits permit *ex parte* seizure of internet domain names. I further discuss this potential solution for copyright infringements in Chapter 9.

The PRO-IP Act is currently the last criminal copyright Act in the United States. Along with most of the digital-phase reasoning for criminal copyright, i.e., the rise in copyright infringements and the perceived need for a higher deterrence, the PRO-IP Act also encompassed national interest reasons, e.g., preventing harm to United States economy.

II EVALUATING COPYRIGHT CRIMINALIZATION IN THE UNITED STATES

Since 1897, when Congress introduced criminal copyright for the first time, it has been repeatedly and extensively extended to more types of works, additional categories of actions, and has increased monetary and nonmonetary sanctions. For example, criminal sanctions for willful and for-profit infringement by an individual began in 1909; it carried a maximum fine of $1,000 and one-year imprisonment. By 1992, the fine reached $250,000 (or twice the gains from the offense) and five-year imprisonment for a first offense or ten-year imprisonment for a second or subsequent offense.[162] Moreover, while only willful, for-profit unlawful performance or representation of a dramatic or musical composition was considered a misdemeanor offense in 1897, "Mass piracy" of all types of copyrighted works (including aiding or abetting) was a felony offense in 1992, and by 1997 the for-profit requirement was extensively loosened.[163]

It is evident that criminal copyright in the United States has dramatically increased since its introduction in 1897. As described, the *low-tech* criminalization phase, 1897–1909, marks the beginning of the process but did not make a significant change to American copyright law, as criminal copyright did not extend to all copyrighted materials, and was only considered a misdemeanor. However, the *high-tech* criminalization phase, both analog and digital sub-phases, marks a significant change toward a more criminally-oriented copyright law with increased scope and sanctions. More specifically, the digital criminalization phase is the most significant phase, both by the increase of penalties and the scope of the offenses.

---

[161] *See* 18 U.S.C. § 2323.

[162] However, as discussed above, different types of works were criminalized in different periods.

[163] In addition, during the years criminal copyright infringement was added to other offenses, i.e., a specified unlawful activity for money laundering and a racketeering activity under RICO, it enabled victims of copyright infringement to submit victim impact statements; it authorized forfeiture of equipment, devices, or materials used to manufacture, reproduce, or assemble counterfeit or illicit labels; and it mandated restitution across the board for all IP crimes.

It is not surprising that during the digital criminalization phase, Congress also strengthened civil copyright enforcement. The statuary damage range, for example, rose dramatically in 1999 to $30,000 per infringed work and up to $150,000 per infringed work for willful infringement.[164] As I further explore in Chapter 5, the digital age posed many threats to the copyright regime, and Congress sought better practices of enforcement. Thus, criminal copyright, mainly in the digital age, should be located within the broader enforcement framework of copyright law. As copyright enforcement has not achieved its goals yet, I argue that the United States is still in the digital criminalization phase, as criminalization of copyright law is likely to continue in the following years.

The long-term review of criminal copyright legislation reveals the declared reasons for the process: (1) increase in criminalization since 1971 was mainly due to industry concerns that civil remedies are ineffective for deterring copyright infringements and cause financial loss (especially the Copyright Act Amendments – 1974; the Copyright Felony Act of 1992; the No Electronic Theft (NET) Act of 1997; the Intellectual Property Protection and Courts Amendments Act of 2004; and the Family Entertainment and Copyright Act of 2005); (2) government concerns over crime (especially the Sentencing Reform Act of 1984, the Anti-Drug Abuse Act of 1988, the Anticounterfeiting Consumer Protection Act of 1996, and the Prioritizing Resources and Organization for Intellectual Property Act of 2008); (3) desire to protect public interests (especially the Copyright Felony Act of 1992, the Anticounterfeiting Consumer Protection Act of 1996, the Intellectual Property Protection and Courts Amendments Act of 2004, and the Prioritizing Resources and Organization for Intellectual Property Act of 2008); (4) adapting copyright law to technological developments and industry and consumer use of digital technologies (especially the Sound Recording Act of 1971, the Copyright Act of 1976, the Piracy and Counterfeiting Amendments Act of 1982, the Copyright Felony Act of 1992, the No Electronic Theft (NET) Act of 1997, and the Intellectual Property Protection and Courts Amendments Act of 2004); and (5) Congress' broad interpretation of international treaties (the Digital Millennium Copyright Act of 1998).

In addition, the legislative overview reveals that throughout the entire criminalization process, industry-related groups were involved in the criminal copyright legislation process, i.e., politics played an important role in copyright criminalization (especially the Copyright Act of 1909, the Sound Recording Act of 1971, the Copyright Act of 1976, the Piracy and Counterfeiting Amendments Act of 1982, the No Electronic Theft (NET) Act of 1997, the Digital Millennium Copyright Act of 1998, the Intellectual Property Protection and Courts Amendments Act of 2004, and the Prioritizing Resources and Organization for Intellectual Property Act of 2008). These characteristics are best summarized in Table 2.

[164] Theft Deterrence and Copyright Damages Improvement Act, Pub. L. No. 106–160, 113 Stat. 1774 (1999).

TABLE 2 *Characteristics of Copyright Criminalization in the United States*

Reasons	United States Legislation
Deterrence due to copyright infringement	• Copyright Act Amendments – 1974 • Copyright Felony Act of 1992 • No Electronic Theft (NET) Act of 1997 • The Intellectual Property Protection and Courts Amendments Act of 2004 • Family Entertainment and Copyright Act of 2005
Government concerns over organized crime and protecting public interests	• Sound Recording Act of 1971 • Sentencing Reform Act of 1984 • Anti-Drug Abuse Act of 1988 • Copyright Felony Act of 1992 • Anticounterfeiting Consumer Protection Act of 1996 • Intellectual Property Protection and Courts Amendments Act of 2004 • Prioritizing Resources and Organization for Intellectual Property Act of 2008
Technology developments	• Sound Recording Act of 1971 • Copyright Act of 1976 • Piracy and Counterfeiting Amendments Act of 1982 • Copyright Felony Act of 1992 • No Electronic Theft (NET) Act of 1997 • Intellectual Property Protection and Courts Amendments Act of 2004
Broad interpretations of international requirements	• Digital Millennium Copyright Act of 1998
Lobbying efforts (politics)	• Copyright Act of 1909 • Sound Recording Act of 1971 • Copyright Act Amendments – 1974 • Copyright Act of 1976 • Piracy and Counterfeiting Amendments Act of 1982 • No Electronic Theft (NET) Act of 1997 • Digital Millennium Copyright Act of 1998 • Intellectual Property Protection and Courts Amendments Act of 2004 • Prioritizing Resources and Organization for Intellectual Property Act of 2008

Thus, much like in the United Kingdom, the legislative overview reveals some of the reasons for the criminalization process: (1) a rise in copyright infringements and infringers, mostly due to technological developments that were not deterred by civil sanctions; (2) national interests; (3) international movements toward criminal copyright; and (4) political power. These, along with other reasons are further discussed in Chapters 5 and 6, and further evaluated in Chapters 8 and 9.

CONCLUSION

The American experience with copyright criminalization tells a story that is not much different from the British one. Copyright law is clearly no longer an exclusive matter of civil liability and criminal copyright legislation continually rises. Examining the American test case through the lens of two phases, low-tech and high-tech, shows that at the beginning, criminal copyright did not mark a drastic change in copyright law's perception. The Second – high-tech – phase, however, might tell a different story. The rapid expansion of criminal copyright legislation could eventually make copyright law criminally-oriented.

Legislation, dramatic however it may be, should not be sufficient to lead to a paradigm shift. Thus, despite the continuous injection of criminal sanctions into copyright law, it is important to evaluate whether copyright infringement is still primarily considered a civil wrong, affecting private commercial interests.[165] In order to evaluate the meaning of criminal legislation in copyright law and to assess whether copyright law is in the midst of a criminal paradigm shift, i.e., expanding from civil-based to both a civil and criminal, the next chapter turns to evaluate the actual enforcement and practical usage of the legislative increase of criminal copyright in the chosen criminal copyright cases, i.e., the United Kingdom and the United States.

---

[165] Penney, *supra* note 8, at 61; Hardy, *supra* note 12, at 310; Benjamin Farrand, *'Piracy. It's a Crime.' – The Criminalisation Process of Digital Copyright Infringement, in* NET NEUTRALITY AND OTHER CHALLENGES FOR THE FUTURE OF THE INTERNET 137, 140–41 (Agustí Cerrillo-i-Martínez et al. eds., 2011).

4

The Criminal Copyright Gap[*]

INTRODUCTION

Copyright law is no longer only a civil matter. As demonstrated in Chapters 1–3, *criminal copyright* has dramatically increased worldwide and in many countries, such as the United Kingdom and the United States. Although civil copyright legislation is still much more extensive than criminal copyright legislation, the increase of criminal provisions in copyright law can lead to the perception that the law is a criminal-oriented law. In other words, the overview of criminal copyright in previous chapters indicates that we may be witnessing a paradigm shift toward criminal copyright.

Legislation alone, however, is insufficient to change the perception of copyright as criminal-oriented law. The perception of criminal copyright also depends on enforcement and not solely on legislation, and thus, the increase of criminal legislation in copyright law could have different meanings, not necessarily resulting in a change of perception, or a paradigm shift, which would be difficult to achieve.

In order to evaluate the meaning of criminal legislation in copyright law and to assess whether copyright law is in the midst of a criminal paradigm shift, this chapter reviews the actual enforcement and practical usages of the legislative increase of criminal copyright in the United Kingdom and in the United States. For this purpose, I present statistical findings on criminal copyright litigation to determine whether it aligns with the relevant criminal copyright legislation. Statistical data in the United States regarding criminal copyright prosecutions is far more extensive than similar data in the United Kingdom. Hence, I primarily focus on the United States. After establishing that the ongoing legislative process of copyright criminalization is not applied in practice, or at least not to as a large extent as expected,

---

[*] For an earlier version of this chapter, see Eldar Haber, *The Criminal Copyright Gap*, 18 STAN. TECH. L. REV. 247 (2015).

I discuss potential explanations of what I call the *criminal copyright gap* – the gap between the scope of criminal copyright liability and sanctions and the infrequency of prosecution and punishment. Finally, I summarize the evaluation and return to the guiding question of this chapter – whether criminal copyright is undergoing a paradigm shift – and also discuss the possible implications of the criminal copyright gap.

I CRIMINAL COPYRIGHT PRACTICAL CHANGES

The ongoing legislative process of copyright criminalization could have us assume that copyright law is in the midst of a paradigm shift from civil to criminal copyright.[1] Despite the continuing legislative process of copyright criminalization, which – one could expect – should lead to an increase in criminal copyright prosecutions, practical observation suggests that copyright in action not only remains mostly a matter of civil law,[2] but that criminal prosecutions are still relatively rare.[3] It is important to note that criminalizing copyright does not necessarily imply that criminal copyright becomes the only responsive measure to copyright infringements, as it is not designed to be the sole and/or main tool to resolve the copyright infringement scheme. This was evident and noted by Janet Reno the (then) U.S. Attorney General: "Civil and administrative remedies will continue to be the primary tool for enforcement of IP rights. That makes sense. But there are some cases where the seriousness of the violation and the egregiousness of the conduct

---

[1] Paradigms are what the members of a scientific community share and conversely, a scientific community consists of men who share a paradigm. *See* THOMAS S. KUHN, THE STRUCTURE OF SCIENTIFIC REVOLUTIONS 176 (2d ed. 1970).

[2] *See* Lanier Saperstein, *Copyrights, Criminal Sanctions and Economic Rents: Applying the Rent Seeking Model to the Criminal Law Formulation Process*, 87 J. CRIM. L. & CRIMINOLOGY 1470, 1506 (1997); U.S. DEP'T OF JUSTICE, PROSECUTING INTELLECTUAL PROPERTY CRIMES 5–6 (3d ed. 2006), *available at* www.justice.gov/criminal/cybercrime/docs/ipma2006.pdf ("[c]riminal copyright penalties have always been the exception rather than the rule."); Timothy D. Howell, Comment, *Intellectual Property Pirates: Congress Raises the Stakes in the Modern Battle to Protect Copyrights and Safeguard the United States Economy*, 27 ST. MARY'S L.J. 613, 646–47 (1996); Sharon B. Soffer, *Criminal Copyright Infringement*, 24 AM. CRIM. L. REV. 491 (1987). For an argument that criminal copyright litigation should have increased due to criminal copyright legislation, see I. Trotter Hardy, *Criminal Copyright Infringement*, 11 WM. & MARY BILL RTS. J. 305, 305 (2002).

[3] *See* Kim F. Natividad, *Stepping It Up and Taking It to the Streets: Changing Civil & Criminal Copyright Enforcement Tactics*, 23 BERKELEY TECH. L.J. 469, 480 (2008). For this data, see JOHN GANTZ & JACK B. ROCHESTER, THE PIRATES OF THE DIGITAL MILLENNIUM 207–08 (2005); Maggie Heim & Greg Geockner, *International Anti-Piracy and Market Entry*, 17 WHITTIER L. REV. 261, 267 (1995); Steven Penney, *Crime, Copyright, and the Digital Age*, in WHAT IS A CRIME? CRIMINAL CONDUCT IN CONTEMPORARY SOCIETY 61, 61 (Law Comm'n of Canada ed., 2004); Hardy, *supra* note 2, at 305.

require imposition of a criminal penalty."[4] However, as a general argument, the increase of criminal copyright legislation should lead to a higher scale of enforcement, if it does not cause copyright infringement to cease, or at least, be substantially reduced.

In order to assess whether copyright law is undergoing a paradigm shift toward criminal copyright, I seek to determine, inter alia, whether the government's understanding of copyright law has changed from a civil to a criminal perspective, by examining whether enforcement of criminal copyright has increased in accordance with the manifold legislation. For this purpose, I analyze and compare available statistical data regarding criminal and civil copyright litigation in the United Kingdom and in the United States, focusing on the United States that provides the most comprehensive statistical data for analysis. My examination highlights different legislative landmarks in criminal copyright that should have led to an increase in the prosecution of copyright infringement.

A *Practical Changes in the United Kingdom*

The detailed overview of copyright legislative history in the United Kingdom in Chapter 2 reveals that until 1982, with the enactment of the Copyright Act 1956 (Amendment) Act of 1982,[5] criminal copyright made only four legislative appearances: in 1862, 1906, 1911, and 1956.[6] Accordingly, until 1982, criminal copyright in the United Kingdom in practice was almost nonexistent. As indicated by Lord Wilberforce in *Rank Film Ltd v. Video Information Centre*:

> In practice, as one might suppose, section 21 [of the 1956 Copyright Act - E. H.] is very rarely invoked: only one case came to our knowledge, namely of a prosecution under the Copyright Act 1911, and potential liability under it might well be disregarded as totally insubstantial. The same argument would apply as regards conspiracy to breach it.[7]

Over a 35-year period, from 1982 through the latest criminal copyright legislation in 2017, United Kingdom criminal copyright legislation expanded repeatedly and extensively.[8] Accordingly, enforcement measures of criminal copyright became

---

[4] Janet Reno, *Statement by the Attorney General Symposium of the Americas: Protecting Intellectual Property in the Digital Age* (Sept. 12, 2000), *available at* www.justice.gov/archive/ag/speeches/2000/91200agintellectualprop.htm.

[5] *See* Copyright Act 1956 (Amendment) Act 1982, c. 35 (U.K.).

[6] Fine Arts Copyright Act, 1862, 25 & 26 Vict., c. 68 (U.K.); Musical Copyright Act of 1906, 6 Edw. VII, c. 36 (U.K.); Copyright Act, 1911, 1 & 2 Geo. V, c. 46 (U.K.); Copyright Act, 1956, 4 & 5 Eliz. II, c. 74 (U.K.).

[7] [1982] AC 380 at 441; *See also* Colin Tapper, *Criminality and Copyright, in Intellectual Property, in* THE NEW MILLENNIUM: ESSAYS IN HONOUR OF WILLIAM R. CORNISH 266, 272 (David Vaver & Lionel Bently eds., 2004).

[8] *See supra* Chapter 2.

more substantial. For example, as the IP Office (IPO) indicated, IP enforcement measures have increased since the introduction of the first United Kingdom IP Crime Strategy in 2004. Since then, according to the IPO, "there has been extensive and consistent marketing, liaison and joint working between law enforcement agencies, government departments and commercial sectors."[9] The IPO further noted "far more agencies are involved in dealing with IP crime, including Regional Asset Recovery Teams (RART), the Serious and Organised Crime Agency (SOCA), Trading Standards, Police Forces throughout the country, but particularly the City of London Police and the National Fraud Intelligence Bureau."[10]

Nevertheless, despite the IPO report, the rise of criminal copyright enforcement does not necessarily correspond with the massive rise in criminal copyright legislation since 1982. As I further show, although in some years there has been a rise in the number of prosecutions of individuals, in other years there was a drop in criminal copyright prosecutions. With that, a caveat is in place: Statistical data of United Kingdom's criminal copyright filing is rather limited. Except for prosecution under the Copyright, Designs and Patents Act of 1988 (CDPA), there is no official statistical data of criminal copyright prosecution per criminal copyright statutes. Even then, official statistical data regarding criminal copyright only began in 2002 and covers the number of individuals cautioned, prosecuted, or indicted under the criminal provisions of the CDPA on instances where the copyright infringement is the primary offence.[11] Moreover, the official statistics regarding the number of flings against individuals ceased in 2012, and since then they report the number of individuals cautioned and prosecuted under the CDPA.[12]

My quest to obtain further statistical data beyond reports on criminal copyright prosecutions continued through submitting several requests to various public authorities under the Freedom of Information Act 2000 (FOIA),[13] while searching for published responses to other Freedom of Information requests for criminal

---

[9] *Prevention and Cure: The UK IP Crime Strategy 2011*, Intellectual Property Office 5 (2011), www.ipo.gov.uk/ipcrimestrategy2011.pdf.

[10] *Id.*

[11] The statistical data regarding the number of individuals proceeded against, found guilty, and cautioned under the criminal provisions of the CDPA (and Trade Marks Act 1994) since 2002, is mainly extracted from The IP Crime Report, produced by the IP Crime Group, founded in 2004 by the Intellectual Property Office. Specifically, the Report's criminal copyright statistics are provided by the Ministry of Justice. *See, e.g.*, IP Crime Group, *IP Crime Annual Report 2012–2013*, Intellectual Property Office (2013), www.ipo.gov.uk/ipcreport12.pdf; For the entire IP Crime Group Reports, see *Annual IP Crime Report*, Intellectual Property Office, www.gov.uk/government/collections/ip-crime-reports#ip-crime-reports (last visited Dec. 1, 2017).

[12] *See, e.g.*, IP Crime Group, *IP Crime Annual Report 2013–2014*, Intellectual Property Office (2014), www.gov.uk/government/uploads/system/uploads/attachment_data/file/374283/ipcreport13.PDF.

[13] Freedom of Information Act 2000, c. 36 (U.K.) [hereinafter FOIA]. The Act grants a statutory right of access to recorded information held by public authorities.

copyright filings.[14] Unfortunately, this too led to limited, additional data on criminal copyright filings, which does not significantly augment the official data provided by the IP Crime Report.[15] The only other publicly available FOIA request regarding this matter was made to the Ministry of Justice by *James Firth*, CEO of the Open Digital Policy Organisation.[16] The Ministry provided Mr. Firth with data on the number of defendants prosecuted in magistrate courts under the CDPA and was limited to England and Wales, from 1994 through 2010. Thus, this information is also limited, as it excludes Scotland and Northern Ireland and is contained to a 16-year period alone.

Importantly, statistical analysis of criminal copyright litigation in the United Kingdom was conducted in 2015. Under an independent IPO Report in 2015 [hereinafter IPO Report 2015], researchers summarized statistics of prosecution and sentence records under CDPA between 2006 and 2013, aggregated mainly from the Ministry of Justice, the Crown Prosecution Service, and Trading Standards.[17]

[14] I filed several requests under FOIA to the Ministry of Justice; the Crown Prosecution Service; the Office for National Statistics; the Federation Against Copyright Theft; and the Intellectual Property Office. I requested statistical data on the annual number of UK criminal copyright prosecutions (filed cases) between 1862 and 2016; annual defendants number of UK criminal copyright prosecutions (filed cases) between 1862 and 2016; annual criminal prosecutions (filed cases of all crimes) between 1862 and 2016; and annual civil copyright infringement lawsuits between 1862 and 2016.

[15] More specifically, the Ministry of Justice replied that "to confirm if the Department holds the information you have requested would exceed the cost limits under the legislation," and declined the request, and that the criminal copyright offenses are "grouped together with offence under other sections of the same Acts and cannot be separately identified." The Ministry of Justice notified me that the requested information on these offences may be held by the courts on individual case files, and that even if I file requests to all magistrates' courts in England and Wales under FOIA, it would exceed the estimated cost limits and that it is very likely that any information that may be held within scope of my request may be exempt from disclosure under the terms of Section 32 (Court Records) and thus rejected; the Crown Prosecution Service replied that "Unfortunately, the CPS does not prosecute offences committed under all the different acts that you have specified in your request and, as such, we do not hold any information regarding the prosecution of most of these types of offences. CPS data records only offences prosecuted by the CPS and does not include any prosecutions commenced by other private prosecutors." However, the Crown Prosecution Service did provide information regarding prosecutions under section 107 of the CDPA, but only since 2004, when the CPS commenced the collection of offence based data; the Office for National Statistics replied that "the information you requested is not held by the Office for National Statistics (ONS);" the Federation Against Copyright Theft replied that "We are not statutory body and as such do not provide this level of detail;" and the Intellectual Property Office replied that "The only relevant information held by the Intellectual Property Office is that published in recent years in our IP Crime Reports." The provided statistical data was also limited to England and Wales. As I did not receive sufficient statistical data in England and Wales, I did not file similar FOIA requests in other part of the United Kingdom, e.g., Scotland and Northern Ireland.

[16] See *Total number of criminal prosecutions and convictions under S.107 Copyright, Designs and Patents Act 1988*, WHATDOTHEYKNOW?, www.whatdotheyknow.com/request/total_number_of_criminal_prosecu (last visited Dec. 1, 2017).

[17] See Martin Brassell & Ian Goodyer, PENALTY FAIR? STUDY OF CRIMINAL SANCTIONS FOR COPYRIGHT INFRINGEMENT AVAILABLE UNDER THE CDPA 1988, IPO (2015) [hereinafter IPO REPORT

These statistics, however, are less relevant for the purposes of this chapter, as they both focused on examining differences between physical and online offences while also focusing on the number of people found guilty (unlike the number of people proceeded against). The IPO Report 2015, however, does shed light on the relatively low rates of convictions under the CDPA.

Accordingly, I make controlled use of the official statistics derived from the IPO reports between 2002 and 2012, while acknowledging the limits of analyzing any findings in my quest to determine whether the government has incorporated into its understanding a copyright paradigm change, by examining whether the enforcement of criminal copyright has increased in accordance with legislation.

Returning to the purposes of this chapter, it is important to be reminded of copyright criminalization in the United Kingdom, which is relevant to the following analysis. Since 2002, the United Kingdom has criminalized copyright law four times – in 2002, 2003, 2010, and 2017 – but has also slightly de-criminalized copyright law in 2010 when Parliament decreased the length of imprisonment for some copyright offenses.[18] However, most criminalization and de-criminalization legislation only changed the scope of criminal sanctions and did not add new offenses; thus, they should not affect the number of criminal prosecutions. The only regulation that added a criminal copyright offense was the Copyright and Related Rights Regulations in 2003, which introduced new criminal offenses to CDPA.[19] Therefore, under the limited official statistical data the evaluation of the impact of 2003 legislation is also very limited, as it is confined to a short period of the United Kingdom criminalization process.

Overall, there is a substantial increase in the number of criminal copyright defendants in the United Kingdom between the years 2002 and 2009. On the one hand, the 2003 regulations had an impact on prosecutions, as the number of individuals prosecuted (2003–2009) under the CDPA increased each year. On the other hand, between 2010 and 2012 the number of criminal copyright defendants

---

2015], www.gov.uk/government/uploads/system/uploads/attachment_data/file/405874/Penalty_
Fair_Study_of_criminal_sanctions_for_copyright_infringement_available_under_the_CDPA_
1988.pdf.

[18] *See* Copyright, etc. and Trade Marks (Offences and Enforcement) Act 2002, c. 25 (U.K.); Copyright and Related Rights Regulations, 2003, S.I. 2003/2498 (U.K.); Digital Economy Act 2010, c. 24 (U.K.); Copyright, Designs and Patents Act 1988 (Amendment) Regulations, 2010, S.I. 2010/2694 (U.K.). For a full overview of criminal copyright legislation in the United Kingdom, see Chapter 2.

[19] Knowingly infringing a copyrighted work by communicating it to the public in the course of a business or to such an extent as to affect prejudicially the owner of the copyright (Copyright and Related Rights Regulations, 2003, S.I. 2003/2498, § 26(1)(b) (U.K.) (codified as § 107(4A)); infringing upon the making available right, in making, dealing with or using illicit recordings in the course of a business or to such an extent as to affect the owner prejudicially (Copyright and Related Rights Regulations §26(1)(b) (codified as § 107(4A)); knowingly engaging in an activity related to devices and services designed to circumvent technological measures (Copyright and Related Rights Regulations § 24 (codified as § 296ZB(1)).

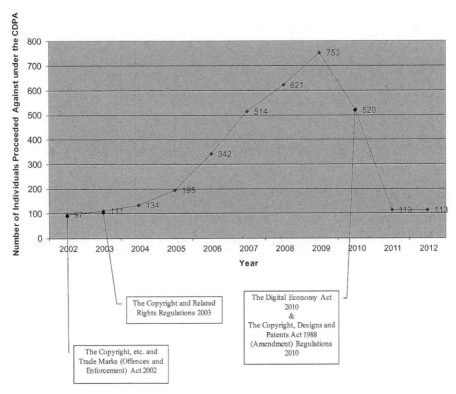

FIGURE 1 Official Criminal Copyright Proceeding in the United Kingdom

dropped. Moreover, if we examine the online criminal provisions of the CDPA, the IPO Report 2015 notes that they were rarely used, if at all.[20] As shown in Figures 1 and 2.[21]

Although Figures 1 and 2 indicate that there had been a growth in the number of defendants in criminal copyright prosecutions in the United Kingdom, since 2010 the trend has reversed. However, as indicated earlier, these limited statistics – which might not tell the full story as previously mentioned – are insufficient to determine whether there is a copyright gap between legislation and enforcement. It is even more limited, as alternative legislation and common law like fraud is often used in the United Kingdom instead of criminal copyright legislation, and thus it is highly difficult to determine the scope of the potential enforcement gap.[22] The IPO Report 2015 also notes that there are other data limitations that are highly relevant for any evaluation. For instance, the gathered data is aggregated from different systems

[20] IPO REPORT 2015, *supra* note 18, at 6.
[21] Figures 1 and 2 are based on statistical data from The IP Crime Report, *supra* note 12.
[22] *See* IPO REPORT 2015, *supra* note 18, at 45.

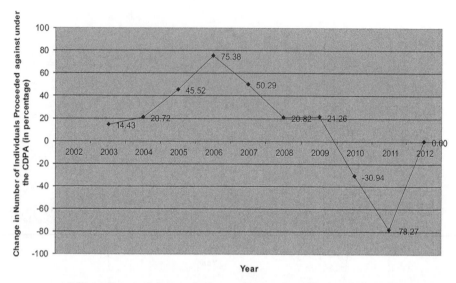

FIGURE 2 Official Criminal Copyright Proceeding in the United Kingdom (Percentage)

which might lead to overlapping results.[23] Thus, without sufficient data to determine the potential gap in the United Kingdom, I turn to evaluate the United States, to determine the scope of criminal copyright enforcement and its possible ramifications.

B *Practical Changes in the United States*

Statistical data regarding criminal copyright prosecutions in the United States between the fiscal years 1955 and 2015[24] seems to indicate that the criminalization process in copyright is limited to legislation. This data was gathered from two sources: first, data for 1955–2008 and 2012–15 is based on the United States Attorneys' Annual Statistical Reports, which provides statistics of overall criminal prosecutions,

---

[23] *Id.* at 48–49.
[24] When criminal copyright was introduced in 1897, the fiscal year started on July 1, 1896, and ended on June 30, 1897. From the fiscal year of 1977, a fiscal year starts on October 1 and ends on September 30 of the next calendar year (Congressional Budget Act of 1974, Pub. L. 93–344, July 12, 1974, 88 Stat. 297 (1974) (currently codified at 31 U.S.C. § 1102)). The data refer to criminal copyright infringement, prosecuted under 17 U.S.C. § 104 (1955–78, due to the Act of July 30, 1947, 61 Stat. 652 which codified the Copyright Act of 1909); 17 U.S.C. § 506 (1978–2016); and 18 U.S.C. § 2319 (1982–2016).

and inter alia, criminal copyright prosecutions, including the number of defendants[25]; second, data for 2008–12 is based on the Department of Justice's Annual Performance and Accountability Report,[26] which provides statistics of criminal copyright prosecutions including the number of defendants.

Here, too, a caveat is in place: there are various factors to take into consideration when analyzing the findings. First, there is no data for the years 1897–1954, and hence, the evaluation of criminal copyright prosecutions during this time is limited. Nonetheless, the lack of official data for 1897–1954 does not hold great significance for my evaluation, as criminal copyright did not play an active role in copyright at that time. Although there are no official statistics on the number of criminal copyright prosecutions at that time, there are some indications that under the 1909 Act, criminal copyright prosecutions were highly rare. For example, as the Supreme Court noted:

> The first full-fledged criminal provisions appeared in the Copyright Act of 1909, and specified that misdemeanor penalties of up to one year in jail or a fine between $100 and $1,000, or both, be imposed upon "any person who willfully and for profit" infringed a protected copyright. This provision was little used.[27]

Also, as recognized by Donald C. Curran, Acting Register of Copyrights in a 1985 Congressional hearing[28]: "Although criminal sanctions have been available for copyright infringement since the 1909 Act, and in a quite limited way even before, these sanctions were seldom invoked before the 1970's [sic]." Thus, official statistics

---

[25] United States Attorneys' Annual Statistical Reports for 1955–2015 are available at *Electronic Reading Room*, UNITED STATES DOJ, www.justice.gov/crt/foia-electronic-reading-room (last visited Dec. 1, 2017). As the Reports stopped indicating criminal copyright infringements prosecutions between 2008 and 2012 (they only mark zero), I used the absent data from the Department of Justice's Annual Performance and Accountability Report (2008–12).

[26] Since 1996, Congress mandated a DOJ report of IP prosecutions brought under §§ 2318, 2319, 2319A and 2320 (2012) of Title 18 of the U.S. Code. *See* Anticounterfeiting Consumer Protection Act of 1996, Pub. L. No. 104–153, 110 Stat. 1386 (1996) (codified originally as 18 U.S.C. § 2320(e), currently under 18 U.S.C. § 2320(h) (2012)); *see, e.g., FY 2004 Performance and Accountability Report*, U.S. DEP'T OF JUSTICE (2004) www.justice.gov/ag/annualreports/pr2004/Appd/A-c.pdf (last visited Dec. 1, 2017); *FY 2012 Performance and Accountability Report*, U.S. DEP'T OF JUSTICE (2012), www.justice.gov/sites/default/files/ag/legacy/2012/11/26/app-d.pdf (last visited Dec. 1, 2017).

[27] *See* Dowling v. United States, 473 U.S. 207, 221–22 (1985).

[28] *See* Civil and Criminal Enforcement of the Copyright Laws: Hearing before the Subcomm. on Patents, Copyrights and Trademarks of the Committee on the Judiciary, 99th Cong. 35 (1985) (statement of Donald C. Curran, active Register of Copyrights). *See also* William Strauss, *Remedies Other Damages for Copyright Infringement*, Studies prepared for the Subcommittee on Patents, Trademarks, and Copyrights of the Committee on the Judiciary, U.S. Senate, Eighty-sixth Congress 111, 124 (Study 24, March 1959), www.copyright.gov/history/studies/study24.pdf (arguing that the criminal section of the copyright act "has rarely been invoked" prior to 1959).

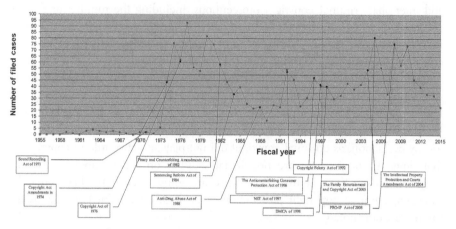

FIGURE 3   Criminal Copyright Filings in the United States

for the years 1955–2015 are sufficient to discuss the criminal copyright gap and are
detailed in Figure 3 (criminal copyright filings in the United States 1955–2015).[29]

Analyzing the data reveals interesting results. First, during the low-tech criminalization phase, and up until the beginning of the analog high-tech phase (1955–71),
criminal copyright prosecutions were scarce: Approximately 26 lawsuits were filed
during a 16-year period. Curran, in a statement before the Subcommittee on Patents,
Copyrights and Trademarks of the Committee on the Judiciary of the Senate,
pointed to four reasons to explain this failure to use the 1897 and 1909 criminal
sanctions until 1970. First, as few offenders were prosecuted, there was limited case
law and thus not many precedents or legal certainty to follow. Apparently, lawyers
were more comfortable recommending civil proceedings, which had a vast case law
history. Second, federal civil remedies were thought to be sufficient punishment for
copyright infringers. Third, criminal penalties were believed to be ineffective to
deter infringement. And finally, liberalization of defendant's rights were thought to
increase the burden of criminal prosecution, thus lawyers opted for the "surer" civil
field when possible.[30] I further analyze these and other possible reasons for the
relatively low-rate of criminal copyright prosecutions in the section below.

The year 1974 brought about an increase in criminal prosecutions with the filing
of 44 criminal lawsuits, which is congruent with increased legislation in the analog
high-tech criminalization phase (1971–88). Criminal prosecutions remained at this
level until 1985, but dropped between 1986 and1991. Moreover, the beginning of the
digital high-tech phase in 1992 did not mark an increase in copyright prosecutions.

[29] Figure 3 is processed from statistical data I extracted from the United States Attorneys' Annual
Statistical Reports (1955–2008, 2012–15) and from the Department of Justice' Annual Performance and Accountability Report (2008–12).
[30] *See Civil and Criminal Enforcement of the Copyright Laws, supra* note 29, at 35–36.

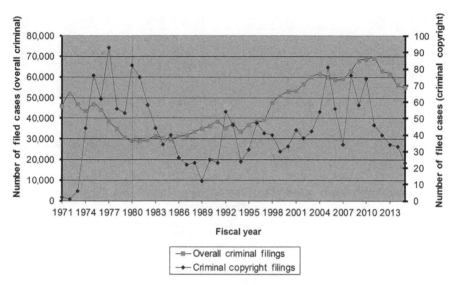

FIGURE 4 Criminal Copyright and Overall Criminal Filings

Especially noteworthy is that the NET Act of 1997 did not lead to a substantial increase of litigation. This is in contrast to what we could have expected from the massive lobbying that preceded the Act. It is not until 2005 that we can identify again an increase in criminal copyright prosecutions – which only resembled the increase in the analog phase and did not exceed it.

In order to evaluate the findings that criminal copyright prosecutions do not always correspond with legislation, it is important to compare the findings to other possible trends that could explain this gap.

First, a decrease in criminal litigation could be a result of a decrease in overall criminal prosecution, for example due to a reduction in criminal justice resources in that same fiscal year. Hence, a reduction in overall prosecutions likely led to a reduction in criminal copyright prosecutions. However, data from the United States Attorneys' Annual Statistical Reports, which provides statistics on overall criminal prosecutions, illustrates that this is hardly the case.[31]

As Figure 4 indicates, criminal copyright prosecutions and overall criminal prosecutions in the high-tech criminalization phase do not follow the same path. For instance, between 1980 and 1990, criminal copyright prosecutions dropped from 82 filings to 25 filings. During that same period, overall criminal filings increased from less than 30,000 annual filings to more than 36,000 annual filings.

Second, since Figure 3 illustrates the number of filings, rather than the number of individuals prosecuted, it is possible that while fewer cases were filed, the cases filed

[31] United States Attorneys' Annual Statistical Reports for 1955–2015 are available at www.justice .gov/usao/resources/annual-statistical-reports.

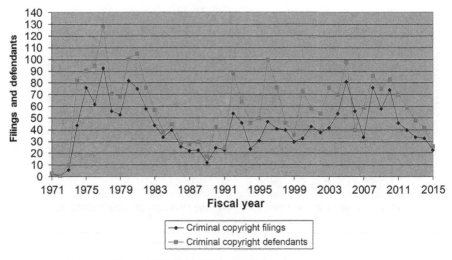

FIGURE 5 Criminal Copyright Filings and Defendants

had multiple defendants, leading to an increase in the number of defendants prosecuted. Thus, it is likely that prosecutors targeted large-scale operations of criminal copyright, which led to more convictions. However, as illustrated in Figure 5, this, too, is not the case.

Although some fiscal years indicate an increase in the number of accused persons, namely, that some prosecutions involved multiple defendants, it is not substantial. Notably, the number of defendants from 1977 to 1978 (which marks only the beginning of the high-tech criminalization phase) is higher than in any other fiscal year.

Third, the decrease in criminal prosecutions could be the result of an overall decrease in both civil and criminal copyright litigation during those years. Hence, analyzing the ratio of civil to criminal copyright lawsuits should reveal whether criminal copyright expanded to encompass a larger portion of litigation annually and, thus, illuminate whether copyright is moving toward a paradigmatic change. The Judicial Business of the U.S. Courts annual reports (1997–2015) (which provides data for the fiscal year ending on September 30 for U.S. courts of appeals, district courts, and bankruptcy courts) together with the probation and pretrial services system and other components of the federal judiciary,[32] illustrates the relationship between filed civil and criminal copyright cases.

As Figure 6 illustrates, from 1996 to 2007, there was a decrease in the percentage of criminal copyright cases filed vis-à-vis civil copyright cases, suggesting that

---

[32] *See Judicial Business of the U.S. Courts*, USCOURTS, www.uscourts.gov/Statistics/JudicialBusi ness.aspx (last visited Dec. 1, 2017).

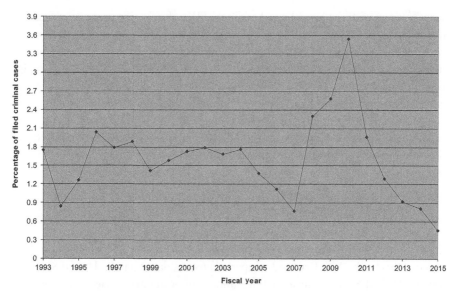

FIGURE 6 Percentage of Criminal Copyright Out of Total Copyright Litigation

criminal copyright itself decreased during these years. On the other hand, from 2007 to 2010, criminal copyright cases increased, as opposed to civil copyright cases. But since 2010, there has been a dramatic decrease in the percentage of criminal copyright cases filed vis-à-vis civil copyright cases. Relatively speaking, criminal copyright seems now to be happening at its lowest rate since 1993. These findings suggest that, although the *civil-criminal copyright ratio* has increased in some years, it was limited, while in other years the ratio remained stagnate or even decreased. Thus, the decrease in criminal litigation is not a result of an overall decrease in copyright litigation.

To conclude this part of the evaluation, while the United Kingdom statistical data was lacking and insufficient to prove or disprove my claim, the United States statistical data revealed interesting results: data from a portion of the low-tech criminalization phase (1955–71) was insignificant to confer the criminal copyright perception, as both legislative acts and criminal enforcement measures were scarce. More meaningful criminalization in the Unites States began with the high-tech criminalization phase. Along with the increase in criminal copyright legislative acts, from 1974 onwards there was a substantial expanse in criminal prosecutions. Surprisingly, the passage of the NET Act and the inclusion of the most stringent criminal-oriented provisions into the copyright code, which were designed to "enable DOJ to prosecute several additional copyright infringement cases each

year,"[33] along with the formation of additional IP enforcement agencies and allocation of financial resources for the purposes of responding to copyright infringements
via criminal law,[34] did not cause copyright prosecutions to increase (considering that
implementation and enforcement does not occur immediately). After eliminating
possible explanations for the criminal copyright gap, i.e., a decrease in overall
criminal prosecution, an increase in the number of defendants prosecuted per case,
and an overall decrease in civil copyright litigation, I conclude that there is a gap
between the scope of criminal copyright liability and penalties on the one hand and
the infrequency of prosecution and punishment on the other. But what is the
significance – or better yet – the implications of the criminal copyright gap?

II EVALUATING THE CRIMINAL COPYRIGHT GAP

Whether or not criminal copyright prosecutions is decreasing globally is beyond the
scope of this book. With that, and as a partial answer, data from the United Kingdom
and the United States indicate that the amount of criminal copyright cases litigated
yearly is erratic and has not increased (as would be expected from the influx of

---

[33] The No Electronic Theft (NET) Act, Pub. L. No. 105–47, 111 Stat. 2678 (1997)) was enacted in
an expectancy to increase prosecutions of criminal copyright infringers. See the first draft of the
NET Act (H.R. REP. No. 105–339, at 6 (1997)): "Based on information from the Department of
Justice (DOJ), CBO expects that enacting this bill would enable DOJ to prosecute several
additional copyright infringement cases each year."

[34] In the United States, it seems that the Department of Justice (DOJ) actively tries to combat
intellectual property criminal infringements. For example, as part of the DOJ strategy to
combat intellectual property crimes, the DOJ developed a team of specially-trained prosecutors
who focus specifically on intellectual property crimes: first, a team of specialists that serve as a
coordinating hub for national and international efforts against intellectual property theft,
entitled the Criminal Division's Computer Crime and Intellectual Property Section (CCIPS);
second, assigning specialized prosecutors entitled "Computer and Telecommunications
Coordinators" (CTCs) to different United States Attorney's Offices; third, adding a "Computer
Hacking and Intellectual Property" (CHIP) units in different cities where IP enforcement is
especially critical; and fourth, creating the National Intellectual Property Law Enforcement
Coordination Council (NIPLECC) to improve coordination of the different law enforcement
agencies. In 2004, CCIPS, CHIP and NIPLECC, along with other investigating and enforcement agencies developed the Strategy Targeting Organized Piracy ("STOP!") Initiative, "to
prosecute organized criminal networks that steal creative works from U.S. businesses and
develop international interest in and commitment to the protection of intellectual property,"
resulting in global large scale action against piracy and counterfeiting networks. *See* United
Stated DOJ, *Report of the Department of Justice's Task Force on Intellectual Property* 13 (2004),
www.justice.gov/olp/ip_task_force_report.pdf (last visited Dec. 1, 2017); Hardy, *supra* note 2, at
323; *Finding and Fighting Fakes: Reviewing the Strategy Targeting Organized Piracy: Hearing
Before the S. Comm. on Oversight of Government Management, the Fed. Workforce, and the
District of Columbia of the S. Comm. on Homeland Security and Governmental Affairs,* 109th
Cong. 76, 79–80 (2005); Grace Pyun, *The 2008 Pro-IP Act: The Inadequacy of the Property
Paradigm in Criminal Intellectual Property Law and its Effect on Prosecutorial Boundaries,* 19
DEPAUL J. ART TECH. & INTELL. PROP. L. 355, 368–71 (2009).

additional criminal copyright legislation). I now turn to analyze this *criminal copyright gap* to understand its reasoning and possible ramifications.

One possible explanation for the *criminal copyright gap* is a result of under-enforcement of criminal copyright law by authorized law enforcement agencies. Reasons for under-enforcement are diverse,[35] e.g., favoritism to or hostility against a specific group,[36] official neglect, prioritizing resources/economic considerations, a conflict between enforcers and legislators over the meaning of the law and its appropriateness, etc.[37] Focusing on general reasons for under-enforcement of criminal law is insufficient on its own to provide a full understating of the criminal copyright gap. As each law has its own unique characteristics, criminal copyright gap should be examined vis-à-vis the unique characteristics of copyright enforcement. Accordingly, I offer several possible explanations for the criminal copyright gap relating to political, economic, and social theories of copyright infringement and enforcement.

First, criminal legislation might be the result of international pressure to legislate but not necessarily enforce legislation. For example, the TRIPS Agreement requires member states to provide for criminal procedures, penalties, and enforcement measures but does not address the scale of enforcement.[38] Enforcement provisions in international agreements are either ineffective[39] or crafted as broad legal standards (rather than concrete rules that can be interpreted differently by member states)[40] and implemented in a different manner.[41] As long as international treaties and agreements focus mostly on regulation and refrain from obligatory enforcement

---

[35] For a comprehensive analysis of under-enforcement in criminal law, see Alexandra Natapoff, *Underenforcement*, 75 FORDHAM L. REV. 1715 (2006).

[36] Tom Stacy & Kim Dayton, *The Underfederalization of Crime*, 6 CORNELL J.L. & PUB. POL'Y 247, 292 (1997); Darryl K. Brown, *Street Crime, Corporate Crime, and the Contingency of Criminal Liability*, 149 U. PA. L. REV. 1295, 1302 (2001).

[37] For these, and more examples, see Natapoff, *supra* note 36, at 1722.

[38] Agreement on Trade-Related Aspects of Intellectual Property Rights art. 3, Apr. 15, 1994, Marrakesh Agreement Establishing the World Trade Organization, Annex 1C, 1869 U.N.T.S. 299, 33 I.L.M. 1197 (1994) [hereinafter TRIPS], which requires member states to provide for criminal procedures and penalties, which should apply at least in cases of copyright piracy on a commercial scale. Although article 41 requires member states to ensure that enforcement procedures are available under their law so as to permit effective action against any act of infringement of IP rights covered by the Agreement, it does not address the scale of enforcement. In addition, article 41.5 states that "this Part does not create any obligation to put in place a judicial system for the enforcement of intellectual property rights distinct from that for the enforcement of law in general, nor does it affect the capacity of members to enforce their law in general."

[39] For more on international IP agreements, e.g., TRIPS, and the reasons why they sometimes fail to provide effective global enforcement of IP rights, see Peter K. Yu, *TRIPS and Its Achilles' Heel*, 18 J. INTELL. PROP. L. 479 (2011).

[40] Jerome H. Reichman & David Lange, *Bargaining Around the TRIPS Agreement: The Case for Ongoing Public-Private Initiatives to Facilitate Worldwide Intellectual Property Transactions*, 9 DUKE J. COMP. & INT'L L. 11, 35 (1998).

[41] *See, e.g., id.* at 36.

measures or do not craft obligatory narrow legal rules for IP enforcement, criminal legislation may to some extent become a dead letter, at least in some countries.[42] It is important to mention the existence of non-traditional international IP forums, usually private or public-private partnership that aim at IP enforcement.[43] Hence, these private partnerships press for enforcement of international agreements and even add additional IP enforcement requirements to the existing agreements.

Second, interest groups lobby to enact some criminal legislation but have less or no power to influence the enforcement of legislation.[44] Thus, the power used by interest groups to lobby for criminal sanctions for IP infringement is not necessarily felt vis-à-vis enforcement agencies. For example, up until year 2000, the Walt Disney Company's attempts to prod the Unites States Attorney to prosecute criminal copyright were often rejected – even after the enactment of the NET Act in 1997.[45] As Peter Nolan, Senior Vice President/Assistant General Counsel of the Walt Disney Company indicated (after being asked "[h]as Disney actually sought a prosecutor to bring a case?"):

> Oh, yes, and been declined on quite a few cases. In large part, it wasn't necessarily anything other than the offices having limited resources. I think this is, by the way, normal human thinking or management thinking. The U.S. Attorney says, 'I have limited resources. I want to go after the person who is causing violence to my fellow citizens in my locality. I'm going to go after them rather than a copyright infringe-ment which has a comparatively low guideline level, and as a result, I'm not going

---

[42] *Cf.* Peter K. Yu, *Enforcement, Economics and Estimates*, 2 W.I.P.O. J. 1, 1 (2010).

[43] *See, e.g.*, The Global Congress on Combating Counterfeiting and Piracy, designed to produce recommendations mainly aimed at government authorities to step up enforcement mechanism and action. The Global Congress on Combating Counterfeiting and Piracy is convened by a public-private partnership with representatives from INTERPOL, the World Customs Organization (WCO), the World Intellectual Property Organization (WIPO), the International Chamber of Commerce/BASCAP initiative (ICC/BASCAP) and the International Trademark Association (INTA). For more examples of IP enforcement initiatives, see Viviana Muñoz Tellez, *The Changing Global Governance of Intellectual Property Enforcement: A New Challenge for Developing Countries*, in INTELLECTUAL PROPERTY ENFORCEMENT: INTERNATIONAL PERSPECTIVES 3, 9–10 (Li Xuan & Carlos M. Correa eds., 2009).

[44] Various interest groups lobby for copyright criminalization. In the U.S., for example, the music, motion picture and computer industries lobbied Congress to strengthen copyright protection and enforcement in the high-tech criminalization phase, resulting in, e.g., the Sound Recording Act of 1971 (Pub. L. No. 92–140, 85 Stat. 391 (1971)), the Copyright Act of 1976 (Pub. L. No. 94–553, 90 Stat. 2541 (1976)), the Piracy and Counterfeiting Amendments Act of 1982 (Pub. L. No. 97–180, 96 Stat. 91 (1982)) and the No Electronic Theft (NET) Act (Pub. L. No. 105–47, 111 Stat. 2678 (1997)). *See* Penney, *supra* note 4, at 63; Mary J. Saunders, *Criminal Copyright Infringement and the Copyright Felony Act*, 71 DENV. U. L. REV. 671, 674–75 (1994). For a general review of the local and global political process of copyright protection, see Michael Birnhack, *Trading Copyright: Global Pressure on Local Culture*, in THE DEVELOPMENT AGENDA: GLOBAL INTELLECTUAL PROPERTY AND DEVELOPING COUNTRIES 363 (Neil Netanel ed., 2008). I further discuss the lobbying efforts of various copyright-related industries in Chapter 5.

[45] The No Electronic Theft (NET) Act.

to bring it. I just don't have the manpower to do it or the money.' And then we as copyright owners decide to go civilly.[46]

However, there are few reports that indicate that some interest groups, such as the RIAA, meet with law enforcement agencies on a regular basis to assist them detect copyright infringements. Thus, it seems that interest groups – while not equal to their lobbying powers – to some extent influence law enforcement agencies in combating copyright and trademark infringements.[47]

Although lacking any official evidence, there is another possible political explanation for the criminal copyright gap. This explanation suggests that low enforcement is a conscientious decision made by the government in an attempt to balance political pressure by the IP industry to enforce copyright protection versus political pressure by other industries that are interested in limited or no enforcement.[48] Under-enforcement of copyright law could also be a result of an intentional policy to refrain from public pressure and the formation of a "police state," due to the nature of copyright infringement detection (which I further explain in this chapter), and the need for comprehensive resources for enforcement.[49] It might also be a conscientious decision by rights holders, as criminal procedures might be perceived as too uncertain, and that civil law would benefit them more financially.[50]

Third, it is plausible that criminal copyright legislation aims to deter simply or mostly through legislation.[51] The fact that criminal litigation has not increased does not necessarily indicate that criminalization has failed.[52] For example, according to the House Report on the enactment of the NET Act, it was only expected to "enable DOJ to prosecute several additional copyright infringement cases each year."[53] Hence, criminal copyright litigation was not supposed to dramatically increase – even after the inclusion of many criminal provisions to copyright law.

Moreover, deterrence is not only measured by quantitative means. It is also measured qualitatively. For example, even if the state's prosecution rate does not increase, one newsworthy, well-publicized case could potentially deter copyright infringement.[54] In addition, longer periods of imprisonment for every case could

---

[46] *Intellectual Property/Copyright Infringement*, UNITED STATES SENTENCING COMMISSION 248 (2000), www.ussc.gov/Research/Research_Projects/Economic_Crimes/20001012_Symposium/tGroupTwoDayTwo.pdf.

[47] *See* PAUL R. PARADISE, TRADEMARK COUNTERFEITING: PRODUCT PIRACY, AND THE BILLION DOLLAR THREAT TO THE U.S. ECONOMY 256 (1999).

[48] *See* Natapoff, *supra* note 36, at 1741; Edward K. Cheng, *Structural Laws and the Puzzle of Regulating Behavior*, 100 Nw. U. L. REV. 655, 714–15 (2006).

[49] Cheng, *supra* note 49, at 659.

[50] *See* IPO REPORT 2015, *supra* note 18, at 74.

[51] For more on deterrence, see *infra* Chapters 7 and 8.

[52] *See* Strauss, *supra* note 29, at 124. *Cf.* Hardy, *supra* note 2, at 323.

[53] *See* H.R. REP. No. 105–339, at 6 (1997).

[54] *See* Salil K. Mehra, *Software as Crime: Japan, the United States, and Contributory Copyright Infringement*, 79 TUL. L. REV. 265, 294 (2004); in addition, criminal arrests, followed by media coverage, could potentially be sufficient to create deterrence due to fear of damage to

also have deterrent effect.[55] As DOJ representative Kevin Di Gregory noted in Congress:[56]

> [E]ven a handful of appropriate and well-publicized prosecutions under the NET Act is likely to have a strong deterrent impact, particularly because the crime in question is a hobby, and not a means to make a living. If these prosecutions are accompanied by a vigorous anti-piracy educational campaign sponsored by industry, and by technological advances designed to make illegal copying more difficult, we are hopeful that a real dent can be made in the practice of digital piracy.

Qualitatively, criminal copyright succeeded to some extent. In the United States, for example, consistent with Congress' objectives for the NET Act to prosecute commercial-scale "pirates,"[57] federal agents brought down "Pirates With Attitude" in 1999[58]; broke the "DrinkorDie" software piracy ring in 2001[59]; and prosecuted other computer software and motion pictures infringers.[60] Thus, under this reasoning, focusing on large-scale operations fulfill part of the intention behind criminal copyright legislation, and furthermore, could be sufficient to create deterrence against infringement. Moreover, targeting large-scale operations could emphasize the argument that criminal copyright mainly serves to complement the civil enforcement system.[61]

However, it seems that this reasoning does not correspond with the current reality that criminal copyright legislation and copyright infringement do not cease. It is debatable, and very difficult to measure, whether copyright infringements and counterfeiting rates increase annually. Some data indicate that copyright infringements and counterfeiting rates grow annually worldwide – specifically in the United States and in the United Kingdom. For example, a study conducted by the International Planning and Research Corporation (IPRC), for the Software Alliance

---

reputation. *See id.* at 297. *See also* Aaron M. Bailey, *A Nation of Felons: Napster, the Net Act, and the Criminal Prosecution of File-Sharing*, 50 Am. U. L. Rev. 473, 476 (2000).

[55] *See, e.g., Civil and Criminal Enforcement of the Copyright Laws, supra* note 29, at 43.

[56] *Implementation of the "Net" Act and Enforcement Against Internet Piracy: Oversight Hearing Before the Subcomm. on Courts and Intellectual Prop., House Comm. on the Judiciary*, 106th Cong. (1999) (statement of Kevin Di Gregory of the United States Department of Justice).

[57] *See* 143 Cong. Rec. S12,689 (daily ed. Nov. 13, 1997) (statement of Sen. Hatch) ("I am also relying upon the good sense of prosecutors and judges. Again, the purpose of the bill is to prosecute commercial-scale pirates who do not have commercial advantage or private financial gain from their illegal activities. But if an over-zealous prosecutor should bring and win a case against a college prankster, I am confident that the judge would exercise the discretion that he or she may have under the Sentencing Guidelines to be lenient. If the practical effect of the bill turns out to be draconian, we may have to revisit the issue.").

[58] "Pirates With Attitude" operated 13 FTP (file transfer protocol) servers hosting more than 30,000 software programs. Peter S. Menell, *This American Copyright Life: Reflections on Re-Equilibrating Copyright for the Internet Age*, 62 J. Copyright Soc'y U.S.A. 201, 289 (2014).

[59] *Id.*

[60] *Id.*; Eric Goldman, *A Road to No Warez: The No Electronic Theft Act and Criminal Copyright Infringement*, 82 Or. L. Rev. 369, 381–92 (2003).

[61] *See* Menell, *supra* note 59, at 295.

(BSA), a trade association mainly representing the software industry, showed that from 1997 to 1999, "software piracy" increased in the United States and in conjunction, global revenue losses to software "piracy" increased from $11.3 billion in 1997 to $12.2 billion in 1999.[62] Another study argued that music sales in the United States have dropped by more than $7 billion dollars, from $14.6 billion before 1999, to $6.97 billion in 2014.[63] Nevertheless, it is safe to argue that criminal legislation does not fully deter copyright infringement simply by the legislative act, or at least not enough.[64]

Fourth, criminal copyright is not designed to eliminate illegal infringements, but rather reduce them to a level that is profitable for rights holders. Under this argument, copyright enforcement will not rise, at least not substantially, as there is a "tolerance rate" in which copyright is still profitable for its rights holders, and criminal copyright only aids in maintaining that infringements remain below this rate.[65] Under this argument, rights holders are not perusing actual enforcement as long as civil remedies are more appealing.[66] However, this is a weak argument in favor of under-enforcement, as even if such tolerance exists, it is unknown and unquantifiable, since it will vary among different rights holders. Even if such a

[62] *See* INT'L PLANNING & RESEARCH CORP., SEVENTH ANNUAL BSA GLOBAL SOFTWARE PIRACY STUDY 6 (2002), www.bsa.org/~/media/Files/Research%20Papers/GlobalStudy/2002/Global_Piracy_Study_2002.pdf; Goldman, *supra* note 61, at 398–99.

[63] RIAA, NEWS AND NOTES ON 2014 RIAA MUSIC INDUSTRY SHIPMENT AND REVENUE STATISTICS www.riaa.com/wp-content/uploads/2015/09/2013-2014_RIAA_YearEndShipmentData.pdf; Sara K. Morgan, *The International Reach of Criminal Copyright Infringement Laws – Can the Founders of The Pirate Bay Be Held Criminally Responsible in the United States for Copyright Infringement Abroad?*, 49 VAND. J. TRANSNAT'L L. 553, 558 (2016).

[64] *See, e.g.,* Miriam Bitton, *Rethinking the Anti-Counterfeiting Trade Agreement's Criminal Copyright Enforcement Measures*, 102 J. CRIM. L. & CRIMINOLOGY 67, 67–68 (2012); In the United Kingdom, file-sharing was reported to increase from £278 million in lost sales in 2003 to £414 million in lost sales in 2005. *See* ANDREW GOWERS, GOWERS REVIEW OF INTELLECTUAL PROPERTY (2006), http://webarchive.nationalarchives.gov.uk/+/http:/www.hm-treasury.gov.uk/d/pbr06_gowers_report_755.pdf (last visited Dec. 1, 2017). However, the true rates of copyright infringement are extremely difficult, if not impossible, to estimate, thus, this data should be examined carefully. *See* United States Government Accountability Office, *Observations on Efforts to Quantify the Economic Effects of Counterfeit and Pirated Goods*, REPORT TO CONGRESSIONAL COMMITTEES (2010), www.gao.gov/new.items/d10423.pdf (last visited Dec. 1, 2017); *see also* the 2010 Annual report by the International Federation of the Phonographic Industry (IFPI), which states:

Although P2P piracy is the single biggest problem and did not diminish in 2009, the illegal distribution of infringing music through non-P2P channels is growing considerably. The research showed the biggest increases in usage for overseas unlicensed MP3 pay sites (47%) and newsgroups (42%). Other significant rises included MP3 search engines (28%) and forum, blog and board links to cyberlockers (18%).

IFPI *Digital Music Report*, IFPI (2010), www.ifpi.org/content/library/DMR2010.pdf (last visited Dec. 1, 2017). *See also* Robin Fry, *Copyright Infringement and Collective Enforcement*, 24 E.I.P.R. 516, 522 (2002).

[65] *See* Ariel Katz, *A Network Effects Perspective on Software Piracy*, 55 U. TORONTO L.J. 155, 191 (2005).

[66] *See* Strauss, *supra* note 29, at 124.

tolerance rate was measurable, it will most likely be highly inaccurate and expensive to measure, as infringement rates change daily.

Fifth, despite government efforts to increase the involvement of enforcement agencies in enforcing copyright offenses, the digital environment possesses many difficulties for enforcement agencies, such as detecting infringement,[67] identifying suspects,[68] identifying infringements that occur in multiple jurisdictions and with overseas operators, as well as problems associated with prosecuting juveniles.[69] Take detection for example. Detecting illegal file-sharing is not an easy task. It is import-ant to first differentiate between civil and criminal enforcement measures because they hold significant differences. In order to detect illegal file-sharing, rights holders will usually connect to a P2P network, search for their copyrighted materials, and track the user's Internet Protocol (IP) address. Civilly, the rights holder can apply for a subpoena to reveal the identities of file sharers in order to file a civil lawsuit against them.[70] Even if some courts will not easily reveal the identity of the file-sharer, this is a relatively easy and inexpensive method to detect and file a civil lawsuit.

Criminal enforcement is different. In the United States, for example, sharing a single song online is probably insufficient to pass the threshold for criminal liability. Rather, the file-sharer will need to be linked to other infringements in a set period. Only then could he or she be liable for criminal prosecution. This raises three main problems:

(1) Without the creation of a database of infringements, it is almost impos-sible to analyze the file-sharer's allegedly illegal activity to determine whether it amounts to criminal activity. Under this scenario, enforce-ment agencies must maintain and operate a database that contains information on every file-sharer's allegedly illegal activity. For this

---

[67] In a different context, see Cheng, *supra* note 49, at 656; Robert A. Kagan, *On the Visibility of Income Tax Violations, in* 2 TAXPAYER COMPLIANCE: SOCIAL SCIENCE PERSPECTIVES 76, 76–78 (Jeffrey A. Roth & John T. Scholz eds., 1989).

[68] Identifying criminal infringers could be proven as a challenge to enforcement agencies: ISPs are currently not obliged to monitor their users online, as to protect their privacy; identifying infringing uses necessitates financial resources which are limited and are more complex: they need to pass a threshold of infringements to be considered criminal. *See,* in the United States, 17 U.S.C. § 512(m); Bailey, *supra* note 55, at 514–15. *See also* David R. Johnson & David Post, *Law and Borders: The Rise of Law In Cyberspace,* 48 STAN. L. REV. 1367 (1996).

[69] The United States Department of Justice terminated federal criminal investigations under the NET Act, when it found the perpetrator was a juvenile and therefore not normally subject to federal prosecution. *See Implementation of the "Net" Act and Enforcement Against Internet Piracy, supra* note 57. *See also* Reno, *supra* note 5.

[70] *See* 17 U.S.C. § 512(h). However, it is not an easy task for courts do decide, due to a possible risk to fundamental human rights, such as free speech and the right to privacy. *See* Michael Birnhack, *Unmasking Anonymous Online Users in Israel,* 2 HUKIM 51, 82 (2010) [Hebrew]. *See generally,* Lyrissa Barnett Lidsky & Thomas F. Cotter, *Authorship, Audiences, and Anonym-ous Speech,* 82 NOTRE DAME L. REV. 1537 (2007); Eldar Haber, *The French Revolution 2.0: Copyright and the Three Strikes Policy,* 2 HARV. J. SPORTS & ENT. L. 297, 317 (2011).

database to be effective, as it is expensive, rights holders must willingly provide enforcement agencies with details on alleged infringements and infringers (IP address). Only then can enforcement agencies decide whether an end-user passes the threshold for criminal prosecution.

(2) As an IP address usually indicates all members of a household, i.e., there is no technological differentiation between each household member, it is almost impossible to analyze who in the household actually infringed, again questioning the validity of the threshold. In order to prosecute a household IP address that passes the threshold, each alleged illegal activity must be analyzed separately to determine which household member actually infringed. This task is of course expensive and problematic.[71] Setting a very high threshold for the entire household would ensure that at least one of its members was engaging in criminal activity, but would still be insufficient to detect the specific alleged criminal infringer.

(3) This method of detecting infringements is almost solely reserved for tracking P2P infringers. Thus, the perceivable outcome of the success of criminal prosecutions which occurred by the database identification, is that users will either encrypt their actions or their IP addresses using various technologies and thus avoid getting caught or use other methods of downloading and data consumption, such as websites that offer streaming of copyrighted materials, direct access to copyrighted materials, and instant messaging and chat software.[72]

Thus, law enforcement agencies face a difficult task when determining who infringed, i.e., the number of criminal prosecutions do not rise.[73] In this case, it is

---

[71] It may require, for example, summoning of witnesses, searches in houses, seizures and examination of computers, etc. For this argument, see Alexander Peukert, *Why do 'Good People' Disregard Copyright on the Internet?*, in Criminal Enforcement of Intellectual Property Law 151, 160 (Christophe Geiger ed., 2012).

[72] *See* Haber, *supra* note 71, at 323–24.

[73] For example, after lack of convictions under the NET Act (No Electronic Theft (NET) Act, Pub. L. No. 105–47, 111 Stat. 2678 (1997)), during the first eighteen months following its enactment, in a hearing of the House Judiciary Committee's Subcomm. on Courts and Intellectual Property in May 1999, Kevin Di Gregory of the United States Department of Justice pointed out several significant challenges to law enforcement: First, unlike physical-world copyright "piracy," which requires expensive manufacturing equipment, storage facilities, and a distribution chain, including middlemen and retailers, illegal digital distribution of copyrighted works requires only a computer and an internet account. Thus, the internet "pirate" is a less obvious focus for a criminal investigation. Second, it is difficult to count the number of illegitimate copies made over the internet and therefore calculate damages and losses. Third, when copyright crimes occur over the internet, where no specific United States Attorney has primary responsibility or jurisdiction, prosecutions often cut across prosecutors' territories, leaving them without a crime to prosecute in their own district. Fourth, investigating digital copyright piracy requires agents that are not only experienced criminal investigators, but also possess special technical skills, and thus are hard to retain. *See Implementation of the "Net"*

crucial that interest groups privately investigate, as well as cooperate with, law enforcement agencies (much like with other criminal offenses). However, as it seems, interest groups choose to take a less active role in prosecution efforts than lobbying efforts.[74] Moreover, copyright owners could be more interested to use criminal law as leverage to settle civil lawsuits, without actually using criminal sanctions: copyright owners may file a complaint against an individual with law authorities, while filing a civil suit as well and in this manner, pressure her to settle. After settlement, some copyright owners could be less motivated to aid law enforcement agencies.

It is worth noting that despite difficulties posed by the digital environment, due to detection technologies and methods, it is potentially easier to catch criminal infringers in a digital environment than in a physical one.[75] Thus, this reason on its own is insufficient to explain the criminal copyright gap.

Sixth, there are no government guidelines for criminal copyright prosecution or those that exist are too vague to be used by the prosecution. Take the United States Attorneys' Manual as an example: the Executive Office for United States Attorneys

---

Act and Enforcement Against Internet Piracy, supra note 57; Goldman, *supra* note 61, at 377–78.

[74] *See, e.g.,* a reported telephone conversation with Joel Schoenfield, RIAA special antipiracy counsel that took place on April 9, 1984. Schoenfield stated that "RIAA is selective in what they refer to Justice, turning over only the most egregious cases." *See Civil and Criminal Enforcement of the Copyright Laws, supra* note 29, at 41; *id.* at 3 (statement of Victoria Toensing, deputy assistant attorney general at the criminal division) (stating that "there has been a history of interest in copyright prosecutions in the Criminal Division," and that Julian Greenspun, a member of the General Litigation Section "communicated to each industry [i.e., the record industry, the motion picture industry and the computer industry – E. H.] an offer that if for some reason they found a certain U.S. attorney's office was unable or did not wish to bring a certain prosecution that we had an offer in the Criminal Division, in the General Litigation Section, to review that case to see if it merited prosecution."). *Cf.* Gregor Urbas, *Criminal Enforcement of Intellectual Property Rights: Interaction Between Public Authorities and Private Interests in* NEW FRONTIERS OF INTELLECTUAL PROPERTY LAW: IP AND CULTURAL HERITAGE, GEOGRAPHICAL INDICATIONS, ENFORCEMENT AND OVERPROTECTION 303, 305 (Christopher Heath & Anselm Kamperman Sanders eds., 2005) (arguing that many industry bodies, e.g., the Motion Picture Association, the International Federation of Phonographic Industries and the Business Software Alliance, take an active role in providing intelligence and operational support in public enforcement activities).

[75] The digital environment offers various methods to detect copyright infringers. For example, using port-based analysis, which is based on the concept that many P2P applications have default ports on which they function, and administrators "observe the network traffic and check whether there are connection records using these ports." Yimin Gong, *Identifying P2P Users Using Traffic Analysis,* SYMANTEC (July 20, 2005), www.symantec.com/connect/articles/identifying-p2pusers-using-traffic-analysis. The second method, known as protocol analysis, uses "an application or piece of equipment [that] monitors traffic passing through the network and inspects the data payload of the packets according to some previously defined P2P application signatures." *See also* Haber, *supra* note 71, at 323; or by using DRM steganography, such as watermarks that can aid detect the internet identity of the User Internet Protocol (IP) address. For more information on steganography, see *Information Hiding: Steganography & Digital Watermarking,* JJTC (last visited Dec. 1, 2017), www.jjtc.com/Steganography.

(EOUSA) publishes and maintains an internal manual for attorneys and other organizational department units involved in prosecution.[76] Until 1985, the manual did not directly address criminal prosecution of copyright infringements. For example, the 1984 revision to the manual stated, "the existing Federal statutory scheme clearly contemplates enforcement primarily by civil means." In other words, the manual perceived criminal remedies to be a mere supplement to civil copyright remedies.[77]

Due to raised concerns by representatives of the motion picture and recording industries that the 1984 manual could be construed to permit declination of criminal copyright cases in favor of civil remedies,[78] in 1985 the Department of Justice revised the manual concluding, "[A]ll criminal copyright matters should receive careful attention by the United States Attorney." This revised section has not been changed since.[79] However, it seems that the DOJ claimed intention does not meet the anticipated increase in federal criminal copyright prosecutions, which shows that since 1985 there was no substantial increase in prosecutions, even though we would seem to think there should have been.

Seventh, enforcement agencies might feel conflicted about the criminal nature or lack thereof of criminal copyright, use prosecutorial discretion, and their individual feelings may override professionalism and "rule of law" norms. Research has shown that some parts of the public have little interest in imprisoning infringers without a profit motive,[80] especially young infringers.[81] This could equally apply on sentencing.[82] Therefore, enforcement agencies might abstain from prosecuting most copyright infringement activities. Under these arguments, the criminal copyright

---

[76] See *Mission and Functions*, UNITED STATES DEPARTMENT OF JUSTICE (last visited Dec. 1, 2017), www.justice.gov/usao/eousa/mission.html.

[77] See *Civil and Criminal Enforcement of the Copyright Laws*, *supra* note 29, at 8 (statement of Senator Mathias).

[78] *Id*. at 15–16 (statement of Victoria Toensing, deputy assistant attorney general at the criminal division).

[79] United States Attorneys' Manual § 9–71.010.

[80] See Jonathan Band & Masanobu Katoh, *Members of Congress Declare War on P2P Networks*, J. INTERNET L. (2003), www.accessmylibrary.com/article-1G1-114008586/members-congress-declare-war.html (noting that enforcement of criminal copyright against non-commercial infringers has not been a priority for the Justice Department, which perceives that the public has little interest in seeing college students sent to prison merely because they traded songs on the internet).

[81] The United States Department of Justice recognized that the "NET Act defendants – because they tend to be young and acting without a profit motive – tend to make more sympathetic defendants than those in most criminal cases, and that U.S. Attorney's Offices are naturally reluctant to bring such prosecutions." See *Implementation of the "Net" Act and Enforcement Against Internet Piracy*, *supra* note 57. See, e.g., *Draft for a Second Act on Copyright in the Information Society*, GERMANY MINISTRY OF JUSTICE 12 (Sept. 27, 2004), www.urheberrecht .org/topic/Korb-2/bmj/760.pdf.

[82] See, for example, in the United Kingdom, whereas statistical data shows that courts many times prescribe relatively low sanctions on criminal infringers. See IPO REPORT 2015, *supra* note 18, at 58–63.

gap occurs due to a conflict between the action, criminal copyright, and social and/
or moral norms that do not consider the actions criminal.[83]

This possible explanation of the criminal copyright gap could be best explained
from Meir Dan-Cohen's identification and distinctions between conduct and decision rules.[84] In his seminal work, Dan-Cohen identifies and distinguished between
two sets of legal rules: the first, conduct rules, designed to guide the general public's
behavior; the second, decision rules, directed to the officials who apply conduct
rules. By offering a model of *Acoustic Separation*,[85] Dan-Cohen exemplifies how
society accommodates competing values at stake in criminal law and raises the issue
of the legitimacy of selective transmission.

The criminal copyright gap could be explained to some extent under this model.
Criminal copyright infringement as a conduct rule, tells society not to infringe
copyright, and upon infringement, they could face a criminal sanction. Criminal
copyright infringement as a decision rule, should instruct law enforcement agencies
on how to enforce infringements. But in this case, the two sets of rules are not
necessarily in harmony, creating selective transmission. In other words, if the public
and the officials receive different normative messages regarding criminal copyright
infringements, selective transmission could occur. This could possibly explain the
existence of low enforcement and, inter alia, the criminal copyright gap.

As we have seen, the criminal copyright gap is most likely caused by under-
enforcement and is a result of various, likely overlapping, reasons. Rights holders
might feel that the criminal law is not practical for their purposes and thus might
invest their efforts primarily on other measures, e.g., taking down infringing websites; taking civil measures against infringers; setting up initiatives that closely work
with ISPs; etc.[86]

Notably, the criminal copyright gap could have various ramifications on copyright
criminalization. Mainly and most importantly, the gap could turn criminal copyright
legislation into almost a dead letter. As long as enforcement measures do not coincide
with legislation, achieving criminal copyright goals will most likely be impossible.

---

[83] *See, e.g.,* Dan Kahan's explanation of the "sticky norms" problem. *Kahan* argues that a law
which conflicts with a social norm could be counter-productive. Kahan further argues that
severe penalties, in oppose to weak penalties, could likely cause governmental actors to override
professionalism and "rule of law" norms due to individual feelings. *See* Dan M. Kahan, *Gentle
Nudges vs. Hard Shoves: Solving the Sticky Norms Problem,* 67 U. CHI. L. REV. 607, 608 (2000);
Cheng, *supra* note 49, at 660.

[84] *See* Meir Dan-Cohen, *Decisions Rules and Conduct Rules: On Acoustic Separation in Criminal Law,* 97 HARV. L. REV. 625 (1984). I am extremely grateful to Peter S. Menell for this
suggestion.

[85] Dan-Cohen exemplifies the Acoustic Separation model through an imaginary universe, in
which two types of people exist: the public and officials. Each of the groups occupies a
different, acoustically sealed chamber. The law is directed to both groups. In a different
manner: the public is guided by conduct rules, while the officials provide guidelines for their
decisions based on the law (decision rules). *See id.,* at 630.

[86] *See* IPO REPORT 2015, *supra* note 18, at 5.

CONCLUSION

Whether or not the increase of criminal copyright legislation leads to a paradigm shift in copyright law is open to dispute. Thus far, the legal community's understanding of copyright law has not changed from a civil to a criminal perspective on copyright, and as such a paradigm shift is not currently underway. I argue that a paradigm shift cannot be merely legislative. Changing the perception of copyright law from civil to criminal requires structural changes in practice, i.e., criminal copyright cannot be mostly a legislative act. Statistics of the two chosen test cases, especially the United States, reveal that criminal litigation does not match the relatively massive inclusion of criminal copyright into legislation. As I note, the criminal copyright gap between the scope of criminal copyright liability and penalties and the infrequency of prosecution and punishment, could be attributed to a variety of reasons: international pressure to legislate criminal copyright without obliging enforcement; political barriers and considerations; achieved deterrence through legislation/other means or a "tolerance rate" of copyright infringements; difficulties for enforcement agencies; social, moral, and economic considerations; and differed prioritization by law enforcement.

The criminal copyright gap demonstrates an important issue: legislation in itself is insufficient to create a paradigm shift, as enforcement of criminal copyright plays an important role in the paradigmatic change to criminal copyright.[87] However, as there is little enforcement of criminal copyright, its reasoning is different from the logic behind the massive legislation insertion of criminalization. In the following two chapters, I search for probable explanations for copyright criminalization and examine what led to the process, arguing that there are two main sets of reasons for the process: internal to copyright (Chapter 5); and external to copyright (Chapter 6).

---

[87] Yu, *supra* note 43, at 1.

5

Internal Reasoning for Criminal Copyright

INTRODUCTION

Criminalization processes in general occur due to various reasons, both external and internal to the activity/behavior at stake. As such, it is important to locate the external and internal reasons, as well as analyze the specific process. This chapter focuses on the internal reasons ("internal analysis"), and locates copyright criminalization in a broader framework of copyright expansion to explain the internal reasons for copyright criminalization. The distinction between the two kinds of reasons is not always clear cut. My treatment of them separately is mostly for purposes of clarity, rather than to indicate a substantive separation.

I first make the case for the need for an internal analysis that is mostly descriptive in nature, but can contribute to the normative debate on both copyright criminalization and the understanding of other criminalization processes. Mainly, the internal analysis aids in understanding copyright criminalization in relation to evaluating the process and to examining its legitimacy and possible ramifications. In addition, the internal analysis could aid future studies in identifying similar patterns in future criminal copyright legislation during the process of legislation. Finally, although each criminalization processes have its own unique characteristics, understanding the internal reasons for copyright criminalization contributes to the wider discussion of external criminalization patterns, e.g., IP criminalization, which is further discussed in Chapter 6.

In order to understand the reasons for copyright criminalization, I intend to scrutinize this field, by reviewing and analyzing the history of the criminalization process through three fields: first, the official reasons for copyright criminalization that are measured using legislation and legislative materials, as shown in the history of legislation in Chapters 1–3; second, I audit secondary sources, primarily, scholarly literature on copyright criminalization, particularly other possible reasons presented in scholarly literature that could be linked to copyright criminalization; third,

I explore possible reasons as presented in the popular media about copyright criminalization, while bearing in mind that this third element is limited due to its impartial nature.

Locating the real, not merely declared, reasons for copyright criminalization is an important element for the normative evaluation of the process and its possible continuance in the future. The declared reasons for copyright criminalization, which I summarize and discuss in the descriptive analysis of legislative materials in Chapters 1–3, reveal that copyright criminalization occurs mostly due to a need for a stronger deterrent against infringement which harms economic, social and/or national interests. The literature on copyright criminalization has identified additional (internal) reasons behind the criminalization process: digital technology, which, inter alia, has increased copyright infringement and (allegedly) reduced the ability to detect infringers; political forces; and the notion of copyright as property. However, these arguments have usually either merely revealed a fraction of copyright criminalization reasons, or have served as explanations for rights holders' success in promoting criminal copyright legislation, not rather that these factors are main reasons for copyright criminalization, regardless of technological developments and potential financial losses.

Thus, as current literature presents incoherent approaches to the reasoning of copyright criminalization, this chapter offers a taxonomy to better understand criminal copyright internal reasons. I conceptualize the internal reasoning for copyright criminalization as an important part of a broader *framework of copyright expansion*. Under this conceptualization, this chapter argues that criminalization, internally to copyright law, is another step in an on-going expansion of copyright holders' rights, which have gradually increased over the years and more extensively in recent decades. This characterization is important both to the understandings of the criminalization process and the normative discussion on whether criminal copyright is justified, which is further analyzed in Chapter 8, and will contribute to current literature on copyright expansion, which does not usually refer to criminal copyright as a form of copyright expansion.

This chapter is mostly descriptive, in that it searches for rationales behind copyright criminalization and does not explore justifications for copyright criminalization (although they sometimes overlap).[1] I intend to clarify the (internal) processes that led to and sustained copyright criminalization, while leaving most of the normative discussion on whether the process is justified to Chapter 8. I begin by briefly reviewing the framework of copyright expansion to understand the logic behind this framework regardless of copyright criminalization and locate criminal copyright in the expansion framework. Then, I turn to explore three major rationales for copyright expansion that are linked to copyright criminalization. First, is the

---

[1] The normative discussion on copyright criminalization is further analyzed in Chapters 8, both from criminal and copyright law perspectives.

negative impact on rights holders' business models, which is attributed mainly to the possible and actual increase of copyright infringement. I explore the various external (to copyright) reasons that are incorporated into this internal reason; namely, technological developments combined with a pro-infringement social norm/lack of moral condemnation against infringement, globalization, and accessibility. I argue that the actual and/or potential harm of copyright infringement has resulted in both legislative and non-legislative response, while criminal copyright is both a preemptive and a reactive measure to copyright infringements.

Second, is the shift toward a pure property paradigm, i.e., the transformation of copyright law from a limited set of exclusive rights granted for purposes of market regulation regime to a property regime. Under this argument, copyright criminalization is directly linked to copyright's (assumed) paradigmatic change to a property regime, which increases the current (low) protection of copyright and adjusts it to tangible property, by among other things, using criminal sanctions.

Third, is the fact of rights holders' increasing and successful political power over the legislature, which results in criminal legislation. This reason is not only the political means which rights holders use to advance criminal copyright, but also serves as an important explanation of the process, as public choice theory implies. Copyright criminalization internal reasons are presented in Figure 7.

I COPYRIGHT EXPANSION FRAMEWORK

Copyright law was not always as broad as it is today. Previously, copyright protection was granted for shorter periods, included fewer types of works that encompassed less exclusive rights, and in some cases, protection was only granted after specific legal formalities and requirements were met.[2] Yet copyright protection has expanded rapidly over the years, especially in the last three decades.[3] There are two primary trajectories of copyright law expansion. First, is an expansion of copyright law to previously unprotected resources or uses. This relates to expansions in subject

---

[2] *See, e.g.,* Rebecca Tushnet, *Copy This Essay: How Fair Use Doctrine Harms Free Speech and How Copying Serves It*, 114 YALE L.J. 535, 541–44 (2004).

[3] *See* DEBORA J. HALBERT, INTELLECTUAL PROPERTY IN THE INFORMATION AGE: THE POLITICS OF EXPANDING PROPERTY RIGHTS 26 (1999); Mark A. Lemley, *Property, Intellectual Property, and Free Riding*, 83 TEX. L. REV. 1031, 1042 (2005); Alex Steel, *Problematic and Unnecessary? Issues with the Use of the Theft Offence to Protect Intangible Property*, 30 SYDNEY L. REV. 575, 599 (2008); Neil Weinstock Netanel, *Why Has Copyright Expanded? Analysis and Critique*, in 6 NEW DIRECTIONS IN COPYRIGHT LAW 3 (Fiona Macmillan ed., 2008). Nevertheless, it is important to note that copyright does not always move in a single direction toward a pure monopoly right, and some cases of weakening protection exist. *See, e.g.,* Neil Netanel, *Recent Developments in Copyright Law*, 7 TEX. INTELL. PROP. J. 331, 340–41 (1999); Laura A. McCluggage, *Section 110(5) and the Fairness in Music Licensing Act: Will the WTO Decide the United States Must Pay to Play?*, 40 IDEA J.L. & TECH. 1, 16–18 (2000).

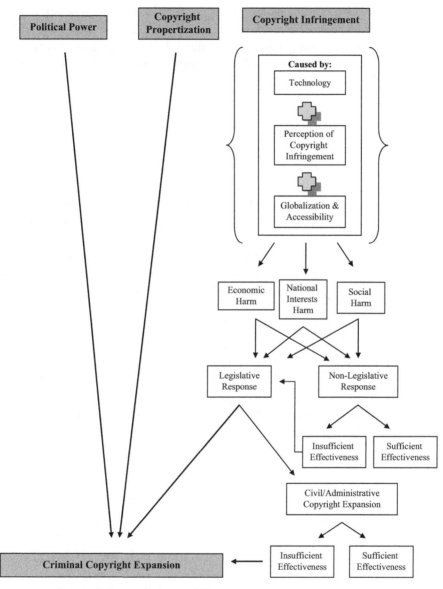

FIGURE 7 Criminal Copyright Internal Reasons

matter, e.g., adjusting copyright laws to new technologies or to the creation of new exclusive rights, e.g., introducing a public performance right.[4] Second, is an

---

4 In the United States, for example, Congress expanded the scope of copyright to include additional rights, e.g., the right of public display in 1976, and the digital public performance right to sound recordings in 1995. *See generally,* Justin Hughes, *Copyright and Incomplete Historiographies: Of Piracy, Propertization and Thomas Jefferson,* 79 S. CAL. L. REV. 993, 1050–51 (2006).

expansion of copyright law to strengthen rights holders' private control, i.e., an expansion of property norms. There are many examples of these expansions[5] – which mainly have occurred through legislation.[6] As this book's purpose is to locate criminal copyright in the framework of copyright expansion, I only briefly review examples of copyright expansions.

A *Examples of Copyright Expansion Framework*

Copyright Term Extension. Over the years and in many countries, and as part of the right holder strengthening movement, the period or term of copyright protection has been lengthened.[7] As further exemplified by the United Kingdom and the United States, this form of copyright expansion was a result of national legislation, which in some instances followed as part of the implementation of multi-national agreements.[8]

Take the example of the United Kingdom, whereas the Statute of Anne provided for a term of 20 years' protection to existing works, and 14 years' protection to new works, a term which was renewable for additional 14 years if the author was alive at

---

[5] There are many examples of copyright's expansion over the years, e.g., the scope of originality and creative appropriation. When copyright was introduced, authors were almost free to make usage of other works as long as their work made substantial contribution and did not displace demand for the works used. However, current copyright law protects works to a much higher extent. *See* NEIL WEINSTOCK NETANEL, COPYRIGHT'S PARADOX 59–60 (2008). For purposes of the discussion here, I only briefly analyze few types of copyright's expansion that strike to me as the most extensive, as these examples are only set to exemplify copyright expansion paradigm.

[6] The expansion of copyright protection is not limited to legislation, and occurred also through judicial decisions, which expanded copyright through interpretations of the statutory limitations on the copyright owner's exclusive rights. *See* Deborah Kemp, *Copyright on Steroids: In Search of an End to Overprotection*, 41 MCGEORGE L. REV. 795, 818 (2010).

[7] For more on copyright term extension in various countries, see, e.g., Samuel Ricketson, *The Birth of the Berne Union*, 11 COLUM.-VLA J.L. & ARTS 9 (1986); Tyler T. Ochoa, *Patent and Copyright Term Extension and the Constitution: A Historical Perspective*, 49 J. COPYRIGHT SOC'Y U.S.A. 19 (2001); Netanel, *supra* note 3, at 3.

[8] The first requirement of a minimal copyright term was set in article 7 of the Berne Convention for the Protection of Literary and Artistic works, as revised at Berlin on Nov. 13, 1908, which at first *recommended* a copyright term for its member of the author's life plus 50 years. In 1948, the Berne Copyright Union changed the recommendation of the Berne Convention to mandate its members to provide a copyright term of the author's life plus 50 years (The Berne Convention for the Protection of Literary and Artistic Works art. 7 (Brussels Text, 1948)). In 1994, the Agreement on Trade-Related Aspects of Intellectual Property Rights, art. 3, Apr. 15, 1994, Marrakesh Agreement Establishing the World Trade Organization, Annex 1C, 1869 U.N.T.S. 299, 33 I.L.M. 1197 (1994) [hereinafter TRIPS], repeated the 1948 Berne Convention in Article 12 to mandate its members to provide a minimum copyright term of the author's life plus 50 years. The European Union has set a higher requirement for its members than the Berne Convention and TRIPS. As of 1993, European Union members are required to provide a copyright term protection of the author's life plus 70 years (Council Directive 93/98/EEC of October 29, 1993 Harmonizing the Term of Protection of Copyright and Certain Related Rights O.J. (L 290)). *See* Sue Ann Mota, *Eldred v. Reno - Is the Copyright Term Extension Constitutional?*, 12 ALB. L.J. SCI. & TECH. 167, 170 (2001).

the time of the first term's expiration.[9] The duration of copyright in books was extended in 1814 to life of an author, or 28 years since the book's publication (without renewal).[10] In 1842, the copyright law accounted for the author's lifespan and the need to protect the authors descendants when Parliament extended the initial term to life plus seven or forty-two years (the longest between the two).[11] In 1911, the United Kingdom enacted the Berne Convention's minimum requirement, and extended the initial term to life plus 50 years with some restrictions, later removed in the 1956 Act.[12] The term was adopted for all literary, dramatic, musical, and artistic works, with the exception of photographs, sound contrivances and works first published after the death of the author. In addition, the 1911 extension was subjected to compulsory licensing in the last twenty-five years. Finally, since January 1st 1996, the United Kingdom copyright term is life plus 70 years.[13]

The United States tells a similar story.[14] The first Copyright Act of 1790 granted a fixed term of copyright protection for a term of 14 years from the date the author filed with the clerk of the District Court, with the possibility of renewal for an additional 14 years.[15] In 1831, Congress extended the initial term to 28 years, which was renewable for another 14 years, i.e., a maximum term of 42 years from the date of filing.[16] As part of the general copyright revision in 1909, Congress extended the renewable term to 28 years, i.e., to a maximum term of 56 years. In addition, Congress changed the term protection requirements to begin from the date of publication rather than

---

[9] Copyright Act 1709, 8 Ann., c. 19 (Gr. Brit.). For a general description of United Kingdom's copyright term expansion, see Lionel Bently, *R. v. The Author: From Death Penalty to Community Service*, 32 COLUM. J.L. & ARTS 1 (2008); JIABO LIU, COPYRIGHT INDUSTRIES AND THE IMPACT OF CREATIVE DESTRUCTION COPYRIGHT EXPANSION AND THE PUBLISHING INDUSTRY 17 (2013); Ronan Deazley, *Commentary on Copyright Act 1814*, in PRIMARY SOURCES ON COPYRIGHT (1450–1900) (Lionel Bently & Martin Kretschmer eds., 2008), http://copy.law .cam.ac.uk/cam/tools/request/showRecord?id=commentary_uk_1814; Ronan Deazley, *The Life of an Author: Samuel Egerton Brydges and the Copyright Act 1814*, 23 GA. ST. U. L. REV. 809 (2007); CATHERINE SEVILLE, LITERARY COPYRIGHT REFORM IN EARLY VICTORIAN ENGLAND: THE FRAMING OF THE 1842 COPYRIGHT ACT 9 (1999); KEVIN GARNETT ET AL., COPINGER AND SKONE JAMES ON COPYRIGHT 375–82 (16th ed. 2011) [hereinafter COPINGER].

[10] Act to Amend Several Acts for the Encouragement of Learning, 1814, 54 Geo. III, c. 156 (U.K.).

[11] Literary Copyright Act, 1842, 5 & 6 Vict., c. 45 (U.K.).

[12] *See* Copyright Act, 1911, 1 & 2 Geo. V, c. 46, § 3 (U.K.); Copyright Act, 1956, 4 & 5 Eliz. II, c. 74, § 3(4) (U.K.).

[13] The Duration of Copyright and Rights in Performances Regulation, 1995, S.I. 1995/3297 (U.K.).

[14] For a general review of the legislative history of copyright term extension in the United States, see, e.g., WILLIAM F. PATRY, PATRY ON COPYRIGHT § 7:1 (2009); Mota, *supra* note 8, at 169. *See also* Eldred v. Ashcroft, 537 U.S. 186 (2003); NETANEL, *supra* note 5, at 57–58; Jenny L. Dixon, *The Copyright Term Extension Act: Is Life Plus Seventy Too Much?*, 18 HASTINGS COMM. & ENT. L.J. 945, 957 (1996); Dennis S. Karjala, *What Are the Issues in Copyright Term Extension- and What Happened?*, OPPOSING COPYRIGHT EXTENSION, http://homepages.law.asu.edu/ ~dkarjala/OpposingCopyrightExtension/what.html (last visited Dec. 1, 2017); Christina N. Gifford, *The Sonny Bono Copyright Term Extension Act*, 30 U. MEM. L. REV. 363, 369 (2000).

[15] Act of May 31, 1790, ch. 15, § 1, 1 Stat. 124 (1790).

[16] Act of Feb. 3, 1831, ch. 16, § 1, 4 Stat. 436 (1831).

the date of filing with copyright notice, or for certain categories of works from registration and deposit with the Copyright Office.[17] Copyright's term was further extended in 1976, as part of the general revision in copyright. Congress extended the duration of copyright protection to the author's life plus 50 years for individual authors, and a 75-year term from publication or 100 years from creation for works made for hire. The Act also added nineteen years to the renewal term for works created prior to the Act, for a total of 75 years.[18] Efforts to reform the term of protection, to follow the Berne Convention recommendation in 1908 of granting copyright protection equal to the life of the author plus 50 years, existed prior to the 1976 Act. From 1962, while examining the need to extend the copyright term protection, Congress enacted a series of one-year term extensions.[19] In addition, in 1964, the working drafts of copyright revision legislation had adopted a basic term of life-plus-50 for most works.[20] In 1998, Congress enacted the Sonny Bono Copyright Term Extension Act (CTEA), which extended the copyright term by twenty years for works created on or after January 1, 1978, from the life of the author plus 50 years to the life of the author plus 70 years. The CETA also extended the term of protection for anonymous, pseudonymous, or works made for hire, which were created on or after January 1, 1978, to 95 years from publication or 120 years from creation, whichever expires first.[21]

The official reasoning behind lengthening the period of protection is the increase in longevity: the original goal of the copyright protected term was to provide copyright protection for two generations following the author's death; hence, as the average lifespan increases, so should the copyright protected period.[22] In a few cases, countries have extended copyright protection to ensure international copyright uniformity (in the sense of copyright duration).[23] Nevertheless, the extension is not just dependent on the increase in longevity as copyright protection was

---

[17] Copyright Act of 1909, ch. 320, § 23, 35 Stat. 1075, 1080 (1909).

[18] Copyright Act of 1976, Pub. L. No. 94–553, 90 Stat. 2541 (1976).

[19] *See* Pub. L. No. 87–668, 76 Stat. 555 (1962); Pub. L. No. 89–142, 79 Stat. 581 (1965); Pub. L. No. 90–141, 81 Stat. 464 (1967); Pub. L. No. 90–416, 82 Stat. 397 (1968); Pub. L. No. 91–147, 83 Stat. 360 (1969); Pub. L. No. 91–555, 84 Stat. 1441 (1970); Pub. L. No. 92–170, 85 Stat. 490 (1971); Pub. L. No. 92–566, 86 Stat. 1181 (1972); Pub. L. No. 93–573, title I, § 104, 88 Stat. 1873 (1974).

[20] *See* PRELIMINARY DRAFT FOR REVISED U.S. COPYRIGHT LAW: DISCUSSIONS AND COMMENTS ON THE DRAFT, HOUSE COMMITTEE ON THE JUDICIARY 88TH CONG., 2D SESS., COPYRIGHT LAW REVISION PART 3, 19–20 (1964); S. REP. NO. 104–315 at 4 (1996).

[21] Sonny Bono Copyright Term Extension Act, Pub. L. No. 105–298, 112 Stat. 2827 (1998) (codified in scattered sections of 17 U.S.C.).

[22] See, e.g., in the European Union's extension of the Berne Convention and TRIPS standards of the author's life plus 50 years (Directive 93/98/EEC, *supra* note 8, at § 5). For criticism on the European Union's reasoning to expand copyright term protection, see Mota, *supra* note 8, at 174.

[23] In the United States, see, e.g., *Eldred*, 537 U.S. ("By extending the baseline United States copyright term to life plus 70 years, Congress sought to ensure that American authors would receive the same copyright protection in Europe as their European counterparts.").

increased behind the years associated with increased longevity.[24] Thus, additional reasons exist for the copyright term extension,[25] which are mostly attributed to the increase in financial elements of the right itself,[26] and are part of a wider expansion of copyright.

Scope: Works Covered. The first copyright acts protected fewer types of works than those currently protected. For instance, in the United Kingdom, the first Copyright Act only granted protection to publishers' rights in printed books.[27] Then in 1735, copyright protection was extended to engravings made from original designs[28]; maps, charts, and plans; engraving from existing designs received copyright protection in 1767; designs for printing on calico in 1787[29]; sculptures in 1798[30]; paintings, drawings, and photographs in 1862[31]; architecture, works of artistic craftsmanship, and sound recordings in 1911[32]; films and broadcasts in 1956[33]; cable programs and typographical arrangements in 1984[34]; computer programs in 1985[35]; and finally, collages in 1988.[36]

---

[24] *See* Kemp, *supra* note 6, at 809.

[25] For example, the United Kingdom's 1842 term extension (Literary Copyright Act, 1842, 5 & 6 Vict., c. 45, § 3 (U.K.)) can be politically attributed to the publishing industry, which witnessed remarkable progress in both technological and organizational innovations. *See* LIU, *supra* note 9, at 17. In addition, the 1976 term extension in the United States can be partially attributed to the advantages of uniformity with a majority of foreign laws. *See* H.R. 1476, 94th Cong. at 135 (2d sess. 1976); S. REP. NO. 104–315 at 4 (1996).

[26] See, for example, the official explanations behind the 1831 and 1909 term extensions in the United States, were that Congress wanted to "ensure that American authors and their dependents receive the fair economic benefits from their works." *See* S. REP. NO. 104–315 at 3–4 (1996); H.R. REP. NO. 94–1476, at 135 (1976), *reprinted in* 1976 U.S.C.C.A.N. 5659, 5751. In addition, in the United States, the CTEA announced purpose was "to ensure adequate copyright protection for American works in foreign nations and the continued economic benefits of a healthy surplus balance of trade in the exploitation of copyrighted works," (see, as originally stated in the context of the proposed Copyright Term Extension Bill in 1995: Copyright Term Extension Act of 1995, S. 483, 104th Cong. (1st Sess. 1995)). Also, the term extension was attributed to the unprecedented growth in technology that "dramatically enhanced the marketable life of creative works, as well as the potential for increased incentives to preserve existing works." *See* S. REP. NO. 104–315 at 6 (1996).

[27] For a summary of the coverage of copyright in the UK, see Bently, *supra* note 9, at 6–7.

[28] Engravers' Copyright Act 1766, 7 Geo. III, c. 38 (U.K.).

[29] Calico Printers' Act 1787, 27 Geo. III, c. 23 (U.K.).

[30] An Act for Encouraging the Art of Making New Models and Casts of Busts, and other things therein mentioned 1798, 38 Geo. III, c. 71 (U.K.).

[31] Fine Arts Copyright Act 1862, 25 & 26 Vict., c. 68 (U.K.).

[32] Copyright Act 1911, 1 & 2 Geo. V, c. 46, §§ 1(1), 19, 35(1) (U.K.).

[33] Copyright Act 1956, 4 & 5 Eliz. 2, c. 74, §§ 13(4), 13(10) (U.K.) (previously protected as photographs or dramatic works, see Copyright Act 1911 § 35).

[34] The Cable and Broadcasting Act 1984, c. 46, § 22 (U.K.).

[35] Copyright (Computer Software) Amendment Act 1985, c. 41 (U.K.). However, computer programs were considered to be protected prior to the enactment by case law. *See* Gates v. Swift [1982] R.P.C. 339; Bently, *supra* note 9, at 7 n.36.

[36] Copyright, Designs and Patents Act 1988, c. 48, §§ 1(1)(a), 4(1)(b) (U.K.).

Similarly, the first Copyright Act in the United States limited protection to charts, books, and maps.[37] In 1802, Congress expanded the scope of protection to engravings, etchings, and prints,[38] and in 1831 to musical compositions.[39] In 1856, the right of publicly performing dramatic compositions received protection,[40] in addition to adding photographs and negatives in 1865.[41] In 1870, Congress added paintings, drawings, chromos, statues, and models or designs intended to be works of fine arts, while allowing authors to reserve the right to dramatize their works.[42] In 1909, protection was expanded to all existing works of authorship that were copyrightable at that time[43]; in 1912, protection was given to motion pictures[44]; in 1971, to sound recordings[45]; in 1980, to computer programs[46]; and in 1990, to architectural works.[47]

The Bundle of Rights; Remedies. Another aspect of copyright expansion is the addition of exclusive rights granted to rights holders. For example, in the United States, the first Copyright Act granted rights holders the exclusive right to control the reproduction and distribution of their protected work.[48] However, copyright law currently grants the rights to reproduce, distribute, prepare derivative works,[49] perform publically,[50] and publicly display protected works.[51] Furthermore, the remedies granted for copyright infringement have also grown substantially.[52] Under

---

[37] Act of May 31, 1 Stat. 124 (1790). However, as noted in Holmes v. Hurst, 174 U.S. 82, 89 (1899), "the word 'book' as used in the statute is not to be understood in its technical sense of a bound volume, but any species of publication which the author selects to embody his literary product." For a full review of the scope expansions in copyright, see Harper & Bros. v. Kalem Co., 169 F. 61, 64–65 (2d Cir. 1909); Tom W. Bell, *Escape from Copyright: Market Success vs. Statutory Failure in the Protection of Expressive Works*, 69 U. CIN. L. REV. 741, 781–83 (2001).

[38] Act of Apr. 29, 1802, 2 Stat. 171 (1802). *See Harper & Bros.*, 169 F. at 64–65.

[39] Act of Feb. 3, 1831, 4 Stat. 436 (1831).

[40] Act of Aug. 18, 1856, 11 Stat. 138 (1856). *See Harper & Bros.*, 169 F. at 64–65.

[41] Act of Mar. 3, 1865, 13 Stat. 540 (1865).

[42] Act of July 8, 1870, 16 Stat. 212 (1870). *See Harper & Bros.*, 169 F. at 64–65.

[43] Copyright Act of 1909, 35 Stat. 1075 (1909).

[44] Act of Aug. 24, 1912, 37 Stat. 488 (1912).

[45] The Sound Recording Act, Pub. L. No. 92–140, 85 Stat. 391 (1971).

[46] Act of Dec. 12, 1980, Pub. L. No. 96–517, 94 Stat. 3015, 3028 (1980).

[47] The Architectural Works Copyright Protection Act, Pub. L. No. 101–650, 701–706, 104 Stat. 5089, 5133 (1990).

[48] Act of May 31, ch. 15, § 1, 1 Stat. 124 (1790).

[49] The 1909 Copyright Act granted authors rights over translations and dramatizations of their works. In 1976, the Copyright Act extended the scope of the 1909 right to the derivative works right, protecting translations; dramatizations; movie versions; fictionalizations; abridgements; "or any other form in which a work may be recast, transformed, or adapted." *See* Tushnet, *supra* note 2, at 541–42; 17 U.S.C. § 101.

[50] The rights holders' exclusive right to authorize public performance was initially granted only to owners of dramatic works, and was expanded to almost all works, while expanding the meaning of "public" to include more types of performances and eliminating the for-profit requirements. *See* Tushnet, *supra* note 2, at 542.

[51] 17 U.S.C. § 106.

[52] For a brief overview of copyright's coverage and remedies expansion, see Bell, *supra* note 37, at 783–84.

the 1790 Act, remedies were confined to destroying infringing works and the receipt of statutory damages.[53]

Under the current act, rights holders can request many types of remedies, e.g., temporary or final injunctions, impounding of infringing articles and devices used in infringement, statutory or actual damages and receipt of profits from infringement, bans on import of infringing products, payment for costs incurred and attorney's fees, and power to subpoena ISPs to disclose the identity of an alleged infringer.[54]

Copyright Formalities. Copyright formalities, a system of procedural mechanisms to which copyright protection is subject, has also played a role in copyright's expansion. In the United Kingdom, the Statute of Anne contained several formalities. For example, in order to receive copyright protection, a rights holder was required to register the title of a literary work with the Stationers' Company prior to publication,[55] and deposit nine copies of each new book prior to publication with the Stationers' Company's warehouse keeper.[56] The Copyright of engravings, prints, and lithographs and for sculptures, models, and casts was subject to a notice requirement.[57] Even more formalities were added throughout the nineteenth century: In 1842, literary works were conditional on a registration and a deposit requirement,[58] and in 1862, the copyright for paintings, drawings, and photographs were also vested through registration.[59] However, since the 1911 implementation on the 1908 Berlin Revision of the Berne Convention for the Protection of Literary and Artistic Works, the United Kingdom did away with all formal copyright requirements.[60] This move certainly points to copyright expansion, since without formalities it is easier to obtain copyright protection; thus, expanding possible rights in works.

---

[53] Act of May 31, § 2, 1 Stat. 124 (1790) (providing for forfeiture of infringing copies to the copyright owner, "who shall forthwith destroy the same," and for payment "of fifty cents for every sheet which shall be found in his or their possession.").

[54] 17 U.S.C. §§ 502–504, 601–603, 505, 512(h).

[55] Copyright Act 1709, 8 Ann., c. 19, § 2 (Gr. Brit.); Stef van Gompel, *Les formalités sont mortes, vive les formalités! Copyright Formalities and the Reasons for their Decline in Nineteenth Century Europe, in* PRIVILEGE AND PROPERTY ESSAYS ON THE HISTORY OF COPYRIGHT 157, 163 (Ronan Deazley, Martin Kretschmer & Lionel Bently eds., 2010).

[56] Copyright Act 1709 § 5; Parliament increased the number of copies to 11 in 1801 (Copyright Act, 1801, 41 Geo. III, c. 107, § 6 (U.K.)), and lowered it to 5 in 1836 (Copyright Act 1836, 6 & 7 Will. IV, c. 110, § 1 (U.K.)); Gompel, *supra* note 55, at 163.

[57] For example, the 1735 Engravers' Copyright Act required the date of first publication and the engraving of the copyright owner on each plate and printed on each print (Engravers' Copyright Act 1735, 8 Geo. II, c. 13, § 1 (Gr. Brit.)). *See* Gompel, *supra* note 55, at 163.

[58] Literary Copyright Act 1842, 5 & 6 Vict., c. 45, §§ 6–10 (U.K.); Gompel, *supra* note 55, at 178.

[59] Fine Arts Copyright Act 1862, 25 & 26 Vict., c. 68, § 4 (U.K.); Gompel, *supra* note 55, at 179.

[60] Copyright Act 1911, 1 & 2 Geo. V, c. 46 (U.K.).

In the United States, the first copyright statute in 1790 gave copyright protection only after meeting various formalities.[61] With that, Congress has eliminated most of these formalities over time that placed a burden on authors. For example, since 1976 copyright protection exists from the moment a work is created.[62] Currently, the United States still has registration and notice procedures, which are not required as a condition of protection, but are necessary requirements if a rights holder of a domestic work wants to sue for copyright infringement and to claim attorney's fees and statutory damages.[63] In 2008, Congress loosened the registration requirement even further: civil copyright law only requires a certificate of registration, regardless of whether the certificate contains accurate information or not.[64]

To conclude, copyright, in many aspects, has expanded rapidly over the years. This expansion can be divided into an expansion of copyright law to previously unprotected resources or uses and an expansion of copyright law to strengthen rights holders' private control. However, as I further suggest, a third method of copyright expansion exists in the form of strengthening rights holders' control through public enforcement measures, namely, the addition of criminal copyright.

B *Criminalization as a Form of Copyright Expansion*

Criminal enforcement adds another measure to existing civil procedures and as such is part of copyright expansion. Under this *expansion of enforcement measures,* policymakers and rights holders do not only view copyright as a bundle of rights, but rather as the ability to protect and enforce those rights.[65] Thus, copyright criminalization is a part of the copyright expansion movement. However, this form of copyright

---

[61] For example, authors needed to register their copyright, give proper notice about their rights (marking their works with an indication of copyright status, provide other information about their ownership, and reregister their work after an initial term. For a full analysis of copyright formalities in the United States, see Christopher Sprigman, *Reform(aliz)ing Copyright,* 57 STAN. L. REV. 485, 491–94 (2004).

[62] Copyright Act of 1976, Pub. L. No. 94–553, 90 Stat. 2541 (1976); *See* Tushnet, *supra* note 2, at 543.

[63] Attorney's fees and statutory damages cannot be claimed unless the work was registered prior to infringement, or within three months of publication. 17 U.S.C. §§ 408–412. This is due to Article 5(2) of the Berne Convention for the Protection of Literary and Artistic Works (1971 Paris text), 24 July 1971, 1161 U.N.T.S. 3 ("The enjoyment and the exercise of these rights shall not be subject to any formality; such enjoyment and such exercise shall be independent of the existence of protection in the country of origin of the work. Consequently, apart from the provisions of this Convention, the extent of protection, as well as the means of redress afforded to the author to protect his rights, shall be governed exclusively by the laws of the country where protection is claimed."). United States ratified the treaty in 1989, and thus was not subjected to its terms earlier.

[64] Unless, however, the inaccurate information was included on the application for copyright registration with knowledge that it was inaccurate and that the inaccuracy of the information, if known, would have caused the Register to refuse registration. *See* 17 U.S.C. § 411(b)(1).

[65] *See* PATRY, *supra* note 14, at § 7:2.

expansion does not always coincide with the other two forms discussed above: the extension of copyright to previously unprotected resources or uses and strengthening rights holders private control. Hence, it is important to understand why rights holders desire criminal legislation, in order to examine the internal reasons for copyright criminalization. However, here, I only briefly summarize the motivation of rights holders and policymakers in this regard, and return to this point in the final chapters.

Policymakers' perspective can be divided into three main fields of interests: economic, national, and social. From an economic perspective, policymakers are interested in protecting rights holders economic incentives[66] and thus introduced criminal copyright to provide infringers with a stronger deterrent than that existing in civil proceedings.[67] Under this perspective, as copyright is integral to the nation's economy,[68] criminal copyright serves as an impetus for economic growth, increasing employment and commerce[69]; maintains the necessary incentive for creation

---

[66] The Copyright Act of 2005 was enacted due to the Motion Picture Association of America (MPAA) claim that illicit "camcording" of motion pictures in motion picture exhibition facilities, causes the movie industry an estimated $3.5 billion in annual losses because of hard-goods "piracy." *See* Family Entertainment and Copyright Act of 2005, Pub. L. No. 109-9, 119 Stat. 218 (2005) (codified as amended at 18 U.S.C. § 2319B (2005)); *See* H.R. REP. No. 109-33, at 2 (2005). Similar arguments can be traces in International agreements, e.g., Anti-Counterfeiting Trade Agreement art. 1, Oct. 1, 2011, 50 I.L.M. 243 (2011) [hereinafter ACTA], which noted that its provisions are due to the notion that "piracy" undermines legitimate trade and sustainable development of the world economy and causes significant financial losses for rights holders and for legitimate businesses.

[67] See, e.g., in the United Kingdom, the Musical Copyright Act of 1906, 6 Edw. VII, c. 36 (U.K.), which was enacted due to a growing practice of unlawfully selling music sheets at very low prices ("I rise to call attention to the serious loss inflicted upon copyright holders of music by the illegal sale in the streets and elsewhere of copyright music by hawkers, and to the impracticability of their obtaining redress under the existing law."). *See* Deb 14 March 1902 vol. 105 cc4–8; COPINGER, *supra* note 9, at 1250. And accordingly, in the United States, Act of Jan. 6, 1897, ch. 4, 29 Stat. 481 (1897), was enacted mainly due to music copyright owners' concern, that civil remedies will not deter unlawful performances of music, as unlicensed performances throughout the country were uneasy to monitor. *See* Dorothy Schrader, *Music Licensing Copyright Proposals: An Overview of H.R. 789 and S. 28*, CRS REPORT FOR CONGRESS 2–4 (1998). *See also* Robin Fry, *Copyright Infringement and Collective Enforcement*, 24 E.I.P.R. 516, 522 (2002).

[68] *See* H.R. REP. No. 110-617 at 21 (2008) ("[i]ncreasing intellectual property theft in the United States and globally threatens the future economic prosperity of our nation.").

[69] For example, the United States Copyright Felony Act of 1992 (Pub. L. No. 102-561, 106 Stat. 4233 (1992)) was partially justified by the need to lower potential losses of jobs and diminution in the number of works created. *See* H.R. REP. No. 102-997 (1992), *reprinted in* 1992 U.S.C.C.A.N. 3569; STEPHEN E. SIWEK, INST. FOR POL'Y INNOVATION, POLICY REPORT 189: THE TRUE COST OF COPYRIGHT INDUSTRY PIRACY TO THE U.S. ECONOMY (2007), www.ipi .org/docLib/20120515_CopyrightPiracy.pdf (arguing that United States economy suffers 373,375 job losses annually). In addition, the PRO-IP Act was among others, due to revenue losses for American companies from copyright infringements and a negative impact on U.S. economy in terms of reduced job growth, exports, and competitiveness. *See* Prioritizing Resources and Organization for Intellectual Property Act, Pub. L. No. 110-403, § 503(1)–(2), 122 Stat. 4256

and investment in copyrighted materials, and protects businesses from financial losses and even bankruptcy[70]; safeguards foreign rights holders, who are unaware or unable to file civil lawsuits[71]; raises author-incentive to create by lowering the expected probability of infringements; reduces judicial burden, as criminal cases are usually decided faster than civil dockets[72]; and finally, could reduce the risk of counterclaims, as people usually sue the government less than they sue a rights holder.[73]

From a *national interest perspective*, policymakers use criminal copyright to reduce other criminal activities that are allegedly related to copyright infringements, usually organized crime and terrorism.[74] Thus, if criminalization of copyright could reach its goal and deter copyright infringement, it might also reduce other, related criminal activities. In addition, if preserving the market of ideas and important

---

(2008). *See also* COMPUTER CRIME AND INTELLECTUAL PROPERTY SECTION, CRIMINAL DIVISION, U.S. DEP'T OF JUSTICE, PROSECUTING INTELLECTUAL PROPERTY CRIMES 1 (3d ed. 2006).

[70] *See, e.g.*, Nadine Courmandias, *The Criminalisation of Copyright Infringement in Japan and What This Tells Us about Japan and the Japanese*, 17 ASIA PAC. L. REV. 167, 172 (2009).

[71] Fry, *supra* note 67, at 516.

[72] Kent Walker, *Federal Remedies for the Theft of Intellectual Property*, 16 HASTINGS COMM. & ENT. L.J. 681, 688 (1994); Fry, *supra* note 67, at 522.

[73] *See* Maggie Heim & Greg Geockner, *International Anti-Piracy and Market Entry*, 17 WHITTIER L. REV. 261, 267 (1995).

[74] *See*, in the United Kingdom, the Copyright, etc. and Trade Marks (Offences and Enforcement) of 2002, c. 25 (U.K.), which was proposed due to an argument that the offences under the Copyright, Designs and Patents Act 1988, c. 48 (U.K.) were insufficient and leading organized criminals into the field (COPINGER, *supra* note 9, at 1253). See also, in the United State, the Anticounterfeiting Consumer Protection Act, Pub. L. No. 104–153, 110 Stat. 1386 (1996); 141 CONG. REC. S18594 (daily ed. Dec. 14, 1995) (statement of Sen. Leahy), which was legislated in order to combat copyright (and trademark) infringements linked to organized crime. *See* S. REP. No. 104–177 (1995). In addition, the Intellectual Property Protection and Courts Amendments Act of 2004 (Pub. L. No. 108–482, 118 Stat. 3912 (2004)) was reasoned by a perceived need of software companies to deter counterfeiting of identification measures to verify computer software authenticity, as they were highly profitable and there was a low risk of detection and prosecution, while software infringements and counterfeiting has become part of an intricate web of international organized crime; *See* H.R. REP. No. 108–600 (2004); *International Copyright Piracy: A Growing Problem with Links to Organized Crime and Terrorism: Hearing Before the Subcomm. on Courts, the Internet, and Intellectual Property*, 108th Cong. 41 (2003) (testimony of Rich LaMagna, a Senior Manager of Worldwide Anti-Piracy Investigations at Microsoft Corporation). Moreover, the Prioritizing Resources and Organization for Intellectual Property Act of 2008 (Pub. L. No. 110–403, § 503(1)–(6), 122 Stat. 4256 (2008)), was, among other things, justified to fight terrorists and organized crime, which utilize copyright infringements to fund some of their activities. See also in International discussion of imposing criminal copyright legislation, e.g., in Directive 2004/48/EC, of the European Parliament and of the Council of 29 April 2004 on the Enforcement of Intellectual Property Rights, 2004 O.J. (L 195). For examples of the possible linkage between crime and terrorism to copyright infringement, see, e.g., Courmandias, *supra* note 70, at 173; Fry, *supra* note 67, at 516; PAUL R. PARADISE, TRADEMARK COUNTERFEITING: PRODUCT PIRACY, AND THE BILLION DOLLAR THREAT TO THE U.S. ECONOMY 21 (1999); Maureen Walterbach, *International Illicit Convergence: The Growing Problem of Transnational Organized Crime Groups' Involvement In Intellectual Property Rights Violations*, 34 FLA. ST. U. L. REV. 591, 592 (2007).

human rights, such as free speech, are considered a national interest, then criminal copyright could help fulfill this interest, as stronger copyright protection could result in better dissemination of ideas, and creation of works.[75] Finally, policymakers use criminal copyright to protect consumer interests, i.e., to protect the public against the threat of counterfeit. Although counterfeit usually refers to trademarks, it has played a role in the reasons behind criminal copyright, as well.[76]

From a *social perspective*, policymakers can use criminal law to shape the social norms regarding infringement. Under this argument, policymakers are aware that society does not consider copyright infringements a universally wrong conduct.[77] Thus, criminal law is partially used to educate society on what is morally wrong.

From rights holders' perspective, copyright criminalization is desirable mostly in the economic sense, i.e., criminal copyright provides them with a financial benefi-cial. There are multiple reasons for this: criminal law avails them with additional enforcement opportunities[78]; it shifts the costs of investigation, enforcement, and litigation to the state's criminal justice system and ultimately to taxpayers[79]; it could improve their reputation within society, which suffers from lawsuits against alleged

---

[75] *See* Cheng Lim Saw, *The Case for Criminalising Primary Infringements of Copyright– Perspectives from Singapore*, 18 INT'L. J.L. & INFO. TECH. 95, 104–05 (2009). By contrast, criminal copyright could also harm national interests of preserving the market of ideas and important human rights as free speech, as it could have a chilling effect on the usage of permitted activities, e.g., the fair use exemption (where it exists), as some people will be afraid from possible criminal prosecution.

[76] In a few cases, criminalization was linked to consumer protection. For example, the United States Copyright Felony Act of 1992 (Pub. L. No. 102–561, 106 Stat. 4233 (1992)) was partially justified by the need to protect consumers, which are "victimized by these acts of piracy." *See Criminal Sanctions for Violations of Software Copyright: Hearing on S. 893 Before the Sub-comm. on Intellectual Prop. and Judicial Admin. of the H. Comm. on the Judiciary*, 102d Cong. (1992) ("[N]ot only is the software industry seriously damaged, but the public is also victimized by these acts of piracy. The consumer is paying full price for a product which he believes is legitimate. However, not only may there be imperfections in the actual reproduction, but the quality of the product is often lower as a result of cheap equipment. Furthermore, the consumer is ineligible for the important support and backup services typically offered by the software publisher."). In addition, the Intellectual Property Protection and Courts Amend-ments Act of 2004 was reasoned, partially by a perceived need to protect consumers from unknowingly purchasing counterfeited products; *See* H.R. REP. No 108–600, at 5 (2004) ("[c]onsumers are now accustomed to looking for these authentication features to protect them-selves from being defrauded into buying counterfeit products."). The criminal provisions in ACTA were also attributed to decrease risks to the public (Anti-Counterfeiting Trade Agree-ment art. 1, Oct. 1, 2011, 50 I.L.M. 243).

[77] *See, e.g.*, Fry, *supra* note 67, at 516.

[78] *Id.* at 522.

[79] *See* Heim & Geockner, *supra* note 73, at 267; Geraldine Szott Moohr, *Defining Overcrimina-lization through Cost-Benefit Analysis: The Example of Criminal Copyright Laws*, 54 AM. U. L. REV. 783, 798 (2005). Moreover, as civil litigation is expensive, rights holders that lack sufficient funds to sue are unable to civilly respond to infringements, i.e., they require the help of the government in filing lawsuits.

end users, and could allow them an avenue to enforce their rights without alienating their existing and potential customers[80]: it could serve as a better deterrent than civil damages and therefore be more effective in fighting copyright infringements[81]; it could provide a better tool than civil enforcement to enforce large-scale operations and cross-border infringements; and it adds nonmonetary, criminal sanctions, i.e., imprisonment. Imprisonment is in itself an alluring sanction for rights holders. First, it can aid against infringers who are not deterred by civil or financial sanctions.[82] Second, imprisonment prevents infringers from continuing their criminal activity, thus resulting in a decrease of future infringements.[83] Third, prisoners face many social costs, e.g., stigma and barriers in trying to re-enter the employment market, and thus many people will be deterred by imprisonment due to its vast social consequences.[84]

Understanding the basic drive to criminalize copyright leads us to explore copyright criminalization under the copyright expansion trend and to identify three main frameworks that explain the process. First, is the *infringement framework*, which was brought about by the negative effects infringement played on rights holders' financial gains. This framework has three main factors: technological developments, social and/or moral norms, and globalization. Second, is the *copyright propertization framework*, a shift toward a pure property paradigm. Third, is the *political framework*, based mainly on public choice theory, which holds that the criminalization process is vastly influenced by political power. It is important to note that the three frameworks could explain the entire process of copyright criminalization independently, even without the external reasons for criminalization set in Chapter 6. However, as I argue, it is much more likely, and as the development of copyright criminalization indicates as well, that the reasons for copyright criminalization are diverse and although some reasons play a bigger role than others in copyright criminalization, the combination of the reasons together is important for the entire process.

---

[80] *See* Moohr, *supra* note 79, at 799; Amy Harmon, *THE NAPSTER DECISION: THE REACTION; Napster Users Make Plans for the Day the Free Music Dies*, N.Y. TIMES (Feb. 13, 2001), www.nytimes.com/2001/02/13/business/napster-decision-reaction-napster-users-make-plans-for-day-free-music-dies.html?src=pm.

[81] I. Trotter Hardy, *Criminal Copyright Infringement*, 11 WM. & MARY BILL RTS. J. 305, 312 (2002).

[82] For example: "judgment proof" infringers, incapable of being deterred by civil damages; or impecunious infringers, which lack the ability to pay any fine and are therefore not deterred by civil damages or criminal fines, as they do not intend to pay them.

[83] *See* Lanier Saperstein, *Copyrights, Criminal Sanctions and Economic Rents: Applying the Rent Seeking Model to the Criminal Law Formulation Process*, 87 J. CRIM. L. & CRIMINOLOGY 1470, 1508 (1997).

[84] *See* Steven Penney, *Crime, Copyright, and the Digital Age, in* WHAT IS A CRIME? CRIMINAL CONDUCT IN CONTEMPORARY SOCIETY 61, 74–75 (Law Comm'n of Canada ed., 2004).

II INCREASE OF COPYRIGHT INFRINGEMENT

The first reason for copyright criminalization, as part of the expansion framework, is the potential and actual increase in copyright infringement. Under this framework, infringing has become much easier due to technological advances combined with the notion that social and moral norms do not prevent infringement, as many do not recognize infringement as wrong. Accordingly, the copyright regime could be at risk. Since copyright infringement reduces monetary incentives to create, it could undermine the copyright regime and result in a possible chilling effect to create and invest in works; hence, rights holders, authors, and society could be harmed. Therefore, the possible and actual threat of copyright infringement, had led rights holders to search for new methods, both preemptive and reactive, to protect their rights and business models and prevent possible revenue loss.[85] Criminal copyright is one of the measures to prevent or at least reduce infringements, as I further explain.

Over the years, rights holders have used many methods to respond to infringement, and it is important to locate the criminalization process within these attempts. The reasons that led to infringement or the possibility to infringe? Technological developments (combined with social/moral norms, and globalization) are not entirely internal reasons to copyright law. However, as these reasons do not by themselves justify the criminalization process externally, as they possess internal influences, I classify them in the internal context, via the *copyright infringement framework*.

A *Reasons of the Increase of Copyright Infringement*

There are three main, interrelated reasons that explain the increase of copyright infringement.[86] First, and perhaps most importantly, are technological

---

[85] For example, some scholars found a negative impact on the music industry due to illegal file sharing. *See, e.g.*, Norbert J. Michel, *Digital File Sharing and the Music Industry: Was There a Substitution Effect?*, 2 Rev. of Econ. Res. on Copyright Issues 41, 50 (2005); Martin Peitz & Patrick Waelbroeck, *The Effect of Internet Piracy on Music Sales: Cross-Section Evidence*, 1 Rev. Econ. Res. On Copyright Issues 71 (2004); Alejandro Zentner, *File Sharing and International Sales of Copyrighted Music: An Empirical Analysis with a Panel of Countries*, 5 Topics Econ. Analysis & Pol'y 1 (2005); Stanley J. Liebowitz, *File-Sharing: Creative Destruction or Just Plain Destruction?*, 49 J.L. & Econ. 1 (2). On the other hand, some researchers stated that it is difficult to argue that weaker copyright protection has had a negative impact on artists' incentives to be creative. *See* Felix Oberholzer-Gee & Koleman Strumpf, *File-Sharing and Copyright* (Harvard Business School, Working Paper No. 09–133, 2009), www.hbs.edu/research/pdf/09-132.pdf; William Patry, Moral Panics and the Copyright Wars 15–16 (2009) (noting that empirical evidence indicates that music and film industries revenue continue to rise each year despite copyright infringements); *Cf.* Stanley J. Liebowitz, *How Reliable Is the Oberholzer-Gee and Strumpf Paper on File-Sharing?* (Sept. 2007) (unpublished manuscript), *available at* http://papers.ssrn.com/sol3/papers.cfm?abstract_id=1014399.

[86] It is important to note that other factors also contributed to the reasons for copyright infringements' rise, e.g., the increasing types of works covered by copyright, etc. However, I will focus on the three main reasons for the increase of copyright infringements, which are closely linked

developments, which have changed the nature of reproducing and distributing works. Second, is a perception of copyright infringement as an acceptable social norm that is not considered morally wrong. Third, is globalization, which has increased the demand for foreign works. This part explores these three reasons.

1 Technology

When copyright protection was first granted, in both the United Kingdom and the United States in the eighteenth century, technology was not a key instrument in copyright infringement. Most infringements were carried out by hand – without the use of technology. Moreover, most individuals did not have the know-how to use available technologies to copyright, and even in those cases, available technology was expensive and highly inaccessible. Over time and as technology advanced, rights holders gained more efficient methods to reproduce and distribute their works. However, technological uses were not only advantageous to rights holders, and copyright infringers too began to benefit as well. Technology provided the public a more affordable and accessible way to copy and distribute works in faster and easier ways, sometimes with lower risk of detection.[87] On the one hand, this conduct could potentially decrease incentives to create certain kinds of creative works and could undermine the copyright regime.[88] On the other hand, technology also benefited rights holders who were also able to produce and distribute their work in faster, easier and cheaper ways, and also increased their control over the work.[89]

In a nutshell, although rights holders benefited from technological developments, they were also harmed by its nature as it led to more infringements. Under this argument, technological developments were a substantial element in the increase of copyright infringement. Accordingly, financial harm caused rights holders to try various methods to reduce potential and actual losses. Criminalizing copyright law was yet another method used by rights holders to maintain maximize profits. This

---

to the criminalization process, as described in the legislative history of copyright criminalization in Chapters 1–3.

[87] Technology can also assist infringers to better conceal their actions. *See* Kim F. Natividad, *Stepping It Up and Taking It to the Streets: Changing Civil & Criminal Copyright Enforcement Tactics*, 23 BERKELEY TECH. L.J. 469, 470 (2008). I. Trotter Hardy refers to this phenomenon as creating "decentralized infringement." *See generally*, I. Trotter Hardy, Copyright and "New-Use" Technologies, 23 NOVA L. REV. 657 (1999).

[88] *Hearing on H.R. 2265 Before the Subcomm. on Courts and Intellectual Property of the House Comm. on the Judiciary*, 105th Cong. (1997) ("[p]iracy acts as a powerful disincentive to entrepreneurs who might otherwise bring new products to market but are worried that they will be unable to do so profitably because of the theft of their products. Software piracy particularly discourages those in our industry who often have the most to offer in terms of new innovation – start-ups, small and medium-sized companies who cannot afford to make the necessary investments in research and development to develop new products without being sure of receiving a return on their investment.").

[89] *See* JESSICA LITMAN, DIGITAL COPYRIGHT 12 (2d ed. 2006).

argument will become more evident after reading the historical description of the various methods used by rights holders to respond to infringements.

The nature of the relationship between technological advances and copyright infringement needs to be developed further to highlight specific connections and the role of the former with the advance of the latter, and more specifically in copyright criminalization.[90] A brief assessment of major technological developments that influenced copyright law (even prior to the criminalization process) is due.

The starting point is the emergence of the analog platform: means for mechanically capturing and reproducing works of authorship.[91] Johann Gutenberg's invention of the printing press (with moveable wooden or metal letters) in the mid-fifteenth century, a new form of reproduction equipment, gave rise to the original need for copyright protection.[92] Before the invention of the printing press, infringing most types of copyrighted works was impossible or required investing many hours of physical labor – thus, making infringement unprofitable.[93] The printing press enabled faster and cheaper production of some works – raising overall revenue.[94] While authors and rights holders could now earn more money, it also opened up the gateway for increased infringement. Technological developments could now become harmful to the copyright regime, in an economic sense, if the expected return for a new work did not exceed the expected cost of its creation.[95]

Since Gutenberg's invention, technological measures, which made copying more efficient and increased the speed of reproduction, have continued to develop. Beginning in the early nineteenth century, additional commercial reproduction methods have emerged: e.g., the invention of stereotyping which allowed an exact copy to be made of a page of type; the invention of the papermaking machine; and developments in the printing press processes and equipment, e.g., displacing iron from wood as the material

---

[90] For a general description of the linkage between copyright protection and technological developments, see Jessica Litman, *Copyright Legislation and Technological Change*, 68 Or. L. Rev. 275 (1989).

[91] Peter S. Menell, *Envisioning Copyright Law's Digital Future*, 46 N.Y.L. Sch. L. Rev. 63, 104 (2002).

[92] *See* Sony Corp. of America v. Universal City Studios, 464 U.S. 417, 430 (1984) ("[i]t was the invention of a new form of copying equipment – the printing press – that gave rise to the original need for copyright protection"); Stephen M. Kramarsky, *Copyright Enforcement in the Internet Age: The Law and Technology of Digital Rights Management*, 11 DePaul J. Art & Ent. L. 1, 3 (2001); Kemp, *supra* note 6, at 808; Seville, *supra* note 9, at 9. For a full analysis of technology history, see Daniel R. Headrick, Technology: A World History (2009).

[93] *See* Paul Goldstein, Copyright's Highway: From Gutenberg to the Celestial Jukebox Hill 31 (2003).

[94] *See id.*; Paradise, *supra* note 74, at 128.

[95] For more on the analysis of the costs of creating a work and the cost of producing the actual copies of the work, see William M. Landes & Richard Posner, *An Economic Analysis of Copyright Law*, 18 J. Legal Stud. 325 (1989); William M. Landes & Richard Posner, The Economic Structure of Intellectual Property Law 37–41 (2003).

from which printing presses were made and the use of steam to power the printing press.[96] By the end of the nineteenth century, technology enabled the recording of sounds, moving photographic pictures, and the multiplication of copies of sheet music in manuscript,[97] through the development of photographic equipment.[98]

By the beginning of the twentieth century, technological developments further changed the nature of the content industry.[99] In 1909, Congress gave new technologies – moving pictures and piano rolls – copyright protection,[100] rejecting the United States Supreme Court view on this matter.[101] By the late 1940s, small-format photographic film made microform reproduction easy and widespread.[102] And in the 1960s, magnetic tape recording and cassette players were introduced commercially.[103] Magnetic tape recording and cassette players availed relatively-high quality, low-cost copying to the public,[104] and led to a fundamental change in the economics of recorded music.[105] Lost revenues from "piracy" were reported at $100 million, in comparison to $300 million for legitimate tape sales.[106] These technological changes also attributed to the enactment of the Sound Recording Act of 1971, which was largely the result of lobbying efforts by record and motion picture industries.

[96] John Feather, Publishing, Piracy and Politics: An Historical Study of Copyright in Britain 174–75 (1994); Liu, *supra* note 9, at 17.
[97] Isabella Alexander, *Criminalising Copyright: A Story of Publishers, Pirates, and Pieces of Eight,* 66 Cambridge L.J. 625, 628–29 (2007).
[98] *Id.* (referencing to Graham Clarke, The Photograph, Oxford History of Art 18 (1997), arguing that "[b]y 1895 a Kodak camera could be purchased for a guinea and by 1900 Kodak Brownies were being sold at 5s"); Feather, *supra* note 96, at 176.
[99] For a list of technological developments in the twentieth century, see Feather, *supra* note 96, at 176.
[100] *See* Copyright Act of 1909, ch. 320, 33 Stat. 1075–82 (1909). *See also* Robert P. Merges, *One Hundred Years of Solicitude: Intellectual Property Law, 1900–2000,* 88 Calif. L. Rev. 2187, 2192 (2000).
[101] See, e.g., the Supreme Court decision in White-Smith Music Publishing Co. v. Apollo Co., 209 U.S. 1 (1908) (holding that a piano roll could not constitute a "copy" of a copyrighted musical composition). However, the Copyright Act of 1909 rejected the Court's definition of a copy, while introducing a protection on piano rolls. See Merges, *supra* note 100, at 2193–94.
[102] Feather, *supra* note 96, at 176.
[103] *See* Register's Report on the General Revision of the U.S. Copyright Law (July 10, 1961), *reprinted in* 5 Melville Nimmer and David Nimmer, Nimmer on Copyright (1998), Appen. 14, at 18 [hereinafter Nimmer on Copyright]; Merges, *supra* note 100, at 2196; Note however that sound recording on magnetic tape had been invented in the 1920s. See Feather, *supra* note 96, at 176.
[104] *See* Penney, *supra* note 84, at 63; Merges, *supra* note 100, at 2197; Office of Technology Assessment, *Copyright and Home Copying: Technology Challenges the Law,* FAS 77 (1989), www.fas.org/ota/reports/8910.pdf.
[105] *See* Merges, *supra* note 100, at 2197; Paul Sugden, *You Can Click but you Can't Hide: Copyright Pirates and Crime – the 'Drink or Die' Prosecutions,* 30 E.I.P.R. 222, 222 (2008).
[106] *See* H.R. Rep. No. 92–487 (1971), *reprinted in* Nimmer on Copyright, *supra* note 103, Appen. 18, at 18–3 (statement of Rep. Kastenmeier).

The analog age was highly profitable for rights holders and did not pose a real threat to their business models[107]: making unauthorized copies was a relatively slow process; it lacked the quality of the original; and the relative ease of detecting unauthorized commercial-scale publication proved as an effective deterrent to copyright infringement.[108] In the analog age, the biggest threat to rights holders was compliance with the public performance right. Both civil and criminal copyright enforcement's timeline align on this matter: the first criminal copyright Act was legislated mainly due to unlicensed performances throughout the country that were difficult to monitor.[109] Accordingly, in the civil realm, the American Society of Composers, Authors and Publishers (ASCAP) was formed in 1914 in order to protect public performance rights.[110] Thus, enforcement of copyright infringement at that time was rather effective, and the usage of criminal copyright was limited.

The change came in the digital age. The introduction of the personal computer into wide use, which enabled the perfect replication of copyrighted works in digital form, again affected copyrights holders and, eventually, led Congress in 1980 to extend copyright protection to computer programs.[111] The development of personal computers, Compact Digital (CD) recording format,[112] cable television, Digital Video Disc formats, digital books, and especially the onset of the internet, which has dramatically grown in size since its inception,[113] probably holds the largest threat to rights holders thus far, forcing Congress again to respond. As noted in Congress[114]:

> Unfortunately, the potential for this problem to worsen is great. By the turn of the century the Internet is projected to have more than 200 million users, and the development of new technology will create additional incentive for copyright thieves to steal protected works. The advent of digital video discs, for example, will enable individuals to store far more material on conventional discs and, at the same time, produce perfect secondhand copies. The extension of an audio-compression technique, commonly referred to as MP3, now permits infringers to transmit large

---

[107] Menell, *supra* note 91, at 105.

[108] *Id.*

[109] Musical Public Performance Right Act of Jan. 6, 1897, ch. 4, 29 Stat. 481 (1897).

[110] ASCAP established boarder copyright protection through litigation. *See, e.g.*, Herbert v. Shanley, 242 U.S. 591 (1917); Jerome H. Remick & Co. v. General Electric Co., 16 F.2d 829 (S.D.N.Y. 1926); Buck v. Lester, 24 F.2d 877 (E.D.S.C. 1928). For more on the formation of ASCAP, see Peter S. Menell, *This American Copyright Life: Reflections on Re-Equilibrating Copyright for the Internet Age*, 62 J. COPYRIGHT SOC'Y U.S.A. 201, 211 (2014; Robert P. Merges, *Contracting into Liability Rules: Intellectual Property Rights and Collective Rights Organizations*, 84 CALIF. L. REV. 1293, 1328–40 (1996).

[111] Act of Dec.12, 1980, Pub. L. No. 96–517, 94 Stat. 3015, 3028 (1980).

[112] Although the compact disk (CD) format was introduced in the 1980s, it only started to pose a threat on the sound recording industry in the mid-1990s, when CD devices of this era enabled consumers to record from or onto this medium. *See* Menell, *supra* note 91, at 109.

[113] *See* Annemarie Bridy, *Is Online Copyright Enforcement Scalable?*, 13 VAND. J. ENT. & TECH. L. 695, 696–97 (2011).

[114] *See* H.R. REP. NO. 105–339, at 4 (1997).

volumes of CD-quality music over the Internet. As long as the relevant technology evolves in this way, more piracy will ensue. Many computer users are either ignorant that copyright laws apply to Internet activity, or they simply believe that they will not be caught or prosecuted for their conduct. In light of this disturbing trend, it is manifest that Congress must respond.

As indicated in Congressional reports, in 1996–1997 lost revenues from "piracy" exceeded $11 billion, and caused substantial unemployment, lost tax revenue,[115] and raised prices for honest purchasers of copyrighted software:[116]

> Copyright piracy flourishes in the software world. Industry groups estimate that counterfeiting and piracy of intellectual property – especially computer software, compact discs, and movies – cost the affected copyright holders more than $11 billion last year (others believe the figure is closer to $20 billion). In some countries, software piracy rates are as high as 90% of all sales. The U.S. rate is far lower (27%), but the dollar losses ($2.3 billion) are the highest worldwide. The effect of this volume of theft is substantial: 130,000 lost U.S. jobs, $5.6 billion in corresponding lost wages, $1 billion in lower tax revenue, and higher prices for honest purchasers of copyrighted software.

Notably, and as further discussed in Chapter 8, it is highly difficult to assert the volume of infringements and losses. Reliance on these statistics, in general, as Eric Goldman argued, is indefensible for two reasons: first, the $11 billion statistic measured worldwide losses and not United States losses; and second, the Study's methodology feigns credibility through complexity that obscures guesswork, subjective judgments, and unreliable data inputs.[117]

As seen, digitization had a vast impact on copyright law. It enables an easy, accessible, affordable and a prefect duplication of a copyrighted work.[118] It also possesses many other attributes: enables recording on small devices; facilitates alteration and integration of different art forms; and with the proper technology,

---

[115] For example, an economic analysis conducted by Stephen E. Siwek, suggests that in the United States, Federal, state and local governments lose at least $2.6 billion in tax revenues annually (up to 2007). *See* SIWEK, *supra* note 69, at i.

[116] *See* H.R. REP. No. 105–339, at 4 (1997).

[117] *See* Eric Goldman, *A Road to No Warez: The No Electronic Theft Act and Criminal Copyright Infringement*, 82 OR. L. REV. 369, 396–99 (2003).

[118] *See* Penney, *supra* note 84, at 66. Peter Menell argues that the most important factors and characteristics responsible for the emergence of the digital content platform are: "(1) dramatic advances in microprocessor speed, memory storage, and data compression; (2) achievement of high sampling rates in capturing digital content; (3) development of improved technologies for perceiving (listening to and viewing) digital content; (4) essentially flawless, inexpensive, and rapid reproduction capabilities; (5) precise manipulability of digital content; (6) archive management and searchability; (7) portability; (8) development of digital networks for distributing content (including broadband); and (9) convergence of distribution platforms." *See* Menell, *supra* note 91, at 110.

worldwide distribution is easier.[119] In an economic sense, digitization is more efficient than analog forms, as it reduces the fixed and marginal costs of copying.[120] But beyond the characteristics of the digital content platform, digital networks posed the biggest threat to the content industries.

The 1980s brought upon technologies such as Usenet and Bulletin Board System (BBS) which enabled users to connect to a central server and download copyrighted materials directly from it.[121] Not long after the creation of the World Wide Web in 1991, technological developments enabled users to transfer files between them, using instant messaging technology: Internet Relay Chat (IRC), ICQ, MSN Messenger, etc.[122] Other users used websites to download songs off the internet. A new generation of file sharing began with the creation of software designed for sharing free music online. Napster was a P2P file-sharing internet service for audio files in MP3 format. But Napster was just the beginning. More file-sharing technologies, some not limited to audio files, were developed and released to the general public: Gnutella, Aimster, Audio-Galaxy, Grokster, KaZaA, eMule, LimeWire, BitTorrent to name a few.[123] Along with P2P file-sharing programs, other technological developments which threatened rights holders emerged. End users could now consume copyrighted materials via the technology of streaming.[124]

Thus, the internet allowed for a rapid and transnational distribution of copyrighted works.[125] Along with the emergence of the internet, the invention of mass-storage capacities such as MP3,[126] file-sharing networks,[127] or new transmission

---

[119] See Goldstein, *supra* note 93, 163–65; for more on the broader implications of the digital platform on the content industry, see Menell, *supra* note 91, at 110–18.

[120] See Penney, *supra* note 84, at 66.

[121] See PCMAG, www.pcmag.com/encyclopedia_term/0,2542,t=BBS&i=38485,00.asp (last visited Dec. 1, 2017).

[122] For an elaboration on these technologies. See PCMAG, www.pcmag.com/encyclopedia_term/ 0,2542,t%3DIRC&i%3D45421,00.asp (last visited Dec. 1, 2017).

[123] For more on the differences between the technologies, see FILESHARINGZ, http://filesharingz .com/guides/filesharing-history.php (last visited Dec. 1, 2017).

[124] Streaming (or webcasting) is a digital form of transmission of a media over a network that results in playing of it, without the storage of a permanent copy at the recipient's end, using online streaming technologies. For a general description of webcasting and streaming, see David L. Hayes, *Advanced Copyright Issues on the Internet*, at 420 (2011), www.fenwick.com/docstore/ publications/ip/advanced_copyright_07-21-08.pdf, and his previous article, David L. Hayes, *Advanced Copyright Issues on the Internet*, 7 TEX. INTELL. PROP. L. J. 1 (1998); Eldar Haber, *Copyrights in the Stream: The Battle on Webcasting*, 28 SANTA CLARA COMPUTER & HIGH TECH. L.J. 769 (2012).

[125] See, e.g., COMPUTER CRIME AND INTELLECTUAL PROPERTY SECTION, *supra* note 69, at 1.

[126] MP3 (Moving Picture Experts Group 1 Audio Layer) refers to both the method for the compression of audio data and the resulting digital format. See PCMAG, www.pcmag.com/encyclope dia_term/0%2C2542%2Ct%3DMP3&i%3D47286%2C00.asp (last visited Dec. 1, 2017).

[127] See Stanley J. Liebowitz, *The Metric Is the Message: How Much of the Decline in Sound Recording Sales Is Due to File-Sharing?* (Sept. 2011) (unpublished manuscript), *available at* http://papers.ssrn.com/sol3/papers.cfm?abstractid=1932518.

methods, e.g., streaming and the expansion of internet bandwidth mainly expedited the spread of copyright infringements.[128] At that stage, Congress sought to expand copyright enforcement, both in the civil and criminal realms. Criminal copyright could be viewed as complementary to the civil enforcement system in those cases where the civil enforcement system does not provide a sufficient deterrent, as well as in those cases where other matters/factors limit private enforcement.[129] To conclude the brief outline, technological advances (mainly digitization) largely affected copyright law. Users now possessed the ability to consume high-quality copyrighted works at virtually no cost, anytime and anywhere.[130] It is, therefore, not surprising that enforcement of copyright infringement, both private and public, enhanced dramatically since the 1980s, mostly due to these technological developments.[131] In this sense, the legislature, through amendments to copyright law, reacts to and includes new technologies and industries, while adapting to new technologies to maintain the balance between creators' financial incentives and the public's interest in free access to information.[132]

But, a second important element in the reciprocal dynamics of copyright and technology is relevant to the criminalization process. As is revealed in the development of new technology, increased infringement of copyright (owing to technology and other factors) harms rights holders. Rights holders have attempted various methods of responding to these infringements: for example, bolstering their rights in non-criminal legislation. However, as we have determined in the outline of criminalization in the United Kingdom and United States, criminalization was applied as a response to copyright infringements caused by technology: at the beginning of the twentieth century, technological developments enabling infringement developed sporadically and were rarely available to the public. While criminal copyright had commenced, it was isolated and limited to specific instances. However, technological developments since the 1960s have changed this reality: recordable audio-cassette tapes and computer floppy disks in the 1960s were the starting

---

[128] Storage capacity is required to enable the storage of media files. Storage capacity in home computers has increased dramatically from thousands to millions, billions, trillions and quadrillions of bytes. Bandwidth has expanded from thousands to million and billions of bits/second. For a brief overview of storage capacity and bandwidth history, see OLIVER WENDT, ASSISTIVE TECHNOLOGY: PRINCIPLES AND APPLICATIONS FOR COMMUNICATION DISORDERS AND SPECIAL EDUCATION 28–29 (2011).

[129] See Menell, *supra* note 110, at 295.

[130] See Menell, *supra* note 91, at 118.

[131] See, e.g., id.

[132] See Note, *The Criminalization of Copyright Infringement in the Digital Era*, 112 HARV. L. REV. 1705, 1705 (1999); David N. Weiskopf, *The Risks of Copyright Infringement on the Internet: A Practitioner's Guide*, 33 U.S.F L. REV. 1, 10 (1998); Sony Corp. of America v. Universal City Studios, 464 U.S. 417, 430 (1984) ("From its beginning, the law of copyright has developed in response to significant changes in technology."); Merges, *supra* note 100, at 2194; Penney, *supra* note 84, at 61; HALBERT, *supra* note 3, at 26; Jessica Litman, *Real Copyright Reform*, 96 IOWA L. REV. 1, 3 (2010).

point. From the 1970s, which brought with it many technologically-relevant developments, we witness a rise in copyright criminalization in both the United Kingdom and the United States. Here, I argue, technological developments played an important role, not only for the entire criminalization process, but also to its acceleration from the 1970s. At this point, modern technology began to challenge copyright law far beyond any prior technological developments. By the same token, copyright law in itself needed to be updated, more than ever before.[133]

The impact of technology on the rise in copyright infringements and the subsequent search for better practices of enforcement could not then (and cannot now) be stressed enough. Copyrighted works have not always needed the strong protections such as they currently receive. Before the 1980s, infringement was difficult, and when it took place, reproductions were usually slow, of poor quality, and easily detectable. Technological developments (mainly having to do with digitization and the internet) proved that the content industries' long-standing business models were no longer resilient.

Hence, technological developments play a key-role in copyright criminalization in both test-cases (when combined with other factors, i.e., the perception of copyright infringement as a socially/morally acceptable norm and along with globalization). In other words, these elements are linked to copyright criminalization with the increase in copyright infringements.[134] However, the fact that copyright law needs to adapt to new technologies and is a threat to right holder business models does not necessarily imply that criminal sanctions should be legislated. Perhaps, other, existing legal models – such as civil copyright – should rise to the infringement challenge? If this is the case, it is important to determine whether civil copyright proves itself to be a sufficiently strong weapon in the battle against new infringing technologies. I further discuss this question in the next section.

2 Perception of Copyright Infringement

Although many users are capable of creating perfect reproductions in their homes, almost free of charge, and in some instances without the risk of detection, not all users infringe. This would seem to suggest that even though for some, infringement

---

[133] *See, e.g.*, Marybeth Peters, *The Spring 1996 Horace S. Manges Lecture: The National Information Infrastructure: A Copyright Office Perspective*, 20 COLUM.-VLA. J.L. & ARTS 341, 342 (1996).

[134] Most scholars argue that copyright criminalization is directly linked to the proliferation of digital technology, which inter alia increased copyright infringements and reduced the detectability of infringers. *See, e.g.*, Note, *supra* note 132, at 1712; Sugden, *supra* note 105, at 223; Diane L. Kilpatrick-Lee, *Criminal Copyright Law: Preventing a Clear Danger to the U.S. Economy or Clearly Preventing the Original Purpose of Copyright Law?*, 14 BALT. INTELL. PROP. L.J. 87, 88 (2005); Penney, *supra* note 84, at 67; Michael Coblenz, *Intellectual Property Crimes*, 9 ALB. L.J. SCI. & TECH. 235, 239–40 (1999).

holds no moral wrong, for others it does.[135] Take committing murder, for example. Assuming that it is easy to commit murder and that detection is almost impossible, people can thus murder other people easily without fear of criminal sanctions. In this scenario, some people, if not most, will still not commit murder, as they find it either morally or socially wrong. In other words, the fact that people can act in a certain manner does not imply that they necessarily will. As for copyright, the fact that technology enables easy infringement with lower detection rates does not imply that all people will infringe, as long as social and/or moral norms prevent them from doing so. To put it differently, for some, infringing is neither morally or socially unacceptable. Hence, the combination of technological developments and the perception of copyright infringement as a socially and/or morally acceptable behavior are necessary to explain the increase in copyright infringements.

It is difficult to assess whether perception of copyright infringement has changed over time. But awareness of the copyright system has certainly changed.[136] People used to have less interaction with the copyright system, because they lacked the ability to infringe. It is also uncertain as to what extent technological innovation in the digital age has changed how copyright infringement is perceived. What is evident, however, is that along with the rise in copyright protection during the digital era, new "pro-copyright-use" social forces have emerged. These new social forces are focusing on innovation, civil liberties, consumer protection, and artists' rights more than ever before.[137] There are few key-examples of such new social forces: the open software movement[138]; rise in the involvement of civil liberties organizations[139]; rise in consumer protection to use technology[140]; the strengthening of Artists' Rights;[141] and a rise in the public's ability to influence legislation.[142] These social forces could support infringement to some extent (i.e., file-sharing rationalization),[143] as a tool to combat the expansion of copyright.[144]

---

[135] It is important to note that there are many criminal offenses, usually categorized as *malum prohibitum* ("wrong because prohibited"), not directly linked to social and/or moral norms. Thus, some people comply with the law only as a measure of compliance, and therefore they will not infringe copyright, event though it could be considered a socially acceptable norm and not morally wrong. I will further elaborate on *malum prohibitum* offenses in Chapter 8.

[136] Menell, *supra* note 110, at 207.

[137] *See* Menell, *supra* note 91, at 180–91.

[138] *See, e.g.,* David McGowan, *The Legal Implications of Open Source Software*, 2001 ILL. L. REV. 241 (2001); Yochai Benkler, *Coase's Penguin, or Linux and the Nature of the Firm*, 112 YALE L.J. 369 (2002); Menell, *supra* note 91, at 181–85.

[139] Menell, *supra* note 91, at 185–87.

[140] *Id.*, at 188.

[141] *Id.*, at 188–90.

[142] The power of the public to influence legislation was demonstrated in the Stop Online Piracy Act (SOPA) (H.R. 3261, 112th. Cong. (2011)) and the PROTECT IP Act (PIPA) (PROTECT IP Act, S. 968, 112th Cong. (2011) (PIPA)).

[143] Menell, *supra* note 110, at 254.

[144] Peter Menell argues that many "consider copyright laws to be punitive, chilling, backward, and poorly attuned to the needs of their generation." *See id.*, at 210.

Examining changes in the public's perception of copyright law is beyond the scope of this book. Even without scrutinizing the changes in copyright perception, it is safe to argue that combining technological developments with the lack of a social and/or moral norm against infringements, leads to an escalation in copyright infringements – which subsequently has led to rights holders' attempts to strengthen enforcement. However, these facts are not directly linked to copyright criminalization, or at least should not be, as other methods of responding to copyright infringement exist, for example by legal, technological, or social measures.

3 Globalization and Accessibility

Globalization is also a factor in the increase in copyright infringements.[145] If at first, with the enactment of the first copyright law in the United States in 1790, economic opportunities were mostly domestic,[146] globalization has since expanded the financial opportunities worldwide. While I do not mean to imply that globalization has turned every creation internationally relevant, it has extended in ways manifold the relevant markets for copyright works. Thus, a global economy has created a world market for copyrighted materials and has provided infringers with sundry infringement opportunities – with increased potential financial losses for rights holders. In addition, the possibilities of copyright infringement of local works have increased internationally[147]: as some copyrighted works expanded their market scope, the incentive for people in foreign countries to infringe has also increased. Thus, globalization is another factor that explains the rise in copyright infringements, as more people have a wider variety of works to consume and, in some cases, infringe.

*

To conclude, a combination of technological developments, low social mores/moral norms associated with infringement, and globalization mainly explain the increase in copyright infringement. However, these reasons do not create a directly causal link between copyright criminalization and copyright infringements, as they only explain the reason rights holders seek a method to protect their business models. Only upon understanding the different measures used by rights holders to respond to copyright infringement can we establish a causal link between copyright expansion and copyright infringements (with criminalization as a form of this expansion).

---

[145] See, for instance, in reference to counterfeit goods, PARADISE, *supra* note 74, at 25.

[146] See, for example, in the United States, NIMMER ON COPYRIGHT, *supra* note 103, § 17.01 ("In decades past, an American copyright practitioner could wind up a career that included only fleeting encounters with foreign and international copyright.").

[147] PARADISE, *supra* note 74, at 25.

B *Responding to Copyright Infringement via Copyright Expansion*

Copyright infringement potentially threatens rights holders' business models. Let us take the music industry for example: If all users illegally obtain a copy of an entire album, rights holders would not earn profits and would incur losses. This might cause them to avoid investing in future works. Yet, we do not need to take it this far. Even if financial losses are not high, rights holders might have less incentive to invest in future works. Altogether, regardless of financial losses, rights holders would still attempt to maximize their profits and receive compensation for their financial loss. After all, many rights holders are for-profit companies.

This takes us to the next step. As a response to copyright infringement, rights holders have tried several different approaches over the years: some *ex ante*, as a preemptive measure, to deter potential infringements,[148] and others *ex post*, as a reactive measure, which also serves as a potential deterrent. In both cases, these measures are usually in the form of expanding their rights. I apply Lessig's famous four modalities (or constraints) for regulating behavior to examine rights holders' *ex ante* measures: law (litigation and private ordering for this matter), market, social norms, and architectural design (code).[149] Under Lessig's modalities, copyright expansion is not necessarily achieved by legal means alone. For example, the usage of technologies such as DRM could also expand rights holders' rights, even beyond those granted to them by law. Therefore, before turning to describe legislative measures, which also examines the criminalization possibility, I briefly discuss non-legislative measures.

1 Non-Legislative Measures: Litigation

In response to copyright infringements, rights holders have tried to sue various "players" in the field.[150] For one, rights holders have tried – and in some cases

---

[148] By, e.g., enhancing civil damages and/or criminal penalties. For example, in 1897, when Congress introduced criminal penalties for the first time, it prescribed civil damages of $100 for the first infringement and $50 for subsequent infringements, while inserting a liability provision of willful unlawful performance or representation of a dramatic or musical composition for profit, liable for imprisonment for up to one year. The enactment was attributed to music copyright owners' concern, that civil remedies will not deter unlawful performances of music, as unlicensed performances throughout the country were uneasy to monitor. *See* Act of January 6, 1897, ch. 4, § 4966, 29 Stat. 481 (1897). This form of deterrence holds much more importance today, as technology evolved and the possibility of undetected infringements rises. Thus, in the digital era, where many people can infringe copyright over the internet, while the probability of detection is very low, rights holders are expanding their rights as a preemptive measure to infringements, and the usage of criminal copyright could be important as it could serve as a higher deterrent than civil sanctions. *See, e.g.,* Peters, *supra* note 133, at 342.

[149] *See* LAWRENCE LESSIG, CODE: VERSION 2.0 120–37 (2006); LAWRENCE LESSIG, FREE CULTURE 116–73 (2004).

[150] For a general description of some copyright "war stories" (in the author's words), see Jessica Litman, *War Stories*, 20 CARDOZO ARTS & ENT. L.J. 337 (2002); Haber, *supra* note 124.

succeeded – to eliminate technologies that enable users to infringe copyright, by suing the manufacturers of these technologies. In the late 1970s, when Sony introduced Betamax – the first home video cassette recorder (VCR) that enabled users to make a copy of a television broadcast – some rights holders embarked on – and lost – a legal campaign against Sony. The Court held that the Betamax was legal since it possess substantial non-infringing uses, and that the recording act is considered as time-shifting, and therefore a fair use under the law.[151]

The legal battle against technology manufacturers rose with the development and addition of infringing technologies that enable sharing copyrighted materials over the internet. Rights holders filed lawsuits against websites that sanctioned users' uploading and downloading of songs to and from the internet.[152] In addition, rights holders filed lawsuits against the manufacturers and operators of shareware software, i.e., P2P file-sharing internet service.[153] Some rights holders unsuccessfully tried to sue ISPs for direct liability,[154] but successfully established legal grounds for contributory or vicarious infringement.[155] The legal struggle continued when rights holders began directly suing end users – a practice that continues today.[156] At the same time,

---

[151] *See* Sony Corp. of America v. Universal City Studios Inc., 464 U.S. 417 (1984); Edward Lee, *The Ethics of Innovation: p2p Software Developers and Designing Substantial Noninfringing Uses under the Sony Doctrine*, 62 J. Bus. Ethics 147 (2005); Wendy J. Gordon, *Fair Use as Market Failure: A Structural and Economic Analysis of the "Betamax" Case and Its Predecessors*, 82 Colum. L. Rev. 8 (222).

[152] *See, e.g.,* UMG Recordings, Inc. v. MP3.com, 92 F. Supp. 2d 349 (S.D.N.Y. 2000), in which MP3.com, a website that enabled users to play music online providing that they already owned the CDs that contain the requested songs, did not have the right to reproduce the recordings. *See also* Peter K. Yu, *Copyright Wars*, 32 Hofstra L. Rev. 907, 913 (2004).

[153] *See, e.g.,* A&M Records, Inc. v. Napster, Inc., 114 F. Supp. 2d 896 (Cal., 2000); A&M Records Inc. v. Napster Inc., 239 F. 3d 1004 (9th Cir. 2001); UMG Recordings, Inc. v. MP3.com, 92 F. Supp. 2d 349 (S.D.N.Y. 2000); Aimster Copyright Litigation Appeal of John Deep, 334 F.3d 643 (7th Cir. 2003); MGM, Inc. v. Grokster, Inc. 545 U.S. 913 (2005); Arista Records LLC v. Lime Group LLC, 532 F. Supp. 2d 556 (S.D.N.Y. 2007); Arista Records LLC v. Lime Group LLC, 715 F. Supp. 2d 481 (S.D.N.Y. 2010).

[154] Religious Tech. Ctr. v. Netcom On-Line Commc'ns Serv., Inc., 907 F. Supp. 1361, 1368 (N.D. Cal. 1995) (the court held that an internet access provider for a Bulletin Board System (BBS) operator was not directly liable for copyright infringement committed by a subscriber to the BBS, where the access provider took no affirmative action to copy work and received no direct financial benefit from the infringement); Central Point Software v. Nugent, 903 F. Supp. 1057 (E.D. Tex. 1995) (holding that a BBS operator is liable for direct infringement in these circumstances).

[155] *Netcom*, 907 F. Supp. at 1373. In addition, as ISPs could play an important role in the preventing copyright infringements or aid rights holders in detecting unlawful activities (at least to some extent), rights holders are consistently trying to make usage of them. For example, in the United Kingdom, rights holders filed lawsuits against ISPs to block access to a website that promotes online piracy and against websites that enabled users to infringe their copyright. *See, e.g., Hollywood Wins Case In UK against Piracy Website*, redOrbit (July 28, 2011), www .redorbit.com/news/technology/2086927/hollywood_wins_case_in_uk_against_piracy_website.

[156] See, in the United States, lawsuits filed against end users by the Recording Industry Association of America (RIAA), which started in 2003. *See, e.g.,* Maverick Recording Co. v. Harper, 598 F.3d 193 (5th Cir. 2010); Capitol Records, Inc. v. Thomas, 579 F. Supp. 2d 1210

rights holders continued the legal battle against various technology manufactur-ers,[157] search engines, website operators, streaming services and cloud-based services.[158]

2 Non-Legislative Measures: Private Ordering

Another legal solution against copyright infringements is private ordering – volun-tary, self-regulation undertaken by private parties.[159] Rights holders use contractual restrictions such as "Terms of Use" on websites and other market agreements in order to restrict access to and use of their works.[160] In 2011, for example, in the United States, the content industry reached an agreement with ISPs, for implement-ing a system of "Copyright Alerts,"[161] a form of private ordering that resembles the

(D. Minn. 2008); Sony BMG Music Entm't. v. Tenenbaum, 721 F. Supp. 2d 85 (D. Mass. 2008). In December 2008, the RIAA announced that they would cease to file lawsuits against users, but a growing group of law firms which are dedicated to pursuing copyright claims, are still filing lawsuits against hundreds and thousands of end users for copyright infringements in the United States. *See, e.g.*, Voltage Pictures, LLC v. Does, 1:10-cv-00873-RMU (D.D.C., filed May 24, 2010); Greg Sandoval, *"Hurt Locker" Downloaders, You've Been Sued*, CNET NEWS (May 28, 2010), http://news.cnet.com/8301–31001_3–20006314–261.html (last visited Dec. 1, 2017); Christopher Siebens, *Divergent Approaches to File-Sharing Enforce-ment in the United States and Japan*, 52 VA. J. INT'L L. 155, 165–168 (2011). In the United Kingdom, this is hardly a new practice. In an attempt to respond to copyright infringements at the end of the nineteenth century, mostly due to multiplication of copies enabled by the recent accessible printing technologies, the music publishers brought civil proceedings against "hawkers." However, rights holders failed to recover most damages, as injunctions were promptly breached. *See* Alexander, *supra* note 97, at 630. For more recent lawsuits, see *Mass BitTorrent Lawsuits Return to the UK*, DELIMITER (Mar. 29, 2012 5:57 PM), http://delimiter.com.au/2012/03/29/mass-bittorrent-lawsuits-return-to-the-uk.
[157] *See, e.g.*, Recording Industry Ass'n of America v. Diamond Multimedia Systems, 180 F.3d 1072 (9th Cir. 1999) (lawsuit against Diamond Multimedia, the manufacture of the "Rio" portable digital audio technology); *see* RealNetworks, Inc. v. Streambox, Inc., 2000 WL 127311 (W.D. Jan. 18, 2000) (suing a manufacture of technology that can decrypt technological protection measures).
[158] *See, e.g.*, Menell, *supra* note 91, at 138–53.
[159] For an excellent example of private ordering in copyright law see Niva Elkin-Koren, *What Contracts Cannot Do: The Limits of Private Ordering in Facilitating a Creative Commons*, 74 FORDHAM L. REV. 375 (2005).
[160] *See* NETANEL, *supra* note 5, at 66–71. As this Chapter is mostly descriptive, I do not attempt to raise the normative debate on the usage of private ordering. However, as a general note, private ordering could be highly problematic for the copyright regime, as it poses dangers for the public domain and the legitimate usage of copyrighted materials. *See, e.g.*, Elkin-Koren, *supra* note 160, at 376; Niva Elkin-Koren, *Copyrights in Cyberspace-Rights without Laws?*, 73 CHI.-KENT L. REV. 1155, 1187–99 (1998); Julie E. Cohen, *Lochner in Cyberspace: The New Economic Orthodoxy of "Rights Management,"* 97 MICH. L. REV. 462, 538–59 (1998).
[161] *See The Copyright Alert Program*, AT&T, https://copyright.att.net/home (last visited Dec. 1, 2017); *See generally*, Sean M. Flaim, *Copyright Conspiracy: How the New Copyright Alert System May Violate the Sherman Act*, 2 N.Y.U. J. INTELL. PROP. & ENT. LAW 142 (2012).

graduated response system. As explained by AT&T (a member of the Copyright Alert Program/System)[162]:

> The Copyright Alert Program was created as part of an industry agreement involving the Motion Picture Association of America (MPAA), the Recording Industry of America Association (RIAA) and the nation's largest internet Service Providers (ISPs), including AT&T. The program is a response to copyright infringement activities on peer-to-peer file sharing networks, and is an effort to educate consumers about the importance of obtaining digital content – like movies and music – legally ... There are two basic elements of the Copyright Alert Program. Content owners identify copyrighted content that is being shared over Peer-to-Peer file sharing networks (such as Bit Torrent) and send AT&T a notice of alleged copyright infringement based on the IP Address of the user. AT&T then identifies the subscriber based on the IP Address and forwards a copyright alert to the subscriber advising them of the allegation and educating them about online copyright infringement. If AT&T receives additional notices for a particular subscriber account, the copyright alerts will escalate, culminating in measures that may impact the customer's high speed internet connection. Whether such activity has been engaged in intentionally or by mistake, we will ask subscribers to stop the activity and ensure others using your network do the same. Importantly, if your home network is not protected or secured by a password or firewall, and unauthorized users are accessing your network, they may be the source of the problem. Your subscriber information is protected – AT&T will not provide your information to content owners unless required to do so by court order.

With potential variations, the alert system is generally triggered when an alleged infringement by a subscriber was discovered, and the ISP is informed. Using the mail account that is registered with the ISP, the subscriber then receives a notice. It begins with two notices of infringement as an educational measure. Upon the third and fourth notices, the subscriber receives messages requiring acknowledgment. The two final notices would then include mitigation measures for subscribers, e.g., reducing their transmission speed, moving them down to a lower-tier service, redirecting them to a landing page that requires subscribers to contact customer service, and perhaps most dramatically, temporarily suspending their internet access.[163]

A "graduated" approach to copyright enforcement has many flaws.[164] It does have benefits, and perhaps mainly, it could be much more than just criminal procedures. Practically, however, within its limitation to track only certain types of

---

[162] See Flaim, *supra* note 162, at 153.
[163] See Ben Depoorter & Alain Van Hiel, *Copyright Alert Enforcement: Six Strikes and Privacy Harms*, 39 COLUM. J.L. & ARTS 233, 245–47 (2015).
[164] For criticism on the copyright alert system, see, e.g., Annemarie Bridy, *Graduated Response American Style: "Six Strikes" Measured against Five Norms*, 23 FORDHAM INTELL. PROP. MEDIA & ENT. L.J. (2012); Sean M. Flaim, *Copyright Conspiracy: How the New Copyright Alert System May Violate the Sherman Act*, 2 NYU J. INTELL. PRPO. & ENT. L. 142 (2012); Margot

infringements, it would be rather limited to challenge new types of content consumption that are outside the scope of detection, at least while basic human rights are safeguarded, like that of privacy. Thus, while private ordering could decrease the level of copyright infringement, it is unlikely to completely prevent it. Thus, although private ordering can aid rights holders, I argue that it is currently an insufficient mechanism to resolve the perceived problem of copyright infringement.

3 Non-Legislative Measures: Technology

Technological Protection Measures (TPMs), such as Digital Rights Management (DRM), are used to prevent copyright infringement.[165] Yet, DRM is not merely a preemptive measure. Some rights holders use DRM to improve their control over the market, while engaging in actions such as price discrimination, to achieve this end.[166] However, for the purpose of the discussion on criminal copyright, I categorize DRM as mostly a preemptive measure to prevent infringements, that is, copyright infringement is an important cause for adding DRM.

Preventive technological methods, such as *encryption, watermarking, digital fingerprinting, spoofing,* and *interdicting,* have been used by rights holders to control access to or the use of creations.[167] One method used was *encryption.* In an attempt to prevent copyright infringement, rights holders encrypted access to media, which in turn was accessible only to authorized consumers with an authorization code that permits decryption.[168] However, although encryption can aid in protecting works, it has been proven ineffective: the encryption can be cracked and the decryption key distributed.

Other methods used were: *watermarking,* which enables rights holders to control different aspects of use, e.g., limiting that use to specific devices or controlling the amount of usage[169]; and *digital fingerprinting,* which enables the accurate

---

Kaminski, *Copyright Crime and Punishment: The First Amendment's Proportionality Problem,* 73 Md. L. Rev. 587 (2014).

[165] DRM attempts to control user's usage of a media and hardware. *See Digital Rights Management,* Electronic Frontier Foundation, www.eff.org/issues/drm (last visited Dec. 1, 2017).

[166] For a comprehensive analysis of the impact of DRM on copyright law, see generally Tarleton Gillespie, Wired Shut: Copyright and the Shape of Digital Culture (2007).

[167] Although similar in propose, encryption and watermarking differ in one major category: encryption refers to a code which a user must break to use a file, while a watermark is a code which is placed on top of the file, requiring that the file be used in conjunction with a compatible secure player or viewer before it is used. For this definition, *see* Damien A. Riehl, *Peer-to-Peer Distribution Systems: Will Napster, Gnutella, and Freenet Create a Copyright Nirvana or Gehenna?,* 27 Wm. Mitchell L. Rev. 1761, 1789 (2001).

[168] *See generally,* Kenneth W. Dam, *Self-Help in the Digital Jungle,* 28 J. Legal Stud. 393, 398–401 (1999); John A. Rothchild, *Economic Analysis of Technological Protection Measures,* 84 Or. L. Rev. 489, 493–96 (2005).

[169] More on watermarking, see Riehl, *supra* note 168, at 1792–93.

identification of media files over the internet, even when the file name is modi-fied.[170] Hence, as a response to copyright infringement over the internet, ISPs could potentially block infringing materials,[171] as well as *spoofing* and *interdicting*, by which rights holders were able to make available media files that were apparently "real media files," seemingly protected by copyright. In actuality, these files con-tained computer-user static, popping, cracking noises, or silence.[172] In addition, rights holders bombarded peer-to-peer networks with many fake requests and "ghost files," i.e., empty files.[173] This method could be classified as "annoyance tactics," which could potentially deter end users from infringing copyright and turning to obtain copyrighted works legally.

Hence, by using various types of TPMs, rights holders expanded their control over their works and prevented access to their works[174] – without seeking legal protec-tion.[175] Preventing access to works can actually reduce permitted uses of copyrighted works and thus strengthen the copyright.[176] One example is the fair use defense. Under the fair use defense, use of a copyrighted material is permitted for, e.g., educational purposes.[177] However, if the desired work is protected by a technological measure that prohibits access to the work, the end user cannot use the work, even for educational purposes. Thus, by using TPMs rights holders can weaken users' rights and strengthen their own.

However, the use of TPMs was, and still is, insufficient in preventing copyright infringement. As technology and ingenuity is never one-sided, infringers have also developed better technology that can "defeat" TPMs.[178] Here, too, Congress attempted to resolve this problem with legislation and enacted the DMCA, which made it illegal to traffic in technologies that defeat TPMs and to engage acts that circumvent TPMs.[179] However, as copyright infringement still exists to a large extent, it seems that TPMs do not effectively eliminate copyright infringements of any kind, even e-books. Thus, as technology has proven to be currently insufficient

---

[170] *See* Joseph A. Sifferd, *The Peer-To-Peer Revolution: A Post-Napster Analysis of the Rapidly Developing File-Sharing Technology*, 4 VAND. J. ENT. L. & PRAC. 93, 108 (2002).

[171] *Id.*

[172] For more on Spoofing, *see* Kristine Pesta, Comment, *The Piracy Prevention Bill H.R. 5211: The Second Generation's Answer to Copyright Infringement over Peer-to-Peer Networks*, 33 SW. U. L. REV. 397, 408–09 (2004).

[173] *Id.* at 409.

[174] This is considered an expansion of rights holders' protection, as copyright law does not grant such right. *See* NETANEL, *supra* note 5, at 68.

[175] Rothchild, *supra* note 169, at 490.

[176] *Id.*

[177] 17 U.S.C. § 107.

[178] Rothchild, *supra* note 169, at 490.

[179] Under § 1204 of the DMCA (Pub. L. No. 105–304, 112 Stat. 2860 (1998)), any person who "willfully or for purposes of commercial advantage or private financial gain" violates §§ 1201 or 1202 is subject to: (1) A fine of up to $500,000 and/or jail sentence of up to five years for the first offense; and (2) A fine of up to $1,000,000 and/or jail sentence of up to ten years for any subsequent offense.

to deter copyright infringement, rights holders should consider other measures of regulations. Accordingly, legal measures, e.g., criminalizing copyright, are another form of legal response to copyright infringements, where other measures have thus far not succeeded.

4 Non-Legislative Measures: Market and Social Norms

There are two main forms of educational measures that are used to decrease copyright infringement. The first is *legal education*. To make the public aware of the difference between legal and illegal copyright actions, the public must first be made aware of what constitutes illegal activity. Moreover, in a complicated legal field such as copyright law, which often deals with new technological developments, legal certainty is not always at hand. Thus, through public awareness of the illegal nature of copyright infringement, some people would cease their actions because of that knowledge, while others would cease because of the now-known legal prohibition.[180] The second form is *social/moral education* – which attempts to change social mores and/or moral norms to recognize the wrongful nature of copyright infringement. By this perception, the technical ability to infringe would become irrelevant, as individuals would avoid infringing merely because it is wrong and/or illegal.

There are various examples of legal and social/moral education. For example, the United States Department of Justice (DOJ) has developed a national education program to teach students the value of IP and the consequences of committing IP crimes developing and using educational materials; creating partnerships with non-profit educational organizations to promote public awareness of IP crimes; producing a video on the negative consequences of IP "theft;" and encouraging federal prosecutors handling IP crime cases throughout the nation to promote DOJ's public awareness programs. The DOJ also proposed educating the public about its policy prohibiting the use of peer-to-peer software on Justice Department computer systems. Finally, the DOJ promoted authorized use of the FBI's new Anti-Piracy Seal and Warning.[181]

In practice, rights holders used legal education methods to educate the public.[182] American interest groups, such as the RIAA and MPAA,[183] distributed letters and

---

[180] As mentioned in *supra* note 136, some people comply with the law simply as a measure of compliance, and therefore they will not infringe copyright, even though it could be considered socially acceptable and not morally wrong.

[181] See *Report of the Department of Justice's Task Force on Intellectual Property*, UNITED STATED DOJ 51 (2004), www.justice.gov/olp/ip_task_force_report.pdf (last visited Dec. 1, 2017).

[182] More on copyright education, see Brett Lunceford & Shane Lunceford, *The Irrelevance of Copyright in the Public Mind*, 7 Nw. J. TECH. & INTELL. PROP. 33 (2008); Haber, *supra* note 151.

[183] The content industries are usually represented through major industry groups, *e.g.*, the Motion Picture Association of America (MPAA), the Recording Industry Association of America

sound bites to institutions, such as colleges and corporations[184]; hired celebrities to convey the message that file-sharing harms artists[185]; hung banners and posters against copyright infringement[186]; required that "pirates" publish apologies in newspapers[187]; encouraged employees to find and report copyright infringement in the workplace[188]; and used the media, such as radio public service announcements, websites, and television commercials to broadcast their messages.[189] To exemplify, browsing to the former file-sharing company "Grokster Ltd." led to the following announcement[190]:

> The United States Supreme Court unanimously confirmed that using this service to trade copyrighted material is illegal. Copying copyrighted motion picture and music files using unauthorized peer-to-peer services is illegal and is prosecuted by copyright owners. There are legal services for downloading music and movies. This service is not one of them. YOUR IP ADDRESS IS **.***.*.*** AND HAS BEEN LOGGED. Don't think you can't get caught. You are not anonymous ... In the meantime, please visit www.respectcopyrights.com and www.musicunited .org to learn more about copyright.

Accordingly, browsing to LimeWire's website in the past led to the following announcement (the source was originally written in upper case letters)[191]:

> ATTENTION LIMEWIRE IS UNDER A COURT ORDER DATED OCTOBER 26, 2010 TO STOP DISTRIBUTING THE LIMEWIRE SOFTWARE. A COPY OF THE INJUNCTION CAN BE FOUND HERE. LIMEWIRE

(RIAA), and the American Society of Composers, Authors, and Publishers (ASCAP). For more on previous education attempts by the RIAA, see Hardy, *supra* note 81, at 330 (describing the RIAA attempts to educate college students into greater respect for copyrights through campaigns).

[184] PARADISE, *supra* note 74, at 252 (noting that in 1997, the RIAA distributed Soundbyting: "a program and teaching module that discusses the ethical issues involved on the internet, the penalties for engaging in music piracy, and other pertinent issues.").

[185] *See* Mike Snider, *Entertainment Industry Widens War*, USA TODAY (Feb. 13, 2003, 8:59 AM), www.usatoday.com/tech/news/2003-02-13-piracy-side_x.htm; *Lily Allen Campaigns against Music Piracy*, THE TELEGRAPH (Sept. 21, 2009, 8:06 PM), www.telegraph.co.uk/culture/music/music-news/6216281/Lily-Allen-campaigns-against-music-piracy.html.

[186] For example, in 1995, the Business Software Alliance (BSA) posted posters and distributed educational flyers in more than 160 computer software stores across the United States. *See* PARADISE, *supra* note 74, at 253.

[187] *Id.* at 252.

[188] For example, the BSA operates a confidential "Anti-piracy" hotline worldwide to report suspected incidents of copyright infringement. *See* REPORT SOFTWARE PIRACY NOW! YOUR REPORT IS CONFIDENTIAL, BSA, https://reporting.bsa.org/r/report/add.aspx?src= us&ln=en-us (last visited Dec. 1, 2017); PARADISE, *supra* note 74, at 253.

[189] Some commercials tried to achieve public deterrence by an analogy of theft, for example. See a sample of such commercial, at: YOUTUBE, www.youtube.com/watch?v=l5SmrHNWhak&fea ture=related (last visited Dec. 1, 2017).

[190] *See* GROKSTER, www.grokster.com (last visited Dec. 1, 2017).

[191] *See* LIMEWIRE, www.limewire.com.

LLC, ITS DIRECTORS AND OFFICERS, ARE TAKING ALL STEPS TO COMPLY WITH THE INJUNCTION. WE HAVE VERY RECENTLY BECOME AWARE OF UNAUTHORIZED APPLICATIONS ON THE INTERNET PURPORTING TO USE THE LIMEWIRE NAME. WE DEMAND THAT ALL PERSONS USING THE LIMEWIRE SOFTWARE, NAME, OR TRADEMARK IN ORDER TO UPLOAD OR DOWNLOAD COPYRIGHTED WORKS **IN ANY MANNER** CEASE AND DESIST FROM DOING SO. WE FURTHER REMIND YOU THAT THE UNAUTHORIZED UPLOADING AND DOWNLOADING OF COPYRIGHTED WORKS IS ILLEGAL. IF YOU HAVE DOWNLOADED LIMEWIRE SOFTWARE IN THE PAST, FILES ON YOUR PERSONAL COMPUTERS CONTAINING PRIVATE OR SENSITIVE INFORMATION MAY HAVE BEEN INADVERTENTLY SHARED AND YOU SHOULD USE YOUR BEST EFFORTS TO REMOVE THE SOFTWARE FROM YOUR COMPUTERS.

In the United Kingdom, the Creative Industries Task Force taught young people to respect IP rights by educating them about the consequences of copyright infringements.[192] However, despite these attempts, social norms have not changed to a large extent, and copyright infringements have yet to cease.[193] Reported infringements rates are still relatively high around the world. For example, research conducted by "Envisional," as requested by NBC Universal in 2011, to analyze bandwidth usage across the internet with the specific aim of assessing how much of that usage infringed upon copyright, concluded that "Across all areas of the global internet, 23.76% of traffic was estimated to be infringing."[194]

5 Legislative Measures

Current methods have not achieved rights holders' desired effects – elimination of or substantial reduction in unlawful infringements. Accordingly, rights holders continue to attempt to strengthen copyright protection and increase their revenues via two main routes: 1) through legislation that enforces their rights,[195] legally

[192] *See* Lauren E. Abolsky, *Operation Blackbeard: Is Government Prioritization Enough to Deter Intellectual Property Criminals?*, 14 FORDHAM INTELL. PROP. MEDIA & ENT. L.J. 567, 601 (2004).
[193] For more on social norms and the morality of infringements, see Joseph P. Fishman, *Copyright Infringement and the Separated Powers of Moral Entrepreneurship*, 51 AM. CRIM. L. REV. 359 (2014).
[194] *See Technical Report: An Estimate of Infringing Use of the Internet*, ENVISIONAL (2011), http://documents.envisional.com/docs/Envisional-Internet_Usage-Jan2011.pdf. However, it is noted that NBC Universal are unlikely an impartial party regarding copyright infringements, but as a general argument, copyright infringements are still occurring worldwide.
[195] Aside from civil law, another form of legislation as a reactive measure is administrative law. Few policymakers adopted a so-called graduated response or Three Strikes Policy (3SP), providing for the termination of subscriptions and accounts of repeat infringers in appropriate circumstances. The three strikes policy, also known as the graduated response or the "digital guillotine," had been implemented by way of legislation in Taiwan (Copyright Act, art. 90quinquies

protects technological measures that aid copyright protection,[196] and expands their potential damages for infringements; or by civil, administrative or criminal legislation.[197]

The expansion of civil copyright, or rather private enforcement methods, are discussed at length in copyright literature. Peter Menell offers a clear outline of civil copyright legislation during the digital age, which I will briefly outline here.[198] It began in 1984, when Congress amended the first sale doctrine and prohibited the rental of sound recordings, due to the sound recording industry's concern of home copying (even prior to the digital age).[199] In 1990, Congress imposed prohibitions on rentals of software.[200] In 1992, Congress imposed technological constraints on the manufacture of

(2007) (Taiwan), *translated in* WIPO, www.wipo.int/wipolex/en/text.jsp?file_id=187795#None (2009)), South Korea (Copyright Act of Korea, art. 133bis (2007) (S. Korea)), France (Projet de loi favorisant la diffusion et la protection de la création sur Internet [Bill supporting the diffusion and the protection of creation on Internet] (2009) (Fr.), *translated in* LA QUADRATURE DU NET, www.laquadrature.net/wiki/HADOPI_full_translation (2010)), the United Kingdom (Digital Economy Act, §§ 124A–124N (2010) (U.K.)) and New Zealand (Copyright (Infringing File Sharing) Amendment Act, 2011 No. 11 § 92A (N.Z.)), and by means of private ordering in Ireland (*See* EMI Records & Ors v. Eircom Ltd, [2010] IEHC 108, www.courts.ie/judgments .nsf/6681dee4565ecf2c80256e7e0052005b/7e52f4a2660d8840802577070035082f?OpenDocu ment). As this attempt is still at an early stage, the outcome for rights holders is still uncertain. For more on the three strikes policy, see PATRY, *supra* note 85, at 11–14; Peter K. Yu, *The Graduated Response*, 62 FLA. L. REV. 1373 (2010); Charn Wing Wan, *Three Strikes Law: A Least Cost Solution to Rampant Online Piracy*, 5 J. INTELL. PROP. L. & PRACT. 232 (2010); Olivier Bomsel & Heritiana Ranaivoson, *Decreasing Copyright Enforcement Costs: The Scope of a Graduated Response*, 6 REV. OF ECON. RES. ON COPYRIGHT ISSUES 13 (2009); Annemarie Bridy, *Graduated Response and the Turn to Private Ordering in Online Copyright Enforcement*, 89 OR. L. REV. 81 (2010); Eldar Haber, *The French Revolution 2.0: Copyright and the Three Strikes Policy*, 2 HARV. J. SPORTS & ENT. L. 297 (2011).

[196] Rights holders also lobbied an amendment to the copyright act, to include legal protection of paracopyright, e.g., technological protection measures, which resulted in the enactment of the DMCA. The DMCA, among other things, forbids the circumvention of technology that controls access to copyrighted materials. *See* Digital Millennium Copyright Act (DMCA), Pub. L. No. 105–304, 112 Stat. 2860 (1998) (codified as amended at 17 U.S.C. §§ 512, 1201–1205, 1301–1332 & 28 U.S.C. § 4001).

[197] Examining the United States, we can witness a rise in civil damages since 1909: in 1909, Congress set an initial rate of $250 as a minimum statutory damage award and $5,000 as a maximum award for each act of knowing infringement (Copyright Act of 1909, ch. 320, § 25(b), 33 Stat. 1075–82 (1909)); In 1976, Congress set an initial rate of $250 as a minimum statutory damage award and $10,000 as a maximum award for each act of knowing infringement (Copyright Act of 1976, Pub. L. No. 94–553, 90 Stat. 2541 (1976), § 504(c)(1) (1978)); for willful infringement, the 1976 Act provided for $150,000 (Copyright Act of 1976 § 504(c)(1) (1978)). Currently, the minimum statutory damage award is $750 and the maximum award is $30,000. However, it is difficult to argue that this rise in civil damages represent anything, as it is not subjected to inflation. For example, $10,000, the maximum award for each act of knowing infringement set in 1976 will be worth $40,939.37 in 2013, thus exceeding the 2013 maximum award of $30,000. For inflation rates, see *US Inflation Calculator*, www.usinflationcalculator.com.

[198] Menell, *supra* note 91.

[199] Record Rental Amendment of 1985, Pub. L. No. 980450, 98 Stat. 1727 (1984).

[200] Computer Software Rental Amendments of 1990, Pub. L. No. 101–650, 104 Stat. 5089, 5134–37 (1990).

copying devices, due to industries' concern about new technologies that enable the making of high quality digital copies of audio recordings.[201] In 1995, in order to add royalties to digital "performances," Congress established an exclusive right to perform sound recordings "publicly by means of a digital audio transmission."[202] In 1998, Congress added anti-circumvention and anti-trafficking bans to the copyright Act.[203] In 1999, Congress dramatically increased the statutory damage range to $30,000 per infringed work and up to $150,000 per infringed work for willful infringement.[204]

These examples of the expansion of civil copyright emphasize how Congress reacted to the changes of the digital era. Criminal copyright was therefore not the only legislative means by which Congress sought enforcement. Private enforcement legislation aligns with the criminalization process, both perceived as a responsive measure to the rise in copyright infringements, which the digital age brought upon rights holders.

To conclude, one of the main internal reasons for the criminalization process is the increase in copyright infringements, which is part of the copyright expansion framework. Over time, technological developments, combined with the perception of copyright infringement as a socially and morally acceptable norm and the globalization process, has expanded the market for copyrighted materials and has increased potential and actual copyright infringement worldwide. In this sense, I categorize criminalization of copyright as another responsive measure to infringements. However, criminal copyright is not solely attributed to copyright infringement, and could also be part of a different, pragmatic change in copyright law.

III COPYRIGHT PROPERTIZATION

Copyright criminalization could also be a result of a shift toward a pure property conception of copyright law.[205] The expansion of copyright protection is attributed,

---

[201] *See* Audio Home Recording Rights Act of 1992, Pub. L. No. 102–563, 106 Stat. 4237 (1992). Under this Act, Congress also imposed a royalty on the sale of devices and blank recording media.

[202] Digital Performance Right in Sound Recordings Act, Pub. L. No. 104–39, 109 Stat. 336 (1995); Menell, *supra* note 91, at 131–33.

[203] Digital Millennium Copyright Act (DMCA), Pub. L. No. 105–304, 112 Stat. 2860 (1998) (codified as amended at 17 U.S.C. §§ 512, 1201–1205, 1301–1332 & 28 U.S.C. § 4001).

[204] Theft Deterrence and Copyright Damages Improvement Act, Pub. L. No. 106–160, 113 Stat. 1774 (1999).

[205] I further discuss the normative debate on whether copyright is property in this chapter. For a discussion of the justification of copyright as property, see generally, ROBERT P. MERGES, JUSTIFYING INTELLECTUAL PROPERTY (2011). Although some scholars attributed copyright propertization to copyright criminalization, most only addressed the usage of property terminology to influence copyright criminalization. Lydia Pallas-Loren, for example, attributed the formation of the NET Act in the United States, to "Digitization and Copyright as 'Property.'" *See* Lydia Pallas-Loren, *Digitization, Commodification, Criminalization: The Evolution of Criminal Copyright Infringement and the Importance of the Willfulness Requirement*, 77 WASH.

inter alia, to the ongoing propertization process, i.e., the transformation of copyright law from a limited set of exclusive rights granted for purposes of market regulation to a property regime.[206] Under a property conception, protection granted should be similarly to tangible property.

Before turning to analyze the possibility that copyright propertization plays a role in copyright criminalization, an important clarification is in place: copyright propertization is debatable in copyright law literature. On this basis, some scholars raised the argument that copyright law is undergoing a propertization process, while others, and perhaps mainly Justin Hughes, criticized this argument.[207]

Without choosing sides in this debate, scholars which do not accept the propertization argument would alternatively attribute copyright criminalization to changes in the norms of copyright law, which led to a strengthening of the exclusive control granted by copyright law. There are two possible frameworks for copyright propertization: first, as a reactive measure for the increase in copyright infringement. Under this approach, policymakers use the rhetoric of property to advance criminalization goals; second, copyright expansion is not directly linked to infringement, but rather the expansion is part of the normative and conceptual agenda of copyright within property law. This approach views the criminalization process as a natural step toward a property regime. Accordingly, the propertization conception of copyright law considers criminalization to be independent to other reasons of copyright criminalization.

This question falls within the greater scheme of whether IP, particularly copyright, should be treated as a tangible item, which is further discussed throughout this book. Here, I only focus on the role of the propertization process in criminal copyright legislation.[208] Thus, I explore the propertization process of IP in general, and copyright in particular, that could explain the expansion of copyright protection and *criminal copyright*. And, I begin with a short review of the history of IP propertization. The linkage between copyright criminalization and copyright propertization is based upon secondary academic literature on IP and copyright propertization in general and on copyright criminalization in particular, as well as on legislative materials, court decisions, and popular-media references to copyright infringement.

U. L.Q. 835, 853–61 (1999). *See also* Irina D. Manta, *The Puzzle of Criminal Sanctions for Intellectual Property Infringement*, 24 Harv. J.L. & Tech. 469, 473 (2011).

[206] *See* Hughes, *supra* note 4, at 996, 1048; Pallas-Loren, *supra* note 206, at 856–61.

[207] *See* Hughes, *supra* note 4.

[208] For more on the debate whether IP qualifies as property, see, e.g., Frank H. Easterbrook, *Intellectual Property Is Still Property*, 13 Harv. J.L. & Pub. Pol'y 108 (1990); Lemley, *supra* note 3; Adam Mossoff, *Is Copyright Property?*, 42 San Diego L. Rev. 29 (2005); Henry E. Smith, *Intellectual Property As Property: Delineating Entitlements in Information*, 116 Yale L.J. 1742 (2007); Stephen L. Carter, *Does It Matter Whether Intellectual Property Is Property?*, 68 Chi.-Kent L. Rev. 715 (1993); Richard A. Epstein, *Liberty Versus Property? Cracks in the Foundations of Copyright Law*, 42 San Diego L. Rev. 1 (2005).

A Surveys of IP Propertization

Copyright is a form of intangible property. In its inception in the eighteenth century, copyright was considered a pure form of property.[209] For example, in the United Kingdom, copyright was considered property almost from the enactment of the first modern copyright law,[210] but it is not evident that every legislator thereafter treated it as such.[211] Nevertheless, it is evident that as copyright law evolved over the years, the IP propertization conception continued to grow, including proprietary concepts in copyright law.[212]

Copyright propertization holds much significance in explaining part of the criminalization process. In this sense, if copyright is similar to tangible property, then criminalization is easier to justify.[213] The use of property terminology over the years, best exemplifies IP propertization vis-à-vis criminal copyright. Under this examination, when copyright is widely referred to as property, policymakers and the general public treat it as such. This in turn enhances the criminalization process.

1 Use of Property Terminology in IP

Terminology could play an important part in shaping the perception of a concept. The repeated placement of property terminology together, or near, copyright allows

[209] For example, in Britain, the Statute of Anne arguably marks "the divorce of copyright from censorship and the reestablishment of copyright under the rubric of property rather than regulation." *See* MARK ROSE, AUTHORS AND OWNERS: THE INVENTION OF COPYRIGHT 48 (1993); FREE CULTURE, *supra* note 150, at 64. On the other hand, other scholars refer to the Statute of Anne simply as a trade-regulation statute which was enacted to bring order to "the chaos created in the book trade by the lapse in 1694," and does not refer to property. *See* LYMAN RAY PATTERSON, COPYRIGHT IN HISTORICAL PERSPECTIVE 143 (1968). For a full analysis on this matter, see Hughes, *supra* note 4. For more discussion on whether IP qualifies as property, see *supra* note 209.

[210] *See* Blackstone's characterization of copyright as property in Perrin v. Blake, (1772) 96 Eng. Rep. 392 (K.B.) stating that: "[t]he law of real property in this country wherever its materials were gathered, is now formed into a fine artificial system, full of unseen connexions and nice dependencies; and he that breaks one link of the chain, endangers the dissolution of the whole."

[211] For an extensive research on copyright propertization, see Hughes, *supra* note 4, at 1009–26; *See also* Shubha Gosh, *Globalization, Patents, and Traditional Knowledge*, 17 COLUM. J. ASIAN L. 73, 75 (2003).

[212] Mark A. Lemley, *Romantic Authorship and the Rhetoric of Property*, 75 TEX. L. REV. 873 (1997); Mark A. Lemley, *The Modern Lanham Act and the Death of Common Sense*, 108 YALE L.J. 1687 (1999); Randal C. Picker, *From Edison to the Broadcast Flag: Mechanisms of Consent and Refusal and the Propertization of Copyright*, 70 U. CHI. L. REV. 281 (2003); Albert Sieber, Note, *The Constitutionality of the DMCA Explored: Universal City Studios, Inc. v. Corley & United States v. Elcom Ltd.*, 18 BERKELEY TECH. L.J. 7, 37 (2003); Melissa A. Kern, *Paradigm Shifts and Access Controls: An Economic Analysis of the Anticircumvention Provisions of the Digital Millennium Copyright Act*, 35 U. MICH. J.L. REFORM 891, 903 (2002).

[213] Manta, *supra* note 206, at 476.

its incorporation into the meaning of copyright.[214] Thus, as a normative matter, the usage of property terminology is important to the criminalization process: it can shape and change social norms regarding copyright infringements, and influence judicial and legislative decisions.[215] The association of copyright infringement with theft allows legislators to criminalize copyright with less public resistance.

COPYRIGHT AS INTELLECTUAL PROPERTY Although IP is commonly referred to as intangible property, it has often been treated as real property. The term intellectual property encompasses the word "property" within it, and thus this terminology implies that it is a form of property. Scholars argue that the phrase "intellectual property" attained formal international recognition in 1893 with the formation of the United International Bureau for the Protection of Intellectual Property (BIRPI), which was established to administer the Berne and Paris Conventions.[216] In the United States, the first mention of the phrase "intellectual property" can be traced back to *Davoll v. Brown*, a 1845 circuit court case.[217] With that, Mark Lemley argues that the common use of the term as a descriptor of the field was in 1967 with the formation of the World Intellectual Property Organization.[218] Thus, as Lemley points out, the phrase "intellectual property," as compared to copyright and patent, is a relatively new term[219]; or to say the least, it has only recently gained general acceptance and continues to grow ever since.[220] Disagreeing with Lemley, Justin Hughes argues that the term intellectual property or "artistic property," which refers to copyright, was used frequently throughout the nineteenth century much prior to the formation of WIPO; and thus the term "intellectual property" as used to describe

---

[214] *See* Patricia Loughlan, *"You Wouldn't Steal A Car": Intellectual Property and the Language of Theft*, 29 E.I.P.R 401, 401 (2007).

[215] Netanel, *supra* note 3, at 12; PATRY, *supra* note 85, at 14–15.

[216] *See, e.g.*, Craig Joyce, *"A Curious Chapter in the History of Judicature"*: Wheaton v. Peters *and the Rest of the Story (of Copyright in the New Republic)*, 42 HOUS. L. REV. 325, 328 (2005).

[217] *See* Lemley, *supra* note 3, at 1033 (citing Davoll v. Brown, 7 F. Cas. 197, 199 (C.C.D. Mass. 1845), calling intellectual property "the labors of the mind" and concluding that they were 'as much a man's own . . . as what he cultivates, or the flocks he rears.'"). Note however, that the Supreme Court referred to copyrighted works as "literary property" prior to 1845 in at least two occasions. *See* Hughes, *supra* note 4, at 1034

[218] Lemley, *supra* note 3, at 1033; Convention Establishing the World Intellectual Property Organization, July 14, 1967, art. 2(viii), 6 I.L.M. 782, 784 (defining the term "intellectual property" to include literary, artistic and scientific works, performances of performing artists, phonograms, and broadcasts, inventions in all fields of human endeavor, scientific discoveries, industrial designs, trademarks, service marks, and commercial names and designations, protection against unfair competition, and all other rights resulting from intellectual activity in the industrial, scientific, literary or artistic fields); Joyce, *supra* note 217, at 328.

[219] Lemley, *supra* note 213, at 895.

[220] Mark Lemley shows "an almost exponential growth" in the use of the term "intellectual property" in United States federal court opinions between 1944–2004. *See* Lemley, *supra* note 3.

copyright had very little to do with the "propertization" of copyright.[221] Hughes continues his argument by indicating that copyright was referred to as a form of property long before the formation of the "intellectual property" phrase.[222] Without picking a side of the argument, it seems that even if the phrase "intellectual property" often appeared in the nineteenth century, it plays a quite dominant role today. The usage of property terminology and rhetoric, when referring to intellectual property and copyright as a part of IP, could influence both policymakers and society's perception of copyright.

COPYRIGHT INFRINGEMENT AS PIRACY AND THEFT Policymakers, scholars, and associated industries, often use property terminology, e.g., "stealing," "theft," and "piracy" to describe copyright infringement.[223] The term "piracy," for instance, was originally reserved for physical property, i.e., maritime piracy, and may have played a crucial role in anchoring the IP propertization paradigm.[224] "Piracy," in relation to unauthorized copying, was widely used prior to the criminalization process,[225] and even prior to modern copyright laws, suggesting that it is not only connected to contemporary lobbying by rights holders.[226] It was also common to treat infringement as theft when there was little distinction between physical works and rights to which they conveyed.[227] Even prior to the enactment of the Statute of Anne in 1709, "piracy" was widely used to describe the unauthorized printing of books, and later for a wide range of perceived transgressions of civility emanating from print's practitioners.[228] Along with "piracy," copyright infringement was routinely equated with shoplifting, letter-picking, purse-cutting, highway robbery, house burgling, and hospital plundering.[229] In the eighteenth century, for example, the London book cartel referred to book copiers as "pirates," while contemporary industries use the term "pirates" more loosely.[230]

---

[221] Hughes, *supra* note 4, at 1005–08.

[222] *Id.* at 1006.

[223] *See, e.g.,* Ariel Katz, *A Network Effects Perspective on Software Piracy*, 55 U. TORONTO L.J. 155, 156 (2005); for criticism of the pervasive rhetorical use of the language of "theft" in intellectual property discourse, see Loughlan, *supra* note 215.

[224] *See* Hughes, *supra* note 4, at 995.

[225] Alexander, *supra* note 97, at 627.

[226] Hughes, *supra* note 4, at 1009–10.

[227] *See* Colin Tapper, *Criminality and copyright, in* INTELLECTUAL PROPERTY IN THE NEW MILLENNIUM: ESSAYS IN HONOUR OF WILLIAM R. CORNISH 266, 267–68 (David Vaver & Lionel Bently eds., 2004) (making a similar argument).

[228] *See* ADRIAN JOHNS, THE NATURE OF THE BOOK 32 (1998); Hughes, *supra* note 4, at 1009; ADRIAN JOHNS, PIRACY: THE INTELLECTUAL PROPERTY WARS FROM GUTENBERG TO GATES 23 (2009).

[229] William St. Clair, *Metaphors of Intellectual Property, in* PRIVILEGE AND PROPERTY ESSAYS ON THE HISTORY OF COPYRIGHT 369, 388 (Ronan Deazley, Martin Kretschmer & Lionel Bently eds., 2010).

[230] *See* Halbert, *supra* note 3, at 6; Lawrence Liang, *Beyond Representation: The Figure of the Pirate, in* MAKING AND UNMAKING INTELLECTUAL PROPERTY 167 (Mario Biagioli, Peter Jaszi & Martha Woodmansee eds., 2011).

Thus, usage of the term "piracy," instead of been conceived as a tool used in the "propertization" of copyright and, i.e., in copyright criminalization, is actually a concept that described unauthorized copying before the concept of copyright ever existed. However, today, more than ever before, any unauthorized usage of copyrighted materials is widely referred to as "piracy."[231] As few scholars have suggested that while today, the term "piracy" in relation to copyright encompasses every copyright infringing activity, in the past, "piracy" was used to describe the large-scale sale of counterfeit copies.[232]

Another example of the use of property terminology is "plagiarism." Although plagiarism is not synonymous with copyright infringement, the two terms do overlap many times. The term *plagiarism* originated from the Latin term *plagiori* (i.e., from "trap" or "snare"), which under Roman law referred to the stealing of a slave or child.[233] Plagiarism is usually characterized as an offense, while the plagiarist is often referred to as a thief or a criminal.[234]

A step-up in the use of terminology is the term *theft* to describe copyright infringement. The usage of "theft" is important. Patricia Loughlan argues that the use of *piracy* to describe and denigrate the unauthorized user of IP is not equivalent to the use of *theft* to describe and denigrate the same conduct.[235] Whereas "the term 'pirate' is clearly metaphorical," Loughlan argues, terms like "theft" and "stealing" to describe and denigrate the unauthorized use of IP are less metaphorical.[236] These terms are more closely linked to describe and denigrate the unauthorized user of IP, as the copyright owner also suffers a form of financial deprivation, namely depreciation in the value of their property as a result of the non-violent theft of another.[237]

Many courts used the rhetoric of theft to describe copyright infringements.[238] For example, in *Grand Upright Music Ltd v. Warner Bros. Records*, the N.Y. District

---

[231] Litman, *supra* note 151, at 349. As a normative argument, the increase usage of terms such as piracy to describe any copyright infringement will not necessarily benefit rights holders in the long run, as the word will lose most of its meaning and become trivial. *See* Jane C. Ginsburg, *How Copyright Got A Bad Name for Itself*, 26 COLUM. J.L. & ARTS 61, 63 (2002).

[232] *See, e.g.,* LITMAN, *supra* note 89, at 85. Other scholars, when referring to IP, use the term "piracy" in quotation marks. This indicates a new context, or rather that the quotation marks are to sensitize to the use of the word. *See* Hughes, *supra* note 4, at 999.

[233] The term "plagiarism" in connection with literary works was first used by Roman poet Martial, who accused his rival, Fidentius, in reciting his works to the crowd, as if they were his own. Bishop Richard Montagu first used the term in English, in 1621. *See* Stuart P. Green, *Plagiarism, Norms, and the Limits of Theft Law: Some Observations on the Use of Criminal Sanctions in Enforcing Intellectual Property Rights*, 54 HASTINGS L.J. 167, 177 (2002).

[234] *See* Green, *supra* note 234, at 169–70.

[235] *See* Loughlan, *supra* note 215, at 402.

[236] *Id.*

[237] *Id.* However, Patricia Loughlan argues that "Copyright infringement is not theft." *See id.* at 403.

[238] *See, e.g.,* Grand Upright Music Ltd v. Warner Bros Records, Inc., 780 F. Supp. 182 (S.D.N.Y.1991) (reciting the Seventh Commandment: "Thou Shalt Not Steal," in a copyright infringement case). *See also* Loughlan, *supra* note 215, at 404.

Court recited the Seventh Commandment: "Thou Shall Not Steal" (*Exodus* 20:15) in a copyright infringement case.[239] Other courts however were not as passionate. For example, the Supreme Court in *Dowling v. United States*, stated that copyright infringement is not equal to physical theft:

> It follows that interference with copyright does not easily equate with theft, conversion, or fraud .... It is less clear, however, that the taking that occurs when an infringer arrogates the use of another's protected work comfortably fits the terms associated with physical removal employed by § 2314. The infringer invades a statutorily defined province guaranteed to the copyright holder alone. But he does not assume physical control over the copyright; nor does he wholly deprive its owner of its use. While one may colloquially link infringement with some general notion of wrongful appropriation, infringement plainly implicates a more complex set of property interests than does run-of-the-mill theft, conversion, or fraud ....[240]

Notwithstanding this decision, legislators and scholars often use the rhetoric of theft as well as other property terms to describe copyright infringement.[241] Terms like "piracy" and "theft" have made many appearances in the history of criminal copyright and can be traced to criminal copyright legislation and legislative materials. Examining criminal copyright legislation reveals that Congress used the term "theft" twice relating to IP infringements[242]: First, with the enactment of the No Electronic *Theft* (NET) Act, noting in the Act's title that the law refers to electronic "theft"; second in the PRO-IP Act of 2008, stating for example, in Section 401(b): "The Office of Justice Programs of the Department of Justice may make grants to eligible state or local law enforcement entities, including law enforcement agencies of municipal governments and public educational institutions, for training, prevention, enforcement, and prosecution of **intellectual property theft** and infringement crimes."[243] [emphasis added – E. H.].

The main uses of property terminology in copyright criminalization can be found in the Congressional hearings on various criminal copyright acts, especially those in the digital phase. For example, in the House Report of the NET Act, Rep. Robert Goodlatte stated:

> Pirating works online is *the same as shoplifting* a videotape, book, or record from a store. Through a loophole in the law, however, copyright infringers who *pirate* works knowingly and willfully, but not for profit, are outside the law. This situation

---

[239] *See Grand Upright Music*, 780 F. Supp. *See also* Loughlan, *supra* note 215, at 404.

[240] *See Dowling v. United States*, 473 U.S. 207, 217–18 (1985).

[241] *See, e.g.,* Loughlan, *supra* note 215, at 404.

[242] Reference to theft and "piracy" in the context of IP infringements, appeared in many proposed bills. *See, e.g.,* S. 1932, 108th Cong. (2003); H.R. 4077, 108th Cong. §§ 108–110 (2004); H.R. 3261, 112th Cong. (2011).

[243] Prioritizing Resources and Organization for Intellectual Property Act, Pub. L. No. 110–403, 122 Stat. 4256 (2008) (codified as amended at 42 U.S.C. § 3713a(B)). This Act refers to IP infringements as theft throughout the Act. *See* §§ 402(a)–(b), 503.

has developed because the authors of our copyright laws could not have anticipated the nature of the Internet, which has made the *theft* of copyrighted works virtually cost-free and anonymous. [emphasis added – E. H.].[244]

In addition, in the PRO-IP Act, Congress used the term "theft" in order to justify criminal copyright provisions: "These industries are suffering from rampant theft of their intellectual property online;"[245] and "[i]ntellectual property is the lifeblood of our economy, and protecting that property from theft ... is important."[246]

Thus, policymakers and rights holders have used the property rhetoric to justify criminal sanctions and shape the public's conception of criminal copyright. Although the use of this terminology to describe copyright infringement can be considered to lack real ramifications, it could also be viewed as a deliberate attempt by copyright industries to tilt the public discussion in their favor,[247] to reshape the public conception and push toward criminal copyright.[248]

B *Expansion of Copyright to Property Rights*

Rights holders attempt to create new property boundaries through legislative and non-legislative means to balance the many adversities they face in protecting their creations.[249] In the United States, for example, Congress has reasoned copyright criminalization by making a direct link to tangible property. As noted by Congress:

> The public must come to understand that intellectual property rights, while abstract and arcane, are no less deserving of protection than personal or real property

[244] *See* 143 CONG. REC. H9883, H9885 (daily ed. Nov. 4, 1997) (statement of Rep. Goodlatte). *See also* the House Report of the Copyright Felony Act (Pub. L. No. 102–561, 106 Stat. 4233 (1992)) in the United States (H.R. REP. No. 102–997, 102d Cong., (1992), *reprinted in* 1992 U.S.C.C.-A.N. 3569) [emphasis added – E. H.]:

> > The purpose of S. 893 is to harmonize the current felony provisions for copyright infringement and to provide an effective deterrence to the *piracy* of motion pictures, sound recordings, computer programs, and other original works of authorship. *Piracy* of copyrighted works costs U.S. industries millions of dollars a year, resulting in losses of jobs and diminution in the number of works created. Effective criminal penalties will aid in preventing such losses.

[245] 154 Cong. Rec. E2141–01, E2141 (daily ed. Sept. 27, 2008) (statement of Rep. Blackburn); Grace Pyun, *The 2008 Pro-IP Act: The Inadequacy of the Property Paradigm in Criminal Intellectual Property Law and Its Effect on Prosecutorial Boundaries*, 19 DEPAUL J. ART TECH. & INTELL. PROP. L. 355, 379–80 (2009).
[246] 154 Cong. Rec. S9583–02, S9589 (daily ed. Sept. 26, 2008) (statement of Sen. Leahy); Pyun, *supra* note 246, at 379–80.
[247] *See* Hughes, *supra* note 4, at 999; Neil Weinstock Netanel, *Impose a Noncommercial Use Levy to Allow Free Peer-to-Peer File Sharing*, 17 HARV. J.L. & TECH. 1, 22 (2003); Litman, *supra* note 151, at 349.
[248] Pyun, *supra* note 246, at 379–80.
[249] *See* Halbert, *supra* note 3, at xi.

rights .... . What we are essentially saying is if you trash somebody else's property, even if you are not doing it for money but you are just doing it because you wanted to show how smart you are and because you are seriously maladjusted and cannot make an impression on anybody in any other way, *it is as criminal as if you stole*. [emphasis added – E. H.].[250]

and

By passing this legislation, we send a strong message that we value intellectual property, as abstract and arcane as it may be, in the same way that we value the real and personal property of our citizens. Just as we will not tolerate the theft of software, CD's, books, or movie cassettes from a store, so will we not permit the stealing of intellectual property over the Internet.[251]

Rights holders have also used property terminology to educate. For instance, global campaigns against copyright infringement compare copyright infringement to theft. For example, one of the MPAA's videos against illegal file-sharing shows a young girl downloading a file to her computer with the following accompanying text: "You wouldn't steal a car. You wouldn't steal a handbag. You wouldn't steal a movie. Downloading pirated films is stealing ... ."[252] By an analogy, illegal file-sharing becomes stealing and is linked to stealing a car and a handbag, and rights holders attempt to influence society's perception of copyright infringements while trying to deter or reduce public resistance to criminal copyright laws.

The transformation of copyright into property occurs in many forms. For example, as discussed earlier, the increase of copyright duration to the life of the author plus 70 years is "functionally perpetual."[253] Thus, it resembles tangible property. Another example is the use of anti-circumvention technologies (such as DRM), which resemble a lock in the physical world. In other words, the inclusion of new copyright violations that outlaw processes that circumvent technological measures could also be considered propertization of copyright.[254] Through anti-circumvention technologies, an owner of a copyrighted work gains "physical" control to their work, at least to some extent, much like tangible property.[255] Although using different means to control the usage of copyright existed prior to anti-circumvention technologies, e.g., locking cinema doors, they were not treated as part of the propertization of copyright.[256]

This leads us to criminal copyright sanctions. If copyright infringement is similar to tangible theft, the property argument would presume that copyright law should be

---

[250] 143 CONG. REC. H9883-H9885 (daily ed. Nov. 4, 1997).
[251] CONG. REC. S12, 689-S12, 691 (1997).
[252] *See Movie Piracy – It's a Crime*, YOUTUBE (May 17, 2006), www.youtube.com/watch?v=l5SmrHNWhak&feature=related (last visited Dec. 1, 2017).
[253] NETANEL, *supra* note 5, at 58.
[254] *See* Picker, *supra* note 213, at 284.
[255] *Id.*
[256] *See* Hughes, *supra* note 4, at 996.

adjusted similarly. Thus, copyright expansion, which partially explains the criminalization process, is directly linked to the propertization of copyright. The best example of the propertization of copyright *vis-à-vis* the criminalization process is the passage of the NET Act in the United States, which criminalized copyright infringement for some non-commercial uses. Under a strict property approach, if copyright is indeed considered as property, then it should not matter whether the "theft" was profitable. Thus, the property approach does not differentiate between commercial and non-commercial uses and advocates criminalizing both. In Chapter 7, I further discuss the normative views of copyright law, both from property and tort law views, to evaluate criminal copyright legislation and its justifications.

Thus, while debatable,[257] copyright criminalization can be viewed as a shift toward a property paradigm, which is not necessarily linked to actual copyright infringements, but rather to a normative justification of this process. If copyright is treated as a tangible item, then copyright criminalization is not only justified, but should also be enhanced to match the criminal protection granted to tangible property, and vice versa: if we reject the "copyright as property" argument, the justification for criminalization is reduced.

IV POLITICAL POWER

The third possible internal reason for copyright criminalization is political power.[258] Organized groups with shared interests and defined goals tend to influence legislation more than the public.[259] This argument is based on the modern public choice theory, i.e., "the economic study of nonmarket decision making, or simply the application of economics to political science."[260] Thus, the public choice theory can, too, provide an explanation for copyrights' expansion.[261] The linkage between copyright criminalization and political power is based upon the legislative history of criminalization set forth in Chapters 2 and 3, which describe various interest groups' involvement in legislation; secondary academic literature on lobbying efforts in copyright in general and in criminal copyright legislation in particular; and other legislative materials.

---

[257] Peter Menell argues that in the past decades we are witnessing a shift towards a regulatory regime. *See* Menell, *supra* note 91, at 194–97.

[258] Some scholars attributed political forces as a possible reason for copyright criminalization. *See, e.g.,* Pyun, *supra* note 246, at 356; Saperstein, *supra* note 83, at 1472; Manta, *supra* note 206, at 505–12.

[259] Netanel, *supra* note 3, at 3.

[260] On modern public choice theory, see JAMES M. BUCHANAN & GORDON TULLOCK, THE CALCULUS OF CONSENT (1965); DENNIS C. MUELLER, PUBLIC CHOICE II: A REVISED EDITION OF PUBLIC CHOICE 1 (1989).

[261] Bell, *supra* note 37, at 786.

Criminalization is a political process.[262] And copyright law is no different, as it is vastly influenced by political power.[263] Legislators are non-autonomous actors who are motivated to be re-elected and depend on the resources and political powers of interest groups.[264] As such, they use their voting privileges to assist dominant interest groups in exchange for their financial and political support.[265] In addition, rights holders spend much effort on political lobbying, which results in the expansion of copyright owners' rights, mainly due to a lack of a competitor on the other side,[266] i.e., the public is systematically underrepresented, if at all.[267]

Over the years, copyright law had become more important to a wider variety of stakeholders.[268] Along with the growth of associated industries, several distinct industry-lobbying groups were formed and advocate the further expansion of IP criminalization and enforcement.[269] In the United States, we witness a linkage between the high-tech analog phase of copyright criminalization[270] and the expansion of the recording and motion picture industries in the 1960s and 1970s,[271] and a linkage between the high-tech digital phase[272] and the expansion of home computing and software industry (and the internet).[273] Thus, another internal explanation for copyright criminalization is political and is directly related to the evolution of

---

[262] See NINA PERŠAK, CRIMINALISING HARMFUL CONDUCT: THE HARM PRINCIPLE, ITS LIMITS AND CONTINENTAL COUNTERPARTS 5 (2007).

[263] See, e.g., in the United States' 1976 copyright revision: Jessica Litman, *Copyright, Compromise, and Legislative History*, 72 CORNELL L. REV. 857, 865–79 (1987).

[264] See Peter Schuck, *Against (and for Madison): An Essay in Praise of Factions*, 15 YALE L. & POL'Y REV. 553, 572 (1997).

[265] *Id.*; Yafit Lev-Aretz, *Copyright Lawmaking and the Public Choice: From Legislative Battles to Private Ordering*, 27 HARV. J.L. TECH. 203, 216 (2012).

[266] See Hardy, *supra* note 81, at 324.

[267] See Note, *supra* note 132, at 1718. For a comprehensive analysis of the politics in copyright law making, see generally LITMAN, *supra* note 89.

[268] See Graeme B. Dinwoodie, *A New Copyright Order: Why National Courts Should Create Global Norms*, 149 U. PA. L. REV. 469, 486 (2000).

[269] Pyun, *supra* note 246, at 356. For more on lobbying in the United Kingdom, see Alexander, *supra* note 97, at 647–48; Pamela Samuelson, *Should Economics Play a Role in Copyright Law and Policy?*, 1 U. OTTAWA L. & TECH. J. 1, 9 (2004); Saperstein, *supra* note 83, at 1483; Litman, *supra* note 132, at 5; Susan K. Sell, *The Global IP Upward Ratchet, Anti-Counterfeiting and Piracy Enforcement Efforts: The State of Play*, 15 PIJIP RESEARCH PAPER 1, 18 (2008).

[270] See *supra* Chapter 3.

[271] See, e.g., James Lincoln Young, *Criminal Copyright Infringement and a Step Beyond*, 30 COPYRIGHT L. SYMP. 157, 159 (1983); For more on the growth of the United States recording industry, see *Copyright and Home Copying: Technology Challenges the Law*, OFFICE OF TECHNOLOGY ASSESSMENT 91–100 (1989), www.fas.org/ota/reports/8910.pdf.

[272] See *supra* note 271.

[273] See United States v. LaMacchia, 871 F. Supp. 535, 540 (D. Mass. 1994) (summarizing the expansion of the recording and motion picture industries and the home computing and software industry).

different copyright-related industries[274] that have accumulated political power to influence policy makers.[275]

Writing from the position of a former counsel for the Subcommittee on Intellectual Property & Judicial Administration, Committee on the Judiciary, United States House of Representatives, William Patry noted:

> Copyright interest groups hold fund raisers for members of Congress, write campaign songs, invite members of Congress (and their staff) to private movie screenings or sold-out concerts, and draft legislation they expect Congress to pass without any changes. In the 104th Congress, they are drafting the committee reports and haggling among themselves about what needs to be in the report. In my experience, some copyright lawyers and lobbyists actually resent members of Congress and staff interfering with what they view as their legislation and their committee report. With the 104th Congress we have, I believe, reached a point where legislative history must be ignored because not even the hands of congressional staff have touched committee reports.[276]

As copyright legislation is mainly economic, and as many copyright industries are wealthy, they influence copyright legislation to be partial to them.[277] Thus, under the guise of various Congressional fiscal committees, copyright industries can push to include criminal copyright legislation. Importantly, these legislative debates often lack transparency and are conducted behind the scenes, without the public's knowledge.[278] Although legislating criminal provision should be of a social importance, when it is legislated as part of a revision to copyright law, it is often debated as legislation that lacks important social and political issues.[279]

Thus, the copyright criminalization process is a result of rights holders' increasing power to influence the legislature, solely for the purpose of increasing their

---

[274] The growth of different industries related to copyright can be attributed to technological changes and advancement in the pharmaceutical, software, audiovisual, chemical and other industries. For this argument, see Viviana Muñoz Tellez, *The Changing Global Governance of Intellectual Property Enforcement: A New Challenge for Developing Countries, in* INTELLECTUAL PROPERTY ENFORCEMENT: INTERNATIONAL PERSPECTIVES 4 (Li Xuan & Carlos M. Correa eds., 2009).

[275] *See, e.g.,* Merges, *supra* note 100, at 2234; Yochai Benkler, *Through the Looking Glass: Alice and the Constitutional Foundations of the Public Domain,* 66 LAW & CONTEMP. PROBS. 173, 196 (2003).

[276] William F. Patry, *Copyright and the Legislative Process: A Personal Perspective,* 14 CARDOZO ARTS & ENT. L.J. 139, 141 (1996). It should be noted that William Patry's perspective captures the political essence of the 1990s, while as further noted, the political landscape regarding copyright legislation is different today.

[277] *Id.* at 145; Litman, *supra* note 151, at 350.

[278] Patry, *supra* note 277, at 146.

[279] William Patry argues that copyright legislation, unlike important social and political issues, takes place at a "very low level:" in the House of Representatives, at the subcommittee level, which results in decisions being made by a very small group of people; in the Senate: where there is no copyright subcommittee, copyright legislation is considered under unanimous consent agreements. *See id.* at 146–48.

income.[280] Through regulatory protection, rights holders use rent-seeking to create greater profits than would be normally gained in a more competitive market.[281] Rent-seeking occurs when resources are used to capture a monopoly right instead of being put to a more productive use.[282] Rent-seeking can explain the actions of various interest groups throughout the criminal copyright process:[283] As rights holders act in a pluralistic environment, they can only attempt to gain an enforceable monopoly over their works, in order to realize all of the revenues from their copyrighted work by eliminating free riders. However, rent-seeking does not necessarily mean lobbying for criminalization. Interest groups will only lobby for criminalization if they gain and receive economic benefits from it. This is the case for criminal copyright.

In addition, rights holders' tremendous influence on the legislative process occurs within a field lacking all opponents, or at least opponents with sufficient political power to block their attempts.[284] In a balanced legislative system, there should be an opposing power to contrast the industries' political power. For example, against Congress' attempts to enact a law that suppresses copyright goals, interest groups, such as law professors, lobbyists for the academic or scientific communities, criminal defense counsels, or consumer protection lobbyists should have the chance to protest legislation of these statutes. However, in practice, this is hardly the case.[285] Take for example the passage of the NET Act. Although this Act is highly controversial, apart for minor concerns regarding some of the Act's provisions,[286] there were no objections raised to its passage before the House Judiciary Committee's Subcommittee on Courts and Intellectual Property, as out of the eight witnesses who testified, two were government employees and the remaining six were industry

---

[280] *See, e.g.,* Ginsburg, *supra* note 232, at 61–62.

[281] Netanel, *supra* note 3, at 3.

[282] *See* Gordon Tullock, *Rent Seeking, in* THE WORLD OF ECONOMICS 604, 604–09 (John Eatwell et al. eds., 1991); Richard L. Hasen, *Lobbying, Rent Seeking, and the Constitution,* 64 STAN. L. REV. 191, 229 (2012); Richard L. Hasen, *Clipping Coupons for Democracy: An Egalitarian/ Public Choice Defense of Campaign Finance Vouchers,* 84 CALIF. L. REV. 1, 9 (1996). The term "Rent Seeking" was first introduced in 1974. *See* Anne O. Krueger, *The Political Economy of the Rent Seeking Society,* 64 AM. ECON. REV. 291 (1974).

[283] *See* Saperstein, *supra* note 83, at 1500–03.

[284] *See* Bell, *supra* note 37, at 786.

[285] *See, e.g.,* Patry, *supra* note 277, at 145.

[286] Three major concerns were raised during the hearing. First, Kevin Di Gregory, a Deputy Assistant Attorney General in the Criminal Division of the United States Department of Justice suggested that "it would be preferable to limit criminal liability for infringement without a profit motive to cases of willful infringement that threaten to cause substantial economic harm" and that the Act might expose libraries, universities and other non-profit organizations to the risk of criminal liability since the retail value limits could easily be surpassed. Second, Professor David Nimmer, testifying on behalf of the U.S. Telephone Association, was concerned with the meaning of the term "willfully" which could potentially expose internet service providers to criminal liability. Finally, Marybeth Peters, the registrar of copyright, raised concerns regarding the language of the Act, which would criminalize minor, isolated instances of willful infringement. *See generally,* Goldman, *supra* note 116, at 376.

lobbyists.[287] Thus, the reason for copyright's growth, in both civil and criminal law, is that there was hardly an opposition to the right holder's political power. However, this scheme is apparently changing.[288]

With the inception of modern copyright laws in the eighteenth century, copyright was mainly relevant to the content industries. As such, rivalry over copyright was between publishers themselves and did not involve end users, who were practically incapable of infringing upon copyrights. However, even in the analog age, various interest groups were against strong copyright protection. One example of such groups is the cable television industry, which at first opposed the 1976 reform and caused its delay.[289] Thus, rights holders did not always seek similar protection, but the balance was still in favor of the industries supporting stronger protection. When technology enabled end users to infringe copyright, this balance started to change with the entrance of end users into the equation. Prima facie, end users do not have the same political power to influence legislation as they are not a well-organized, cohesive group with shared interests and defined goals. However, technological and industrial developments are likely to change that outcome.

The political landscape surrounding copyright law is far more complicated now.[290] The internet enables more people to communicate and facilitates the organization of communities with shared interests and goals, which could amount to creating an opposition to rights holders. For example, forming a group in social media network, e.g., Facebook, can aid in achieving different goals. Second, the industry is much more diverse and does not share the same goals today. During most part of the first half of the twentieth century, the players involved in legislation shared a common interest: protecting content.[291] Today, many companies, e.g., Google, play on both sides of the field: they are interested in copyright protection but also desire the free, unencumbered flow of copyrighted materials. Other companies, e.g., Megaupload, rely mostly (or even entirely) on the lack of copyright protection, and therefore, would likely advocate for less-strict copyright protection.

This political power is not theoretical and could actually work to decriminalize the Copyright Act: in 2011, Congress proposed two bills, the Stop Online Piracy Act (SOPA)[292] and the PROTECT IP Act (PIPA),[293] which both addressed the perceived problem of non-American websites that were engaged in infringing copyright

---

[287] *See Copyright Piracy, and H.R. 2265, the No Electronic Theft (NET) Act: Hearings on H.R. 2265 Before the Subcomm. on Courts and Intellectual Prop. of the House Comm. on the Judiciary,* 105th Cong. (1997). Only after Congress' hearings, on November 25, 1997, a letter was sent to President William J. Clinton from Dr. Barbara Simons, on behalf of a group of scientists, asking to veto the Act. *See Goldman, supra* note 116, at 376–77.

[288] *See Lev-Aretz, supra* note 266, at 236.

[289] Menell, *supra* note 110, at 212.

[290] *Id.,* at 194–97.

[291] *Id.*

[292] Stop Online Piracy Act, H.R. 3261, 112th. Cong. (2011) (SOPA).

[293] PROTECT IP Act, S. 968, 112th Cong. (2011) (PIPA).

activity. The two bills aimed to prevent online copyright infringement by requiring that American internet intermediaries block access to infringing foreign websites and prevent their flow of revenues. Among other possible ramifications, the proposed bills would have led to the censorship of foreign websites that appear to infringe or induce copyright infringements.

Opposition to enact the two bills came quickly from those industries affected by them. It began with an open letter to Congress, calling to help protect internet innovation and to stop the two bills' enactment,[294] and ended with a "blackout" of many internet websites. For example, on January 18, 2012, Wikipedia was blacked out.[295] Under this blackout, Goggle reported that in one day, 4.5 million people signed a petition to oppose these measures.[296] Following the protest against the two bills, PIPA and SOPA were "postponed."[297] The true meaning of these actions is that the political power to influence legislation is no longer exclusively in the hands of rights holders seeking to enhance copyright protection. Moreover, as long as industries with political power are interested in "under-protection" of copyright law, political compromises on copyright criminalization will most likely occur.[298]

To conclude, politics plays an important part in the expansion of copyright. In this sense, politics, when viewed as an internal reason for copyright's growth, vastly influences the shaping of copyright law, usually in favor of rights holders. Copyright criminalization is strongly linked to the politics of expanding rights holders' rights, both as an external measure (as will be described in Chapter 6) and as an internal measure.

CONCLUSION

Copyright criminalization occurs, inter alia, due to internal reasons. As long as copyright protection continues to grow, the criminalization process will continue. In

---

[294] *Open Letter from Mark Andreessen et al. to Washington* (Dec. 14, 2012), https://dq99galanzv66m
    .cloudfront.net/sopa/img/12–14-letter.pdf (last visited Dec. 1, 2017); Annemarie Bridy, *Copyright Policymaking as Procedural Democratic Process: A Discourse-Theoretical Perspective on ACTA, SOPA, and PIPA*, 30 CARDOZO ARTS & ENT. L.J. 153, 159 (2012).

[295] *See SOPA Protests Planned by Google, Wikipedia and Others on Jan. 18*, WASHINGTON POST (Jan. 17, 2012), www.washingtonpost.com/business/economy/sopa-protests-planned-by-googlewi kipedia-and-others-on-jan-18/2012/01/17/gIQALKBL6P_story.html; *End Piracy, Not Liberty*, GOOGLE, www.google.com/takeaction (last visited Dec. 1, 2017) (reporting that over 115,000 websites participated in the blackout).

[296] *See* Deborah Netburn, *Google Says 4.5 Million People Signed Anti-SOPA Petition Today*, L.A. TIMES (Jan. 18, 2012, 4:00 PM), http://latimesblogs.latimes.com/technology/2012/01/google-anti sopa-petition.html; Bridy, *supra* note 295, at 159.

[297] *See* Carl Franzen, *How the Web Killed SOPA and PIPA*, TPM (Jan. 20, 2012, 6:11 PM), http:// idealab.talkingpointsmemo.com/2012/01/how-the-web-killed-sopa-and-pipa.php.

[298] *See, e.g.*, Edward K. Cheng, *Structural Laws and the Puzzle of Regulating Behavior*, 100 Nw. U. L. REV. 655, 714–15 (2006).

the normative sense, rights holders' legal protection should amount to the point at which "legislation will stimulate the producer" more than the monopoly rights given to the owner will harm the public.[299] Thus, expansion was not always justified from a normative point of view, and copyright criminalization as a form of copyright expansion is not always justified. I further address this important question in Chapters 7–9.

The growth of copyright holders' rights and the linkage to copyright criminalization were divided into three categories. First, is a financial reason: under this category, copyright criminalization is mostly attributed to the possible and actual financial losses of rights holders, which is usually, but not always, linked to technological developments and the civil law's inability to solve this problem.[300] Second, is propertization of copyright law: under this category, copyright criminalization is part of the pragmatic change toward a pure property paradigm. As such, copyright is criminalized in accordance to property laws. Third and finally, is political power: under this category, copyright criminalization is a political process, which is a result of the rights holders' increasing power to influence the legislature.

However, understanding copyright criminalization's wider aspects requires zooming out. The internal reasons provide a valid explanation for why copyright was and still is criminalized, but does not provide any external reasons that might play a role in the process. In order to understand the external reasons of copyright criminalization, I turn, in Chapter 6, to analyze the three main frameworks composing criminal copyright: the *IP framework*, which locates copyright criminalization in a wider framework of IP law; the *technological framework*, which locates copyright criminalization within various legal fields that are criminalized due to similar technological developments; and the *legal framework*, which locates copyright criminalization in the wider context of general criminalization of the law, and encompasses both the IP and the technological frameworks.

---

[299] H.R. Rep. No. 60–2222, at 7 (1909); Note, *supra* note 132, at 1718.

[300] For example, in the early 1930s, there was a rise in criminal copyright proposed bills to revise the Copyright Act of 1909, which seemingly resulted partially from the activities of "song hawkers" during that period and a fear that civil remedies do not serve as an adequate deterrent. For this argument, see Robert S. Gawthrop, *An Inquiry into Criminal Copyright Infringement*, *reprinted in* 20 Copyright L. Symp. 154, 157 (1972).

6

External Reasoning for Criminal Copyright

This chapter continues to explore criminalization of copyright law, and adds external, non-copyright explanations to the examination ("external analysis"). Over the years, various legal fields have undergone a process of criminalization, some of which are partially linked to copyright criminalization. As discussed in Chapter 5, there are various forms of internal reasons for copyright criminalization, which are all part of the copyright expansion paradigm. However, these internal reasons only provide a narrow view of larger processes in the legal field. In other words, copyright criminalization does not only occur because of internal reasons; it is also affected by external reasons that are linked to other criminalization processes.

The external analysis, much like the internal analysis in Chapter 5, is mostly descriptive and based on an analysis of criminalization legislation and literature in various legal fields. Normative evaluations of the reasons behind copyright criminalization are limited in this chapter, and only serve as explanatory notes for the process and its evaluation.

The declared reasons for copyright criminalization, as summarized and discussed in the descriptive analysis of legislative materials in Chapters 2 and 3, mostly exclude external reasons for copyright criminalization and instead, focus on internal reasons. In addition, the literature on copyright criminalization does not directly address external reasons behind the criminalization process, but rather points out other considerations that could be characterized as both internal and external concurrently.[1] My intention, however, is not to decide whether a specific reason for copyright criminalization, e.g., technological developments, is classified correctly,

---

[1] Comparing copyright criminalization to other criminalization process in current literature is limited to the United States and to a comparison between copyright and other IP laws, namely, patent and trademark criminalization. *See, e.g.,* Irina D. Manta, *The Puzzle of Criminal Sanctions for Intellectual Property Infringement,* 24 HARV. J.L. & TECH. 469 (2011).

but rather to evaluate the reasons in their correct framework – which allow under-standing of the process as a whole, while evaluating its validity and necessity.

Criminal copyright is part of three main frameworks: first, an *IP framework*, which locates copyright criminalization in a broader framework of IP law; second, a *technological framework*, which views copyright criminalization within the same scheme as other legal fields that have undergone criminalization due to similar technological developments; third, a *legal framework*, which locates copyright criminalization in the wider context of general criminalization of law and covers both the IP and the technological frameworks. These frameworks are illustrated in Figure 8.

As shown in Figure 8, criminal copyright, which has its internal dynamic toward criminalization (discussed in Chapter 5), is part of other external frameworks – which sometimes affect each other and are all part of the general criminalization legal framework. Criminal copyright is part of both IP and technological frame-works, which in turn are elements in the general criminalization movements.

This chapter locates copyright criminalization in the wider aspect of the crimin-alization legal frameworks. Part I briefly examines criminalization in various fields of law, highlighting their common grounds. In short, although various global movements toward criminalization are fundamentally different in justifications and circumstances, they can have similarities, particularly in the political sense. Part II focuses on the technological framework, which locates copyright criminal-ization as part of other fields of law that have undergone a criminalization process due to technological developments. This part focuses on one technological devel-opment, the internet, as the guiding force for criminalizing different activities, which are usually referred to as "cybercrimes." Within this discussion, I locate one segment of copyright criminalization in the technological framework, discuss the internet, and examine whether it serves as a catalyst for criminalization. Part III asks whether copyright criminalization is part of an IP paradigmatic change that is shifting from mostly-civil to mostly-criminal law. As copyright law is part of the IP

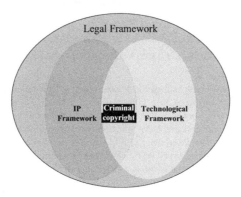

FIGURE 8 Criminalization Frameworks

framework, I examine patent and trademark law as well, while reaffirming that a similar process occurred only in the latter. Finally, I conclude that copyright criminalization is partially a result of external reasons. Nevertheless, I argue that although criminal legislation has been enhanced in many fields of law, including copyright law, the political linkage between the various processes is insufficient to explain each of the criminalization processes on their own. I conclude that copyright criminalization is partially linked to an ongoing process of IP and cybercrime criminalization, but this linkage is only part of the reason behind the copyright criminalization process. I point out that internal reasons play a more dominant role in explaining considerations behind copyright criminalization.

I LEGAL FRAMEWORK: GENERAL CRIMINALIZATION

The legal framework is general and covers all criminalization processes in all related legal fields. As I define it, this framework covers not only the transformation of a non-criminal law to a criminal one, but also the increase of criminal sanctions in existing criminal laws. Before turning to the common ground of the general process of criminalization, we need to understand the nature of different processes.

Whether or not there is a linkage between other fields of law and copyright criminalization requires scrutiny. It is difficult to compare criminal copyright to criminalization processes in other legal fields, as each field has its particular, different justifications, methods, and structures. Each unique criminalization process has unique characteristics that play an important factor in criminalization, which may not play a role in other fields, and therefore comparing two processes could disregard internal reasons of a criminalization process. If we take copyright as an example, as discussed in Chapter 5, infringements of copyright (which I classify en masse as an internal reason for copyright criminalization) have this unique characteristic: potential revenue loss usually means that a single rights holder's loss is attributed to a large number of users. This phenomenon is unique to copyright law. With this caveat in mind, I briefly review some basic elements of other criminalization processes.

Current literature on criminalization reveals that other fields of law are undergoing a similar process in many countries. To name a few, criminalization occurs in corporate law,[2]

---

[2] As of the mid-1990s many countries began to impose criminal liability for cartel participation (see, e.g., Austria, Brazil, Canada, Chile, Croatia, France, Germany, Greece, Ireland, Israel, Italy, Korea, Japan, Mexico, Norway, Slovak Republic, South Korea, Switzerland, the UK, and the United States). For more on cartel criminalization, see, e.g., Renato Nazzini, *Criminalisation of Cartels and Concurrent Proceeding*, 24 E.C.L.R. 483 (2003). Cartel criminalization in the United States began in 1890, several years before copyright criminalization, and continued in the late 1950s. More recent cartel criminalization continued in the last three decades, and match copyright criminalization timeframes, as described in Chapter 3, but not necessarily for the same reasons, as these laws are inherently different in nature. *See* Caron Beaton-Wells, *The Politics of Cartel Criminalisation: A Pessimistic View from Australia*, 3 E.C.L.R 29 (2008);

environmental law,[3] and health law (AIDS transmission).[4] However, the reasons behind any specific criminalization process cannot always be established,[5] and it is important to differentiate among various forms of criminalization. Yet, as these processes originate from the same legal framework, there are some similarities. What is most evident in the literature on various criminalization processes is that the process is attributed to political power.[6] As illustrated in Chapter 5, copyright criminalization as a form of copyright law's expansion is attributed, inter alia, to politics, which I classified as an internal reason. I argued that political reasons are directly linked to copyright law, such as the increase in specific copyright-related industries.

Herein I locate five main political reasons in criminalization's legal framework. First, is the *public choice theory*, which explains various criminalization processes.[7] One form of this theory, which is also used in the copyright criminalization process, holds that organized groups with shared interests and defined goals tend to influence legislation more than the general public.[8] Accordingly, criminalization is partially due to the substantial political influence of interest groups, which we can find in almost any legal field.[9]

Christopher Harding, *Business Collusion as a Criminological Phenomenon: Exploring the Global Criminalisation of Cartels,* 14 Critical Criminology 181 (2006); Caron Beaton-Wells & Ariel Ezrachi, Criminalising Cartels: Critical Studies of an International Regulatory Movement (2011).

[3] *See* Charles J. Babbitt, Dennis C. Cory & Beth L. Kruchek, *Discretion and the Criminalization of Environmental Law,* 15 Duke Envt'l. L. & Pol'y 1 (2004).

[4] *See, e.g.,* Heather Sprintz, *The Criminalization of Perinatal AIDS Transmission,* 3 Health Matrix 495 (1993); Richard H. Shekter, *The Criminalization of AIDS in Canada,* 19 Legal Med. Q. 13 (1995); Erin Dej & Jennifer M. Kilty, *Criminalization Creep: A Brief Discussion of the Criminalization of HIV/AIDS Non-Disclosure in Canada,* 27 Can. J.L. & Soc. 55 (2012); Sun Goo Lee, *Criminalization of HIV in Korea: Fundamental Rights and International Perspectives,* 15 Quinnipiac Health L.J. 65 (2011).

[5] *See* Douglas Husak, Overcriminalization – The Limits of the Criminal Law 10 (2008).

[6] There are also other patterns that are similar in various criminalization processes, such as their timeframe. The end of the twentieth century marks an increase of criminalization in many areas, including copyright (as discussed in the cases of the United Kingdom and United States in Chapters 2 and 3, criminal copyright legislation enhanced since the 1970s in the United States and since 1982 in the United Kingdom), and the reasons for that could be external. In other words, the end of the twentieth century could possibly mark a change in the legislative approach to criminal legislation. However, this criterion is not explanatory, but rather indicatory, in the sense that it does not provide an explanation of the process, but only refers to the time it occurred. For more on general criminalization timeframe, see Sara Sun Beale, *The News Media's Influence on Criminal Justice Policy: How Market-Driven News Promotes Punitiveness,* 48 Wm. & Mary L. Rev. 397 (2006).

[7] On modern public choice theory, see James M. Buchanan & Gordon Tullock, The Calculus of Consent (1965); Dennis C. Mueller, Public Choice II: A Revised Edition of Public Choice 1 (1989).

[8] *See* Neil Weinstock Netanel, *Why Has Copyright Expanded? Analysis and Critique, in* 6 New Directions in Copyright Law 3 (Fiona Macmillan ed., 2008).

[9] *See* Peter Schuck, *Against (and For Madison): An Essay in Praise of Factions,* 15 Yale L. & Pol'y Rev. 553, 572 (1997).

Second, politicians often face external pressures to "do something."[10] One reaction to these pressures is to legislate harsher criminal penalties in order to ensure the public that they are taking a strong stance against crime.[11] In this sense, it is important to note that the public tends to assume that crime rates increase annually – though this assumption has been disproved recently in many countries.[12] Thus, the public's beliefs about crime could lead to criminalization.[13]

Third, criminal sanctions have been enacted because there are few legislative barriers, and legislators are not directed by a principled theory of criminalization.[14] Criminalization occurs when some legislators, lacking legislative guidelines that differentiate between civil and criminal legislation, enact more criminal laws than needed. This reason works in coordination with public pressure on politicians to "do something." Politicians do not always receive proper guidance when faced with a decision about whether to enact a civil or a criminal law. Some of them lack a principled means to limit the scope of criminal law, which could be manipulated by interest groups and/or the public to legislate in the manner they see fit – but is not really in the best interest of society and could be avoided if legislatures possessed better tools.[15]

Fourth, is that, when deciding whether to enhance existing penalties in criminal legislation, legislators could tend to be over-inclusive rather than under-inclusive in a criminalization process, i.e., they prefer to have more criminal sanctions than less.[16] Due to this tendency, many laws include criminal sanctions as a cautionary measure against under inclusiveness, and as such might contain more criminal sanctions than socially desirable.[17]

Fifth, criminalization is a direct response to a perceived sustained increase in general crime rates.[18] Accordingly, sanctions need to be strengthened to compete with increased crime, since weaker sanctions are obviously ineffective. Nevertheless, and as I note above generally, statistics of estimated crime rates in the United States,

---

[10] See Husak, *supra* note 5, at 15–16.

[11] Sara Sun Beale, *What's Law Got to Do with It? The Political, Social, Psychological and Other Non-Legal Factors Influencing the Development of (Federal) Criminal Law*, 1 Buff. Crim. L. Rev. 23, 29 (1997).

[12] For general statistics on crime perception in the United States, see *Public attitudes toward crime and criminal justice-related topics*, Sourcebook, www.albany.edu/sourcebook/tost_2 .html#2_j (last visited Dec. 1, 2017). For a thorough analysis of crime perception, see Sun Beale, *supra* note 6.

[13] Sun Beale, *supra* note 6, at 420; Sun Beale, *supra* note 11, at 25.

[14] For more on the theories of political realism, see Hans J. Morgenthau, Politics Among Nations: The Struggle for Power and Peace 4–14 (1978).

[15] See Husak, *supra* note 5, at 58.

[16] See Paul Rosenzweig, *Over-Criminalization: An Agenda for Change*, 54 Am. U. L. Rev. 809, 810 (2005).

[17] *Id.* at 810.

[18] See, e.g., David Garland, The Culture of Control: Crime and Social Order in Contemporary Society (2001).

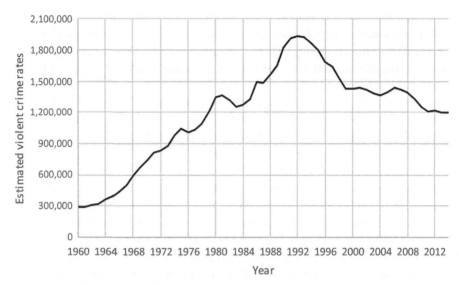

FIGURE 9 Estimated Violent Crime Rates in the Unites States (1960–2014)

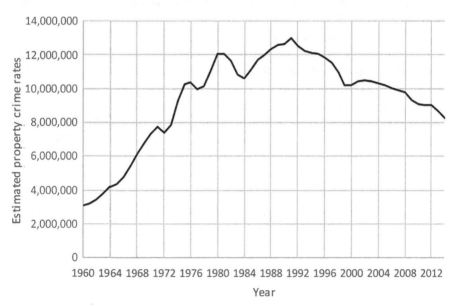

FIGURE 10 Estimated Property Crime Rates in the Unites States (1960–2014)

for both violent and property crimes between the years 1960 and 2014, suggests that general crime rates are no longer increasing.[19] As indicated in Figures 9 and 10,

---

[19] I obtained crime rates statistics in the United States from the Bureau of Justice Statistics website, which provides crime rate statistics between 1960 and 2014. The national or state offense totals are based on data from all reporting agencies and estimates for unreported areas.

since 1992 the general increase of crime rates has ceased. This statistical evidence for this reason would seem to be counter-intuitive, and one would expect to find instead that criminalization is ceasing or even shifting toward a de-criminalization process,[20] lowering the likelihood that the current criminalization process is triggered by this assumption (Figures 9 and 10).

The estimated crime rate in the United States has dropped since 1992. However, since the American Bureau of Justice statistics do not distinguish between criminal copyright and other offenses, it is impossible to learn about a specific criminalization process, e.g., copyright criminalization.

These reasons, separately discussed in academic literature on various criminalization processes, can either be part of external reasoning of any criminalization process, but can also be combined with internal reasons for criminalization. Moreover, these reasons can also explain the criminalization of copyright in a different manner: that there is a general political tendency to expand criminal legislation, regardless of copyright law and copyright-related industries.[21] Thus, copyright law might be just another piece in a general picture. For the current purposes, it suffices to note that categorizing copyright criminalization as a mere, general political movement is inaccurate, as discussed in Chapter 5. Nevertheless, the legal framework does play a role in copyright criminalization, and is important in understanding each criminalization process.

To conclude, the legal framework of criminalization consists of a general, political tendency to expand criminal legislation, regardless of copyright law.[22] This agenda is attributed to the public choice theory; to public pressure on politicians; to lack of legislative barriers; to a tendency to be over-inclusive; and to a direct response to a sustained increase in general crime rates. Thus, under this view, any law, copyright law included, can be criminalized, not only due to internal reasoning of that law, but also due to external reasons.

However, the legal framework is insufficient to explain copyright criminalization's external reasons. In order to have a better understanding of this, it is important to locate the legal framework within other criminalization frameworks. As such, the next two parts explore the technological and IP frameworks.

See *U.S. Bureau of Justice Statistics*, www.bjs.gov/ucrdata/Search/Crime/State/TrendsInOne Var.cfm (last visited Dec. 1, 2017); *see also* Sun Beale, *supra* note 6, at 408–10; ALFRED BLUMSTEIN & JOEL WALLMAN, THE CRIME DROP IN AMERICA (2000).

[20] Figures 9 and 10 are processed from statistical data I extracted from the Bureau of Justice Statistics website (see *supra* note 19).

[21] *See* Rosenzweig, *supra* note 16, at 810. Political reasoning could be both external and internal to copyright. For example, a possible general preference of legislators to legislate criminal laws could be linked to every field of law, and not only to copyright law. However, there are some political reasons that are directly linked to copyright criminalization, discussed in Chapter 5.

[22] *See id.* at 810.

II TECHNOLOGICAL FRAMEWORK

Criminal copyright is part of a general criminalization paradigm. As there are various legal fields that are criminalized with similar reasons, a micro-level analysis is necessary. A closer examination of legal fields that have undergone criminalization reveals that copyright criminalization has common grounds with two of their main frameworks. The first is the technological framework. Technology (combined with other considerations) has played and still plays a leading role in copyright criminalization. Reviewing the legislative history (Chapters 2 and 3), revealed that various technologies, and especially the internet, are closely linked to the rise in criminal copyright legislation.[23] Thus, technology, and especially the internet's infrastructure, combined with the proliferation of various digital technologies, plays a key role in copyright criminalization, and as I explore below, in various criminalization processes.

Copyright infringement over the internet is often linked to cybercrime or computer crime.[24] When the term "computer crime" was first used, as early as the 1960s and the 1970s, it played a limited role in any criminalization process, as it was usually related to theft of telecommunication services and fraudulent transfer of electronic funds.[25] However, beginning in the early 1990s, the internet infrastructure, combined with the proliferation of various digital technologies, has been integral to many criminalization processes.[26]

According to *Jonathan Clough*, the internet facilitates the perpetration of unlawful activities due to six key factors:[27] (1) The *scale* of potential offenders, which could not be achieved offline;[28] (2) high *accessibility* to illegal activities; (3) *anonymity*, which reduces detection; (4) *portability and transferability*, i.e., the ability to store enormous amounts of data in a small space and to replicate that data with no appreciable diminution of quality; (5) *global reach* of the internet and unlimited financial possibilities that broaden the scope and opportunities for unlawful activities[29]; and (6) the *absence of capable guardians*, i.e., the perceived, decreased risk of detection and prosecution.

---

[23] *See* Chapters 2 and 3.

[24] The very notion of the word "crime" to describe copyright infringement could be troublesome, and is part of a political/propertization process which copyright undergoes, as discussed in Chapter 3.

[25] JONATHAN CLOUGH, PRINCIPLES OF CYBERCRIME 3–4 (2010); SUSAN W. BRENNER, CYBERCRIME: CRIMINAL THREATS FROM CYBERSPACE 10–37 (2010).

[26] CLOUGH, *supra* note 25, at 3–4.

[27] *See generally, id.* at 5–8.

[28] As indicated in the Internet World Stats website, on June 30th, 2017, there were 3,885,567,619 internet users worldwide. *See Internet Usage Statistics*, INTERNETWORLDSTATS, www.internetworldstats.com/stats.htm (last visited Dec. 1, 2017); CLOUGH, *supra* note 25, at 5–8.

[29] *See* Michael Edmund O'Neill, *Old Crimes in New Bottles: Sanctioning Cybercrime*, 9 GEO. MASON L. REV. 237, 253 (2000).

Before I continue to compare and contrast the legislative responses of cybercrime and copyright law, a clarification of cybercrime is required. There are three categories of cybercrime.[30] First, are "target cybercrimes": when a computer itself is the target of the criminal activity and includes three online activities – hacking, malware, and distributed denial of service (DDoS) attacks.[31] Target cybercrimes justify legislating cybercrime-specific laws, "because the conduct involved in the commission of and/or the 'harms' inflicted by target cybercrimes do not fit into traditional criminal law."[32] Second, are "tool cybercrimes": when a computer is the tool of, i.e., used for, the criminal activity, e.g., theft, fraud, and extortion via computer.[33] Third, are "computer incidental cybercrimes": when the use of a computer is incidental to the commission of the crime. This category encompasses crimes in which the computer is used as secondary tool for the crime and a source of evidence, e.g., when murder suspects use a computer to learn how to commit murder prior to the act.[34]

When cybercrime was born, many types of copyright infringement were already a criminal offense in both test-case countries: the United Kingdom and the United States. Although in both cases, criminal copyright was considered primarily a civil wrong, affecting private commercial interests, it was still a criminal offense, at least for some types of infringements. Under the three categories of cybercrime, copyright infringement could be labeled as a tool of cybercrime, since a computer (with the internet) is used as a tool to infringe copyright, while the possible harm inflicted on rights holders, society, and the government does not necessarily fit into traditional criminal law. Thus, copyright infringement is perceived as being in need of revision.

However, compared to other cybercrime offenses, copyright law is mostly a civil law, especially before the internet emerged. Therefore, copyright criminalization generally relates to the transformation of a mostly civil-based law into a criminal-based law. Unlike copyright infringements, most cybercrimes, (e.g., fraud, online gambling, and terrorism) apply existing criminal offenses to a new environment (the digital one) and commit the same crime in a nuanced manner.[35] Thus, although, in some instances, copyright criminalization also applies existing criminal offenses to the digital environment (even if new, enhanced legislation has been enacted for cybercrime for these offenses), it does not resemble copyright's criminalization process entirely.

Although criminal copyright is different from most cybercrimes, in the sense that copyright was not originally a criminal offense and is generally still a civil-based law,

---

[30] BRENNER, *supra* note 25, at 39; Computer Crime and Intellectual Property Section, *The National Information Infrastructure Protection Act of 1996, Legislative Analysis*, US DEPARTMENT OF JUSTICE (1996), www.cybercrime.gov/1030analysis.html; CLOUGH, *supra* note 25, at 10.

[31] For more on hacking, malware, and Distributed Denial of Service (DDoS) attacks, see BRENNER, *supra* note 25, at 49–71.

[32] *Id.* at 73.

[33] For more on target cybercrimes, see *id.* at 73–102.

[34] For more on computer incidental crimes, see *id.* at 103–19.

[35] For a full analysis of cybercrime offenses, see CLOUGH, *supra* note 25.

there are some similarities within the technological framework's criminalization reasoning: mainly, the nature of the internet and of digital technologies has created the necessity to enhance criminal penalties or to adapt the current law to the new digital reality. However, criminal copyright remains the exception to the technological framework, as it was never entirely a criminal law, and there are no similar cybercrimes that resemble criminal copyright legislation. While technology has played an important role in copyright criminalization, and its characteristics are inherently different from other criminalization processes in the technological framework, the underlying reasons for criminalization of most cybercrimes (criminal copyright included) are similar, and thus, part of the same framework. Accordingly, technology is both an internal (as discussed in Chapter 5) and an external reason for copyright criminalization.

III IP FRAMEWORK

The second framework that criminal copyright plays a part in is IP criminalization. The IP framework is in itself part of the general legal framework and is similar to the political explanation. However, as the legal framework is too broad and covers many laws that are inherently different, copyright criminalization should be compared to its closest legal fields. As such, I compare copyright criminalization to other IP fields, namely patent law and trademark law,[36] while reaffirming that a similar process has occurred only in the latter.[37]

A *Trademark Criminalization*

1 United Kingdom Trademark Criminalization

In 1988, the United Kingdom introduced criminal trademark by enacting the Copyright, Designs and Patents Act,[38] which amended the Trade Marks Act of 1938.[39] The Act added the offense of a fraudulent application or use of "a mark

---

[36] *See* Manta, *supra* note 1, at 476. Criminal sanctions also exists in other forms of IP, e.g., trade secrets, but on a limited scale. *See* Economic Espionage Act of 1996, Pub. L. No. 104–294, 110 Stat. 3488 (codified as amended at 18 U.S.C. §§ 1831–39). For more on trade secrets criminalization in the United States, see Ronald D. Coenen Jr., Jonathan H. Greenberg & Patrick K. Reisinger, *Intellectual Property Crimes*, 48 Am. Crim. L. 849, 852 (2011); Geraldine Szott Moohr, *The Problematic Role of Criminal Law in Regulating Use of Information: The Case of the Economic Espionage Act*, 80 N.C. L. Rev. 853 (2002).

[37] I do note that there are significant differences between copyright and trademark law, and I only examine their similar common commercial characteristics regarding the criminalization process. *See* Alex Steel, *Problematic and Unnecessary? Issues with the Use of the Theft Offence to Protect Intangible Property*, 30 Sydney L. Rev. 575, 599 (2008). *See also* Miriam Bitton, *Rethinking the Anti-Counterfeiting Trade Agreement's Criminal Copyright Enforcement Measures*, 102 J. Crim. L. & Criminology 67, 84–89 (2012).

[38] The Copyright, Designs and Patents Act 1988, c. 48 (U.K.).

[39] *Id.* § 300; Trade Marks Act 1938, c. 22, § 58A (U.K.).

identical to or nearly resembling a registered trade mark" on goods "which are not connected in the course of trade with the registered trademark owner . . . without the consent of the trademark right holder."[40] The offense was punishable on a summary conviction indictment by up to six months imprisonment or a fine not exceeding the statutory maximum, or both, and on conviction on indictment to a fine or imprisonment for a term not exceeding ten years, or both.

In 1994, Parliament replaced the Trade Marks Act of 1938 with the 1994 Trade Marks Act to implement the EC Trade Marks Directive.[41] The new act added a trademark criminal offense for actions meant to gain – or with intent to cause loss – by applying to goods or packages a mark that is identical to (or likely to be mistaken for) a registered trademark. In addition, the Act proscribes the sale, hire, offer, or promotion for sale or distribution of goods/packaging that bear an infringing or mistakenly similar mark. The Act also outlaws the possession, custody, and control within the course of business of such goods with criminal intent to sell, hire, offer, or promote for sale or distribution of goods/packaging bearing infringing or mistakenly similar mark.[42]

In addition, subject to some provisions, the new Act inserted a trademark criminal offense for the use of a sign that is identical or likely to be mistaken for a registered trademark, to material intended to be used for labeling, packaging goods, and as a business paper. Moreover, the Act proscribes the usage of such material in the course of business, or the possession of it, or having custody or control of such material in the course of a business, with a view to the doing of anything, by himself or with another, which would be an offense under paragraph 92(2)(b).

The Act also criminalizes making, possession, custody, and control of an article specifically designed or adapted to make infringing marks, when the individual is aware or has reason to believe that it has been or will be used to produce goods, labeling, packaging material, and business stationery, or to advertise goods.[43] Under the 1994 Act, the offenses are punishable, on summary conviction to imprisonment for a term not exceeding six months or a fine not exceeding the statutory maximum, or both; and upon conviction on indictment to a fine or imprisonment for a term not exceeding ten years, or both.[44]

In 2002, Parliament enacted the Copyright, etc. and Trade Marks (Offences and Enforcement) Act,[45] which was partially proposed to harmonize the copyright and

[40] The Copyright, Designs and Patents Act 1988 § 300; *see also* Paul Rawlinson, *The UK Trade Marks Act 1994: It's Criminal*, 17 E.I.P.R. 54, 55 (1995).
[41] Council Directive 89/104 of 21 December, 1988 to Approximate the Laws of the Member States Relating to Trade Marks, 1989 O.J. (L 40). For an overview of United Kingdom trademark criminalization, see Rawlinson, *supra* note 40.
[42] Trade Marks Act 1994, c. 26, § 92 (U.K.); Rawlinson, *supra* note 40, at 55–56.
[43] Trade Marks Act 1994 § 92(3); Rawlinson, *supra* note 40, at 56.
[44] Trade Marks Act 1994 § 92(6).
[45] Copyright, etc. and Trade Marks (Offences and Enforcement) Act 2002, c. 25 (U.K.).

trademark regimes.[46] As for trademarks, the Act expanded the scope of search warrants and powers of seizure (sec. 92A).[47] Although the Act did not make any changes to the scope of trademark offenses, and hence it did not add criminal provisions, this is another step in the trademark criminalization process.[48]

2 United States Trademark Criminalization

Congress introduced the first comprehensive trademark legislation in 1870,[49] which at first did not contain criminal sanctions for trademark infringements. In 1876, in an attempt to punish the counterfeiting of trademark goods and the sale or commerce in counterfeit trademark goods, Congress added criminal penalties to the existing Penal Act for violations of trademark laws.[50]

The 1876 Act listed many fraudulent activities, which affixed with registered trademarks in the United States, and proscribed a punishment of up to $1,000, or imprisonment not more than two years, or both, and a punishment of up to $500, or imprisonment not more than one year, or both for willfully and knowingly aiding and abetting any of the violations in the Act.[51] Nevertheless, as determined by the Supreme Court in 1879,[52] the federal regulation of trademarks was in "exercise of a power not confided to Congress."[53] The Court held that Congress did not have the power to regulate trademarks under the IP clause, and in addition, Congressional regulations were only available to interstate commerce, i.e., with foreign nations, and among the several states, and with the Indian tribes.[54] Accordingly, the then-existing trademark legislation was declared unconstitutional, and therefore, void.[55]

In 1881 under the Commerce Clause, Congress adopted the Supreme Court's interpretation of the Constitution and reenacted several acts to regulate commercial

---

[46] *See* Kevin Garnett et al., Copinger and Skone James on Copyright 1253 (16th ed. 2011).

[47] Copyright, etc. and Trade Marks (Offences and Enforcement) Act 2002 § 6.

[48] Notably, for another form of IP, in 2014 Parliament legislated the Intellectual Property Act 2014 which, inter alia, amended the Registered Designs Act 1949 and subsequently harmonized the maximum custodial sentence of ten years for unauthorized copying of design in course of business. *See* Intellectual Property Act 2014, c. 18, §§ 35ZA-35ZD (U.K.).

[49] Act of July 8, 1870, ch. 230, §§ 77–84, 16 Stat. 198 (1870). For a detailed history of trademark legislation in the United States, see Brian J. Kearney, *The Trademark Counterfeiting Act of 1984: a Sensible Legislative Response to the Ills of Commercial Counterfeiting*, 14 Fordham Urb. L.J. 115 (1986).

[50] Act of Aug. 14, 1876, ch. 274, 19 Stat. 141–142 (1876).

[51] *Id.* §§ 1–8.

[52] The Trade-Mark Cases, 100 U.S. at 82 [hereinafter Trade-Mark Cases].

[53] *Id.* at 97; Kearney, *supra* note 49, at 127.

[54] Trade-Mark Cases, *supra* note 52, at 96; U.S. Const. art. 1 § 8, cl. 3; Kearney, *supra* note 49, at 127.

[55] Trade-Mark Cases, *supra* note 52, at 82, 98–99; Kearney, *supra* note 49, at 127; Craig O. Correll, *Using Criminal Sanctions to Combat Trademark Counterfeiting*, 14 AIPLA Q.J. 278, 279 (1986).

trademarks – without enacting criminal provisions.[56] Following this path, the Lanham Act, 1946 (named after Representative Fritz G. Lanham of Texas),[57] did not contain criminal sanctions for trademark infringements. In the early 1980s, following a global increase in trademark, counterfeit American-made goods, the newly formed International Anti-Counterfeiting Coalition (IACC) lobbied Congress for greater trademark protection.[58]

In 1984, due to a lack of sufficiently severe civil sanctions, which allegedly caused an "epidemic of commercial counterfeiting," defrauding consumers out of billions of dollars each year in the United States,[59] Congress enacted the Trademark Counterfeiting Act, criminalizing trademark counterfeiting and imposing penal penalties for the first time.[60] The 1984 Act provides criminal sanctions for intentional trafficking, or attempting to traffic,[61] in goods or services and knowingly[62] using a counterfeit mark on or in connection with goods or services.[63] This insertion of criminal penalties into trademark law was lobbied for by different industry groups, including the IACC.[64]

In 1994, Congress continued trademark criminalization with the enactment of the Violent Crime Control and Law Enforcement Act, which increased the penalties for trafficking in counterfeit goods and services.[65] Congress continued on this path

---

[56] *See* Trade-Mark Act of March 3, 1881, ch. 138, 21 Stat. 502 (1881); Trade-Mark Act of Feb. 20, 1905, ch. 592, 33 Stat. 724 (1905); Kearney, *supra* note 49, at 128–30.

[57] Trademark Act of 1946, Pub. L. 79–489, 60 Stat. 427 (1946); Kearney, *supra* note 49, at 130.

[58] *See* Grace Pyun, *The 2008 Pro-IP Act: The Inadequacy of the Property Paradigm in Criminal Intellectual Property Law and Its Effect on Prosecutorial Boundaries*, 19 DEPAUL J. ART TECH. & INTELL. PROP. L. 355, 363 (2009).

[59] S. REP. NO. 98–526, at 1–6 (1984), *reprinted in* 1984 U.S.C.C.A.N. 3182, 3631. Congress argued counterfeiters treated civil penalties as the "cost of doing their illegal business," and thus criminal prosecutions became necessary for deterrence. *See* David J. Goldstone & Peter J. Toren, *The Criminalization of Trademark Counterfeiting*, 31 CONN. L. REV. 1, 10 (1998); Lauren D. Amendolara, *Knocking Out Knock-Offs: Effectuating the Criminalization of Trafficking in Counterfeit Goods*, 15 FORDHAM INTELL. PROP. MEDIA & ENT. L.J. 789, 794–95 (2005).

[60] The Trademark Counterfeiting Act of 1984, Pub. L. No. 98–473, 98 Stat. 2178–83 (1984) (codified as amended at 18 U.S.C.A. § 2320).

[61] *Id.* § 1502(a). "Traffic" means to transport, transfer, or otherwise dispose of, to another, for purposes of commercial advantage or private financial gain, or to make, import, export, obtain control of, or possess, with intent to so transport, transfer, or otherwise dispose of. *See* 18 U.S.C. § 2320(f)(5).

[62] Knowledge refers to actual knowledge that the goods or services are counterfeit. *See* S. REP. NO. 98–526, at 11–12 (1984); Michael Coblenz, *Intellectual Property Crimes*, 9 ALB. L.J. SCI. & TECH. 235, 277 (1999).

[63] 15 U.S.C. § 1114(1) (1984).

[64] Amendolara, *supra* note 59, at 796.

[65] *See* Violent Crime Control and Law Enforcement Act of 1994, Pub. L. No. 103–322, § 320104 (a), 108 Stat. 1796 (1994). The Act increased the penalties from a maximum fine of $250,000 or imprisoned not more than five years to $2,000,000 or imprisoned not more than 10 years, while for a first offense of a person other than an individual, the Act increased the maximum fine from $1,000,000 to $5,000,000. In cases of a second or subsequent offense, the Act increased

and added trademark counterfeiting to the list of specified unlawful activities under the money laundering statute.[66] Much like the earlier addition of copyright infringement into the Anti-Drug Abuse Act of 1988,[67] classification of criminal trademark as a specified unlawful activity is important due to the relatively steep sanctions that now could be imposed: a convicted trademark infringer is liable to a $500,000 fine or twice the value of the work involved in the transaction (whichever is greater) or imprisonment of up to 20 years or both.[68]

In 1996, Congress increased penalties for criminal violations of trademark rights by enacting the Anticounterfeiting Consumer Protection Act,[69] which made trademark counterfeiting a predicate offense to racketeering under the RICO Act.[70] RICO violations raised fines to twice the gross profits or other proceeds of the illegal activity.[71] In addition, it allows the seizure of counterfeit goods and of any "personal and real estate assets connected with the criminal enterprise."[72]

In 2006, Congress closed a loophole in the interpretation of the Trademark Counterfeiting Act,[73] by enacting Stop Counterfeiting in Manufactured Goods Act.[74] The Act prohibited the intentional or attempted trafficking of counterfeit "labels, patches, stickers, wrappers, badges, emblems, medallions, charms, boxes, containers, cans, cases, hangtags, documentations, or packaging of any type or nature," even in those cases these marks are separate from the goods.[75] Congress expanded the definition of "trafficking" to include the import or export of

penalties from a maximum fine of $1,000,000 or imprisoned not more than fifteen years to $5,000,000 or imprisoned not more than 20 years, while for a second or subsequent offense of a person other than an individual, the Act increased the maximum fine from $5,000,000 to $15,000,000.

[66] Violent Crime Control and Law Enforcement Act of 1994 § 320104(b) (amending 18 U.S.C. § 1956(c)(7)(D) (1994)). *See* Manta, *supra* note 1, at 487; Coenen Jr., Greenberg & Reisinger, *supra* note 36, at 870.

[67] Anti-Drug Abuse Act of 1988, Pub. L. No. 100–690, § 6466, 102 Stat. 4181 (1988).

[68] In addition to a civil penalty of not more than $10,000 or the value of the funds involved in the transaction, whichever is greater. *See* 18 U.S.C. § 1956 (1994).

[69] Anticounterfeiting Consumer Protection Act, Pub. L. No. 104–153, § 3, 110 Stat. 1386 (1996); Goldstone & Toren, *supra* note 59, at 6.

[70] 18 U.S.C. § 1961 (1996). In an effort to fight organized crime in the United States, RICO was enacted as title IX of the Organized Crime Control Act, Pub. L. No. 91–452, 84 Stat. 941 (1970). For an overview of criminal trademark provisions in the United States until 1998, see Goldstone & Toren, *supra* note 59.

[71] 18 U.S.C.A § 1963(a) (1996); Coenen Jr., Greenberg & Reisinger, *supra* note 36, at 870.

[72] Coenen Jr., Greenberg & Reisinger, *supra* note 36, at 870–71.

[73] After the passage of the Trademark Counterfeiting Act, United States courts interpreted "goods" in various ways, creating a loophole as people trafficked labels and component parts to circumvent the Act, instead of the whole good. *See, e.g., id.* at 867; United States v. Giles, 213 F.3d 1247 (10th Cir. 2000); Manta, *supra* note 1, at 486.

[74] Stop Counterfeiting in Manufactured Goods Act, Pub. L. No. 109–181, 120 Stat. 285 (2006) (codified as amended at 18 U.S.C. § 2320).

[75] 18 U.S.C.A. § 2320 (a).

counterfeit goods or distribution of counterfeit goods for commercial advantage or private financial gain.[76]

In 2008, Congress enacted the Prioritizing Resources and Organization for Intellectual Property Act of 2008, amending the Trademark Counterfeiting Act.[77] The Act created a new position, Intellectual Property Enforcement Coordinator, to serve within the Executive Office of the President.[78] Moreover, the Act expanded treble damages liability to suppliers of goods or services to counterfeiters with the intent to provide assistance.[79] In addition, the Act doubled compensation for infringement,[80] and prohibited transshipment through and the export from the United States of trademark infringing goods.[81] It should be noted that section 2320 was amended a few times since 2008, but these amendments are less relevant for the purpose of the discussion here, as they mainly relate to counterfeit drug and counterfeit military goods and services.

3 Trademark vs. Copyright Criminalization

Surveying the trademark criminalization process reveals that although it is considered one of the branches of IP law, it is treated differently. As a general argument, the trademark criminalization process is shorter than the copyright criminalization one and has a narrower scope. In both the United Kingdom and United States, copyright criminalization began in the nineteenth century, much earlier than trademark criminalization, which first appeared as late as the twentieth century. As a matter of *legislative acts*, copyright was criminalized in no less than twelve separate acts in the United Kingdom, compared with only three acts for trademark criminalization,[82] and fifteen different acts in the United States compared to five acts for trademark criminalization. Finally, copyright criminalization in both the United Kingdom and United States is wider in *scope*, i.e., criminal trademark

---

[76] *Id.* § 2320 (e)(2) (as part of the Protecting American Goods and Services Act of 2005, Pub. L. No. 109–181, § 2, 120 Stat. 285 (2005)). "Financial gains" are defined to include "receipt or expected receipt" of anything of value." (18 U.S.C.A § 2320(e)(3)). *See* Coenen Jr., Greenberg & Reisinger, *supra* note 36, at 867; Manta, *supra* note 1, at 486.

[77] Prioritizing Resources and Organization for Intellectual Property Act of 2008, Pub. L. No. 110–403, 122 Stat. 4256 (2008). For a brief overview of the PRO-IP criminal amendments to the Trademark Counterfeiting Act, see Coenen Jr., Greenberg & Reisinger, *supra* note 36, at 868.

[78] 15 U.S.C. § 8111.

[79] *Id.* § 1117.

[80] *Id.* § 1117(c).

[81] 18 U.S.C. § 2320(h).

[82] Acknowledging that prior to the Copyright Act, 1911 (1 & 2 Geo. V, c. 46 (U.K.)), copyright protection was scattered in various acts, criminal copyright only occurred twice (Fine Arts Copyright Act, 1862, 25 & 26 Vict., c. 68 (U.K.); Musical Copyright Act of 1906, 6 Edw. VII, c. 36 (U.K.)). Thus, even after the unified copyright law in 1911, parliament criminalized copyright in no less than 9 separate acts compared with only three acts for trademark criminalization.

infringement is limited to counterfeiting and does not cover many civil trademark infringements. For example, it does not cover those instances that the question of infringement is close in meaningful ways; whether or not the infringement is willful; or when the mark does not cause confusion with the registered mark; and dilution.[83]

There are some similarities between the two criminalization processes. In both cases, one of the main reasons to criminalize is the need for deterrence due to possible financial loss of the right holder. Thus, the criminalization could be a means to achieve deterrence from infringing their IP rights. In addition, much like many copyright infringement, trademark trafficking is many times done in small, local operations with no formal organization and are hard to detect.[84] Thus, justification for both criminalization processes include imposing criminal sanctions to deter illegal actions that in many cases are hard to detect.[85] The political reasons are also quite similar in each case, beyond the broader sense of political reasons of the legal framework reasoning. As evident in the 1984 addition of criminal sanctions to trademark law in the United States and in Chapter 3, discussing the political influences on criminal copyright legislation, interest groups played an important role in both criminalization processes.

Yet, the processes are also distinct from one another. The main difference is that while copyright and trademark are both types of IP, they possess fundamental internal differences, which affect the criminalization decision.[86] To name a few of these differences, trademarks are part of a separate legal framework[87]; trademarks also have characteristics of private goods, in the economic sense, whereas copyright has characteristics of public goods[88]; unlike copyright, trademark law is not concerned with dissemination of knowledge, but rather information, and does not enrich the public domain[89]; trademark protection is (potentially) longer than

---

[83] For these arguments, see Manta, *supra* note 1, at 487.

[84] *See* Lucas G. Paglia & Mark A. Rush, *End Game: The Ex-Parte Seizure Process and the Battle against Bootleggers*, 4 VAND. J. ENT. L. & PRAC. 4, 5 (2002); Amendolara, *supra* note 59, at 795.

[85] Amendolara, *supra* note 59, at 795.

[86] *See, e.g.*, David W. Barnes, *A New Economics of Trademarks*, 5 NW. J. TECH. & INTELL. PROP. 22, 22 (2006); Sonya Katyal, *Trademark Intersectionality*, 57 UCLA L. REV. 1601, 1613 (2010).

[87] For example, in the United States, trademark law originated from the Commerce Clause, and is not governed by the Copyright (and Patent) Clause. *See* Trade-Mark Cases, *supra* note 52, at 82, 93–94 (1879) ("[a]ny attempt, however, to identify the essential characteristics of a trademark with inventions and discoveries in the arts and sciences, or with the writings of authors, will show that the effort is surrounded with insurmountable difficulties").

[88] William M. Landes & Richard A. Posner, *The Economics of Trademark Law*, 78 TRADEMARK REP. 267, 276 (1988); Mark A. Lemley, *Ex Ante Versus Ex Post Justifications for Intellectual Property*, 71 U. CHI. L. REV. 129, 143 (2004). *But see* David W. Barnes, *Trademark Externalities*, 10 YALE J.L. & TECH. 1, 6 (2007); Glynn S. Lunney, Jr., *Trademark Monopolies*, 48 EMORY L.J. 367, 463 (1999); Katyal, *supra* note 86, at 1618.

[89] Katyal, *supra* note 86, at 1615.

copyright protection[90]; trademark infringements are usually easier to prove and the law allows fewer defense options than it does for copyright infringement[91]; trademarks are concerned with the marketplace of goods whereas copyright mainly concerns the marketplace of ideas.[92]

Moreover, trademark criminalization could be less justified than copyright criminalization. Under a property approach to copyright, infringement is considered theft. On the one hand, the "thief" steals creativity as well as effort costs invested to make the product unique.[93] On the other hand, in trademarks, the counterfeiter, or thief, utilizes the public's goodwill associated with the product and brand recognition of the trademark owner. The potential financial loss is many times lower than in copyright.[94]

However, in some cases, particularly when concerning public safety, trademark (and patent) criminalization have stronger justifications than copyright criminalization. Health and safety risks are a reasonable basis for criminalizing behavior. For example, counterfeit medicine, infant formula, or car parts can pose a real health or safety risk.[95] According to INTERPOL, counterfeit medicine is a global phenomenon affecting all.[96] The World Health Organization (WHO) estimates that in the developed world, up to 1% of available medicines are counterfeit; globally this percentage rises to 10%. Furthermore, it claims that in some areas of Asia, Africa, and Latin America, counterfeit goods can compromise up to 30% of the market.[97] In addition, other counterfeit goods can also pose a safety risk, e.g., electronics,

---

[90] Although a registered trademark lasts ten years, it can be renewed indefinitely every ten years, as long as the mark is still in use. *See, e.g.*, in the United States, 15 U.S.C.A. §§ 1058(a), 1059(a); Manta, *supra* note 1, at 495.

[91] *See* Robin Fry, *Copyright Infringement and Collective Enforcement*, 24 E.I.P.R. 516, 516 (2002).

[92] *But see* Katyal, *supra* note 86, at 1617.

[93] *See* PAUL R. PARADISE, TRADEMARK COUNTERFEITING: PRODUCT PIRACY, AND THE BILLION DOLLAR THREAT TO THE U.S. ECONOMY 3 (1999).

[94] *Id.*

[95] Reports indicated that in 2004, more than 200 babies died in China after been given counterfeit infant formula with harmful ingredients. *See* Michael Backman, *China's counterfeit culture is quite an education*, THE AGE (Mar. 28, 2007), www.theage.com.au/news/business/chinas-coun terfeit-culture-is-quite-an-education/2007/03/27/1174761469475.html; Nadine Courmandias, *The Criminalisation of Copyright Infringement in Japan and What This Tells Us about Japan and the Japanese*, 17 ASIA PAC. L. REV. 167 (2009); *The Dangers of Counterfeit Medical Products*, INTERPOL, www.interpol.int/Public/PharmaceuticalCrime/dangers.asp (last visited Dec. 1, 2017); Amy M. Bunker, *Deadly Dose: Counterfeit Pharmaceuticals, Intellectual Property and Human Health*, 89 J. PAT. & TRADEMARK OFF. SOC'Y 493 (2007). There is no doubt that an IP owner can also manufacture a good that be proven as a health risk. See, e.g., in Israel, "Remedia's" baby formula, which caused the deaths of three infants and severely debilitated 20 others in 2003, due to the lack in vitamin B1 (Thiamine). *See* Yuval Yoaz, *Remedia execs to be tried for allegedly causing infants' death*, HAARETZ (Sept. 10, 2006, 12:00 AM), www.haaretz .com/news/remedia-execs-to-be-tried-for-allegedly-causing-infants-death-1.196950; moreover, counterfeits are not always inferior to the original product, and do not always harm the consumer, see Peter K. Yu, *Enforcement, Economics and Estimates*, 2 W.I.P.O. J. 1, 12 (2010).

[96] *See The Dangers of Counterfeit Medical Products*, *supra* note 95.

[97] *Id.*

cigarettes, sunglasses, alcohol, batteries, perfumes, and toys, to name a few.[98] While copyright law does not pose a health risk, "pirated" items can also negatively affect consumers. For example, customers do not receive accompanying product documentation, ongoing customer support, or future product updates.[99] Thus, as copyrighted works do not generally possess the ability to risk public safety, justification for copyright criminalization should be lower than the justification for trademark criminalization.

To conclude, much like copyright law, trademark law has also been criminalized, although in a different manner. What is similar in both processes is the need to deter illegal behavior (infringement) to prevent potential revenue loss to the right holder. Moreover, the similarity between some characteristics of copyright and trademark also played a role in their criminalization, e.g., in the role of specific interest groups in the process. Although I have highlighted several possible reasons for criminalizing both laws, the more substantial normative debate on the question – which, if any, criminalization process is justified – extends beyond the purpose of the current chapter. The normative debate as to whether copyright criminalization is justified is discussed in Chapters 8 and 9.

B *Patent Criminalization*

Both the United Kingdom and United States have not criminalized patent infringement, at least not for direct infringements. In the United Kingdom, despite some inventors' demands,[100] patent law is completely devoid of criminal liability. Whether or not the United Kingdom and United States will criminalize patent law in the future is yet to be seen, but criminalization is likely as many other countries have criminalized patent infringement.[101]

Simply to exemplify, Japan provides criminal patent provisions, such as a five-year imprisonment with labor or up to ¥5,000,000 fine, for an infringement of a patent right or an exclusive license.[102] In Norway, intentional or accessory infringement of

---

[98] See *The Dangers of Fakes*, THE ANTI-COUNTERFEITING GRP., www.a-cg.org/guest/pdf/ Dangers_of_Fakes08.pdf (last visited Dec. 1, 2017); Ryan Rufo, *Below the Surface of the ACTA: The Dangers that Justify New Criminal Sanctions against Intellectual Property Infringement*, 39 AIPLA Q.J. 511, 522–23 (2011).

[99] See Courmandias, *supra* note 95, at 172.

[100] For example, Trevor Baylis, the inventor of the wind-up radio, urged the United Kingdom's business secretary to criminalize the theft of patents, as it should be treated as a white collar crime. See Nick Higham, *Inventor Urges Patent Law Change*, BBC NEWS (Sept. 2, 2009), http://news.bbc.co.uk/2/hi/uk_news/8232130.stm.

[101] For more on worldwide criminal patent provisions, e.g., Japan, Brazil and Thailand, see Noel Mendez, *Patent Infringers, Come Out with Your Hands Up!: Should the United States Criminalize Patent Infringement?*, 6 BUFF. INTELL. PROP. L.J. 34, 63–64 (2008).

[102] Patent Law, No. 116, § 196 (1994) (Japan), *translated in* WORLD INTELLECTUAL PROPERTY ORGANIZATION, DATABASE OF INTELLECTUAL PROPERTY LEGISLATIVE TEXTS, *available at* www.wipo.int/clea/docs_new/pdf/en/jp/jp006en.pdf).

the exclusive patent right is penalized by fine or imprisonment for a term not exceeding three month.[103] In Denmark, intentional patent infringement is penalized by fine or imprisonment up to one and a half years, and can amount to a heavier punishment in aggravating circumstances under the Danish Penal Code.[104] In Germany, patent infringement is penalized by fine or imprisonment for a term not exceeding three years, and in case the perpetrator acts professionally, the penalty is imprisonment for up to five years or a fine.[105] In France, knowingly infringing a patent is liable to a three-year imprisonment and a fine of €300,000; and when committed by an organized crime group, or when the acts are committed on goods dangerous for the health or security of humans and animals, the penalties will be increased to a five-year imprisonment and a fine of €500,000.[106] In Austria, a patent infringer is liable to be fined for up to 360 times the "per diem rate," and a commercial infringement is liable to detention for up to two years.[107]

1 United Kingdom Patent Criminalization

United Kingdom patent law is almost entirely civil. There are no criminal penalties for the infringement of patents associated with selling, distributing, and importing products.[108] However, there are a number of criminal offenses related to patents. First, is the filing or the causing to file a false entry in the patent registry.[109] The maximum penalty on indictment is imprisonment for two years and/or a fine. On summary conviction, the maximum penalty is a fine of up to the prescribed maximum. Second, is the false representation that anything disposed of for value is a patented product.[110] The penalty for such offense, only triable summarily, is a fine. Third, is the false representation that a patent has been applied for in respect of any article disposed of for value, or if the patent application has been withdrawn or refused.[111] Here too, penalty for such offense, only triable summarily, is a fine. Fourth, is the use of "Patent Office" to describe a place of business or on any document to suggest a relationship with the Patent Registry, which is an offense –

---

[103] Act No. 9 of December 15, 1967 on Patents § 57 (The Norwegian Patents Act)); an unofficial translation of the Norwegian Patents Act is available at www.patentstyret.no/en/For-Experts/Patents-Expert/Legal-texts/The-Norwegian-Patents-Act.

[104] Danish Patent Act Art. 57.

[105] Para. 142(2) Patentgesetz (The German Patent Act).

[106] Article L. 615–14 IPC. In addition, in the event of repetition or if the offender is or has been contractually bound to the aggrieved party, the penalties involved shall be doubled (Article L. 615–14-1 IPC).

[107] Austrian Patent Act, art. 159 (English translation is available at www.patentamt.at/Media/PatG_englisch.pdf).

[108] *See generally*, DAVID I. BAINBRIDGE, INTELLECTUAL PROPERTY 498–99 (7th ed. 2009).

[109] Patents Act 1977, c. 37, § 109 (U.K.); BAINBRIDGE, *supra* note 108, at 498.

[110] Patents Act 1977 § 110; BAINBRIDGE, *supra* note 108, at 498.

[111] Patents Act 1977 § 111; BAINBRIDGE, *supra* note 108, at 498.

and, if convicted, the offending party is liable on summary conviction to a fine.[112] Appropriate officers, i.e., directors, managers, secretaries or other similar officers, or any person purporting to act in such a capacity, which consents to or connives in the commission of any offense under the Act is also guilty of the relevant offense.[113] Fifth, is falsely representing a patent agent, conducting business under a name or description containing the words "patent agent" or "patent attorney," or if in the course of business, one describes oneself or permits oneself to be described as a "patent agent" or "patent attorney."[114] Here the maximum penalty is a fine.

Thus, although there are several criminal offenses associated with patent infringement, generally, the core of patent law is not criminal and has not undergone a criminalization process. Therefore, copyright and patent legislation in the United Kingdom differ in this respect.

2 United States Patent Criminalization

United States patent law is mostly civil, and contains only two criminal provisions, which are both of relatively modest importance and do not criminalize direct patent infringement.[115] The first prohibits anyone who falsely makes, forges, counterfeits, or alters any letters patent, or anyone who passes, utters, publishes, or attempts to pass, utter, or publish as genuine, any such letters patent, knowing the same to be forged, counterfeited, or falsely altered.[116] This offense is punishable by a fine or imprisonment of up to ten years, or both.[117] The second provision prohibits the intentional false marking of a patent and is punishable by a fine of up to \$500 for each offense.[118]

However, no criminal provisions of "regular" patent infringement exist, leaving patent law in the United States mostly civil. Thus far, patent law has not undergone a criminalization process, neither through legislation nor litigation.[119]

3 Patent vs. Copyright Criminalization

There are several possible explanations why patent law has not been criminalized, whereas copyright law has, and the distinctions between these different forms could play a role in criminalization. In order to understand the reasons for the differential

---

[112] Patents Act 1977 § 112; BAINBRIDGE, *supra* note 108, at 498.

[113] Patents Act 1977 § 113(1); BAINBRIDGE, *supra* note 108, at 498.

[114] Copyright, Designs and Patents Act 1988, c. 48, § 276 (U.K.); BAINBRIDGE, *supra* note 108, at 499.

[115] *See generally*, BAINBRIDGE, *supra* note 108, at 498–99; Mendez, *supra* note 101; Manta, *supra* note 1, at 488.

[116] 18 U.S.C. § 497.

[117] *Id.*

[118] 35 U.S.C. § 292.

[119] *See generally*, Manta, *supra* note 1, at 488.

legal treatment, it is important to inquire as to the benefits of criminalizing patent infringements.

First, unlike most copyright infringements, patent litigation is much more complex, expensive, uncertain, and lays a heavy burden plus risks of invalidation on patent owners.[120] Thus, criminal prosecutions of patent infringements could reduce litigation costs for patent owners, therefore reducing losses.[121] In addition, patent criminalization could deter patent infringers from infringing again, and in this matter reduce patent infringement. In both cases, criminal patents could be justified as a means to incentivize the creation and investment in patents.[122]

Second, the current status of patent infringers, which is presently only a civil wrong, differentiates between the public's perception of patent infringement from copyright and trademark infringements, as the lesser evil.[123] Thus, although usually harder to commit and requiring more financial resources and expertise, patent infringement could have more appeal than copyright and trademark infringements.

Third, patents are protected for a much shorter period than copyright works. Therefore, it may be more justifiable to impose criminal sanctions in patent law, where the incentive to invent could be reduced more substantially than copyright or trademark protection.[124]

Fourth, under one approach, copyright and patent law should both be treated equally as property. As such, the infringement of each should be considered theft: the thief steals the invention, creativity, and associated creation costs that make the invention unique.[125] Thus, legislators should grant patent owners a higher level of

---

[120] For example, the American IP Law Association reported in 2003 that the median patent discovery and litigation costs are $2.5 million and $4 million respectively in the case of litigations involving claimed damages in excess of $25 million. *See* AM. INTELLECTUAL PROPERTY LAW ASS'N, REPORT OF THE ECONOMIC SURVEY 22 (2003)); Jonathan M. Barnett, *Property as Process: How Innovation Markets Select Innovation Regimes*, 119 YALE L.J. 384, 397 (2009); James Bessen & Michael J. Meurer, *Lessons for Patent Policy from Empirical Research on Patent Litigation*, 9 LEWIS & CLARK L. REV. 1, 2 (2005). For a study on patent invalidation through litigation, see John R. Allison & Mark A. Lemley, *Empirical Evidence on the Validity of Litigated Patents*, 26 AIPLA Q.J. 185, 205 (1998).

[121] *See* Manta, *supra* note 1, at 493–94. However, criminal prosecutions of patent infringements would shift the litigation costs to the State, which might lack sufficient knowledge on the patent and its validity.

[122] *Id.* at 493–94.

[123] *Id.*

[124] Patent protection usually expires after twenty years from the filing date for utility patents and fourteen years from issue date for design patents. *See, e.g.*, in the United States, 35 U.S.C. § 154 (a)(2); 35 U.S.C. § 173. On the other hand, copyright protection will in most cases be much longer, i.e., it usually expires after the life of the author plus seventy years. *See, e.g.*, in the United States, 17 U.S.C. § 302(a). Manta, *supra* note 1, at 494.

[125] *See* Nigel Stirk, *Intellectual Property and the Role of Manufacturers: Definitions from the Late Eighteenth Century*, 27 J. HIST. GEOGRAPHY 475, 478 (2001); Manta, *supra* note 1, at 470–71; PARADISE, *supra* note 93, at 3.

protection for their product, as they usually invest more time and money in the procedural process and on the inventions than do rights holders.[126]

Fifth, as previously discussed, public safety concerns are relevant to both patent and trademark infringements. For instance, counterfeit medicine, infant formula, and car parts can pose real health and safety risks, even if we simply account for potential manufacture error.[127] Thus, as most copyrighted materials do not generally have the potential to harm public safety, it may be less justified to impose criminal sanctions on copyright than on trademark and patent laws.

However, setting a criminal bar for patent infringements has many intricacies.[128] While in copyright law, individuals commit most infringements, and criminal sanctions could deter their actions, most patent infringements are committed by companies that are less likely deterred by criminal sanctions.[129] With that, individuals are less rational than companies and, in this manner, criminal sanctions could deter infringing activities by companies. In addition, as *Kent Walker* argues, due to the arcane nature of the patent prosecution process, criminal intent is more difficult to prove in patent infringement than in copyright infringement.[130] Also, patent infringement could be incidental, as opposed to copyright infringement, because many inventors may not be aware that they are infringing upon a right.[131] Hence, criminal patent infringement must require a higher level of willfulness than copyright law, which is more complex in the patent context and could be problematic in prosecution.[132] Moreover, the possibly chilling effect on patent inventiveness due to over-deterrence could be more harmful to society, at least to some extent. Whereas in copyright, the possible ramifications of over-deterrence could give some creators pause, which will of course deprive society, over-deterrence in inventions could limit and block important inventions in life-saving medicine and quality-of-life technologies.[133] Generally speaking, as important as free speech is, I believe that

---

[126] Copyright has less formal requirements to receive protection, and is less expensive to register – where such registration is required. The estimated application costs for a patent varies. However, generally speaking, the estimated application costs for a patent is estimated between $10,000 to $30,000 per patent, while copyright registration of a basic claim in an original work of authorship, costs in the United States $35, and trademark registration will usually cost between $275 and $375 (www.uspto.gov/inventors/trademarks.jsp). *See* Manta, *supra* note 1, at 495; Mark A. Lemley, *Rational Ignorance at the Patent Office*, 95 Nw. U. L. Rev. 1495, 1498 (2001); Fees, U.S. Copyright Off., www.copyright.gov/docs/fees.html (last visited Dec. 1, 2017); *Trademarks*, U.S. Patent and Trademark Off., www.uspto.gov/inventors/trademarks .jsp (last visited Dec. 1, 2017).

[127] *See supra* note 95.

[128] For a general review of patent vs. "soft IP" criminalization, see Manta, *supra* note 1, at 495–99.

[129] *Id.* at 504; John R. Allison & Mark A. Lemley, *Who's Patenting What? An Empirical Exploration of Patent Prosecution*, 53 Vand. L. Rev. 2099, 2117 (2000).

[130] For this argument, *see* Kent Walker, *Federal Remedies for the Theft of Intellectual Property*, 16 Hastings Comm. & Ent. L.J. 681, 686–87 (1994).

[131] *See* Manta, *supra* note 1, at 495.

[132] *Id.* at 495–96.

[133] *Id.* at 498–99.

life-saving medicine has greater significance on society. Finally, copyright claimants face more hurdles in proving infringement than do claimants in patents infringement, because copyright law allows for more exemptions and requires additional elements of proof.[134]

These considerations are only some reasons for the differences in the criminalization of patent and copyright law.[135] I submit that the main difference between copyright and patent law criminalization is the distinct nature of infringement, its scope, and the perceived need to increase deterrence, rather than existing procedural obstacles that each hold. On the one hand, patent infringements are rarer than copyright infringements, more detectable by rights holders, and usually require some sort of expertise and financial resources. On the other hand, copyright infringement, especially in the digital age, is usually more affordable, accessible, and easier, sometimes even with lower risks of detection. Thus, rights holders in copyright-related industries are more concerned about copyright infringements than rights holders in patent-related industries, and thus the political influence on criminal copyright is greater.

Even if copyright law criminalization is more justifiable than patent criminalization,[136] it does not suggest that it is justified. However, the non-criminal nature of patent law, in comparison to copyright criminalization, is valuable in understanding criminal copyright, since it reveals that internal considerations are generally more relevant to criminalization than are external ones. As Chapter 5 shows, copyright criminalization is driven by three main considerations: copyright infringements, copyright propertization, and political power. However, patent law is not equally affected by these reasons. First, patent infringement was affected less by technological developments,[137] which were partially responsible for the increase of copyright infringements (combined with a pro-infringement social norm/lack of a moral norm against infringement, globalization, and accessibility). Second, patent law did not transform from a limited set of exclusive rights granted for purposes of market regulation regime into a property regime – as did copyright. And third, patent holders seem less involved in lobbying for legislative changes than rights holders. For all three reasons, patent law is currently excluded from the legal framework of criminalization and accordingly from the IP framework, as the external reasons for criminalization, namely political considerations, are insufficient on their own to cause criminalization. However, although patent law has not yet begun a criminalization process in both the United Kingdom and the United States, as has copyright

---

[134] *See* Fry, *supra* note 91, at 516.
[135] For more reasons, see Manta, *supra* note 1, at 492–505.
[136] The evaluation of patent criminalization is beyond the scope of this book. For such evaluation, see *id.*
[137] *Id.* at 501.

and trademark, this is not a claim that it will not happen in the future and eventually be part of the legal and IP frameworks.[138]

To conclude, unlike copyright and trademark, patent law has not yet been criminalized in the United Kingdom and the United States. Thus, the IP framework is mostly composed of trademark and copyright. The IP framework, which is a part of the general legal framework, does provide a narrower set of reasons to criminalize it, other than political. In other words, examination of any criminalization process should encompass a narrower framework than the general one, when it is possible to locate, understand, and analyze it, as it could further advance the analysis of the process. In this part, I have chosen the IP framework as a pre-determined legal field that copyright is a part of. However, since this choice does not always exist, other similar frameworks could be examined (such as the technological framework in copyright criminalization).

CONCLUSION

Criminalization processes occur in many fields of law. Each process possesses a unique set of reasons, which are internally linked to the criminalized law under review. However, there are some external measures that are also at play and are part of the legal framework of criminalization. Specifically, in copyright criminalization, there are two main frameworks: first, the *IP framework*, which locates copyright criminalization in a wider framework of IP law; and second, the *technological framework*, which locates copyright criminalization within other legal fields that are criminalized due to similar technological developments. The application of these frameworks, along with the internal reasons in Chapter 5, are important to the criminal copyright analysis, as they shed light on the process. The importance of the six (mostly descriptive) chapters of this book to the normative debate on whether copyright law should be criminalized, and if so to what extent, is discussed further in Chapters 7 and 8, which examine copyright criminalization from the normative viewpoint of criminal and copyright theories.

---

[138] There are few indicators for a possible future patent criminalization process, such as discussions and compromises in international treaties and agreements, that could bind the United States and the United Kingdom criminalize patent law. *See id.* at 492.

7

The Copyright–Criminal Integration

INTRODUCTION

Copyright criminalization affects both criminal and copyright law. When policy-makers criminalize copyright infringement, they reshape both fields to include new offenses.[1] Thus, in order to avoid over criminalization of copyright law, we need to figure out whether such regulation aligns with both criminal and copyright law theories. But even before such an examination can take place, we need to undertake a descriptive analysis of current criminal and copyright frameworks. The current chapter argues that copyright criminalization should be examined *via* a structured principled approach, which integrates perspectives from both criminal and copyright theories. While few criminalization theories exist, they are inconsistent and also are insufficient to examine copyright criminalization in some legal systems, as they do not account for various perceptions of criminal law theories. Therefore, this chapter suggests an integrated approach toward copyright criminalization, while differentiating between the main approaches to criminal law. Understanding the various approaches to both criminal and copyright laws, will set the groundwork for a thorough evaluation of the criminalization of copyright infringement, a task I partake in Chapter 8.

Justification for imposing criminal sanctions should rely on a principled crimin-alization theory, which also takes into account the underlying theories of criminal law and of the particular legal field. Reviewing the academic literature determining which conduct should be regulated by criminal law (rather than administrative or civil laws) reveals that the criminalization theories used are diverse and inconsist-ent.[2] Only in recent years, have we witnessed the emergence of a more substantive

[1] However, during my analysis in Chapters 2 and 3, and for the purpose of this book, I have also included an increase in penalties for old offenses.
[2] *See, e.g.*, Paul H. Robinson & John M. Darley, *The Utility of Desert*, 91 Nw. U. L. Rev. 453, 454 (1997).

academic discussion on criminalization. The fundamental question underlying these theories is which conduct should be criminal? Theories have either focused on the notion of potential or actual *harm* to individuals and to society, and/or whether the conduct is inherently immoral and should be criminalized due to its *wrongful nature*. Another approach, advocated by a few legal systems, which primarily emphasizes the protection of social values, suggests that criminalizing behavior should mostly rely on identifying an important *protected social interest/value*, which could justify the reason why a particular conduct should be prohibited by criminal law.[3] Few theories further analyzed the question of criminalization by locating the state interest in criminalizing conduct and examined whether the state interest is substantial and legitimate. Some theories examined the efficiency of criminal sanctions in achieving the substantial and legitimate state interest; and whether criminal law is the most efficient mechanism to regulate the conduct. Other scholars suggested using law and economics theories in criminalization. Finally, some scholars suggested examining the consequences of criminalization.

I suggest that current criminalization theories do not directly take into account the various approaches to criminal and copyright law that hold great importance in the outcome of criminalization. In order to implement criminal theory in copyright, we first need to examine copyright law theories. Various copyright law theories would approach criminalization in a different manner. The difference between the notions of criminalization is based on the various accounts of copyright law theories, and how they perceive copyright. Within the European continent, copyright is usually perceived as having roots in natural law and natural rights, while in Anglo-American jurisdictions the basis for copyright protection is mostly utilitarian.[4] More closely, there are four main theories that justify copyright protection on different grounds: *Incentive/Utilitarian* theory, *Personality* theory, *Labor-Desert* theory, and *Users' Rights* theory. Thus, as copyright law is justified on different grounds, criminalization could be supported by distinct views that could lead to unique determinations of the criminalization question.

Hence, due to the inconsistency in criminalization theories and their overlooking of criminal approaches, this chapter provides a structured principled approach to examine copyright criminalization from an integrated criminal and copyright theory perspective. I begin by examining the main theoretical frameworks of criminalization discussed in the literature. First, I examine single-element approaches to

---

[3] For an example of such justification of imposing criminal sanctions, see, e.g., Tatjana Hörnle & Mordechai Kremnitzer, *Human Dignity as a Protected Interest in Criminal Law*, 44 Isr. L. Rev 143 (2011); Mordechai Kremnitzer & Khalid Ghanayim, *Proportionality and the Aggressor's Culpability in Self-Defense*, 39 Tulsa L. Rev. 875, 879 (2003).

[4] *See* Wendy J. Gordon, *Intellectual Property*, in The Oxford Handbook of Legal Studies 617, 623–24 (Peter Can & Mark Tushnet eds., 2003); Geraldine Szott Moohr, *The Crime of Copyright Infringement: An Inquiry Based on Morality, Harm, and Criminal Theory*, 83 B.U. L. Rev. 731, 746–47 (2003).

criminalization, namely, harmfulness and wrongfulness. After concluding that single-element approaches are insufficient to provide an adequate criminalization theory, I turn to evaluate multiple-element approaches, as suggested by Joel Feinberg and further developed by Andrew Simester and Andreas von Hirsch. Then, I review principled criminalization theories based primarily on a *principled* approach to criminalization,[5] formulated by Jonathan Schonsheck and Douglas Husak. By extracting the main elements of the principled criminalization approaches that are relevant to copyright criminalization, I set the ground for the normative evaluation in Chapter 8.

This *integrated approach* to criminalization consists of four main elements, namely, harm and wrongfulness (either examined separately or combined); substantial public interest/protected social interest; efficiency of criminalization; and consequences of criminalization. Arguing that any criminalization theory should be adapted to the criminalized law theories, the chapter turns to explore the main theories of copyright law. I begin by briefly reviewing copyright's main theoretical frameworks. I then offer a general query as to whether these frameworks justify criminal legislation, an evaluation which will be further analyzed in Chapter 8.

I CRIMINALIZATION THEORIES

A crucial step in imposing criminal sanctions from a criminal law perspective first requires understanding the important role criminal law plays and its distinct nature as opposed to that of civil law. While criminal and civil law share some similar rationales, they also possess various differences and usually rely on distinct justifications.[6] Prima facie, criminal punishment is the state's most intrusive means of prohibiting illegal conduct.[7] This general statement is best exemplified using imprisonment (and capital punishment where it exists), as imprisonment means the loss of liberty, and potential

---

[5] The balancing approach, suggests that a legislature that seeks to criminalize an activity of some sort, should weigh all the reasons for criminalizing the particular action and all the reasons against it, while the weightier set of reasons should prevail. The principled approach, favored in Anglo-American legal philosophy, represents an attempt to limit the power of the state to criminalize and thus ensure that they meet some basic standards. *See* JONATHAN SCHONSHECK, ON CRIMINALIZATION 29–38 (1994); NINA PERŠAK, CRIMINALISING HARMFUL CONDUCT: THE HARM PRINCIPLE, ITS LIMITS AND CONTINENTAL COUNTERPARTS 10–12 (2007).

[6] Although Oliver W. Holmes argued that "the general principles of criminal and civil liability are the same," most scholars reject an underlying unity of criminal and tort. *See* OLIVER W. HOLMES, THE COMMON LAW 44 (1881); Jerome Hall, *Interrelations of Criminal Law and Torts*, 43 COLUM. L. REV. 753 (1943). Other utilitarians have suggested that there is no meaningful distinction between tort and crime. *See, e.g.,* JOHN AUSTIN, LECTURES ON JURISPRUDENCE 416, 517 (4th ed. 1879). For more on key-distinctions between criminal and civil law, see Jason M. Solomon, *What Is Civil Justice*, 44 LOY. L.A. L. REV. 317 (2010); Moohr, *supra* note 4, at 747.

[7] Nils Jareborg, *Criminalization as Last Resort (Ultima Ratio)*, 2 OHIO ST. J. CRIM. L. 521, 526 (2005).

stigmatization and humiliation.[8] Under some approaches to criminal law, when deciding to regulate conduct, the state should only resort to criminalization as an *ultima ratio* – a last resort. However, regulating some conduct could also be justified even when other measures, e.g., civil or administrative law, prove to be more efficient measures to regulate particular, immoral activities.

Perhaps surprisingly, the goal of criminal law is disputable. Criminal punishment is usually justified on grounds of incapacitation, desert/retribution, deterrence, rehabilitation, and/or restorative justice.[9] Academic literature on the scope of criminal punishments mainly focuses on two approaches. The *retributivism* approach views criminal law through its system of sanctions.[10] Under this approach, criminal law is a distinct body of law that is motivated by concern for the imposition of sanctions as punishments. Punishments used in other fields of law are usually considered incidental. In other words, the *retributivism* approach views criminal law as a tool to punish people for culpable misconduct.[11] A second *utilitarian/regulatory* approach does not refer to the punishing act itself, but rather views criminal law as an additional state regulatory tool that exists to deter misconduct otherwise not deterred by other sanctions.[12] The retributivist and utilitarian approaches represent two distinct views of criminal law's aims. Without answering the question, which view is more persuasive, both do not explain the complexity of the criminalization process and do not provide a structured theory of criminalization. Therefore, over time, additional criminalization approaches have emerged, which usually vary with the Anglo-American and Continental legal systems on opposing sides. The distinctive element between these theories is usually their reliance on either the *harmfulness* or *wrongfulness* elements of a conduct, the possibility of using economic analysis of crime, and the number of elements that are required for criminalization.

A *Single-Element Criminalization Approaches*

Until recently, a discussion on the principles of criminalization was almost non-existent.[13] Prior to 1994, the few scholars who had addressed the process of criminalization regarded it mostly as a single-element approach, meaning that criminalization requires the fulfillment of a single element. These theories relied on either *harmfulness*

---

[8] *Id.*; Dan Markel, *How Should Punitive Damages Work?*, 157 U. PA. L. REV. 1383, 1429 (2009).

[9] *See* ANDREW ASHWORTH, SENTENCING AND CRIMINAL JUSTICE 77–91 (2010); GEORGE P. FLETCHER, RETHINKING CRIMINAL LAW 409 (2010); Paul H. Robinson, *Criminalization Tensions: Empirical Desert, Changing Norms, and Rape Reform*, in THE STRUCTURES OF THE CRIMINAL LAW 186, 187 (Antony Duff et al. eds., 2010).

[10] For a full explanation of the nature of criminalization, see ANDREW SIMESTER & ANDREAS VON HIRSCH, CRIMES, HARMS, AND WRONGS: ON THE PRINCIPLES OF CRIMINALISATION 3–5 (2011).

[11] *Id.* at 3–4; Andrew Simester, *Enforcing Morality*, in THE ROUTLEDGE COMPANION TO PHILOSOPHY OF LAW 481, 483 (Andrei Marmor ed., 2012).

[12] SIMESTER & VON HIRSCH, *supra* note 10, at 4; Richard A. Posner, *An Economic Theory of the Criminal Law*, 85 COLUM. L. REV. 1193 (1985).

[13] *See, e.g.*, Kimberly Kessler Ferzan, *Prevention, Wrongdoing, and the Harm Principle's Breaking Point*, 10 OHIO ST. J. CRIM. L. 679, 679 (2013).

or *wrongfulness* elements of a conduct to criminalize behavior, but without formulating a theory of criminalization.[14] In other words, the decision to criminalize a conduct relied solely on two elements: first, as generally favored in Anglo-American legal systems, criminalization prevents harm to others and is thus justified, and second, as favored in Continental legal theories, criminalization is justified when conduct is morally wrongful. These two single-element approaches, have created a lively debate over the years within the political theory of criminalization.[15] However, since 1994, and mainly in recent years, scholarly discussion of a normative principled theory of criminalization has increased,[16] and as current literature reveals, these two elements do not provide a complete, adequate theoretical basis for criminalization that properly answers the question as to which conduct should be criminalized

For purposes of examining copyright criminalization through a structured principled theory, it is first important to understand the general outlines of the two different and sometimes incompatible, single-element approaches. Only upon understating the basic elements can we turn to examine the structured theories of criminalization, extract their main components, form an integrated approach to criminalization, and examine copyright criminalization through its lens.

1 Harm Principle

John Stuart Mill first articulated the *harm principle* as the main principle of Anglo-American legal systems to justify criminalization of a conduct (or limiting criminalization).[17] Under a liberal position, the *harm principle* justifies restricting individual liberty when individual conduct causes harm to others in society.[18] In Mill's words:

---

[14] As I further elaborate, Joel Feinberg did offer a multiple element theory of criminalization, but not a principled approach. I discuss the elements of harmfulness, wrongfulness, offense, and legal paternalism throughout this Chapter. *See* Andreas von Hirsch, *Harm and Wrongdoing in Criminalisation Theory*, 12 CRIM. L. & PHIL. 1, 2 (2012).

[15] There is an academic debate as to which of the two principles is more important in criminalizing behavior. For example, H. L. A. Hart advocated the harm principle approach, while Lord Devlin advocated the morality approach. *See* H. L. A. HART, LAW, LIBERTY, AND MORALITY (1963); *Cf.* PATRICK DEVLIN, THE ENFORCEMENT OF MORALS (1965).

[16] A different form of debate on criminalization, which began in the 1960s, focused on the practical realities of criminalizing behavior. This approach to criminalization deals with the variety of costs that the criminal law imposes, e.g., enforcement and privacy costs, in order to decide whether to criminalize a behavior. *See, e.g.,* HERBERT PACKER, THE LIMITS OF THE CRIMINAL SANCTION (1968); NORVAL MORRIS & GORDON HAWKINGS, THE HONEST POLITICIAN'S GUIDE TO CRIME CONTROL (1970); Sanford Kadish, *The Crisis of Overcriminlization*, 374 ANNALS AM. ACAD. POL. & SOC. SCI. 157 (1967). For more on the history of criminalization, see Michael S. Moore, *A Tale of Two Theories*, 28 CRIM. JUST. ETHICS 27 (2009).

[17] For a general explanation of the harm principle in Anglo-American legal systems, see Andrew Simester & Tony Smith, *Criminalization and the Role of Theory, in* HARM AND CULPABILITY 1, 4–6 (Andrew Simester & Tony Smith eds., 1996).

[18] JOHN STUART MILL, ON LIBERTY 8–9 (New York: Penguin 1982) (1859); *See also* JOEL FEINBERG, OFFENSE TO OTHERS (1984); PERŠAK, *supra* note 5, at 13.

The sole end, for which mankind are warranted, individually or collectively, in interfering with the liberty of action of any of their number is self-protection. That the only purpose for which power can be rightfully exercised over any member of a civilised community, against his will, is to prevent harm to others.[19]

Mill's harm principle, although not solely reserved for criminal legislation,[20] is often characterized as a *positive approach* to criminalization,[21] as harmfulness is sufficient in justifying coercive measures in criminal law.[22] Under this approach, criminalizing conduct is legitimate *only* when it is subscribed to prevent harm to others.

The harm principle appeared in a more moderate liberal position after being developed further by Feinberg,[23] who argued thus: "[I]t is always a good reason in support of penal legislation that it would be effective in preventing (eliminating, reducing) harm to persons other than the actor (the one prohibited from acting) and there is no other means that is equally effective at no greater cost to other values."[24] Under Feinberg's version of the harm principle, harm is defined as a "thwarting, setting back, or defeating an interest."[25] In contrast to Mill, harm is not necessarily the *only* reason to criminalize, but rather *a good reason* that can coexist with other principles.[26] Feinberg's harm principle can be characterized as a *negative approach* to criminalization, as preventing harm is an additional reason to favor criminalization, but is not a sufficient reason alone for criminalization.[27]

Following Feinberg, many scholars continued to develop the harm principle.[28] For example, Duff et al., found that the harm principle can be interpreted as providing a negative constraint on criminalization – which should not be justified

---

[19] MILL, *supra* note 18, at 14.
[20] *See* ANTONY DUFF, LINDSAY FARMER, SANDRA E. MARSHALL & VICTOR TADROS, THE TRIAL ON TRIAL, TOWARDS A NORMATIVE THEORY OF THE CRIMINAL TRIAL 16 (2007).
[21] Although Mill's Harm Principle is often characterized as a *positive approach* to criminalization, it can be viewed as both positive and negative. Michael S. Moore argues that the harm principle is positive, in the sense that "it permits the use of the criminal law to prohibit behavior harmful to people other than the actor or those who consent to the behavior," and that the harm principle is negative in the sense that "it forbids the use of the criminal law to prohibit behavior that is merely offensive or that is popularly regarded as immoral, even if such behavior is not harmful to anyone, and it forbids the use of the criminal law to prohibit behavior that harms only the actor himself." For this observation, see Moore, *supra* note 16.
[22] MILL, *supra* note 18; Antony Duff, *Towards a Modest Legal Moralism* at n.3 (2013), *available at* http://link.springer.com/article/10.1007%2Fs11572-012-9191-8#page-1.
[23] Unlike Mill's harm principle, Feinberg's version is characterized as a moderate liberal position as it can coexist with other principles. *See* PERŠAK, *supra* note 5, at 13.
[24] JOEL FEINBERG, THE MORAL LIMITS OF THE CRIMINAL LAW: HARMLESS WRONGDOING xix (1988).
[25] JOEL FEINBERG, THE MORAL LIMITS OF THE CRIMINAL LAW: HARM TO OTHERS 33 (1984).
[26] For this interpretation of Feinberg's harm principle, see PERŠAK, *supra* note 5, at 13.
[27] Duff, *supra* note 22, at n.3; Bernard E. Harcourt, *The Collapse of the Harm Principle*, 90 J. CRIM. L. & CRIMINOLOGY 109, 114 (1999).
[28] *See, e.g.*, JOSEPH RAZ, THE MORALITY OF FREEDOM (1986). Raz accepts the harm principle, but nevertheless supports it by the principle of autonomy, and thus suggests a "autonomy-based harm principle."

unless it prevents harm.[29] However, other scholars have also criticized the harm
principle over the years. For example, James Fitzjames Stephen criticized Mill's
harm principle, by insisting that "criminal law is in the nature of a persecution of the
grosser forms of vice," and that vicious conduct is criminalized and punished "for
the sake of gratifying the feeling of hatred – call it revenge, resentment, or what you
will – which the contemplation of such conduct excites in healthily constituted
minds."[30] Generally, one of the main criticisms against Mill's harm principle is that
Mill mistook harm for wrong.[31] Other scholars have criticized the harm principle as
being too vague.[32] For the purpose of the current focus on copyright, the harm
principle suffices as an important factor in the criminalization process, but is
insufficient on its own to criminalize conduct, as Feinberg acknowledged.

What does constitute harm to fulfill the principle is not easy to answer.[33] Mill did
not offer a clear definition.[34] Feinberg, however, offered some clarifications:[35] One's
interests are distinguishable components of his well-being, which are decided by
examining whether the conduct had "set back an interest is whether that interest is
in a worse condition than it would otherwise have been in had the invasion not
occurred at all."[36] Thus, the harm principle is confined to conduct that damages
another's interests.[37] But what about indirect harm to a person's interests? Should
harm be broadly defined to include indirect damage to another's interests? Under
this category, harm is not limited to damaging a single person, or only to human

[29] For this argument, see DUFF ET AL., *supra* note 20, at 17.
[30] *See* JAMES FITZJAMES STEPHEN, LIBERTY, EQUALITY, FRATERNITY 152 (1874). For more on this
critique, see DUFF ET AL., *supra* note 20, at 17–18. For more criticism on the harm principle,
see. e.g., Arthur Ripstein, *Beyond the Harm Principle*, 34 PHIL. & PUB. AFF. 215 (2006); Hamish
Stewart, *The Limits of the Harm Principle*, 4 CRIM. L. & PHIL. 17 (2010); Cass R. Sunstein,
Legal Interference with Private Preferences, 53 U. CHI. L. REV. 1129, 1131 (1986); Harcourt, *supra*
note 27, at 113; PERŠAK, *supra* note 5, at 14.
[31] *See generally*, RAZ, *supra* note 28; Moore, *supra* note 16, at 28–29.
[32] *See, e.g.*, PERŠAK, *supra* note 5, at 14, 60–61.
[33] There are various propositions for examining harm. For example, Feinberg offered several tools
to examine harm: (1) gravity of the possible harm; (2) the degree of probability; (3) the
magnitude of the risk of harm; and (4) the social value of the conduct to be prohibited. *See*
FEINBERG, *supra* note 25, at 215–16; Cheng Lim Saw, *The Case for Criminalising Primary
Infringements of Copyright–Perspectives from Singapore*, 18 INT'L J.L. INFO. TECH. 95, 105
(2009). In addition, Asaf Harduf offered a taxonomy of criminalization based on the harm
principle. *See* Asaf Harduf, *How Crimes Should Be Created: A Practical Theory of Criminalization*, 49 CRIM. L. BULL. 31 (2013).
[34] SIMESTER & VON HIRSCH, *supra* note 10, at 36.
[35] Feinberg defined harm as a "thwarting, setting back, or defeating of an interest." *See* FEINBERG,
supra note 25, at 33.
[36] Id. at 33–34.
[37] SIMESTER & VON HIRSCH, *supra* note 10, at 338.

beings,[38] but rather also applies to damage caused to society. Hence, it refers to harms that are "public wrongs" – i.e., a breach or violation of the public's interests and as such appropriately concerns the public.[39] I claim that the harm principle should not be limited to direct harms, but also should apply, in some circumstances, to indirect harms that are remote,[40] or secondary reactive harms.[41] Moreover, the harm principle could also encompass Feinberg's *offense principle* to some extent (which I further explain below), as some offensive behavior may contain other forms of harm.[42] Still, the harm principle should refrain from over-broadness, which could easily make it an empty concept.[43] Hence, the harm principle should be limited to objective harmful consequences.[44]

2 Wrongfulness

The second single-element approach to criminalization, often associated with retributivism, is based on legal moralism and relies on wrongfulness as a basis for criminalization.[45] Legal moralism advocates for the criminalization of a morally wrongful conduct, perpetrated with a culpable state of mind due to its wrongfulness.[46] Feinberg had his hand, too, in formulating the principle: "[I]t can be morally legitimate to prohibit conduct on the ground that it is inherently immoral, even

---

[38] The harm principle should also encompass "non-human beings with interests that merit the law's protection," i.e., the public is not only concerned with harm or risk of harm which is inflicted on other people, but also to harm of non-human beings, e.g., animals, to protect the public interest. *See* ANTONY DUFF, ANSWERING FOR CRIME: RESPONSIBILITY AND LIABILITY IN THE CRIMINAL LAW 124 (2007).

[39] For this proposition, see *id.* at 140–46. Feinberg, for example, identifies two types of "harms": harm as a setback to interests, and harm as a wrong to another person. *See* FEINBERG, *supra* note 25, at 31–38; Antony Duff, *Harms and Wrongs*, 5 BUFF. CRIM. L. REV. 13, 17 (2001); Moohr, *supra* note 4, at 752.

[40] For example, incitement to murder. For more on indirect and remote harms, see SIMESTER & VON HIRSCH, *supra* note 10, at 53–88, 346–47.

[41] Secondary reactive harms occur when "people are affected by the prospect, rather than the actuality, if a wrongful action." *See id.* at 47–50.

[42] *See id.* at 92–107.

[43] Harcourt, *supra* note 27, at 113.

[44] *See* DENNIS J. BAKER, THE RIGHT NOT TO BE CRIMINALIZED 8 (2011).

[45] Von Hirsch, *supra* note 14, at 8. It is important to distinguish between two forms of wrongness: prima facie wrongness and wrongness all things considered. Killing someone could be considered a prima facie wrongness in society; however, if it's committed in self-defense, it is not necessarily wrongful all things considered. Thus, applying an approach of wrongness all things considered will examine the wrongfulness in its context. For this example, see Victor Tadros, *Wrongness and Criminalization, in* THE ROUTLEDGE COMPANION TO PHILOSOPHY OF LAW 157, 159 (Andrei Marmor ed., 2012). It is also worth mentioning that wrongfulness can be related or grounded in harm.

[46] *See* DUFF ET AL., *supra* note 20, at 17.

though it causes neither harm nor offense to the actor or to others."[47] These two main approaches in legal moralism theories regarding criminalization, divided into positive and negative approaches:[48] under a *positive legal moralism* approach, "an action can warrant proscription simply on the ground of its moral wrongfulness."[49] However, positive legal moralism theories vary on their approach to criminalization. Some scholars view moral wrongfulness as a constraint on criminalization, i.e., that only morally wrongful conduct can be criminalized, but wrongfulness is insufficient on its own.[50] A stricter approach claims that only a conduct that is morally wrong (independent of criminal law) or wrong because it has been criminalized[51] could be a part of criminal law.[52]

Another view of legal moralism is that criminalization should be reserved solely for *publicly* wrong conduct, i.e., reserved for wrongs concerning the public.[53] Take, for example, tax evasion. Under this view, tax evasion becomes wrong when its objective is to protect the public, and thus in those instances is justifiably criminalized.

The second type of moralistic approach, often characterized as a *negative approach*, views wrongfulness only as an additional reason in favor of criminalization.[54] Thus, wrongfulness is a necessary condition for criminalization but cannot stand on its own. We may not criminalize conduct unless it is wrongful, but wrongdoing is an insufficient element of criminalization.[55] Hence, under the *negative moralist approach*, wrongdoing does not provide any positive reason to criminalize. The negative approach's downfall is that it does not provide criteria for criminalizing conduct; rather, it provides a tool to revoke conduct that should not be criminalized.[56]

In practice, the issue of moral considerations in criminalization is too vague and thus causes conflicts. Similar to the harm principle, morality of conduct should be

---

[47] FEINBERG, *supra* note 24, at 27.

[48] For this distinction, see Duff, *supra* note 22.

[49] *See* Simester, *supra* note 11, at 481.

[50] Tadros, *supra* note 45; *See also* MICHAEL S. MOORE, PLACING BLAME: A THEORY OF THE CRIMINAL LAW 33–35 (1997).

[51] *See generally*, Tadros, *supra* note 45.

[52] Michael Moore offers a similar approach. *See* MOORE, *supra* note 50; Tadros, *supra* note 45, at 157.

[53] For this view, see generally Sandra E. Marshall & Antony Duff, *Criminalization and Sharing Wrongs*, 11 CAN J.L. & JURIS. 7 (1998); Antony Duff & Sandra E. Marshall, *Public and Private Wrongs, in* ESSAYS IN CRIMINAL LAW IN HONOUR OF GERALD GORDON (2010). For a discussion of this view, see Tadros, *supra* note 45, at 159–62; Duff, *supra* note 22, at 6.

[54] *See* Tadros, *supra* note 45, at 157–58; MOORE, *supra* note 50. Antony Duff argues that wrongfulness "is not just a necessary condition of criminalisation, but its proper focus." *See* DUFF, *supra* note 38, at 80.

[55] Duff, *supra* note 22, at 2.

[56] *Id.*

examined objectively.[57] Prima facie, under the general moralist approach to criminalization, *malum prohibitum* offenses, i.e., offenses that are wrong because they are prohibited,[58] are unjustified and should not be criminalized.[59] For example, driving on the other side of the road or tax evasion are not pre-legally wrong, and therefore the state should not criminalize these actions. However, some legal moralists can justify criminalization of some *malum prohibitum* offenses, not pre-legally wrongful, under these approaches, as they argue that conduct become wrong by virtue of their regulation.[60] In other words, when examining a conduct, it does not need to be wrongful independent *of the law as a whole*.[61] Otherwise, only *malum in se* offenses would be criminalized.[62] Thus, conduct such as tax evasion would not be considered criminal. With this in mind, when regulation is crafted to serve society's common good and does not surpass the expected burden imposed on citizens as part of their civic duty, then the conduct (even non-pre-legally) is wrongful in itself.[63]

B Multiple-Elements Criminalization Approaches

Single-element approaches to criminalization posit that criminalization should rely on either harm or wrongfulness. A few scholars have suggested that there are possibly other reasons to criminalize, while sometimes combining both harm and wrongfulness to justify criminalization.[64] Feinberg suggested the first multiple-element approach that advocated four main "liberty-limiting principles" of criminalization and added the *offense principle* and *legal paternalism* as potential liberty-limiting principles to harmfulness and wrongfulness. Andrew Simester and Andreas von Hirsch suggested their Feinbergian version of criminalization, combining the two single-element approaches of harm and wrongfulness to formulate a dual-element approach to criminalization.

---

[57] NICHOLAS RESCHER, OBJECTIVITY: THE OBLIGATIONS OF IMPERSONAL REASON 3 (1997); BAKER, *supra* note 44, at 5.

[58] *See, e.g.,* Tadros, *supra* note 45, at 157.

[59] *Id.* at 157.

[60] *Id.* at 170. *See also* Antony Duff, *Crime, Prohibition and Punishment,* 19 J. APPLIED PHIL. 97 (2002). On the other hand, Douglas Husak argues that *mala prohibita* cannot be justified under this approach. *See* Douglas Husak, *Malum Prohibitum and Retributivism, in* DEFINING CRIMES: ESSAYS ON THE CRIMINAL LAW'S SPECIAL PART 65 (Antony Duff & Stuart Green eds., 2005).

[61] *See* Duff, *supra* note 22, at 3.

[62] *See, e.g.,* Richard L. Gray, *Eliminating the (Absurd) Distinction between Malum In Se and Malum Prohibitum Crimes,* 73 WASH. U. L. Q. 1369, 1370 (1995).

[63] For a full analyses of *malum prohibitum* offenses and legal moralism, see *id.* at 3.

[64] DUFF ET AL., *supra* note 20, at 58.

1 Feinberg's Approach to Criminalization

The harm principle and legal moralism in Feinberg's criminalization theory are only two elements of his four main "liberty-limiting principles" of criminalization.[65] Feinberg takes an integrated approach to harmfulness and wrongfulness. Unlike Mill, Feinberg did not fully reject paternalism and legal moralism and accepted that some harmless wrongs still provide justification for criminalization.[66] In this sense, Feinberg's theory is moralistic.[67] As the offense principle and the criminalization of paternalistic coercion will not always harm the person coerced, Feinberg acknowledged that there are other supplementary factors to the harm principle: offense, legal paternalism, and legal moralism.[68] I briefly explain Feinberg's liberty-limiting principles.

Feinberg suggested that the *offense principle* targets all undesired mental states, and added additional reasons for criminalization.[69] Under the *offense principle*, Feinberg asserts, "[i]t is always a good reason in support of a proposed criminal prohibition that it is necessary to prevent serious offense of persons other than the actor and would be an effective means to that end if enacted."[70] Under this approach, offensive conduct is justifiably criminalized (or at least supports it) when the conduct is wrongful to another party and causes a severely offended mental distress, e.g., disgust, shame, hurt, anxiety.[71] Examples of offensive behavior include using obscenity, causing loud or raucous noise, or engaging in sexual acts in public.

Feinberg also suggested using the *legal paternalism* principle, under which criminalization of self-harm could be justified[72]: "[I]t is always a good and relevant (though not necessarily decisive) reason in support of a criminal prohibition that it will prevent harm (physical, psychological, or economic) to the actor himself."[73] In other words, legal paternalism supports criminalization, to prevent self-harmfulness,

[65] *See generally*, FEINBERG, *supra* note 25.
[66] *See generally*, FEINBERG, *supra* note 24; DUFF ET AL., *supra* note 20, at 19.
[67] DUFF ET AL., *supra* note 20, at 19.
[68] FEINBERG, *supra* note 25, at 78; JOEL FEINBERG, THE MORAL LIMITS OF THE CRIMINAL LAW: OFFENSE TO OTHERS (1985); JOEL FEINBERG, THE MORAL LIMITS OF THE CRIMINAL LAW: HARM TO SELF, ch. 18–19 (1986); DUFF ET AL., *supra* note 20, at 19.
[69] FEINBERG, *supra* note 18. Feinberg's principle means that if the seriousness of the wrongful offense outweighs its reasonableness, then criminalization is justified. *See also* Harlon L. Dalton, *Book Review: Offense to Others: The Moral Limits of the Criminal Law (vol. 2), by J. Feinberg*, 96 YALE L.J. 881 (1987); PERŠAK, *supra* note 5, at 13.
[70] FEINBERG, *supra* note 18; FEINBERG, *supra* note 24, at xix.
[71] *See* FEINBERG, *supra* note 18, at 1; PERŠAK, *supra* note 5, at 14.
[72] *See* PERŠAK, *supra* note 5, at 17.
[73] FEINBERG, *supra* note 68, at 4.

but under Feinberg's "soft-paternalism" principle, only when self-harmfulness is involuntary.[74] For example, the state can prohibit conduct such as suicide because of the presumption that no one would voluntarily choose to kill herself.[75] This approach was criticized by many scholars, particularly on the grounds of interfering with the notion of autonomy and the expression of autonomy to voluntarily choose, or interfering with the notion of individuality, i.e., what is good for one person is not good for another.[76]

2 Simester and von Hirsch's Approach to Criminalization

Andrew Simester and Andreas von Hirsch suggested a *dual-element perspective* to criminalize behavior, arguing that criminal prohibition of any conduct is dependent on both wrongfulness and harmfulness;[77] albeit, each element is insufficient on its own.[78] Under this theory, the harm principle is important to construct criminalization, as criminal law is conceived as a regulatory tool "with a distinctively moral voice."[79] Thus, the state should only criminalize a behavior that is both harmful and morally wrong, because people have "a moral right not to be falsely censured as criminals."[80]

Simester & von Hirsch's approach to criminalization, which builds on Feinberg's theory, is important in the formulation of a criminalization theory, as it mediates between two approaches of criminalization. However, this approach does not provide a full taxonomy of criminalization: although Simester and von Hirsch address external considerations for criminalizing a conduct,[81] it is insufficient to formulate a fully principled criminalization theory. For example, a certain conduct,

[74] Feinberg rejected the criminalization of hard-paternalism, noting that "[h]ard paternalism will accept as a reason for criminal legislation that it is necessary to protect competent adults, against their will, from the harmful consequences even of their fully voluntary choices and undertakings." *Id.* at 12.

[75] Feinberg gives an example of a policeman which sees a "John Doe" about to chop off his hand with an ax. In this example, the policeman "is perfectly justified in using force to prevent him because of the presumption that no one would voluntarily choose to do such a thing. The presumption, however, should always be taken as rebuttable, in principle. If there were an official tribunal to investigate such matters, it would require that once the presumption against voluntariness is established (perhaps by expert witnesses, perhaps from its own records), it must be overturned by evidence from some source or other, including the voluntary testimony of the petitioner, Doe himself." *See id.* at 125.

[76] PERŠAK, *supra* note 5, at 17–18.

[77] *See* SIMESTER & VON HIRSCH, *supra* note 10. For a brief overview of Simester and von Hirsch's dual-element criminalization theory, see von Hirsch, *supra* note 14.

[78] However, Simester & von Hirsch do not provide a criterion for determining wrongfulness; rather they offer differing wrongfulness-arguments. *See* SIMESTER & VON HIRSCH, *supra* note 10, at 44–46, 100; von Hirsch, *supra* note 14, at 8.

[79] SIMESTER & VON HIRSCH, *supra* note 10, at 4.

[80] *Id.* at 20.

[81] *Id.* at Chap. 11.

e.g., drug use, could be considered harmful (to society) and morally wrong, but should not necessarily be criminalized when more efficient regulatory mechanisms exist to deter drug use.

C *Principled Criminalization Theories*

For the purpose of this book, I need not decide which theory, i.e., the harm principle or legal moralism, is more important in criminalizing a behavior, as their preference changes in different legal systems.[82] Without deciding which single-element or multiple-element approach is more convincing, it is important to note that taken separately they do not offer adequate criteria for criminalization. When formulating a structured criminalization theory, two main approaches should be kept in mind: the *balancing* approach and the *principled* approach. The *balancing* approach refers to the idea of weighing all the reasons in favor of and against criminalizing, while the "weightier set of reasons is [meant] to prevail."[83] The *principled* approach strives to ensure that certain standards are met before criminalizing a conduct and sets limits on the state's power to enact criminal legislation.[84] Although both approaches can potentially examine criminalization, they differ in their ability to provide a proper structured approach. Balancing is more likely to be perceived as a technique (albeit it, too, encompasses normative evaluations), but not as a general principle. The *balancing* approach might lack any specifications of a

---

[82] For example, American courts consider the harm principle as the guiding theory of criminalization. *See* Lawrence v. Texas, 539 U.S. 558, 577 (2003) (concluding that the government must justify criminalization by demonstrating a specific provable harm). For a general discussion on this matter, see Kelly J. Strader, *Lawrence's Criminal Law*, 16 BERKELEY J. CRIM. L. 41 (2011); Eric Tennen, *Is the Constitution in Harm's Way? Substantive Due Process and Criminal Law*, 8 BOALT J. CRIM. L. 3 (2004); Suzanne B. Goldberg, *Morals-Based Justifications for Lawmaking: Before and After Lawrence v. Texas*, 88 MINN. L. REV. 1233 (2004); Lloyd L. Weinreb, *Desert, Punishment, and Criminal Responsibility*, 49 LAW & CONTEMP. PROBS. 47, 49 (1986).

[83] For this explanation of the balancing approach, see SCHONSHECK, *supra* note 5, at 29–38; PERŠAK, *supra* note 5, at 10–11. There are different suggestions in the literature regarding the reasons for a criminalization process. For example, as described by Nils Jareborg, many scholars argue that there are several principles that should be accounted in criminalizing a behavior, as follows. 1) *Blameworthiness.* Does the conduct deserve the censure that punishment expresses? Under blameworthiness, it is important to examine what values and interests have been infringed or threatened, and whether the conduct involves actual harm/creates a danger/is related to such harm in some distant way. In addition, blameworthiness depends on the guilt or culpability exhibited by actors in their conduct. 2) *Need.* Can the conduct be deterred by less intrusive or costly means? 3) *Moderation.* Is the punishment excessive or indefensibly intrusive? *Inefficiency.* Is the usage of criminalization economically efficient? 4) *Control Costs.* Do alternative measures require significantly greater resources? 5) *The Victim's Interests.* Will it be easier for a victim to be vindicated and compensated? These arguments, however, are based on the balancing approach, which does not provide a sufficient taxonomy to criminalize a behavior and will not therefore be used separately. *See generally*, Jareborg, *supra* note 7, at 527–31.

[84] PERŠAK, *supra* note 5, at 12.

hierarchy between two "weights," presuming that they are on the same normative level, which could be incommensurable.[85] Moreover, although weighing can take into account differences to some extent, as some reasons for criminalization could be inherently different in nature, it will be difficult to "weigh" them against each other.[86] Therefore, I advocate using a structured approach, namely a *principled* approach, to evaluate criminalization since it is more accurate and offers a critical analysis of the criminalization in process.[87] Nevertheless, the *principled* approach does use balancing techniques and applies these techniques, which are helpful within a given principle.[88]

Although scholars have addressed general principles of a criminalization process, until 1994 none of the theories provided a structured set of principles to examine a particular criminalization process.[89] In 1994, Schonsheck suggested the first principled formula of criminalization, and it includes three elements: the *principle filter*, the *presumptions filter*, and the *pragmatics filter*. In 2008, Husak suggested a second principled formula of criminalization and argued that criminal laws must satisfy seven different internal and external constraints (to criminal law).

1 Schonsheck's Theory of Criminalization

Jonathan Schonsheck formulated a theory of criminalization, probably for the first time.[90] Using a principled approach, Schonsheck suggested setting limits to state power to enact criminal legislation by using a "filtering" procedure. Actions are justifiably criminalized when they successively and successfully pass each filter: *principles, presumptions,* and *pragmatics*.[91]

According to the *principles filter*, a process must correspond to at least one of the four criminal principles: the *harm principle* (justifies restricting individual liberty when the conduct causes harm to others);[92] the *offense principle* (targets all undesired mental states);[93] *legal paternalism* (prevents harm to the actor, not to others); and *legal moralism* (when the conduct is inherently immoral, even though it causes neither harm nor offends the actor or others). According to the

---

[85] *Id.* at 11; SCHONSHECK, *supra* note 5, at 7.

[86] *See* SCHONSHECK, *supra* note 5, at 15; PERŠAK, *supra* note 5, at 11–12.

[87] *See* PERŠAK, *supra* note 5, at 12.

[88] *Id.* at 12.

[89] *See, e.g.,* PACKER, *supra* note 16; Kadish, *supra* note 16. *See also* DOUGLAS HUSAK, OVER-CRIMINALIZATION: THE LIMITS OF THE CRIMINAL LAW 59 (2008).

[90] While Feinberg suggested four main "liberty-limiting principles" of criminalization, they are insufficient as a full-complex theory of criminalization. *See* SCHONSHECK, *supra* note 5. It is very unfortunate that, for some unknown reason, Schonsheck's theory is not commonly discussed in criminalization literature. For a similar observation, see DUFF, *supra* note 39, at 80.

[91] SCHONSHECK, *supra* note 5, at 25.

[92] *See* MILL, *supra* note 18; FEINBERG, *supra* note 25.

[93] *See* FEINBERG, *supra* note 18.

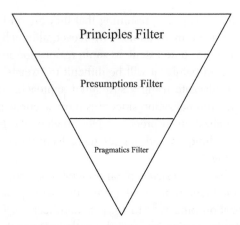

FIGURE 11 Schonsheck's Criminalization Filters

presumptions filter, the legislature must seek less restrictive measures than criminal law. Passing the *principles and presumptions filters*, leads to the final test, the *pragmatics filter*, in which the legislature must examine the repercussions of criminalization by conducting a cost-benefit analysis of the consequences of imposing criminal law.[94] Schonsheck's theory of criminalization is shown in Figure 11.[95]

As a fairly obvious example, consider the act of committing murder. Murder is a harmful and wrongful activity. Its criminalization is justified on both grounds of the *harm principle* and *legal moralism*. It passes the principles filter causing the legislature to examine a less restrictive measure, for instance, civil law, to regulate murder. If no other less restrictive measure exists, then murder passes the presumptions filter. Under the pragmatics filter, the legislature must conduct a cost-benefit analysis of the consequences of treating murder as a criminal offense. Only if the benefits outweigh the costs, is regulating murder through criminal law justified. Less obvious examples could lead to different outcomes. A breach of a contract, for example, would be considered harmful and most likely wrongful enough to pass the principles filter. However, as breach of contracts are common, civil law is probably a more efficient mechanism than criminal law. Therefore, it will not pass the presumptions filter. Thus, under this evaluation, breach of contract should remain in the realm of civil law.

Unfortunately, Schonsheck's theory is rarely discussed in academic literature, and thus lacks a substantial discussion of its possible drawbacks. Of the few scholars who did address this theory, Asaf Harduf argues that Schonsheck's theory is set at a lofty conceptual level and "does not bring us any closer to clear considerations of

---

[94] SCHONSHECK, *supra* note 5, at 16.
[95] The illustration of the criminalization filters was suggested by Schonsheck. *See id.* at 26.

criminalization than does sticking to general constitutional doctrines for reviewing legislation."[96] Harduf further argues that such concrete levels of analysis do "not provide clear insights regarding other forms of conduct."[97]

To a large extent, I agree with Harduf's arguments. The main problem of Schonsheck's theory is its vagueness. While the first filter provides a relatively structured method of criminalizing, the second and third filters allow differential assessment by a variety of legislators, and there is no structured mechanism to judge their outcomes. However, such a structured mechanism is practically impossible to craft. Thus, one solution is to implement balancing techniques to resolve the problem, at least to some extent. Moreover, an additional and important drawback in Schonsheck's theory is its failure to address the various perceptions of criminal law. A positive legal moralist, for example, will reject Schonsheck's theory. Finally, Schonsheck did not address the question of a legitimate and substantial state interest or a protected social interest in criminalization. Indeed, not every approach to criminal law would agree that such components should be part of a criminalization theory. However, the importance of such elements in criminalization is protecting the communities' shared values and interests and not merely the interests of individuals (although such interests could also be considered as part of the shared values and interests of communities). Thus, at the very least, any criminalization process should include the possible inclusion of such an element in examining criminalization.

2 Husak's Theory of Criminalization

In perhaps the most extensive work on criminalization thus far, Douglas Husak offered a theory of criminalization or "a decision procedure for justifying criminal laws,"[98] which consists of seven general principles or constraints designed to limit state authority to enact penal offenses.[99] Husak sorted these constraints into two general categories:[100] first, four internal constraints derived from criminal law itself; and second, three external constraints dependant on a relatively-controversial normative theory imported from outside of criminal law.[101] In this part, I briefly explore

---

[96] Harduf, *supra* note 33, at 38–39.
[97] *Id.*
[98] Husak presupposes the existence of a legitimate state, and focuses on the question as to whether "[w]hat must be true before the state is permitted to resort to the criminal sanction in particular." *See id.* at 55–56.
[99] *Id.* at 55.
[100] However, note that Husak argues that there the contrast between the two categories is a bit artificial, and that they sometimes overlap enormously. *See id.* at 57, 121.
[101] *Id.*

Husak's theory of criminalization, discussed at length in recent academic literature,[102] in order to understand whether it can aid in my assessment of copyright
criminalization.

Internal Constraints. Husak argues that criminal laws must satisfy four internal
constraints (to criminal law) in order to be justified. First, the *nontrivial harm or evil*
constraint suggests that criminal liability may not be imposed unless statutes are
designed to prohibit a nontrivial harm or evil.[103] Second, the *wrongfulness* constraint
suggests that criminal liability may not be imposed unless the defendant's conduct is
wrongful, at least to some extent.[104] Third, the *desert* constraint suggests that
punishment is justified only when, and to the extent, it is deserved, i.e., undeserved
punishments are unjustified.[105] Fourth, the *burden of proof* constraint suggests that
the state bear the burden of proof in justifying the infringement of rights.[106] Taking
murder again as an example, it should pass Husak's internal constraints. It is a
wrongful conduct that causes nontrivial harm or evil. To properly criminalize
murder, the state should impose a deserved/proportional punishment for the murder
while proving that murder is justified as a criminal offense.

External Constraints. Unlike Husak's internal constraints, the external constraints address not only those punished but also the citizens who are asked to create
and maintain a system of punitive sanctions.[107] Husak argues that criminal laws must
satisfy each of three external constraints (to criminal law) in order to be justified:
First, the state must have a substantial interest in the statute's objective. Legislators
must identify a state interest, determine its legitimacy, and decide whether that
interest is substantial.[108] The state interest is partially determined by examining the
harm or evil proscribed.[109] The determination whether the state has a legitimate
interest in resorting to the penal sanction is achieved by examining whether given
wrongs are inflicted not only upon individual victims but also on the shared values
and interests of communities.[110] Regarding substantial interest, Husak notes that
determining whether a given legitimate state interest qualifies as substantial requires

---

[102] *See, e.g.,* Re'em Segev, *Is the Criminal Law (so) Special? Comments on Douglas Husak's
Theory of Criminalization,* 1 Jrslm. Rev. Legal Stud. 3 (2010).
[103] Husak, *supra* note 89, at 66.
[104] *Id.* at 66.
[105] *Id.* at 82.
[106] *Id.* at 99–100. Husak states that the fourth constraint, i.e., the burden of proof, differs
categorically from the other internal constraints, because although particular offenses might
violate one or more of the other constraints, allocations of the burden of proof cannot show any
given statute to be unjustified.
[107] *Id.* at 121.
[108] *Id.* at 132.
[109] *Id.* at 133. However, Husak argues that we should not generalize from hard cases to conclude
that the whole enterprise of identifying statutory purposes is hopeless.
[110] *Id.* at 136–37. Husak argues that unless some wrongs are done not only to individual victims but
also to the community at large, it will be hard to explain why the state has a legitimate interest
in responding with the hardship and censure inherent in punishment.

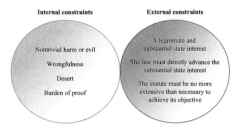

FIGURE 12 Husak's Theory of Criminalization

a theory of the state.[111] Lacking a theory of the state, Husak suggests that determining whether the state interest is substantial could be determined by a few elements, e.g., preventing physical and economic harm,[112] and securing public goods.[113]

Second, the law must directly advance the substantial state interest. This part requires empirical evidence,[114] rather than unsupported speculation, that the legislative purpose will actually be served.[115] Specifically, Husak demands more than a merely rational basis for believing that the law might produce its intended benefits. He specifically claims that criminal legislation should not exist when there is little reason to suppose it would be effective, i.e., Husak demands that all criminal statutes must withstand empirical scrutiny.[116]

Third, the criminal statute must be no more extensive than necessary to achieve its objective.[117] If, according to Husak, a less intrusive alternative exists that is equally effective, the statute in question is less criminally-justified – i.e., that alternatives to given laws should be identified and assessed.[118] In requiring that no alternative that is equally effective be less extensive than the statute in question, Husak imposes a presumption against overinclusive criminal laws.[119] He limits their application to instances where the substantial state objectives cannot otherwise be achieved.[120] To conclude, Husak offers a criminalization theory based on internal and external constraints, as indicated in Figure 12.

---

[111] See *id.* at 137.

[112] For example, forced transfers of property rights. See *id.* at 138.

[113] See *id.* at 138.

[114] Husak notes that empirical evidence requirement jeopardizes an enormous amount of criminal legislation, and cannot be met by facile allegations that a statute is justified simply because it will deter. See *id.* at 145.

[115] *Id.* at 145.

[116] *Id.* at 153.

[117] *Id.* at 132, 153.

[118] And functions as an important tool in combating the perceived problem of overcriminalization. See *Id.* at 154, 158.

[119] An offense is considered overinclusive when its justificatory rationale applies to some but not all of the conduct it proscribes, and considered underinclusive when its justificatory rationale applies to more conduct than it proscribes. See *id.* at 154 (explaining the terms "overinclusive" and "underinclusive" while referring to FREDRICK SCHAUER: PLAYING BY THE RULES 31–34 (1991)).

[120] HUSAK, *supra* note 89, at 156.

Husak's suggestion of a criminalization theory is perhaps the most extensive work encountered thus far. But his theory is criticized in academic literature, mainly on the grounds that he provides a conceptual level only of criminalization without clear considerations.[121] Harduf noted that Husak's theory has greatly enriched the criminalization discourse, but argues that the search for options (aside from criminal legislation), as well as assessing its consequences, are important for any kind of legislation.[122] I beg to differ on this matter and argue that the search for alternatives and assessing consequences is far more important for criminalization, due to criminal law characteristics and the impact on society. Thus, criminal law should be implemented as an *ultima ratio*. Mainly, his theory provides general outlines that are important for any criminalization process. Much like Schonsheck's theory, the vagueness of Husak's constraints [123] should be further analyzed through the lens of the various perceptions of criminal law, while analyzing its consequences.

*

While Husak's theory of criminalization is probably the most extensive work encountered thus far in literature, it should be noted that other scholars, like Asaf Harduf, have offered other theories that, inter alia, greatly rely on previously formulated theories. Harduf offers an analytical examination of criminalization and suggests a *ladder of criminalization* that "conceptualizes, formulates, and distinguishes general considerations of criminalization, and offers the method and coherency."[124] The *ladder of criminalization* comprises four steps: first, identifying a specific type of offensive conduct; second, examining the ability of criminal law to successfully confront that conduct; third, examining alternatives to criminalization; and fourth, assessing the social costs associated with solutions to the offensive conduct.[125]

The first step of the criminalization ladder requires the legislature to identify the offensive conduct, the behavioral causation between the conduct and the harm, and to evaluate the harm itself.[126] The second step of the ladder requires "*purposiveness*": causation between the ability of the criminal law to effectively reduce the harmfulness of the conduct.[127] Within this step of evaluation, we examine the enforceability of a conduct, namely, whether criminal law is capable of detecting

---

[121] Harduf, *supra* note 33, at 39; Miriam Gur-Arye, *Comments on Douglas Husak's Overcriminalization*, 1 Jrslm. Rev. Legal Stud. 21, 21 (2010). For other forms of criticism, see Stuart P. Green, *Is There Too Much Criminal Law?*, 6 Ohio St. J. Crim. L. 737 (2009); Darryl K. Brown, *Can Criminal Law Be Controlled?*, 108 Mich. L. Rev. 971 (2010).

[122] Harduf, *supra* note 33, at 39.

[123] *See* Segev, *supra* note 102, at 7.

[124] Harduf, *supra* note 33, at 32.

[125] *Id.*

[126] *Id.* at 40–47.

[127] *Id.* at 47–60.

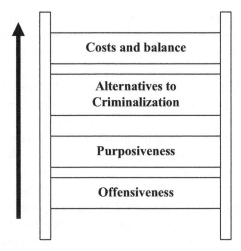

FIGURE 13 Harduf's Ladder of Criminalization

the harm (and perpetrators of the harm), apprehending and detaining the perpetrators, gathering evidence sufficient for prosecution, and reducing the proscribed conduct through punishment. The second step then examines whether criminal law is capable of preventing the relevant harm. The third step of the ladder requires searching for less restrictive alternatives to achieve the purposes.[128] Within this third step, legislators should analyze pre-behavioral, behavioral, and post-behavioral causation interventions, which all target examining other methods to prevent harm.[129] The fourth and final step of the ladder assesses whether the available solutions are the best regulatory choice. Under this step, relying on balancing techniques, legislators should examine criminalization costs to determine whether reducing such costs is possible while maintaining purposiveness.[130] Harduf's ladder of criminalization is shown in Figure 13.

Although a novel attempt, the criminalization ladder possesses drawbacks. For example, the ladder's use will differ with various perspectives of criminal law. A legal moralist, for example, would not necessarily agree with Harduf, arguing that the moral wrongfulness of a conduct is a sufficient (and perhaps the only) condition to justify criminalization. Thus, the ladder of criminalization contains "steps" that may be irrelevant in many legal systems, as their approach toward criminalization might differ. Under this notion, the legal moralist will not search for alternatives, nor will she assess criminal law's ability to achieve the goals and the social costs of such imposition. Harduf is aware of this gap, noting, "[t]hose who find one or more

---

[128] *Id.* at 61–62.
[129] *Id.* at 60–66.
[130] *Id.* at 66–72.

considerations irrelevant might still utilize the rest of the ladder,"[131] and that the ladder is "not a complete guide for legislators."[132] However, in order to properly use this theory, legislators should reconstruct it according to their perception of criminal law.

In addition, the first step of the criminalization ladder mostly revolves around the harm principle and questions whether the conduct causes harm. Although Harduf noted that his adherence to the harm discourse does not preclude considering the issue of moral wrongfulness,[133] a more thorough usage of the wrongfulness requirement is absent, and mainly, Feinberg and Simester & von Hirsch's approaches to wrongfulness. Stated differently, reliance on the harm principle as a requirement to pass the first step of the criminalization ladder could be proven problematic. Moreover, the ladder of criminalization does not sufficiently address all the elements from Husak's theory, e.g., the question of whether the state has a substantial interest in whatever objective the statute is designed to achieve or the burden of proof in justifying the infringement of rights, on the state that resorts to criminal sanctions.[134] Even if Husak's elements should not be part of a criminalization theory, or rather, should only apply in some jurisdictions that share Husak's view of criminalization, Harduf did not provide clear justifications for their absence. Although Harduf criticized Schonsheck's theory as vague, he does not provide any clear mechanism to aid in determining the steps of the ladder, which remain abstract. Usage of economic analysis of law, which Harduf does not refer to, could aid in determining the second and third steps of the ladder. The next part addresses these difficulties while integrating the suggested criminalization theories into four main elements.

3 Integrated Criminalization Approach

Many scholars argue that determinate criminalization criteria are difficult or even impossible to craft, and therefore this task is undesirable.[135] Other scholars argue that a general normative criminalization framework is possible to craft, and also, important for any criminalization process.[136] I do not attempt to suggest a new principled criminalization theory. More accurately, I am not proposing new elements that are

---

[131] *Id.* at 73.

[132] *Id.* at 44.

[133] *Id.* at 43.

[134] HUSAK, *supra* note 89, at 99–100.

[135] *See, e.g.,* DUFF, *supra* note 39, at 80. However, there are various suggestions as to finding the right formula for defining criminalization principles. For example, Donald Dripps suggested content-neutral norms to limit the criminal sanction. Dripps further proposes to fight over-criminalization through criminal procedures, e.g., that penal laws will pass by a higher majority in the legislative house. *See* Donald A. Dripps, *The Liberal Critique of the Harm Principle,* 17 CRIMINAL JUSTICE ETHICS 3, 12 (1998).

[136] *See generally,* SCHONSHECK, *supra* note 5; PERŠAK, *supra* note 5; HUSAK, *supra* note 89.

absent from the current criminalization literature. My contribution in the field of criminalization theories is modest. I suggest an integrated approach toward the existing criminalization theories (mainly Schonsheck and Husak),[137] which is derived from extracting their main elements. I suggest that combining their theories, which overlap to some extent, could aid in determining criminalization in any legal system and under every approach to criminal law.

Although a combination of two theories could sometimes be perceived as problematic, as I further explain, this integrated approach allows for the disintegration of stages which do not fit the legislature's legal system approach. In this sense, if policymakers view Schonsheck's and Husak's respective theories as non-complementary, they could adapt the integrated approach stages to their preferences. In this integrated approach, which examines copyright criminalization, I suggest mechanisms to examine each stage of the evaluation, attempting to clear up the vagueness behind some elements of their excellent theories. Although I provide the general outlines of the integrated approach in the following sections, in order to reduce repetitiveness, a more thorough analysis of each stage's evaluation methodology is explained in Chapter 8, which examines copyright criminalization.

An important caveat is due: the integrated approach serves as an indicator to support or frustrate criminalizing a conduct. Principled criminalization theories should provide legislators with legal tools to evaluate whether a specific conduct should be criminalized, but they are incapable of providing a determinant answer for all conduct at any given time. For example, society might wish to criminalize certain types of *malum in se* conduct, e.g., rape or murder, as a form of condemnation and of society's morality. Under this view, criminal law also has an expressive function and does not exist solely to decrease criminal behavior.[138] Hence, certain types of conduct will be criminalized, without turning to questioning criminal law's efficiency or examining alternatives to it. Moreover, while examining the criminalization of a certain conduct, the integrated approach can be broken-down to serve the state's view of criminal law. For example, if legislators base their criminalization on a strict, positive, legal-moralism approach, then they may disintegrate the theory to include only moral considerations.

Thus, I argue that policymakers should use an integrated approach, examine current principled theories of criminalization, and construct a principled theory that aligns with its criminal law perspective. As a general matter, I suggest an integrated

[137] Schonsheck & Husak's principled theories of criminalization could be viewed as similar in many aspects. Husak's internal constraints are equivalent, in a sense, to Schonsheck's principles filter, while adding desert and burden of proof as constraints on criminalization (even as Schonsheck adds legal paternalism and legal moralism). In addition, Husak's external constraints resemble the presumptions and pragmatics filters. There are minor differences between the scope of each constraint/filter, which could be addressed in a single, unified criminalization theory.

[138] *See generally*, JOEL FEINBERG, DOING AND DESERVING 95 (1970).

approach to criminalizing copyright law, which is composed of various reasons to criminalize, as suggested in the literature (each legislature could "remove" the stages which are irrelevant in its legal system's view), while I further analyze criminal copyright through the various copyright law theories. This integrated approach should not be treated as "stepwise," i.e., legislators would not need to evaluate each criterion if those preceding it are satisfied, but rather disintegrate the theory and examine the stages that align with their perception of the criminal system.

The first stage of the integrated approach to criminalizing copyright law is to identify the elements of Husak's and Schonsheck's respective principled theories that are irrelevant to copyright criminalization examination. First, according to Schonsheck's *principles filter*, the *offense principle* and *legal paternalism* – copyright infringements are neither "offensive"[139] nor do they cause self-harm. Second, the fourth internal constraint suggested by Husak, which places the burden of proof in justifying the infringement of rights on the state's uses of criminal sanctions, is relevant for any legislation, and therefore is not unique to copyright criminalization. Other than these factors, I extract the main elements of criminalization theories and place them in the integrated approach.

The integrated approach to criminalization comprises four main elements of inspection. The first stage is based on the main single-element approaches of criminalization, as they appear in the various approaches described previously. The main elements are harmfulness and wrongfulness. Depending on the legal approach, criminalization requires either harmfulness/wrongfulness or both. During this first stage, policymakers should also determine whether the conduct is *mala in se*, in the sense of legal moralism's approach to criminalization. If a conduct is inherently immoral, i.e., murder, then it does not necessarily need to pass other stages of the integrated approach to criminalization that query the efficiency and consequences of criminalization. In other words, as a *mala in se* offense, murder should be a criminal offense, even if civil or administrative laws could serve as better deterrents and/or that criminal law does not deter murder. Under the single-elements legal approach, passing this stage could be sufficient to establish criminalization. However, as principled theories of criminalization suggest, there are other important elements that should be considered.

The second stage examines whether the state has a substantial interest in the statute's objectives. Deriving from the first stage of Husak's external constraints (and absent from Schonsheck's theory), and from a few legal systems' approach to criminal law, which primarily emphasizes the protection of social values, this stage identifies the state/public interest or a protected social interest, determines its legitimacy, and decides whether that interest is substantial. Under this stage, the

---

[139] Although some rights holders might argue that copyright infringement causes harm to society, it is not "offensive" per se, in the sense of Feinberg's principle.

law under review will be upheld when it achieves a compelling, essential, governing purpose.[140] For example, while keeping the streets clean could be considered a social/governmental interest, this is not substantial enough to criminalize public spitting. The safety of citizens, on the other hand, should be considered consequential enough to criminalize conduct such as armed robbery.

For clarification purposes, it is important to note that unlike Husak's reliance on constitutional law in the United States while forming his internal constraints, this stage could vary depending on each legal system. Moreover, this stage encompasses the view that criminalizing a behavior should mostly rely on identifying an important *protected interest/value*, which could justify prohibiting a conduct by criminal law. Each policymaker should use this stage according to her legal system's view of criminal and constitutional law. In this second stage, criminalization is not supported when there is a lack of a substantial state interest/protected interest to criminalize a conduct. However, this second stage of evaluation could be controversial, as deciding what constitutes a substantial public interest is disputable and could be considered vague. Thus, as this integrated approach suggests, policymakers could break-down this stage of evaluation if it does not correspond to their perception of the legal system, and continue evaluating criminalization without searching for a state or a socially protected interest.

The third stage examines whether criminal law will directly advance the substantial state interest/protected interest, and whether it is more efficient than other measures, e.g., civil and administrative law. This stage encompasses two of Husak's external constraints requiring that the law directly advance the substantial state interest (in empirical evidence rather than unsupported speculation), and that no alternative, which is equally effective and less extensive than the statute in question exists; Schonsheck's *presumptions filter*, that requires that the legislature seek less restrictive measures than criminal law; and Harduf's second and third steps of the *ladder of criminalization* that examine the ability of criminal law to successfully confront that conduct and offer alternatives to criminalization. Under the third stage, policymakers must assess and identify alternatives to criminal law and examine whether they are more or equally efficient. This stage is comprised of two forms of evaluation: an *ex-ante* evaluation that is mainly based on economic analysis of crime, absent from Husak's and Harduf's respective theories, which examines whether other forms of legislation do not internalize the costs of an unlawful act, and achieve optimal enforcement;[141] and an *ex-post* evaluation, when available, that is based on evidence from implementing criminal provisions in the past.

---

[140] HUSAK, *supra* note 89, at 123.
[141] To be clear, I am not proposing to use economic analysis of law as a complete theory of criminalization. Many scholars oppose any implementation of such usage regarding criminalization. *See, e.g.,* GEORGE P. FLETCHER, THE GRAMMAR OF CRIMINAL LAW: AMERICAN, EUROPEAN, INTERNATIONAL 59 (2007); Husak, *supra* note 89, at 180. However, because other scholars have suggested general principles that purport to govern the imposition of criminal sanctions, I implement some observations of law and economics regarding the third stage of the

The fourth and final stage of the integrated approach to criminalization, examines consequences of criminalization. This final stage encompasses Schonsheck's *pragmatics filter* that requires the legislature to examine consequences of criminalization, by conducting a cost-benefit analysis of the consequences of implementing criminal law and Harduf's fourth step of the *ladder of criminalization*. For example, assuming that drug use is a harmful and wrongful conduct, the state has a substantial interest in preventing drug use (due to its dangerous nature), and criminal law acts as the available mechanism to regulate drug use. However, under the fourth stage, if for example, 90% of the population uses a certain drug regularly, the consequences of criminalization could mean criminalizing most of the population – an act that is not beneficial for society. Thus, when examining drug use, legislators should conduct a cost-benefit analysis, and decide whether criminalizing a conduct leads to positive or negative consequences. Fulfilling the fourth stage requirements supports criminalization. The integrated approach to copyright criminalization and the implementation of criminalization theories into the integrated approach are summarized in Figure 14 and Table 3, respectively.

Examining criminalization through the integrated approach requires scrutiny of the two main approaches of criminalization: *macro-evaluation* and *micro-evaluation*. Macro-evaluation builds on criminal law theories. Under macro-evaluation, the legislature must first determine its general approach to criminalization in general. There are two main approaches to criminalization, which could be both positive and negative: *liberal* and *legal moralism* positions. Each position will apply the integrated approach differently. Beginning with the most extreme position, the *positive legal moralist* will only examine the component of wrongfulness to determine the legitimacy of criminalization. The positive legal moralist will stop here and will not examine other elements of the first stage or the other stages of evaluation. Under a second form of evaluation, the *negative legal moralist* will first examine the wrongfulness of a conduct. Only after this element is fulfilled will it continue to evaluate criminalization based on the other factors of the first, and other, stages of evaluation. Under the third form of evaluation, the *positive liberalist* will refer to the harm principle as a sufficient condition on its own to justify criminalization, and once fulfilled, criminalization is justified. Under the fourth form of evaluation, the *negative liberalist* will require fulfilling the harm principle requirement, and once fulfilled, will turn to the other factors of the first stage and the other stages of evaluation. Thus, various forms of evaluation of

---

integrated approach, evaluating efficiency of other measures, e.g., civil and administrative law, to advance the substantial state interest or the protected interest by evaluation of the most optimal enforcement mechanism. For more on economic analysis of crime, see, e.g., Gary S. Becker, *Crime and Punishment: An Economic Approach*, 76 J. POL. ECON. 169 (1968).

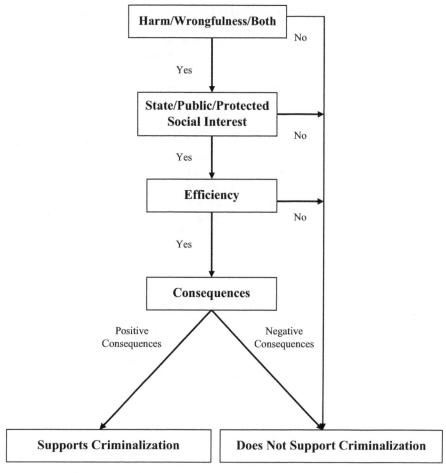

FIGURE 14 The Integrated Approach to Criminalization

the integrated approach exist and eventually can lead to different outcomes. The macro-evaluation of the integrated approach is best exemplified in Table 4.

The second form of criminalization examination, micro-evaluation, turns to copyright law theories. Under micro-evaluation, the legislature should criminalize a conduct depending on which theory copyright law is based upon. Micro-evaluation searches for the possible outcomes of each stage in the integrated approach separately, while visiting the entire stages of the integrated approach.

Thus, after deciding on the macro-approach to criminalization, policymakers should examine each component of the stages – in light of copyright law theories. Before turning to examine the micro-approach through the lens of the integrated approach of criminalization, the four main approaches to copyright law need an explanation.

TABLE 3 *The Implementation of Criminalization Theories into the Integrated Approach*

The Integrated Approach	Derived From
Harm/Wrongfulness/Both (I)	Single-element approaches; multiple-elements approaches; Schonsheck's *principles filter*; Husak's *nontrivial harm or evil* and *wrongfulness* constraints; and Harduf's first step of the *ladder of criminalization* (to some extent)
State/Public Interest (II)	Husak's external constraints; and the perception of social values as advocated in few legal systems
Efficiency (III)	Two of Husak's external constraints (to some extent); Schonsheck's *presumptions filter*; and Harduf's second and third steps of the *ladder of criminalization*
Consequences (IV)	Schonsheck's *pragmatics filter; and* Harduf's fourth step of the *ladder of criminalization*

TABLE 4 *The Macro-Evaluation of Criminalization*

	Positive Approach	*Negative Approach*
Liberalism	*Harm*	*Harm* & Other Stages of the Integrated Approach
Moralism	*Wrongfulness*	*Wrongfulness* & Other Stages of the Integrated Approach

II COPYRIGHT LAW THEORIES

Although there are many conceptualizations of copyright law,[142] copyright's main theoretical framework is primarily composed of four theories, as follows: *Incentive/ Utilitarian* theory, *Personality* theory, *Labor-Desert* theory, and *Users' Rights* theory. Each of these theories could possibly view criminal copyright in a different perspective, and therefore, evaluate the consequences of copyright criminalization differently. The first section of this part briefly reviews the four theories that justify copyright protection. I then examine the general take of each theory on copyright criminalization, laying the groundwork for a specific evaluation of each stage of the

---

[142] For example, the "democratic paradigm" of copyright law suggests that copyright should query the social advantages of knowledge, and serve a productive and a structural function. *See* Neil W. Netanel, *Copyright and a Democratic Civil Society*, 106 YALE L.J. 283 (1996); Michael D. Birnhack, *More or Better? Shaping the Public Domain, in* THE FUTURE OF THE PUBLIC DOMAIN 59, 79–82 (Lucie Guibault & Bernt Hugenholtz eds., 2006). For more theories on copyright law, e.g., ecological, radical/socialist, distributive justice, unjust enrichment, see Peter S. Menell, *Intellectual Property: General Theories, in* ENCYCLOPEDIA OF LAW AND ECONOMICS 129 (Boudewijn Bouckaert & Gerrit D. Geest eds., 2000).

integrated approach to criminalization (in Chapter 8), while distinguishing between various types of copyright infringements.

A Overview of Copyright Frameworks

Incentive/Utilitarian Theory. This theory employs the familiar utilitarian guideline (the lawmakers' beacon when constructing property rights), which is to maximize net social welfare. It requires lawmakers strike an optimal balance between the power of exclusive rights (to stimulate the creation of works) and the (partially offsetting) tendency of such rights to curtail widespread public enjoyment of those creations.[143] This approach normally holds that copyright should provide economic incentives[144] that are essential to create new works and prevent market failure[145]; therefore the legislature should grant certain exclusive rights to authors.[146] Many scholars criticized the utilitarian approach to copyright, inter alia, on the notion that either there are other non-utilitarian factors that provide adequate rewards for creators and copyright protection is not necessarily required[147]; or that there are not enough empirical data to support the policy goals to maximize social welfare.[148]

Personality Theory. Derived from the writings of Kant and Hegel, this theory argues that private property rights are crucial to satisfy some fundamental human needs.[149] It views authors' creations as "spiritual children," part of their inner personality.[150] Under this view, policymakers should strive to create and allocate entitlements to resources in the way that best enables people to fulfill those needs. Therefore, IP rights should be justified on the ground that they prevent appropriation or modification of artifacts through which authors and artists have expressed

---

[143] *See* William Fisher, *Theories of Intellectual Property, in* NEW ESSAYS IN THE LEGAL AND POLITICAL THEORY OF PROPERTY 168, 169 (Stephen R. Munzer ed., 2001) (analyzing the *utilitarian* theory *guidelines*).

[144] William M. Landes & Richard Posner, *An Economic Analysis of Copyright Law*, 18 J. LEGAL STUD. 325 (1989).

[145] Diane L. Zimmerman, *Copyrights as Incentives: Did We Just Imagine That?*, 12 THEORETICAL INQ. L. 29, 30 (2011) (reviewing American incentive theory in copyright law); Landes & Posner, *supra* note 144.

[146] However, these rights must be balanced with the interests of users. *See* RICHARD A. POSNER, ECONOMIC ANALYSIS OF LAW 53 (8th ed. 2011).

[147] Arnold Plant, *The Economic Theory Concerning Patents for Inventions*, 1 ECONOMICA 30 (1934); Menell, *supra* note 142, at 148.

[148] Richard A. Spinello & Herman T. Tavani, *Intellectual Property Rights: From Theory to Practical Implementation in Intellectual Property Rights, in* A NETWORKED WORLD: THEORY AND PRACTICE 1, 15 (Richard A. Spinello & Herman T. Tavani eds., 2005).

[149] For a comprehensive analysis of the personality theory, see ROBERT P. MERGES, JUSTIFYING INTELLECTUAL PROPERTY 68–101 (2011).

[150] For more on the personality theory, see Neil Netanel, *Copyright Alienability Restrictions and the Enhancement of Author Autonomy: A Normative Evaluation*, 24 RUTGERS L.J. 347 (1993); Kim Treiger-Bar-Am, *Kant on Copyright: Rights of Transformative Authorship*, 25 CARDOZO ARTS & ENT. L.J. 1059 (2008); GRAHAM DUTFIELD & UMA SUTHERSANEN, GLOBAL INTELLECTUAL PROPERTY LAW 55–56 (2008).

their will, or on the ground that they create social and economic conditions that are conducive to creative intellectual activity, which in turn is important to human development.[151]

The personality theory was criticized, inter alia, in that some works reflect little or none of an author's personality[152]; in that the theory is applied distinctly to different IP rights[153]; and in that the linkage between the artist's and the public's interests do not necessarily coincide.[154]

Labor-Desert Theory. One of the most influential theories of copyright protection was derived from a Lockean perception.[155] This theory, based on *John Locke's* natural rights theory of private property, suggests that all resources given by God are part of the "commons," and that persons who labor upon resources (neither owned nor "held in common") have a natural property right to the fruits of their efforts, and that the state has a duty to respect and enforce that right.[156] When persons mix their labor with objects from the commons (public realm), they are entitled to that property, but only as long as they have left the commons "enough, and as good" for others to use.[157]

The labor-desert theory and its implementation on intangible property was criticized by many scholars. Their arguments were many: first, that it uses seventeenth century rhetoric and applies it to modern intangible rights[158]; second, that it does not necessarily apply to IP rights[159]; third, that some copyrighted works have no apparent

---

[151] *See* Fisher, *supra* note 143, at 171; ROBERTA R. KWALL, THE SOUL OF CREATIVITY: FORGING A MORAL RIGHTS LAW FOR THE UNITED STATES (2010); MARGARET JANE RADIN, REINTERPRETING PROPERTY (1993); JEREMY WALDRON, THE RIGHT TO PRIVATE PROPERTY (1988); ELIZABETH ADENEY, THE MORAL RIGHTS OF AUTHORS AND PERFORMERS – AN INTERNATIONAL AND COMPARATIVE ANALYSIS 11–68 (2006); Justin Hughes, *The Philosophy of Intellectual Property*, 77 GEO. L. J. 287, 330–65 (1988).

[152] *See* Hughes, *supra* note 151, at 339.

[153] *Id.* at 340.

[154] Amy M. Adler, *Against Moral Rights*, 97 CALIF. L. REV. 263, 273–79 (2009).

[155] *See* John Locke, *Second Treatise of Government*, in TWO TREATISES OF GOVERNMENT §§ 138–40 (Peter Laslett ed., 1963) (3d ed. 1698); Gordon, *supra* note 4, at 624. For a comprehensive analysis of the labor-desert theory, see MERGES, *supra* note 149, at 31–67; Hughes, *supra* note 151, at 296–30.

[156] *See* JOHN LOCKE, SECOND TREATISE OF GOVERNMENT Chap V, sec. 26. (1690), *available at* www.constitution.org/jl/2ndtro5.htm ("[e]very Man has a Property in his own Person ... The Labour of his Body, and the Work of his Hands, we may say, are properly his"); Fisher, *supra* note 143, at 170; DUTFIELD & SUTHERSANEN, *supra* note 150, at 54.

[157] Gordon, *supra* note 4, at 624.

[158] DUTFIELD & SUTHERSANEN, *supra* note 150, at 54; Jeremy Waldron, *From Authors to Copies: Individual Rights and Social Values in Intellectual Property*, 68 CHI.-KENT L. REV. 842, 871, 879–80 (1993).

[159] *See, e.g.,* Seana Valentine Shiffrin, *Lockean Arguments for Private Intellectual Property*, in NEW ESSAYS IN THE LEGAL AND POLITICAL THEORY OF PROPERTY 138, 143, 154–57 (Stephen R. Munzer ed., 2001).

social value or require no labor to produce[160]; and fourth, that it applies only to subject matter of finite capacity and thus does not apply to IP.[161]

Users' Rights Theory. Copyright law also promotes public enjoyment of creation by granting rights to users. The contemporary framework of users' rights was first conceptualized by Patterson & Lindberg more than 25 years ago,[162] and is now revived and reinvigorated by Cohen and others.[163] Users' rights theory generally accepts the incentive theory and is based on the argument that copyright law cannot achieve its goals if users do not have the liberties necessary to enjoy copyrighted works.[164] This theory supports both authors and users.[165] Accordingly, copyright law grants users with rights, such as fair use, personal non-commercial use, and public domain works. On the other hand, users' rights critics argue that, inter alia, copyright did not intend to grant rights to users, and treats fair use and the like only as an affirmative defense,[166] while advocating the need to redefine them.[167]

*

How does copyright criminalization fair in light of these four theories? Any one of these theories could (possibly and differently) affect any stage of the integrated approach. For example, notions of harm or wrongfulness will not necessarily be viewed similarly under each copyright theory, and could possibly lead to distinct outcomes. However, before turning to evaluate each of the integrated approach components in Chapter 8, the general take of each theory on the notion of criminalization is examined.

B *Copyright Criminalization under Copyright Law Theories*

The question of whether copyright criminalization is justified can be answered differently, depending on the chosen theoretical framework. A *utilitarian* approach to copyright will inquire as to whether the protection of copyright *via* criminal sanctions preserves the incentive to create and determines what are the costs and benefits of such imposition. Under the personality and labor-desert approaches, criminalization could be justified as copyright is a natural right. Finally, under the users' rights approach to copyright, some forms of criminalization are not necessarily

---

[160] *See* Hughes, *supra* note 151, at 339.

[161] DUTFIELD & SUTHERSANEN, *supra* note 150, at 54.

[162] L. RAY PATTERSON & STANLEY W. LINDBERG, THE NATURE OF COPYRIGHT: A LAW OF USERS' RIGHTS (1991).

[163] Julie E. Cohen, *The Place of the User in Copyright Law*, 74 FORDHAM L. REV. 347 (2005).

[164] Jessica Litman, *Lawful Personal Use*, 85 TEX. L. REV. 1871, 1889 (2007).

[165] PATTERSON & LINDBERG, *supra* note 162, at 3–5.

[166] David R. Johnstone, *Debunking Fair Use Rights and Copyduty under U.S. Copyright Law*, 52 J. COPYRIGHT SOC'Y U.S.A. 345, 357 (2005).

[167] Jessica Litman, *The Exclusive Right to Read*, 13 CARDOZO ARTS & ENT. L.J. 29 (1994).

justified, as they can create a potentially chilling effect on using copyrighted works and thus negatively affect the liberties necessary to enjoy these works. This part briefly examines the various approaches to criminalization and explores each one's respective take on criminalization. However, this part is limited to a general discussion of copyright law theories only in light of criminalization, and serves to emphasize the main approach of each theory to criminalization. Further evaluation of each theory's view on specific criminalization components is examined in Chapter 8.

1 Incentive/Utilitarian Theory

Under a regulatory conception of copyright law, i.e., that copyright is not a natural right, criminalization will not necessarily be justified (or at least, not all forms of infringement). Analyzing copyright criminalization under the incentive/utilitarian theory requires identifying the optimal balance between, on the one hand, the power of exclusive rights to stimulate the creation of works of authorship and, on the other hand, the partially offsetting tendency of such rights to curtail widespread, public enjoyment of those creations. In other words, does copyright infringement reduce the economic incentive to create works to such a degree that requires the addition of criminal sanctions? What is the impact on the public's access to such works due to criminalization?

An example of the incentive/utilitarian theory can be traced back to the American constitutional approach, whereas copyright promotes the progress of science,[168] and thus protects economic incentives to create works of authorship – which is important for society.[169] Copyright infringements could potentially reduce the incentive to create and negatively influence the market of works and ideas. Does criminal law achieve the optimal balance between the power of exclusive rights and the partially offsetting tendency of such rights to curtail widespread public enjoyment of those creations? Criminal copyright can probably aid in preserving the incentive to create copyright works. On this ground, criminalization is justified. The question is, what are the costs of such imposition on the creation of other works that could potentially infringe copyright, and thus could be negatively incentivized? The additional question, under this theory, is whether the widespread public enjoyment of copyright works could be negatively influenced by criminalization. On these grounds, criminalization is not necessarily justified. Although criminal copyright plays an important part in preserving the incentives to create, it can also create a chilling effect from using other works, and therefore negatively affect the theory's goals.

---

[168] See, e.g., in the United States in U.S. CONST. art. I, sec. 8, cl. 8. The *incentive/utilitarian* theory can be traced earlier to England in 1709, when the Statute of Anne was enacted for the purpose of encouragement of learned men to compose and write useful books. *See* Copyright Act 1709, 8 Ann., c. 19 (Gr. Brit.).

[169] Landes & Posner, *supra* note 144.

Thus, criminalization is partially justified under the *incentive/utilitarian* theory, but should also be limited only to infringements that threat the incentive to create works. Chapter 8 returns to this statement, while differentiating between various types of infringements, e.g., infringements for commercial advantage or private financial gain and infringements without commercial advantage or private financial gain, while also differentiating between their commercial scales.

2 Personality and Labor-Desert Theories

Under a proprietary concept of copyright law, i.e., the personality theory and the labor-desert theory, copyright is a natural right; hence, criminalization could be justified much like real property. Whether copyright is a natural right or a limited statutory monopoly is debatable.[170] If copyright is treated as property, i.e., unauthorized copying of copyrighted materials is theft, imposing criminal sanctions on copyright infringements is justified and should apply to every form of infringement.[171] Thus, under the personality theory and the labor-desert theory, the current status of criminalization is not only justified, but criminal law should play an even more dominant role in the shaping of copyright law.

It is important to assess whether there is a normative justification for copyright propertization, i.e., whether copyright is property.[172] Although I do not attempt to resolve this debate, I briefly review some of the arguments for and against viewing copyright as property or as a limited statutory monopoly, as they are crucial for copyright criminalization. Then, I argue that the notion of copyright as property holds much importance to explaining and justifying criminal copyright. I also note that even property could be limited; therefore, criminalization is not justified on every ground.

There are different views on the nature of property, e.g., under a "Blackstonian conception"[173] or a realist/pragmatist view.[174] However, as a general argument, there

---

[170] *See*, e.g., Lydia Pallas-Loren, *Digitization, Commodification, Criminalization: The Evolution of Criminal Copyright Infringement and the Importance of the Willfulness Requirement*, 77 WASH. U.L.Q. 835, 856–61 (1999); Alfred Yen, *Restoring the Natural Law: Copyright as Labor and Possession*, 51 OHIO ST. L. REV. 517 (1990).

[171] *See*, e.g., Pallas-Loren, supra note 170, at 858; Paul Sugden, *You Can Click but You Can't Hide: Copyright Pirates and Crime – the 'Drink or Die' Prosecutions*, 30 E.I.P.R. 222, 223 (2008).

[172] For more on copyright as a form of property and the shaping of the public domain, see Hanoch Dagan, *Property and the Public Domain*, 18 YALE J.L. & HUMAN. 84 (2006).

[173] William Blackstone characterized property as "that sole and despotic dominion which one man claims and exercises over the external things of the world, in total exclusion of the right of any other individual in the universe." *See* WILLIAM BLACKSTONE, 2 COMMENTARIES ON THE LAWS OF ENGLAND 1 (1765).

[174] For more on the realist view of property, see Felix S. Cohen, *Dialogue on Private Property*, 9 RUTGERS L. REV. 357 (1954); David B. Schorr, *How Blackstone Became a Blackstonian*, 10 THEORETICAL INQUIRIES L. 103 (2009).

are several distinctions between copyright law and real (and mostly Blackstonian) property law.[175]

The first set of differences is the practical usage of copyright. While copyright may be recognized as property, it usually has a more limited duration than "real" property. For example, the duration of copyright is limited, whereas property rights are potentially infinite.[176] Moreover, copyright has limitations, e.g., fair use, while property owners enjoy broad exclusion rights.[177] The second set of differences relies on theory: property rights and copyrights are designed to promote different agendas. Property rights are mostly designed to avoid breaches of the peace; copyrights, at least under few approaches, are mostly designed to provide an incentive to create.[178] The third set of differences is the nature of the right. Tangible property requires the owner's prior consent before taking it, while copyright could be appropriated without the use of force.[179] Moreover, property is linked with actual possession, resulting in a right to exclude other people from it; whereas copyright, as a pure public good,[180] is *non-excludable*, i.e., it is impossible to restrict the usage of a good for all costumers, once it was provided to a single customer.[181] In addition, the notion of harm could be different: although both tangible and intangible

---

[175] For a full analysis, see Stewart Sterk, *Intellectualizing Property: The Tenuous Connections between Land and Copyright*, 83 WASH. U.L.Q. 417 (2005).

[176] Sterk notes that there are exceptions to the infinite nature of real property, e.g., of state statutes that limit the duration of possibilities of reverter or rights of entry. *See id.* at 446.

[177] Sterk, *supra* note 175, at 446. Sterk also suggests that "[i]njunctive relief is the standard remedy for encroachment on real property rights, while in a significant subset of copyright cases courts have limited copyright holders to money damages." *Id.*

[178] *Id.* at 421.

[179] With exceptions, e.g., usage of DRM. Randal C. Picker, *From Edison to the Broadcast Flag: Mechanisms of Consent and Refusal and the Propertization of Copyright*, 70 U. CHI. L. REV. 281, 283 (2003); Irina D. Manta, *The Puzzle of Criminal Sanctions for Intellectual Property Infringement*, 24 HARV. J.L. & TECH. 469, 475 (2011).

[180] *See* POSNER, *supra* note 146, at 52; Ben Depoorter & Francesco Parisi, *Fair Use and Copyright Protection: A Price Theory Explanation*, 21 INT'L REV. L. & ECON. 453, 465 (2002); Stephen Breyer, *The Uneasy Case for Copyright: A Study of Copyright in Books, Photocopies, and Computer Programs*, 84 HARV. L. REV. 281, 281 (1970); Wendy J. Gordon, *Fair Use as Market Failure: A Structural and Economic Analysis of the Betamax Case and Its Predecessors*, 82 COLUM. L. REV. 1600, 1610–11 (1982); Landes & Posner, *supra* note 144, at 326. *Cf.* Christopher S. Yoo, *Copyright and Public Good Economics: A Misunderstood Relation*, 155 U. PA. L. REV. 635 (2007).

[181] *See* Yoo, *supra* note 180, at 637 (explaining pure public goods). See also Justice Holmes' opinion in White–Smith Music Publishing Co. v. Apollo Co., 209 U.S. 1 (1908), noting that:

> The notion of property starts, I suppose, from confirmed possession of a tangible object, and consists in the right to exclude others from interference with the more or less free doing with it as one wills. But in copyright property has reached a more abstract expression. The right to exclude is not directed to an object in possession or owned, but is in vacuo, so to speak. It restrains the spontaneity of men where, but for it, there would be nothing of any kind to hinder their doing as they saw fit. It is a prohibition of conduct remote from the persons or tangibles of the party having the right. It may be infringed a thousand miles from the owner and without his ever becoming aware of the wrong.

infringements could deprive and reduce some of the economic value of the rights holder's goods and incentives to invest in them,[182] the non-rivalrous nature of copyright will usually cause harm and effect the loss of potential sales differently than in property crimes,[183] as the rights holder usually will not be deprived of the good and will still retain the ability to sell it.[184] Unlike tangible property, in which owners suffer definite losses, copyright infringement does not necessarily result in such losses, except, perhaps, in the loss of a "right."[185] Finally, copyright infringements are less likely to be intentional than average property crimes.[186]

Thus, copyright and property are not necessarily synonymous, because they possess different characteristics. Even if we consider copyright to be a form of property, copyright characteristics could change the legislature's decision to criminalize it. Accordingly, copyright law should be carefully criminalized (if at all). Copyright infringement is not always certain, like tangible theft. Whereas downloading copyrighted materials from the internet may be legal because of copyright law's limitations and exceptions, stealing a book from a store, even for the same purposes, will not enjoy the same limitations and will be deemed theft. In addition, the lack of prior consent of the tangible property owner aids (in most cases) in attributing a tangible property theft to an individual. However, in intangible property, the owner is not always aware that her rights were infringed, and cannot necessarily attribute the infringement to a specific person or may find it difficult to prove.[187] Moreover, as a public good, copyright has a *non-rivalry* use, i.e., the consumption of the work by one person does not reduce the availability or quality of that work to another person.[188] Finally, a copyright infringer will usually not result in endangering the safety of the rights holder, like some property crimes do.[189]

---

[182] Glen O. Robinson, *On Refusing to Deal with Rivals*, 87 CORNELL L. REV. 1177, 1210 (2002); Manta, *supra* note 179, at 479–80.

[183] Manta, *supra* note 179, at 475.

[184] *See* Grace Pyun, *The 2008 Pro-IP Act: The Inadequacy of the Property Paradigm in Criminal Intellectual Property Law and its Effect on Prosecutorial Boundaries*, 19 DEPAUL J. ART TECH. & INTELL. PROP. L. 355, 381 (2009).

[185] Stuart P. Green argues that making unauthorized copies of a book is depriving the author of royalties that he otherwise would have earned. I however, disagree with this assumption, as the copier of the book would not necessarily buy the book if he had not made a copy of it. *See* Stuart P. Green, *Plagiarism, Norms, and the Limits of Theft Law: Some Observations on the Use of Criminal Sanctions in Enforcing Intellectual Property Rights*, 54 HASTINGS L.J. 167, 213 (2002); For an opposite argument related to trade secrets, see Neel Chatterjee, *Should Trade Secret Appropriation Be Criminalized?*, 19 HASTINGS COMM. & ENT. L.J. 853, 867–68 (1997).

[186] Manta, *supra* note 179, at 480; Green, *supra* note 185, at 214; Geraldine Szott Moohr, *Federal Criminal Fraud and the Development of Intangible Property Rights in Information*, 2000 U. ILL. L. REV. 683, 731 (2000).

[187] *See* Green, *supra* note 185, at 213.

[188] *See* Yoo, *supra* note 180, at 637; Stewart E. Sterk, *Rhetoric and Reality in Copyright Law*, 94 MICH. L. REV. 1197, 1236 (1996).

[189] *See* Manta, *supra* note 179, at 480.

This justifications for copyright expansion, discussed in Chapters 5–6, holds much importance to explain and justify criminal copyright. If copyrighted works are treated as tangible objects, then infringements should be considered theft. In other words, if infringing copyright causes the same harm as with tangible property, it is justified to impose similar liabilities. However, even then, pragmatic or institutional differences could justify distinct treatment. Moreover, in the normative sense, it seems that this comparison is inaccurate, as the harm caused by copyright infringement is not necessarily similar to theft.[190] While copyright law resembles property in some ways, it is not inherently property,[191] and thus should not be treated similarly.[192] I suggest that it is more accurate to describe, and treat, copyright as a unique kind of property,[193] rather than as a pure property.[194] However, even if copyright is referred to as pure property, it does not necessarily mean that it is a broad, perpetual right. Property rights could be narrow, riddled with exceptions, short-lived, and subject to forfeiture.[195] However, generally speaking, these approaches would consider infringement theft, pure and simple. This notion could change when examining specific conducts, as I further explain in Chapter 8.

3 Users' Rights Theory

Under a users' rights theory, does copyright criminalization harm liberties necessary to enjoy copyrighted works? What is the impact of rights, such as fair use, personal non-commercial use, and works in the public domain? The main impact of copyright criminalization on users is a possible chilling effect on exposure to works and the creation of new works that rely on existing ones. Take for example the fair use defense in the United States. Fair use allows some uses of copyrighted material without requiring permission from the rights-holders, such as criticism, comment, news reporting, teaching (including multiple copies for classroom use), scholarship, or research.[196] Thus, users have a right to use works, as long as they comply with the

---

[190] *See id.*; Miriam Bitton, *Rethinking the Anti-Counterfeiting Trade Agreement's Criminal Copyright Enforcement Measures*, 102 J. CRIM. L. & CRIMINOLOGY 67, 72 (2012); Green, *supra* note 185.

[191] *See* Neil Weinstock Netanel, *Impose a Noncommercial Use Levy to Allow Free Peer-to-Peer File Sharing*, 17 HARV. J.L. & TECH. 1, 24 (2003); Pallas-Loren, *supra* note 170, at 857; Dowling v. United States, 473 U.S. 207, 216 (1985).

[192] *See, e.g.*, Brian M. Hoffstadt, *Dispossession, Intellectual Property, and the Sin of Theoretical Homogeneity*, 80 S. CAL. L. REV. 909, 958 (2007).

[193] ROBERT A. GORMAN, JANE C. GINSBURG & R. ANTHONY REESE, COPYRIGHT, CASES AND MATERIALS 13 (2011).

[194] *See, e.g.*, L. Ray Patterson, *Copyright and "The Exclusive Right" of Authors*, 1 J. INTELL. PROP. L. 1, 37 (1993).

[195] *See* Neil Weinstock Netanel, *Why Has Copyright Expanded? Analysis and Critique*, in NEW DIRECTIONS IN COPYRIGHT LAW 3, 13 (Fiona Macmillan ed., 2008); Pallas-Loren, *supra* note 170, at 858.

[196] 17 U.S.C. § 107.

fair use requirements. Criminal copyright however, could potentially create a chilling effect of using this right, as people could fear criminal sanctions. This becomes more evident when the fair use exemptions are not always clear, and courts could interpret each differently. When persons are unable to tell whether their actions are exempt from liability under the fair use exemption, there is a real possibility that criminal sanctions will deter them from their lawful rights.

Thus, copyright criminalization could have a vast impact on users' rights – which are important for copyright protection. This notion could possibly be applied differently in different cases of infringement. Copyright infringement for commercial advantage or private financial gain will not likely be deemed fair use, as fair use examines, inter alia, whether "the purpose and character of the use, including whether such use is of a commercial nature or is for nonprofit educational purposes."[197] Along these lines, copyright infringements for commercial advantages or private financial gains will not likely be affected by copyright criminalization as much as copyright infringements without commercial advantages or private financial gains. Accordingly, criminalization of copyright infringements for commercial advantage or private financial gain could be justified under the users' rights theory. Despite this, copyright infringements without commercial advantages or private financial gains should not necessarily be criminalized, as they can negatively affect the rights of users, which are important for the copyright regime. These categorizations are discussed further in Chapter 8.

*

Examining copyright law theories leads to diverse conclusions, as the different theories of copyright law do not necessarily coincide on their view of copyright criminalization. Copyright criminalization is more likely to be justified under the personality theory and the labor-desert theories rather than the incentive/utilitarian and users' rights theories. Compliance with copyright criminalization has three levels. The *strong-linkage* to criminalization is based on the personality and the labor-desert theories. Criminalization could mostly be justified under these theories as the notion of property best supports criminalization. The *moderate-linkage* to criminalization is based on the incentive/utilitarian theory. Under this middle level of compliance, criminalization will be based on a balance between the power of exclusive rights and the partially offsetting tendency of such rights to curtail widespread public enjoyment of those creations. Thus, the incentive/utilitarian theory justifies criminalization more than users' rights theory, but less than the personality and the labor-desert theories, as it will take into account the perseverance of incentives. The *weak-linkage* to criminalization is based on users' rights theory. Under this theory, any criminalization process that could potentially harm the rights

[197] *Id.* § 107(1).

granted to users is undesired, and hence, unjustified. Hence, any legal system could take a different approach to criminalization, depending on the chosen theoretical approach to copyright.

CONCLUSION

There are various approaches to criminalization. At first, scholars suggested single-elements approaches, which rely on either harm or wrongfulness. Other scholars later suggested multiple-element approaches, expanding possible considerations to criminalization. Only recently, the debate on criminalization shifted and now offers principled criminalization theories. However, examining criminalization under any principled theory could possibly lead to different outcomes, depending on the approach of criminal law and on the approach of regulated legal field at stake. Thus, I propose an integrated approach to criminalization. Under this integrated approach, a legislature should identify the main elements of criminalization, as suggested in literature, which best fits its view of criminal law. Then, the legislature should apply the integrated approach to the regulated field, and examine criminalization through its lens.

The next chapter turns to a full evaluation of criminalization through the integrated approach of copyright criminalization. Only upon understanding the complexity of copyright approaches within each of the components of the integrated approach, could I evaluate the outcomes of criminalization and understand its ramifications on both criminal and copyright laws.

8

An Integrated Approach for Copyright Criminalization

INTRODUCTION

Criminalization should never be arbitrary. When policymakers consider legal measures to regulate a conduct and turn to criminal law as one form of regulation, they should apply a principled approach that accounts for underlying principles of both criminal law in general and those of the legal field that they consider regulating. Thus, examining copyright criminalization requires reviewing whether the conduct of copyright infringement should be regulated through criminal law. Moreover, in terms of the criminal sanction, policymakers could differentiate between kinetic and online infringements. Under a case-by-case analysis, policymakers could decide that, due to the elements that are scrutinized through the integrated approach, one form of infringement deserves a higher criminal sanction than the other, and they could be sanctioned differently. Hence, the fact that an exclusive right is criminally sanctioned in the kinetic world does not imply that it should be similarly sanctioned for similar online infringement, unless the integrated approach supports both similarly. However, it should be further stressed that this book does not address the exact level of sanctions or potential sentencing guidelines, but rather deals with the question of criminalization in general.

This chapter provides a heuristic for policymakers under the various criminalization approaches, and chiefly, evaluates whether copyright criminalization is justified using the integrated approach of criminalization, introduced in the previous chapter. Under the integrated approach, I examine criminalization through four stages of evaluation, while the fulfillment of the four stages supports criminalizing copyright infringements. However, as this approach integrates different approaches to criminal law, policymakers should disintegrate the stages of the theory and apply those stages which fit their view of the criminal system. *Disintegration* is important for the various possible evaluations of criminalization, which are currently absent from criminalization theories. I would not, however, advise policymakers to remove the fourth stage of the analysis, which examines the consequences of criminalization, due to its importance in protecting both criminal and copyright regimes. Criminal law theories are one prong of the analysis. The second prong requires that we examine criminal copyright under the main copyright law theories and distinguish between infringements: for commercial advantages or financial gains and without commercial advantages or financial gains, while all the time distinguishing between small-scale and large-scale infringement.[1] It should be further stressed that policy-makers must also examine each right that is granted under their regime of exclusive rights separately. In other words, when deciding to criminalize, policymakers must differentiate between exclusive rights of rights holders (e.g., reproduction, distribution, and the making available) and examine them on their own. The fact that one exclusive right is criminalized does not imply that criminalizing a different right is also justified.

The integrated approach takes us to four main stages of evaluation. The first stage examines whether copyright infringement is either harmful or wrongful, or both. I argue that, generally, copyright infringement can cause both financial and social harm to various players in the field, and thus can potentially fulfill the harm principle requirement. Nevertheless, infringements for commercial advantages or financial gains are not necessarily harmful in the same sense as infringements without commercial advantages or financial gains. Thus, not every infringement act meets the harm principle's requirements. Examining the wrongfulness of copyright infringements, which I classify as a *mala prohibita* offense (wrong because prohibited) and not a *mala in se* offense (wrong in itself), leads to the conclusion that they could be wrongful to some extent, but nevertheless, not necessarily wrongful for every type of infringement. Thus, not every act of infringement meets the wrongfulness requirements.

Although, generally, the first stage of criminalization could also inquire into other Feinbergian's "liberty-limiting principles," namely, the offense principle and legal paternalism, they are irrelevant in discussing the criminalization of copyright, as copyright infringements are not "offensive" in the sense of Feinberg's formulation of the principle, while there are no paternalistic elements in copyright infringements.[2] Thus, depending on the legislators' criminal view, I argue that criminal copyright for at least some types of infringements should pass the first stage of criminalization, while it is highly doubted that it applies to all types of infringements.

The second stage examines whether the state or society has a substantial interest in the statute's objective. This stage identifies the public interest (state interest/

---

[1]   Although the commercial nature of infringements and their scope are not necessarily the only available measures to distinguish between infringements, they are the most debated measures discussed in criminal copyright legislation, and thus will serve as my baseline for distinguishing between infringements.

[2]   For this conceptualization, see ANTONY DUFF, ANSWERING FOR CRIME: RESPONSIBILITY AND LIABILITY IN THE CRIMINAL LAW 123–26 (2007).

protected social interest), determines its legitimacy, and decides whether that interest is substantial. I argue that criminal copyright passes this test. I locate, inter alia, the state interest of protecting the creation and dissemination of copyrighted works for both authors and the public welfare, and find that it is both legitimate and substantial.

The third stage examines whether criminal law will directly advance the substantial state interest, and whether it is more efficient than other measures, e.g., civil or administrative law. Under the third stage, policymakers must assess and identify alternatives to the criminal law, and examine whether they are more efficient. Here, I use two different forms of evaluation: an *ex-ante* evaluation, based on economic analysis of crime (along with its limitations) and an *ex-post* evaluation, based on evidence from implementing criminal copyright in the past, and determine whether the results of this addition corresponds to the efficiency stage requirements. I argue that criminal law can advance the state interest of some infringements, but that criminal law is not necessarily the optimal enforcement mechanism to regulate other forms of infringements, e.g., infringements without commercial advantage or financial gain, mainly on a small scale since criminalization is not always justified by legislators who share this stage's view of criminal law.

Finally, the fourth stage examines consequences of criminalization. This stage requires that the legislature examine the consequences of criminalization by conducting a cost-benefit analysis of the consequences of implementing the criminal law. I conclude that criminal copyright is not always justified, as the potential drawbacks for some types of activities supports non-criminalization for any policymaker.

Examining copyright criminalization through the integrated approach reveals that the process is not always justified. Depending on the legal system's approach to both criminal and copyright laws, this would lead to different criminalization outcomes. Mainly, criminalization under a *natural-right* justification for copyright protection would justify criminalization more than under an incentive/utilitarian and users' rights approaches. Moreover, scrutinizing the various types of copyright infringements under the incentive/utilitarian approach, would lead to different outcomes depending on the type of infringement. Accordingly, this chapter concludes that copyright criminalization should be carefully implemented, only when the integrated approach – which is designed by the specific view of a criminal law – supports it.

I EXAMINING CRIMINAL COPYRIGHT

The outcome of a decision to criminalize depends on both criminal and copyright law perspectives. When scrutinizing copyright criminalization through the integrated approach to criminalization an evaluation of each stage of the theory under the viewpoint of each copyright theory separately is required. Moreover, under the examination of each copyright theory, a distinction among four types of copyright infringement is important, as each could produce different outcomes. I examine copyright criminalization through these types of infringements: first, infringement committed for commercial advantage or private financial gain ("commercial gain infringement"); and second, infringement committed without consideration of commercial advantage or private financial gain ("non-commercial gain infringement"). These two fundamental forms of copyright infringement may be further divided into two sub-categories: commercial scale/large scale and non-commercial scale/small scale, depending on the magnitude of the infringement.[3]

A Criminalization First Stage: Harmfulness of Copyright Infringement

The *harm principle* is an essential element of most criminalization theories.[4] The first stage in determining whether copyright criminalization is justified requires assessing whether copyright infringement is harmful, and if so, whether it meets the harm principle's requirements. Evaluating the harm principle in its broader sense could reflect possible damage – and not only individual damage, but damage to the public interest. Even in cases where rights holders are not harmed by unlawful infringements, the broader question is whether the community is harmed by this conduct, even if the harm is remote and nonspecific.[5] Thus, the harm principle requires examining both harm to individuals and to the public.

Likewise, harm is not only associated with physical damage but can be measured by financial damage. In the realm of criminal law, copyright infringement could be classified as a white-collar crime.[6] As such, infringement will rarely include physical harm or violence,[7] but still might include financial harm. Thus, two types of harm are linked to copyright infringements. First, is *financial harm* inflicted upon various

---

[3] In addition, copyright criminalization is a generic term for every criminalized conduct; however, not all conducts are similar. For example, the question of criminalization could take various forms within copyright law, and refer to different types of actions, e.g., making, distributing, and making available. When examining whether to criminalize a specific action, e.g., reproduction or making available, policymakers must scrutinize them separately through the integrated approach.

[4] For discussion on harm as an important element in most criminalization theories, see Chapter 7.

[5] JOEL FEINBERG, THE MORAL LIMITS OF THE CRIMINAL LAW: HARM TO OTHERS 11 (1984).

[6] Although white-collar crimes used to be attributed to respectable persons of high social status who committed the acts during or through their employment, current thinking has redefined this term to attribute crimes to persons using sophisticated resources that are readily available. *See* I. Trotter Hardy, *Prosecuting White Collar Crime: Criminal Copyright Infringement*, 11 WM. & MARY BILL OF RTS. J. 305, 306–07 (2002).

[7] *Id.* at 308; Irina D. Manta, *The Puzzle of Criminal Sanctions for Intellectual Property Infringement*, 24 HARV. J.L. & TECH. 469, 475 (2011).

entities: authors; rights holders (who are not necessarily authors)[8]; intermediaries (e.g., suppliers and distributors); society; and possibly domestic and international economies (e.g., employment and government revenue loss).[9] Second, is a *social harm* that is inflicted on society and national policies.[10] I further explore the various kinds of harm, dividing them into the distinct ways in which copyright is perceived, while examining four types of copyright infringement.

1 Financial Harm

The scope of potential harm caused by copyright infringement could be enormous: for example, loss of sales for rights holders, e.g., photographers, songwriters, authors, and various industries (such as film and music). These losses could also potentially harm a multitude of intermediaries, both suppliers and distributors, who are involved in either the production of works and/or their distribution. Additionally, consumers could be forced to pay higher prices for copyrighted products because of free riders, which potentially harm society. Finally, sale losses also potentially harm domestic and international economies, as government revenues from the copyright industry, mostly obtained from taxes, will be reduced, and jobs could also be lost due to the industries' harm.[11]

With that, copyright infringements are not necessarily economically harmful, that is, when they do not constitute a substitute good.[12] If someone decides to illegally obtain a copy of a copyrighted album without paying for it, e.g., by downloading it from the internet for free, but otherwise did not intend to purchase the album, the rights holder is not economically harmed by that person's action. Unlike tangible property, categorized as rivalrous goods, downloading an album from the internet

---

[8]   *See* Diane L. Kilpatrick-Lee, *Criminal Copyright Law: Preventing a Clear Danger to the U.S. Economy or Clearly Preventing the Original Purpose of Copyright Law?*, 14 BALT. INTELL. PROP. L.J. 87, 118 (2005).

[9]   For example, an economic analysis conducted by Stephen Siwek suggests that the United States suffers an economic loss of $58 billion in total output annually, including 373,375 jobs, and at least $2.6 billion in tax revenues annually (which also includes revenue and related measures of gross economic performance). *See* STEPHEN E. SIWEK, INST. FOR POL'Y INNOVATION, POLICY REPORT 189: THE TRUE COST OF COPYRIGHT INDUSTRY PIRACY TO THE U.S. ECONOMY i (2007), *available at* www.ipi.org/docLib/20120515_CopyrightPiracy.pdf. Siwek has published various studies on behalf of interest groups, e.g., the International Intellectual Property Alliance. The research findings should be carefully examined. *Cf.* A recent report by LSE Media Policy Project, contradicts claims regarding the decline of the United Kingdom's creative industries because of copyright infringement. *See* Bart Cammaerts, Robin Mansell & Bingchun Meng, *Copyright & Creation: A Case for Promoting Inclusive Online Sharing*, LSE (2013), *available at* www.lse.ac.uk/media@lse/documents/MPP/LSE-MPP-Policy-Brief-9-Copyright-and-Creation.pdf (last visited Dec. 1, 2017).

[10] Cheng Lim Saw, *The Case for Criminalising Primary Infringements of Copyright – Perspectives from Singapore*, 18 INT'L J.L. INFO. TECH. 95, 104 (2009).

[11] *See supra* note 9.

[12] Hardy, *supra* note 6, at 308.

does not affect the "real" copy of the album nor does it necessarily deprive the rights holders of profits. Profit is not lost and the rights holder is subsequently not harmed when the downloader decides to download the album illegally for free, when the downloader would not otherwise would have paid for the album.[13] Put simply, not every copyright infringement is a lost sale.

Evaluating the financial harm for rights holders is a difficult, if not an impossible, task. However, as a general matter, not every copyright infringement should be treated as a loss to copyright owners. In some instances, infringements might be economically beneficial, e.g., when monopoly prices are charged above marginal costs, creating deadweight losses that can be inefficient.[14]

Moreover, reported losses by rights holders are probably higher than actual losses. Eric Goldman argues that the "overcounting" of rights holders' losses is "because individuals have heterogeneous reservation prices for copyrighted works, so some individuals may procure a cheap infringing copy (where the cost is below their reservation price) but would not have procured a more expensive copy (where the cost exceeds their reservation price)." Moreover, as Goldman argues, the "over-counting" phenomenon is most obvious in cases where infringing copies can be procured for free, whereas "the infringing work's 'cost' (zero) is below everyone's reservation price, and thus more copies are made than would have occurred at a higher price." The actual loss could theoretically be calculated "by recreating a demand curve and excluding all copies procured by infringers whose reservation price was below the retail value." In addition, as Goldman argues, some rights holders may implicitly desire copyright infringements, as a method to price discriminate or to create barriers to entry by locking in users. Thus, an "overcounting" of rights holders' losses occur.[15] The actual magnitude of harm is probably somewhere in between.

The harm element is crucial in a copyright criminalization decision, as under-evaluating harm could lead to under-criminalizing law and over-evaluation could achieve the opposite.[16] In evaluating the possible harm caused by copyright infringements, I refer to two sets of considerations: first, to the different types of infringements of commercial and non-commercial gain, committed either on a commercial or non-commercial scale; and second, to the copyright law approach, which could evaluate harm differently.

Commercial gain infringements do not necessarily resemble non-commercial gain infringements vis-à-vis harm to the rights holder. Presumably, in both cases of commercial and non-commercial gain infringement, harm inflicted on rights

---

[13] *See, e.g.,* Eric Goldman, *A Road to No Warez: The No Electronic Theft Act and Criminal Copyright Infringement,* 82 OR. L. REV. 369, 426–27 (2003).

[14] Jonathan S. Masur & Christopher Buccafusco, *Innovation and Incarceration: An Economic Analysis of Criminal Intellectual Property Law,* 87 S. CAL. L. REV. 276, 295–96 (2014).

[15] *See* Goldman, *supra* note 13, at 426–28.

[16] *Id.* at 426.

holders is the loss of profits from not selling or licensing works. However, commercial gain infringement also possesses other important elements that may increase the notion of harm[17]: commercial gain infringers are often the competitors of the rights holder, and, therefore, the harm could potentially threaten the rights holder's position in the market.[18] In addition, commercial gain infringers can potentially cause greater harm than can the individual non-commercial infringer.[19] On the one hand, if someone decides to illegally make 10,000 copies of an album for commercial sale, the rights holder will most likely suffer substantial harm. On the other hand, if one decides to download the same CD from the internet for free, for one's own personal use, the rights holder does not incur substantial financial loss, if any. It would require many end users doing so to cause substantial harm.[20] Thus, only when 10,000 end users (with the previous intent of purchasing the CD) download it instead for free, could the harm become equivalent to that in the physical world.

But not all non-commercial gain infringers are similar. Some non-commercial gain infringers only cause small-scale harm to rights holders, if any. Others could cause large-scale harms, especially due to digitization, and particularly on the internet, which changes the possible harm that a single non-commercial gain infringer can cause. One of the most famous cases is that of David LaMacchia, which I discussed earlier and which eventually led to the enactment of the No Electronic Theft (NET) Act.[21] In establishing the BBS, LaMacchia encouraged his correspondents to upload popular software applications and computer games, which he made accessible to other users to download.[22] LaMacchia did not derive any financial benefit from his actions, i.e., he was a single non-commercial gain infringer who caused some rights holders revenue loss, presumably more than one million U.S. dollars.[23] Over the internet, even a person with basic computer skills can use P2P networks to infringe and make a work available on a large scale – which could harm rights holders significantly. Thus, in the sense of the harm principle, non-

---

[17] For a similar argument on the difference between commercial and non-commercial gain infringements, see Geraldine S. Moohr, *The Crime of Copyright Infringement: and Inquiry Based on Morality, Harm, and Criminal Theory*, 83 B.U. L. REV. 731, 755–57 (2003).

[18] *Id.* at 755.

[19] *Id.* at 755–56.

[20] *Id.* at 756–57.

[21] No Electronic Theft (NET) Act, Pub. L. No. 105–47, 111 Stat. 2678 (1997) (codified as amended at 17 U.S.C. §§ 101, 506, 507; 18 U.S.C. §§ 2319, 2320; 28 U.S.C. § 1498). For more on the NET Act and David LaMacchia's actions, see *supra* Chapter 3.

[22] *See* United States v. LaMacchia, 871 F. Supp. 535 (D. Mass. 1994).

[23] According to the indictment, LaMacchia's bulletin board system had as its object the facilitation "on an international scale" of the "illegal copying and distribution of copyrighted software" without payment of licensing fees and royalties to software manufacturers and vendors. The prosecutors alleged that LaMacchia's scheme caused losses of more than one million U.S. dollars to software copyright holders. However, the prosecutor's loss estimate was unsupported. *See* Goldman, *supra* note 13, at 372; Joseph F. Savage, Jr. & Kristina E. Barclay, *When the Heartland Is "Outside the Heartland:" The New Guidelines for NET Act Sentencing*, 9 GEO. MASON L. REV. 373, 377 (2000).

TABLE 5 *Harm of Copyright Infringements*

	Non-Commercial Scale	Commercial Scale
Non-Commercial Gain	*No/Low Harm*	*Possible Harm*
Commercial Gain	*Probable Harm (Low or High)*	*Harm*

commercial gain infringers on a commercial-scale should not be treated equally with the non-commercial gain infringers on a non-commercial scale, as their potential scope of harm is different. The problem will be delineating the elements constituting a commercial-scale infringement.

The linkage between non-commercial gain infringers and harm is probably the most debatable question in copyright criminalization.[24] In contrast, a single act of infringement by a non-commercial gain infringer should not amount to harm in the sense of criminalization. As previously noted, unlike physical theft of property, the infringer does not deprive the owner of any tangible items, and in some cases, never intended to buy the work – thus, not harming the rights holder financially. Harm is caused when there are a vast number of infringers. According to this scenario, even though not all non-commercial-gain infringers cause harm, there is a statistically high probability that at least one infringement will cause harm. If this is the case, criminalization could be justified on these grounds (under the first stage). The problem under this scheme is the over-inclusiveness of criminal law to encompass conduct, which is not harmful on its own, but rather harmful when actions by a certain number of people result in definite harm. It criminalizes conduct of some infringers that do not cause harm. The various notions of harm in copyright are evident in Table 5.

To conclude, under the first stage of the integrated approach, there is a difference between the four types of activities. While commercial gain infringers cause harm that is generally sufficient for the harm principle requirements (yet, not always), non-commercial gain infringers cause harm that is potentially sufficient to withhold the harm principle, but only when it is committed on a commercial scale. However, turning to the second form of evaluation, the notion of harm requires further analysis of relevant copyright law theories, because each would evaluate harm differently.[25]

Under a natural-right conception of copyright law, namely the personality or labor-desert theories, copyright infringement causes harm from both commercial and non-commercial gain infringement, without turning to the question of the

[24] It is important to note that criminalizing a type of behavior does not imply that all the exclusive rights of a copyright owner are affected similarly. See, for instance, in the United States, 17 U.S.C. § 106 (2012).
[25] Under the evaluation of the first stage of the integrated approach, users' rights theory should not change the notion of financial harm.

commercial scale of the infringements. The harm from infringement is self-evident in the theories, and thus fulfills the harm principle requirements.

Under the incentive/utilitarian theory of copyright law, the question of harm is examined through its impact on the incentive of rights holders. Harm principle requirements are partially fulfilled under the incentive/utilitarian theory, as the harm of copyright infringement could possibly create a chilling effect on the creation of new works. However, not every copyright infringement necessarily reduces the incentive to create. According to this notion, commercial-gain infringement is more criminally justifiable than non-commercial gain infringement. However, even non-commercial gain infringement could potentially cause financial harm to an extent that it would reduce the incentive to create. Copyright infringements on a commercial scale, such as David LaMacchia's actions,[26] are potentially no less harmful than other infringements for commercial advantage or private financial gain, and by this theory should be criminalized. However, as harm is not evident in this scenario, the harm principle requirements are only partially fulfilled. Thus, commercial scale infringers should not be treated in the same manner as non-commercial scale infringers, because their potential impact on copyright incentives is different.

To conclude the discussion of the harm principle, financial harm to rights holders should be attributed to some commercial gain infringement and perhaps to infringement on a commercial-scale without commercial gain. The question of whether such criminalization should apply to the non-commercial scale without commercial gain infringers is debatable.[27] However, I argue that the possible over-inclusiveness of these infringers should be a constraint on their criminalization, as the potential harm of non-commercial scale and gain infringers is not evident, and if it exists, it will usually be relatively low.

2 Social Harm

From a social perspective, harm done to rights holders' does not qualify for criminalization when it does not also involve harm to a community and/or a national interest. From an economic perspective, social harm requires proof that the infringers have materially increased the risk of economic dislocation or inefficient

---

[26] See *LaMacchia*, 871 F. Supp.

[27] Certain uses of copyrighted material might be in violation of the statute, but do not necessarily violate the statute's purposes. Various considerations, e.g., an existence of a market failure; when transfer of the use to defendant is socially desirable; and when awarding the end user a non-commercial personal use right would not cause substantial injury to the incentives of the plaintiff copyright owner. However, a non-commercial personal use right does not apply to every form of copyrighted works, and the various considerations would not apply to every usage by an end user. For more on non-commercial personal use under the fair use exemption, see Wendy J. Gordon, *Fair Use as Market Failure: A Structural and Economic Analysis of the Betamax Case and Its Predecessors*, 82 COLUM. L. REV. 1600 (1982).

financial markets.[28] Thus, the broader question is whether copyright infringement causes social harm and is of a magnitude sufficient to criminalize this conduct.

Under a natural-right conception of copyright law, i.e., personality or labor-desert theories, examining copyright infringement's social or financial harm will provide similar outcomes, whether committed commercially on a small scale or on a large scale. Accordingly, the outcomes of examining both social and financial harm will be similar under the incentive/utilitarian theory of copyright law, but perhaps on different grounds. Copyright infringements could potentially impair the incentive to create, and negatively influence the market of works and ideas. With this possibility, copyright infringement could harm the social policy that encourages creativity,[29] and criminal legislation could be an appropriate response. The main social harm that could suffice for criminalization is the protection of national policies and interests, such as copyright. Protecting the copyright regime is an important social policy for various reasons. One such reason is that it provides an incentive to create works of original expression. Thus, if copyright infringement lowers the incentive to create, then the copyright regime is potentially at risk: fewer works means fewer possibilities for society and, ultimately, shrinkage of the public domain.[30]

B *Criminalization First Stage: Wrongfulness of Copyright Infringement*

Using a retributivist approach, blameworthiness is justified when a conduct breaches a moral norm. Is copyright infringement morally wrong? Unfortunately, there is no single or easy answer to this complex question, and various views of copyright law might answer differently on the possible scope of immorality that inheres in copyright infringements.

The first stage in evaluating the wrongfulness of copyright infringements, without turning to a specific copyright law theory, is determining whether the conduct is a *mala in se* offense: if conduct is morally wrong, intrinsically bad, or evil,[31] then other considerations could be irrelevant for the question of criminalization. Take, for

[28] *See* Peter Alldridge, *The Moral Limits of the Crime of Money Laundering*, 5 BUFF. CRIM. L. REV. 279, 302–15 (2001); Moohr, *supra* note 17, at 763.

[29] *See* Moohr, *supra* note 17, at 757.

[30] However, lowering the incentive to create does not necessarily lead to a social harm. Any activity could possibly be socially harmful, but does not necessarily increase the risk of economic dislocation or inefficient financial markets. As evident from Chapters 2 and 3, although copyright has been undergoing a criminalization process for more than a century in both the United Kingdom and United States, criminal enforcement is very low. Nevertheless, although reports indicate that copyright infringements are still happening at a high rate, the copyright regime still exists; and it is debatable whether it is currently threatened, as the industries still thrive. Thus, even if there is a social harm to a community interest and/or a national interest, it does not necessarily amount to being harmful in the sense of criminalization.

[31] *See, e.g.*, Richard L. Gray, *Eliminating the (Absurd) Distinction between Malum In Se and Malum Prohibitum Crimes*, 73 WASH. U. L. Q. 1369, 1370 (1995).

example, homicide – a classic example of a *mala in se* offense. Homicide is morally wrong, intrinsically bad, and considered evil conduct; therefore, it should be a criminal offense. Whether there are less extreme or better alternatives than criminalization, and whether criminal law directly advances the substantial state interest in reducing murder rates and protecting the public, could be irrelevant to the question of criminalization, as this conduct deserves the highest form of social condemnation. Thus, under a moralist view, murder should be a crime, even if criminal law is not the most effective regulatory mechanism. Copyright infringement, however, is different, and classifying copyright infringement as *mala in se* offense is generally misleading, for it is not an intrinsically wrongful behavior.[32]

Turning to a more specific examination of wrongfulness under copyright law theories – specifically the labor-desert theory, which conceptualizes copyright as property – infringement should be considered morally wrong because it resembles stealing authors' livelihoods and that of other intermediaries who are linked to the commercial aspects of the work, while reducing their incentives to create and by that harm society.[33] Because theft is an antisocial assault on property rights, as a means of retribution it should earn society's moral condemnation.[34] The labor-desert theory could even categorize copyright infringement as intrinsically bad or evil and classify it as a *mala in se* offense.[35] Thus, similar to the conception that unauthorized taking of property is criminally culpable (along with being a civil wrong),[36] copyright law should also be criminalized.[37] Under this argument, the moral voice of tangible and intangible property is no different, and thus, should be similarly criminalized.[38] Harm in this matter is irrelevant as well. The unauthorized seizure of property from a person, even if it is intangible and does not cause harm, should be sufficient grounds to determine whether it is an immoral act, or at least immoral enough to pass the wrongfulness requirement.

Under the incentive/utilitarian theory, even when copyright is not treated as tangible property, the conduct of copyright infringement could still be considered morally wrong. Even copyright infringement for personal use, e.g., non-commercial gain infringement, is morally wrong, at least to some extent, as the infringer does not

---

[32] *See* Steven Penney, *Crime, Copyright, and the Digital Age, in* WHAT IS A CRIME? CRIMINAL CONDUCT IN CONTEMPORARY SOCIETY 61, 71 (Law Comm'n of Canada ed., 2004).

[33] *See* Kilpatrick-Lee, *supra* note 8, at 95; Moohr, *supra* note 17, at 765.

[34] *See* John Lindenberg-Woods, *The Smoking Revolver: Criminal Copyright Infringement,* 27 BULL. COPYRIGHT SOC'Y 63, 67 (1979).

[35] *See, e.g.,* WILLIAM BLACKSTONE, COMMENTARIES ON THE LAWS OF ENGLAND 54 (15th ed. 1809); Gray, *supra* note 31, at 1375.

[36] There are some possible exceptions to criminal unauthorized taking of property, e.g., in cases of necessity, duress, and self-defense. *See* Penney, *supra* note 32, at 69.

[37] Lydia Pallas-Loren, *Digitization, Commodification, Criminalization: The Evolution of Criminal Copyright Infringement and the Importance of the Willfulness Requirement,* 77 WASH. U.L.Q. 835, 858 (1999).

[38] Penney, *supra* note 32, at 69.

pay for the work, and potentially deprives the rights holder of profits.[39] Nevertheless, as previously argued, is it immoral to infringe copyright for personal use, even when the act of infringement does not deprive profits from the rights holders, and subsequently does not cause harm? How can we decide whether copyright infringement is considered immoral when portions of the public, perhaps its majority even, do not share this view?[40] The approach of the incentive/utilitarian theory to the wrongfulness of copyright infringement is debatable. However, as a general note, it seems that if the infringement does not reduce the incentive to create, infringement could not be deemed immoral, because it does not negatively affect the rights holder. Thus, according to this notion, the wrongfulness and harmfulness outcomes under the incentive/utilitarian theory are similar.

Under the personality theory, which conceptualizes copyright as an extension of the self, copyright infringement could be morally wrong as the author's "spiritual children" are at risk. The outcome of evaluating this type of wrongfulness does not depend on the various forms of infringement. Whether the infringer acts for personal profit or does not, and whether such an infringement is committed on a large or a small scale is irrelevant to the question of morality and wrongfulness under this theory.

To conclude, the harmfulness and wrongfulness requirements for criminalization of copyright vary across legal systems and across approaches to criminal and copyright law and are applied differently to distinct types of actions. With a natural-right perspective, copyright infringements are both harmful and wrongful enough to pass the first stage of evaluation. However, with the incentive/utilitarian approach, the harmfulness and wrongfulness of copyright infringement are evident only in commercial gain infringement, while policymakers should generally abstain from criminalizing non-commercial gain infringement, and definitely when the infringements are small scale.

C Criminalization Second Stage: Substantial Public Interest

During the second stage of the integrated criminalization approach, mainly derived from Husak's external constraints, justifying criminalization requires a substantial public interest in whatever objective the statute is designed to achieve. Under this stage, the public interest can be also interpreted as a protected social interest, as advocated by some legal systems; and policymakers should adjust this evaluation, depending on their view of criminalization in general. As for copyright criminalization, we should identify the state interest, determine its legitimacy, and decide

---

[39] See, e.g., Moohr, supra note 17, at 765.
[40] See Stuart P. Green, Plagiarism, Norms, and the Limits of Theft Law: Some Observations on the Use of Criminal Sanctions in Enforcing Intellectual Property Rights, 54 HASTINGS L.J. 167, 238 (2002); PAUL R. PARADISE, TRADEMARK COUNTERFEITING: PRODUCT PIRACY, AND THE BILLION DOLLAR THREAT TO THE U.S. ECONOMY 249 (1999).

whether that interest is substantial. On this matter, Husak, forming a test of inter-mediate scrutiny, argues that in order for an interest to be considered substantial, it must be greater than the requirement that it be rational, and less than the require-ment that it be compelling.[41] While copyright theories might vary on the notion of state interests, each should pass this first stage of evaluation, as each identifies a different state interest.

The incentive/utilitarian theory to copyright identifies the state interests in crim-inalizing copyright as protecting the creation and dissemination of copyrighted works that are endangered due to the perceived risk to incentive. Natural-right theories identify the state interest as follows: the protection of authors and the rewards to them. Under the users' rights approach to copyright, the state interest in criminalizing copyright is important for protection of the public welfare and, eventually, the public domain, as both could be endangered.

Protecting the state interest in the production and dissemination of copyrighted works and preventing economic harm is both legitimate and substantial. First, protecting the copyright regime is important under all copyright theories and is all-important for society.[42] Second, protecting copyright is important for preserving and maximizing the public domain.[43] If copyright infringement reduces the incen-tive to create, then the public domain will ultimately contain fewer works. Third, copyright law is an engine of free expression.[44] Protecting copyright, thus, advances free speech (but also restricts it), which is usually considered to be a highly important right.[45] Fourth, copyright law is significant to a nation's economy, accounting for an increasing share of jobs and trade.[46] As such, the interest in criminalizing copyright is high.

To conclude, copyright infringement passes the second stage of the integrated criminalization approach for policymakers that view this stage as important. It locates a substantial state interest in the objective the statute is designed to achieve,

---

[41] See Douglas Husak, Overcriminalization – The Limits of the Criminal Law 129 (2008).
[42] William M. Landes & Richard Posner, An Economic Analysis of Copyright Law, 18 J. Legal Stud. 325 (1989).
[43] Cf. Robert P. Merges, Justifying Intellectual Property 6–7 (2011).
[44] Harper & Row, Publishers, Inc. v. Nation Enters., 471 U.S. 539, 558 (1985).
[45] In the United States, for example, free speech is protected by the First Amendment to the U.S. Constitution (U.S. Const. amend. I). It is also recognized globally as a human right in various forms of international legislation, agreements, and declarations. See Universal Declaration of Human Rights, art. 19, G.A. Res. 217 (III) A, U.N. Doc. A/RES/217 (III) (Dec. 10, 1948). For more information on free speech and copyright, see generally Copyright and Free Speech: Comparative and International Analyses (Jonathan Griffiths & Uma Suthersanen eds., 2005); Neil Weinstock Netanel, Copyright's Paradox (2008); Michael D. Birnhack, Copyright Law and Free Speech After Eldred v. Ashcroft, 76 S. Cal. L. Rev. 1275 (2003); Michael D. Birnhack, The Copyright Law and Free Speech Affair: Making-Up and Breaking-Up, 43 IDEA 233 (2003).
[46] See, e.g., H.R. Rep. No. 110–617 at 21 (2008) ("[i]ncreasing intellectual property theft in the United States and globally threatens the future economic prosperity of our nation.").

while the state interest in protecting copyright law is legitimate and substantial enough to qualify for criminalization.

D *Criminalization Third Stage: Efficiency*

Under the third stage, justifying criminalization requires two elements. First, criminal law directly advances the substantial state interest. In other words, the question is as follows: Does criminal copyright directly mitigate the perceived economic and social harm that copyright infringements can cause to authors, rights holders, and the public at large? Second, are there alternatives that are equally effective and less extensive than criminalization? Within the latter sub-category, I examine whether there are less restrictive measures than criminal law to address and resolve the conceived problem of copyright infringement and consider whether they are more efficient. The methodology for reviewing the efficiency of criminal copyright is important for the outcome of the evaluation, and could differ according to the variety of approaches to criminalization. In this part, I apply two different forms of evaluation: an ex-ante evaluation (mainly based on an economic analysis of crime) that is absent from current criminalization theories; and an ex-post evaluation that is based on evidence from implementing criminal copyright in the past. This will enable us to evaluate whether the results of criminalization correspond to the efficiency stage requirements.

A caveat is in place: economic analysis of criminal law is controversial in criminalization literature. Mainly, economic analysis has been criticized as being insufficient in determining whether copyright should be criminalized. Along with the claim that economic analysis is not always applicable to many aspects of copyright infringement, and it is often non-measurable, it also possesses two main drawbacks.

First, economic analysis relies on human *rationality*, which is not always an exact measurement. A cost-benefit analysis of crime does not consider non-rational actors, and thus does not apply to all viable players in the field.[47] This applies to individuals who are risk-neutral (indifferent regarding two outcomes that have the same expected value), risk-preferring (with the same expected value, always preferring the maximum potential return of their choice), and risk-averse (with the same expected value, always preferring the choice with the least risk).[48]

Second, an *information gap* of many users as to the scope and possible ramifications of their actions (infringing copyright) and the possible sanctions they might face, if caught, could influence the economic model.[49] Furthermore, the economic

---

[47] *See* Robin Andrews, *Copyright Infringement and the Internet: An Economic Analysis of Crime,* 11 B.U. J. Sci. & Tech. L. 256, 274 (2005).

[48] *Id.* at 276–77.

[49] *Id.* at 275–76.

analysis of law is often criticized and is not expected to provide a criminalization theory.[50] However, because some scholars have suggested general principles, which purport to govern the imposition of criminal sanctions, and furthermore have suggested including economic analysis in criminalization theories,[51] I implement some observations of law and economics when evaluating efficiency of other measures, e.g., civil and administrative law, to advance the substantial state interest or the protected interest by evaluation of the most optimal enforcement mechanism.[52] Thus, bearing in mind its shortcomings, I apply economic analysis as part of this examination, as it provides important insights into copyright criminalization.[53] Policymakers who resist the application of economic analysis in criminal law, can disintegrate this stage of evaluation, to use other forms of evaluation or encompass only the ex-post evaluation, which is based on evidence from implementing criminal copyright in the past.

1 Advancing the Substantial Public Interest

The state's interest in criminalizing copyright law is the protection of the perceived economic and social harm caused by copyright infringement. Under this subcategory of criminalization, I examine whether the imposition of criminal sanctions in copyright law can advance the state interest at all,[54] and not whether it is the optimal enforcement scheme, which I examine in the next sub-phase.

Meeting the state interest mostly relies on deterrence and enforceability. Can criminal sanctions deter copyright infringement? Will criminal sanctions affect individual behavior?[55] And is copyright infringement publically enforceable?

---

[50] For further criticism on implementing economic analysis of law in criminal legislation, see, e.g., GEORGE P. FLETCHER, THE GRAMMAR OF CRIMINAL LAW: AMERICAN, EUROPEAN, INTERNATIONAL 59 (2007); HUSAK, *supra* note 41, at 180–87.

[51] For a proposition to apply law and economics in criminalization theories when examining alternative mechanisms, see Roger Bowles, Michael Faure & Nuno Garoupa, *The Scope of Criminal Law and Criminal Sanctions: An Economic View and Policy Implications*, 35 J.L. & SOC. 389, 390 (2008).

[52] For more on economic analysis of crime, see, e.g., Gary S. Becker, *Crime and Punishment: An Economic Approach*, 76 J. POL. ECON. 169 (1968).

[53] *Cf.* Stephen J. Schulhofer, *Is there an Economic Theory of Crime?* in NOMOS XXVII: CRIMINAL JUSTICE 329, 330 (J. Roland Pennock & John W. Chapman eds., 1985) ("[L]egal scholars must also accept that the problem of protecting society from crime while protecting offenders from unnecessarily stringent sanctions, that is, the problem of optimal resource, allocation, is central to the work they should be doing. Thus, the work and interests of many, criminal justice scholars is seriously incomplete."); Andrews, *supra* note 47, at 262.

[54] My evaluation is different from Husak's proposal, which requires empirical evidence rather than unsupported speculation that the law advances the state interest. Although I use economic analysis, Husak's theory does not generally support the integration of economic analysis into criminalization theories. See HUSAK, *supra* note 41, at 145.

[55] *Paul Robinson & John Darley* argue that a rule can be expected to change behavior only when three assumptions are satisfied: awareness of the rule; possession of knowledge that influences behavior as decisions are being made; and the individual believing that the perceived costs

Criminal copyright could advance the state interest through deterrence based on the use of criminal sanctions and due to other possible benefits of criminal enforcement. Criminal law can achieve some level of deterrence for four main reasons. First, criminal sanctions, and especially nonmonetary sanctions, e.g., imprisonment, can deter potential infringers from infringing copyright. Nonmonetary criminal sanctions can either deter potential infringers who fear such sanctions, and/or deter potential infringers who are effectively "judgment proof," and will not be deterred by either civil damages or criminal fines.[56] Moreover, due to criminal law's expressive value, sanctions can deter some potential positivist infringers, which view any criminal prohibition as a wrong, simply because it is criminal, even lacking moral justifications for the criminalization.[57]

Second, criminal sanctions can create stigma that could deter some potential infringers from infringing copyright.[58] Criminal law can also aid in shaping a moral and/or a social norm against infringement, thereby reducing it. Public perception of copyright infringement as a morally or socially wrong behavior can potentially be achieved by enacting criminal sanctions. However, this is not a simple task, because the public should perceive copyright law as just and fair. As Jessica Litman argues, "[i]f the public perceives copyright law to give it a poor return on its investment, it may well respond by divesting – either pressing its elected representatives to enact additional limitations and privileges, or simply failing to comply with rules it no longer perceives as legitimate."[59] Taking this argument further, most of the public are not likely to accept criminal copyright unless the social norm of infringing copyright rises to a level in which it is perceived by them as a socially wrong behavior.

Third, criminal enforcement has many procedural benefits that could possibly reduce copyright infringement and therefore advance the state interest.[60] Thus, governmental resources can aid in advancing the state interest, especially in cases

---

outweigh the perceived benefits of offending. *See* Paul H. Robinson & John M. Darley, *Does Criminal Law Deter? A Behavioral Science Investigation*, 24 OXFORD J. LEGAL STUD. 173 (2004).

[56] *See, e.g.,* Richard A. Posner, *An Economic Theory of the Criminal Law*, 85 COLUM. L. REV. 1193, 1195 (1985).

[57] For the positivistic approach to criminal law, see Henry M. Hart, *The Aims of the Criminal Law*, 23 LAW & CONTEMP. PROBS. 401, 404 (1958); DENNIS J. BAKER, THE RIGHT NOT TO BE CRIMINALIZED 2 (2011).

[58] For more on stigma of criminal sanctions, see Eric Rasmusen, *Stigma and Self-Fulfilling Expectations of Criminality*, 39 J.L. & ECON. 519, 519–44 (1996); Alon Klement & Alon Harel, *The Economics of Stigma: Why More Detection of Crime May Result in Less Stigmatization*, 36 J. LEGAL STUD. 355, 355–78 (2007); Bowles, Faure & Garoupa, *supra* note 51, at 392; *Cf.* Penney, *supra* note 32, at 76.

[59] Jessica Litman, *Real Copyright Reform*, 96 IOWA L. REV. 1, 17–18 (2010).

[60] For example, the identity of the person who initiates the procedure: in criminal law, the State brings criminal proceedings; and in civil law, the injured party usually initiates the proceedings; a different statute of limitations for initiating a civil and a criminal suit; etc. *See supra* Chapter 1.

where rights holders do not possess sufficient knowledge, funds, or expertise to file civil lawsuits and fund litigation.[61] Additionally, criminal procedures could further advance the state interest, as it sometimes requires less formality requirements than does civil copyright litigation. For instance, in the United States, criminal prosecution of copyright infringement does not require registration or preregistration of a work.[62]

Fourth, criminal copyright could aid in the rehabilitation of infringers,[63] thus reducing future infringement and advancing the state interest.[64] Using rehabilitation programs, copyright infringers could possibly cease or at least reduce their infringing activities, therefore, reducing copyright infringements.

To such a degree, the insertion of criminal sanctions into copyright law can potentially advance the state interest, mostly through deterrence. The question is whether criminal copyright will succeed in achieving such deterrence is mostly obtained through the question of deterrence and enforceability. As previously mentioned, the question of deterrence and enforceability is examined ex-ante by an economic analysis of crime.[65]

Under the deterrence theory, assuming that people are rational utility maximizers and risk neutral, deciding to commit a crime is much like any other decision people make.[66] Decisions are largely based on the net benefit, which is composed of a cost-benefit analysis: individuals weigh the benefits of an act against the probability and magnitude of punishment,[67] and only comply with the law when the benefits of compliance outweigh their costs.[68] Specifically, an act will be deterred when

---

[61] Under this assumption, not all rights holders are wealthy industries, and therefore do not necessarily possesses sufficient knowledge, funds, and expertise to file civil lawsuits. Not all individual artists are able to file multiple lawsuits or embark on investigating the possibility of the infringement of their rights.

[62] 17 U.S.C. §§ 408–412.

[63] Nevertheless, it is not evident that rehabilitation of copyright infringers is necessary or even desired by society.

[64] *See, e.g.,* Katarina Svatikova, Economic Criteria for Criminalization: Optimizing Enforcement in Case of Environmental Violations 25 (2012).

[65] Gary Becker offered the first comprehensive economic theory of crime in 1968. Since then, there has been extensive research on this matter which mainly focuses on searching for the most efficient enforcement system, criminal, administrative or civil, to deter unlawful acts, and to what extent. *See* Becker, *supra* note 52; Andrea Wechsler, *Criminal Enforcement of Intellectual Property Law: An Economic Approach, in* Criminal Enforcement: A Blessing or a Curse for Intellectual Property? 128, 128–29 (Christophe Geiger ed., 2012). Becker's theory of crime was widely criticized. *See, e.g.,* Avraham D. Tabbach, *The Social Desirability of Punishment Avoidance,* 26 J.L. Econ. Organ. 265 (2010).

[66] Becker, *supra* note 52, 83–85; Wechsler, *supra* note 65, at 142. As mentioned earlier, the cost-benefit analysis of crime does not consider non-rational actors, and thus does not apply to all possible players in the field. Thus, I also include an ex-post analysis of criminalizing copyright, which could aid in filling this information gap of nonrational actors.

[67] Jeremy Bentham, An Introduction to the Principles of Morals and Legislation 178–88 (Oxford: Clarendon Press, 1996) (1789); Penney, *supra* note 32, at 75.

[68] Svatikova, *supra* note 64, at 77.

expected costs are higher than expected benefits.[69] Or in other words, deterrence is achieved when the sanction is much higher than the damage caused.[70] The cost-benefit results would primarily depend on the level of deterrence.[71]

Deterrence can be divided into two different types: marginal and general deterrence.[72] Marginal deterrence encourages possible criminals to less socially, costly crimes, i.e., it increases the gap of punishment between different crimes.[73] Under general deterrence, criminal law should not seek to punish ex-post crimes, but rather prevent them ex-ante, assuming that people will choose their course of action by examining the expected results.[74] Deterrence could be accomplished through various methods, which could potentially involve different sorts of economic variables, e.g., increasing the probability of detection, apprehension, conviction, and/or punishment.[75] The expected sanction is determined by the probability of detection and conviction is multiplied with the scale of the sanction.[76]

Consider a copyright-related scenario to illustrate this point. Assume that while copyright infringement is illegal people have the technological ability to freely download any song they wish, and as much as they like. Each song is valued at $2. However, the ability to download the song is insufficient to determine whether the action is profitable. To assess profitability, we must consider the potential cost and the probability of getting caught. For the purpose of this discussion, consider that detection is equal to cost, i.e., every person caught downloading a song will be forced to pay $2.[77] Profitability in this case will differentiate scenarios, which could potentially lead to different outcome:[78]

Scenario 1: The chance of being caught downloading a song is 0. In this case, as the probability is 0, the cost is 0 ($2 * 0% = 0), so the expected value is $2 (100%).

---

[69] *Id.* at 77; Becker, *supra* note 52.
[70] Bowles, Faure & Garoupa, *supra* note 51, at 402.
[71] While Congress used deterrence as a justification for criminal insertion, it is a prime mover of economic analysis. *See* Penney, *supra* note 32, at 75.
[72] Andrews, *supra* note 47, at 262.
[73] For example, if an offender receives the same punishment for crimes which are different in scope, e.g., is to be executed for a minor assault just the same as for a murder, then there is no marginal deterrence to murder, which might thus be preferable. *See* RICHARD POSNER, AN ECONOMIC ANALYSIS OF LAW 282 (8th ed. 2011); George J. Stigler, *The Optimum Enforcement of Laws*, 78 J. POL. ECON. 526, 527 (1970); Andrews, *supra* note 47, at 262–63.
[74] *See* Kenneth G. Dau-Schmidt, *An Economic Analysis of the Criminal Law as a Preference-Shaping Policy*, 1990 DUKE L.J. 1 (1990); Andrews, *supra* note 47, at 261–62.
[75] Becker, *supra* note 52; Wechsler, *supra* note 65, at 142–45.
[76] Becker, *supra* note 52; SVATIKOVA, *supra* note 64, at 77; Wechsler, *supra* note 65, at 142.
[77] Although this scenario implements monetary fines, which could also be applicable to non-criminal sanctions, it could also be applied in nonmonetary criminal sanctions.
[78] For similar scenarios, see Hardy, *supra* note 6, at 312–14.

Scenario 2: The chance of being caught downloading a song is 100%. In this case, as the probability is 100%, the cost is $2 ($2 * 100% = $2), so the expected value is 0 (0%).

Scenario 3: The chance of being caught downloading a song is 50%. In this case, as the probability is 50%, the cost is $1 ($2 * 50% = $1), so the expected value is $1 (50%).

Clearly with scenarios 1 and 3, people have an economic motivation to download the song. In scenario 2 there is no such motivation: that is, deterrence plays a role in economic justification to commit the offense. However, in these scenarios, punishment was set only to the amount of the cost. Raising punishments could easily change the outcomes of the scenarios. Now consider similar scenarios under a new proscribed $10 fine for downloading a song from the internet, valued at $2:

Scenario 1: The chance of being caught downloading a song is 0. In this case, as the probability is 0, the cost is 0 ($10 * 0 = 0), so the expected value is $2 (100%).

Scenario 2: The chance of being caught downloading a song is 100%. In this case, as the probability is 100%, the cost is $10 ($10 * 100% = $10), so the expected value is -$8 (-400%).

Scenario 3: The chance of being caught downloading a song is 50%. In this case, as the probability is 50%, the cost is $5 ($10 * 50% = $5), so the expected value is -$3 (-150%).

The new punishment of a $10 fine for downloading a song changes the outcome of the scenarios. In scenarios 2 and 3, users have no economic motivation to download the song, which remains profitable only in the first scenario. In other words, in those scenarios where the chance of being caught downloading a song is higher than 0%, users are deterred from their actions, since the cost exceeds its benefits.[79]

Therefore, the magnitude of the sanction plays an important role in shaping actions of future infringers. Increasing enforcement for a copyright infringer should be set at a value that outweighs the expected benefit to the infringer.[80] However, there are social barriers to increasing the severity of punishment. If punishment exceeds social norms they are less likely to be fully enforced.[81] When a community does not desire to enforce a law, it can influence enforcement agencies, and in so doing curtail the usage of the law,[82] causing the *inverse sentencing effect*,[83] i.e., high penalties could decrease convictions instead of increasing them.[84] The effect could

---

[79] *Id.*

[80] *See* STEVEN SHAVELL, FOUNDATIONS OF ECONOMIC ANALYSIS OF LAW 551 (2004); Wechsler, *supra* note 65, at 142–43.

[81] *See* Penney, *supra* note 32, at 75.

[82] *See* Stigler, *supra* note 73, at 534; Penney, *supra* note 32, at 75.

[83] *See* Neal Kumar Katyal, *Deterrence's Difficulty*, 95 MICH. L. REV. 2411, 2450 (1997).

[84] *Id.* at 2450.

occur when penalties are viewed by the public as nonproportional to the offense, causing the police, prosecutors, jurors, and judges to exercise discretion in imposing sanctions.[85] In addition, if the public does not view the "crime" as wrong, it will be difficult to create such deterrence.[86] Hence, increasing the severity of punishment would not necessarily serve as a deterrent against those crimes, and could potentially induce people to commit more serious offenses with similar penalties.[87] Moreover, prison sentences might not deter large infringing operations, e.g., organized crime, as they could use scapegoats to serve time, and simply restart the company again.[88]

The purpose of this analysis is not to discuss the magnitude of punishment that the legislature should seek, but rather argue that criminal law could potentially achieve deterrence. Thus, under deterrence theories, criminal law could possibly prevent potential infringers from infringing copyrighted materials and advance the substantial state interest of the perceived economic and social harm that copyright infringement causes. Now, I move on to answer the question: Is criminal law the most efficient method to regulate infringement?

2 Examining Alternatives to Criminal Law

If more efficient legal mechanisms exist it could be irrelevant that criminal law could possibly advance the state interest or the protected interest. The normative justification for this reason is mostly utilitarian,[89] founded on what is often referred to in literature as the *ultima ratio* principle – criminal sanctions should be applied only when other measures fail.[90] Under this argument, for legislators who view criminal law as *ultima ratio*, unless private and administrative law measures have failed, copyright law should remain non-criminal. However, some approaches to criminal law might find this assumption false: a positive legal moralist, for example, might not search for alternatives, as criminal law serves an important expressive value. Thus, such legislators can separate this stage of evaluation and disregard its potential outcomes. For policymakers who view criminal law as an *ultima ratio*, the

---

[85] *Id.* at 2451; Penney, *supra* note 32, at 75.

[86] *See* Penney, *supra* note 32, at 75; Dan M. Kahan, *Between Economics and Sociology: The New Path of Deterrence*, 95 MICH. L. REV. 2477, 2481 (1997).

[87] *See* Penney, *supra* note 32, at 76.

[88] *See* Martin Brassell & Ian Goodyer, PENALTY FAIR? STUDY OF CRIMINAL SANCTIONS FOR COPYRIGHT INFRINGEMENT AVAILABLE UNDER THE CDPA 1988, IPO 71 (2015), www.gov.uk/ government/uploads/system/uploads/attachment_data/file/405874/Penalty_Fair_Study_of_crim inal_sanctions_for_copyright_infringement_available_under_the_CDPA_1988.pdf.

[89] There are possible other normative justifications for the requirement of efficiency in applying criminal law, e.g., on the possible negative effects of criminalization on constitutional rights.

[90] Nils Jareborg, *Criminalization as Last Resort (Ultima Ratio)*, 2 OHIO ST. J. CRIM. L. 521, 525 (2005); *Cf.* Malcolm Thorburn, *Constitutionalism and the Limits of the Criminal Law*, in THE STRUCTURES OF THE CRIMINAL LAW 101 (Antony Duff et al. eds., 2011).

alternatives for criminalization first require determining whether private and administrative law measures are ineffective in regulating copyright infringements.[91]

I use two methods to determine the optimal enforcement scheme: first, an ex-ante evaluation, applying an economic analysis of crime to assist in determining whether criminal copyright is more efficient than other measures to regulate copyright infringement and advance the state interest most efficiently. This method is also very limited as some economic considerations are absent. Second, an ex-post evaluation, through the practical use of non-criminal measures to regulate behavior and consider whether criminal copyright was implemented as a last resort.

Ex-Ante Evaluation. Assuming that copyright infringement is a harmful activity, the basic economic criterion for criminalization is whether criminal legislation achieves a social, optimal level of harmful activity, than other forms of legislation.[92] As a general argument, criminal law is preferable in those instances where civil or administrative laws do not internalize the costs of an unlawful act,[93] and criminal law achieves optimal enforcement.[94] The optimal enforcement theory focuses on overall social costs of crime and costs of crime enforcement to improve society.[95] On the one hand, society benefits from imprisonment due to four main elements: deterrence, retribution, rehabilitation, and incapacitation.[96] On the other hand,

---

[91] At this stage, Husak examines the overinclusivness of criminal laws in a constitutional manner. I, however, offer the implementation of both economic analysis of crime and an ex-post evaluation of actual success of criminal copyright. For more on Husak's examination of the alternatives to criminal law, see HUSAK, *supra* note 41, at 154–59.

[92] Bowles, Faure & Garoupa, *supra* note 51, at 390, 395. Steven Shavell locates the following factors, relevant to the choice between monetary and nonmonetary sanctions (and consequently, sometimes between criminal and non-criminal legislation): level of wealth; private benefits from committing acts; probability of imposition of sanctions; and expected harmfulness of acts. *See* Steven Shavell, *The Optimal Structure of Law Enforcement*, 36 J.L. & ECON. 255, 266 (1993).

[93] ROBERT COOTER & THOMAS ULEN, LAW AND ECONOMICS 452 (4th ed. 2004); If one person's actions impinge negatively on one or more third parties, it results in negative externalities. For example, a polluting factory could potentially cause a negative externality if it adversely affects neighbors. If the state imposes liability on the factory owner, the consequences become internalized as to whether to build the factory or how to handle possible pollution. For a similar argument, see Bowles, Faure & Garoupa, *supra* note 51, at 396–97. In addition, the Coasean approach to externalities will justify public enforcement when high transaction costs between parties are likely to fail. *See* Ronald Coase, *The Problem of Social Cost*, 3 J. LAW & ECON. 1 (1960); Guido Calabresi & Douglas Melamed, *Property Rules, Liability Rules, and Inalienability: One View of the Cathedral*, 85 HARV. L. REV. 1089 (1972). However, the application of a Coasean approach could be problematic as IP transaction costs are usually higher than physical property. *See* Salil K. Mehra, *Software as Crime: Japan, the United States, and Contributory Copyright Infringement*, 79 TUL. L. REV. 265, 301.

[94] Andrews, *supra* note 47, at 262; Wechsler, *supra* note 65, at 136.

[95] Andrews, *supra* note 47, at 263.

[96] Another mentionable element is restitution. *See* SHAVELL, *supra* note 80, at 550–52; ANDREW ASHWORTH, SENTENCING AND CRIMINAL JUSTICE 77–91 (2010); GEORGE P. FLETCHER, RETHINKING CRIMINAL LAW 409 (2010); Paul H. Robinson, *Criminalization Tensions: Empirical Desert, Changing Norms, and Rape Reform*, in THE STRUCTURES OF THE CRIMINAL LAW 186, 187 (Antony Duff et al. eds., 2010).

imposing criminal sanctions is not always economically efficient: criminalization increases social costs from imposing criminal sanctions as the state's involvement requires funding, e.g., detecting infringers, investigating, prosecuting, building, maintaining, and staffing prisons, losing potential workers, business, and so forth.[97]

To evaluate optimal enforcement, this part discusses the main conditions that should be satisfied to justify criminalization as the most efficient instrument to internalize social costs and as suggested in the academic literature and summarized by Katarina Svatikova.[98] It is based on the economic analysis of the role of victims and the nature or magnitude of harm.[99] These conditions are *mens rea* (intent), imperfect/low probability detection, the level of harm, compensatory vs. punitive, and enforcement costs.

Mens rea. The criminal intent principle, or *mens rea*, relates to a person's state of mind, meaning that under some exceptions,[100] a person will only be held criminally liable for actions that person intended to do.[101] If intent is present, under the assumption that actors are conscious of the scale of their damage,[102] public enforcement will be preferred over private enforcement – mainly because intent to cause harm increases the probability of actually causing harm and decreases the probability of detection. It also results in a need for a funding agency to allocate funds, acquire information, and to investigate.[103]

What should be the mental element necessary for the commission of copyright crime?[104] Put differently, should copyright infringement require intent or should it be a strict liability offense? Criminal copyright infringement usually requires the presence of intent through the element of willfulness. In the United States, which requires a willfulness element for criminal copyright prosecution, the exact meaning

---

[97] See Wechsler, *supra* note 65, at 144–45. Annual costs of incarceration vary throughout states and countries. For example, to keep an adult inmate incarcerated in the State of Indiana costs an average of $54.28 per day, or $19,812 annually. *See* Indiana Department of Correction, www.in.gov/idoc/2378.htm. *See also* David C. Leven, *Curing America's Addiction to Prisons,* 20 FORDHAM URB. L.J. 641, 643–44 (1993).
[98] See SVATIKOVA, *supra* note 64, at 71–84. *See also* Masur & Buccafusco, *supra* note 14, at 284–85.
[99] See Bowles, Faure & Garoupa, *supra* note 51, at 396.
[100] Criminal law does not always require actual intent, e.g., negligence and recklessness. *See id.* at 399.
[101] See SVATIKOVA, *supra* note 64, at 73.
[102] See Bowles, Faure & Garoupa, *supra* note 51, at 299.
[103] In addition, the willingness to enter into private negotiations could also serve as distinctive criteria, whereas with deliberately caused harm, the offender does not likely wish to enter into private negotiations with the potential victim in the first place. *See* SVATIKOVA, *supra* note 64, at 73.
[104] Stuart P. Green argues that plagiarism should also require intent or "deliberate indifference," much like theft does under criminal law. Green differentiates between a "mistake of fact" and a "mistake or ignorance of the law," and suggests that only the latter should apply in the context of plagiarism. Under this argument, copyright infringement should also require intent or "deliberate indifference" to establish *mens rea*, including a mistake or ignorance of the law. *See* Green, *supra* note 40, at 182–85; Dan M. Kahan, *Ignorance of the Law Is an Excuse – But Only for the Virtuous,* 96 MICH. L. REV. 127, 128, 135 (1997).

of this requirement is vague, as it is not defined by the law.[105] While some courts interpret willfulness to mean a "voluntary, intentional violation of a known legal duty,"[106] other courts have held that willfulness means only intent to copy, not intent to infringe.[107]

Intent could play an important role in distinguishing between different kinds of copyright infringements. People who engage in copyright infringement for commercial advantage or private financial gain will most likely be acting intentionally. Thus, these activities should be sufficient to meet the *mens rea* requirement. Yet, many people who engage in copyright infringements for non-commercial advantage or private financial gain, are often unaware of the infringement, and therefore should not be held criminally liable. This became evident with the proliferation of the internet, which enabled end users to infringe copyright in many everyday activities with spectacular ease; one that they are not always aware of.[108] Nonetheless, criminal law could play an educational role for these infringers, and hence they will ultimately have sufficient awareness about copyright infringements, fulfilling the *mens rea* requirement. Generally, criminal copyright under this criterion should only be reserved for intentional infringements and not merely intent to copy. As long as criminal copyright is reserved for willful actions, it could be sufficient to pass the *mens rea* requirement. However, even if applicable to all copyright infringements, intent represents a weak basis for public enforcement, in general, and an economic analysis of criminal law, in particular, because of its subjective assessment difficulties and diverse nature.[109]

Imperfect/Low Probability Detection. Imperfect detection in the realm of the economic analysis refers to the relatively lower likelihood of detecting an offense as a private citizen as opposed to an arm of public law enforcement.[110] In some cases, there may be a relatively high degree of damage and a relatively low chance of catching the offender.[111] Imperfect detection is a result of various distinctions between private and public enforcement. First, each have different motives in suing, in addition to a collective action problem resulting from a low expected return from prosecution.[112] Second, public agencies could have an informational

---

[105] *See* 17 U.S.C. § 506.
[106] *See* United States v. Moran, 757 F. Supp. 1046, 1049 (D. Neb. 1991).
[107] *See* United States v. Taxe, 380 F. Supp. 1010, 1017 (C.D. Cal. 1974).
[108] For examples of how ordinary Americans become mass copyright infringers with spectacular ease, see JOHN TEHRANIAN, INFRINGEMENT NATION: COPYRIGHT 2.0 AND YOU 2–14 (2011).
[109] By "diverse nature," I am referring to the fact that some crimes do not require proof of intent, e.g., regulatory offenses; and on the other hand, some intentional torts require some form of intent, but are not considered criminal. *See* SVATIKOVA, *supra* note 64, at 73–74; Bowles, Faure & Garoupa, *supra* note 51, at 399–400.
[110] *See* SVATIKOVA, *supra* note 64, at 74.
[111] Bowles, Faure & Garoupa, *supra* note 51, at 401–402.
[112] *See* Steven Shavell, *The Fundamental Divergence between the Private and Social Motive to Use the Legal System*, 26 J. LEGAL STUD. 575 (1997); Bowles, Faure & Garoupa, *supra* note 51, at 400; SVATIKOVA, *supra* note 64, at 75.

advantage.[113] Third, private rights holders may not possess the "right" technology, lacking economies of scale or profit orientation, which would not prevent efficient detection.[114] Fourth, regulatory intervention might be more effective than a private injunction in the sense that it might be more difficult for private right holders to cease unlawful activities ex ante.[115] Fifth, public agencies have potentially better success pursuing suspects globally.[116] And finally, fear from retaliation could prevent victims or witnesses from engaging in private prosecution.[117]

Imperfect private detection could be a valid reason for public enforcement by copyright criminalization.[118] Since the birth of criminal copyright in both the United Kingdom and United States, as discussed in Chapters 2 and 3, imperfect detection was a main cause for copyright criminalization. In the United Kingdom, the 1906 Act, which criminalized copyright was enacted due to a growing practice of the unlawful sale of music sheets.[119] In the United States, the introduction of criminal provisions to copyright law under the 1897 Act, was due to music copyright owners' concerns that civil remedies did not deter unlawful performances of music, as unlicensed performances throughout the country were difficult to monitor.[120] Thus, in both countries imperfect/low detection served as an important justification for criminalization. Moreover, at the beginning of the twentieth century, imperfect detection was limited to only specific types of copyrighted works. The digital era, however, marks a major change in this regard. Digital technology provides the public with a more affordable and accessible manner by which to copy and distribute works, in faster and easier ways, and sometimes with lower risks of detection. Thus, as the possibility of detection has decreased over time, to some extent, public enforcement could still be more efficient than private enforcement. However, it does not distinguish between administrative and criminal law. Moreover, the efficiency of public enforcement is not evident. Many rights holders could possess greater financial funds than the government, and therefore could invest more resources in detecting and filing suit against infringers. Other rights holders,

---

[113] However, note that, generally, private parties should possess superior information about violations due to their direct involvement in harmful activities. The limitation on information is caused when the information is needed to be developed or if special expertise in needed for its evaluation. *See* Steven Shavell, *Liability for Harm Versus Regulation of Safety*, 13 J. LEGAL STUD. 357 (1984); SVATIKOVA, *supra* note 64, at 74; Bowles, Faure & Garoupa, *supra* note 51, at 400.

[114] *See* Gary S. Becker & George J. Stigler, *Law Enforcement, Malfeasance, and Compensation of Enforcers*, 3 J. LEGAL STUD. 1 (1974); Bowles, Faure & Garoupa, *supra* note 51, at 400.

[115] Bowles, Faure & Garoupa, *supra* note 51, at 400.

[116] Kent Walker, *Federal Remedies for the Theft of Intellectual Property*, 16 HASTINGS COMM. & ENT. L.J. 681, 688 (1994).

[117] Bowles, Faure & Garoupa, *supra* note 51, at 400.

[118] *See* Wechsler, *supra* note 65, at 137–38.

[119] Musical Copyright Act of 1906, 6 Edw. VII, c. 36 (U.K.). *See supra* Chapter 2.

[120] Musical Public Performance Right Act of Jan. 6, 1897, ch. 4, 29 Stat. 481 (1897). *See supra* Chapter 3.

who do not possess these financial resources, are less likely than the government to detect and file lawsuits.

The Level of Harm. The level of harm could potentially serve as a criterion for criminalization due to the assumption that, the more harmful an activity is, the more it should be controlled by the most coercive mechanism.[121] Thus, the question is whether the harm caused by copyright infringement is substantial enough for criminalization. As discussed earlier, there are two main kinds of harm linked to copyright infringements: financial harm and social harm. Financially, copyright infringement can cause direct and indirect harm to rights holders, intermediaries, consumers, and the public at large. However, the scope of this financial harm is practically unmeasurable, if not highly debatable. Although some scholars and industry representatives report that copyright infringement causes a substantial financial harm due to (potential) loss of sales,[122] other scholars argue that copyright infringement's harm is not substantial, if it exists at all.[123] Furthermore, it is difficult to evaluate whether money that is not spent on purchasing legal copies represents a loss to the economy, as it could be spent on other purchases (including, perhaps, of services or products of the rights holder, like concert tickets or other merchandise).[124]

Although the industry may inflate the magnitude of financial harm caused by copyright infringements, it suffices to argue that some financial harm exists, but its magnitude is debatable and difficult to measure. Recognizing this, social harm is even more difficult to measure than financial harm. Even if copyright infringements cause social harm, i.e., harm to a community interest and/or a national interest, it

---

[121] SVATIKOVA, *supra* note 64, at 76.

[122] *See*, e.g., Norbert J. Michel, *Digital File Sharing and the Music Industry: Was There a Substitution Effect?*, 2 REV. ECON. RES. COPYRIGHT ISSUES 41, 50 (2005) (arguing that there appears to be mounting evidence that digital copying negatively impacted music sales); Martin Peitz & Patrick Waelbroeck, *The Effect of Internet Piracy on Music Sales: Cross-Section Evidence*, 1 REV. ECON. RES. ON COPYRIGHT ISSUES 71 (2004) (finding that music downloading could have caused a 20% reduction in music sales worldwide between 1998–2002); SIWEK, *supra* note 9, at i (arguing that United States economy suffers 373,375 job losses annually); H.R. REP. NO. 105–339, at 4 (1997) (arguing that industry groups estimate that "piracy" of intellectual property cost the affected copyright holders more than $11 billion in 1996, and that the effect of this volume of theft is substantial: 130,000 lost U.S. jobs, $5.6 billion in corresponding lost wages, $1 billion in lower tax revenue, and higher prices for honest purchasers of copyrighted software).

[123] *See* Felix Oberholzer-Gee & Koleman Strumpf, *File-Sharing and Copyright* (Harvard Business School, Working Paper No. 09–133, 2009), www.hbs.edu/research/pdf/09-132.pdf; WILLIAM PATRY, MORAL PANICS AND THE COPYRIGHT WARS 15–16 (2009) (noting that empirical evidence indicates that music and film industries revenue continue to rise each year despite copyright infringements). *Cf.* Stanley J. Liebowitz, *How Reliable Is the Oberholzer-Gee and Strumpf Paper on File-Sharing?* (Sept. 2007) (unpublished manuscript), *available at* http://papers.ssrn.com/sol3/papers.cfm?abstract_id=1014399 (arguing that Oberholzer-Gee and Strumpf results should have come to a different conclusion, i.e., that sharing has a positive impact on sound recordings).

[124] *See* Brassell & Goodyer, *supra* note 88, at 21.

requires proof that the infringers actually and materially increase the risk of economic dislocation or inefficient financial markets.[125] Even if copyright infringements apparently cause social harm, this does not necessarily amount to
criminally harm. It is even more doubtful as to whether small scale, non-
commercial infringements cause social harm – especially when this harm is minor
and its impact on creativity and the incentive to create is probably low. It is notable
that this could change with a large number of such infringements, which, when
integrated, could cause substantial harm.

To conclude, copyright infringement causes both financial and social harm, but
these harms are practically unmeasurable and debatable. Hence, economic analysis
of this stage is problematic and cannot serve as an indicator to determine whether
copyright infringements should be criminalized.

Compensatory vs. Punitive. Internalization of harm in civil law is imperfect.
Even if victims receive substantial financial compensation, they will not be in the
position they were in prior to the act, resulting in an ineffectual deterrence from an
economic standpoint.[126] Robert Cooter argues that, whereas civil law fixes a price for
behavior in the form of a sanction, criminal law aims at deterring behavior by
imposing a sanction.[127] Therefore, the aim of public and private systems is different.
However, criminal sanctions are not necessarily "more punitive" than civil sanctions.[128] Although as a general argument, criminal sanctions are more drastic than
civil sanctions,[129] in fact, in many cases, civil sanctions are no less punitive than
criminal sanctions.[130] Thus, in some cases, private law resembles public law. For
example, punitive damages, which can increase compensation,[131] carry criminal law
characteristics, resulting in a vague boundary between public and civil law. Hence,
the nature of compensatory versus punitive actions causes an imperfect boundary
between private and public law.[132] The general argument is that a criminal conviction is likely to pose a harsher punishment than civil damages and could cause
greater deterrence.[133]

---

[125] See Alldridge, *supra* note 28, at 302–15; Moohr, *supra* note 17, at 763.

[126] Bowles, Faure & Garoupa, *supra* note 51, at 402–403.

[127] Robert D. Cooter, *Prices and Sanctions*, 84 COLUM. L. REV. 1523 (1984); Bowles, Faure & Garoupa, *supra* note 51, at 403.

[128] See, e.g., Kenneth Mann, *Punitive Civil Sanctions: The Middle Ground Between Civil and Criminal Law*, 101 YALE L.J. 1795, 1798 (1992).

[129] Imprisonment imposes high personal opportunity costs, and thus potentially represent a greater deterrent than monetary sanctions. For this argument, see Bowles, Faure & Garoupa, *supra* note 51, at 398; *See also* WAYNE R. LaFAVE, CRIMINAL LAW 15 (2003).

[130] See JEREMY BENTHAM, RATIONALE OF PUNISHMENT 12 (Kessinger Publishing, LLC, 2010) (1830); Moohr, *supra* note 17, at 747.

[131] Robert D. Cooter, *Economic Analysis of Punitive Damages*, 56 S. CAL. L. REV. 97 (1982); Bowles, Faure & Garoupa, *supra* note 51, at 403.

[132] Bowles, Faure & Garoupa, *supra* note 51, at 404.

[133] See Hardy, *supra* note 6, at 312; Daniel S. Nagin, *Criminal Deterrence Research at the Outset of the Twenty-First Century*, 23 CRIME & JUST. 1, 3 (1998).

Examining current civil copyright remedies in both the United Kingdom and United States, revealed that civil copyright law does provide substantial financial remedies for infringement – usually meant to return rights holders to the same position they were in prior to the act, if not an improved one. Thus, the internalization of harm in civil copyright law could be perfect to some extent, as it fixes a relatively high price for behavior in the form of a sanction. However, some copyright infringers who are effectively judgment proof, might not have the ability to compensate rights holders, and therefore, the victim will not receive substantial financial compensation for infringement. In these instances, public law, and more specifically criminal law, might be the only available mechanism.

Enforcement Costs. Adhering to criminalization should take into account enforcement costs.[134] On a high level of enforcement costs, the public enforcer will have a high incentive to act only when the harm is substantial, due to a social gain of achieving deterrence, as opposed to an insubstantial harm, which causes a sunk cost for a relatively small benefit.[135] Generally, relatively small harms should not be enforced through public law, because enforcement costs are greater than deterrence benefits.[136] From an economic perspective, the optimal law enforcement mechanism is obviously the cheapest.[137] Criminal (and public) enforcement includes costs to the public system and for compliance from private parties with public regulations.[138] Mainly, these costs are used for detecting infringers, investigating, interrogating, prosecuting, building, maintaining, and staffing prisons, loss of potential workers and business, judicial costs, etc.[139] Private enforcement includes the expenses of private parties (including time and effort) as well as public expenses of private litigation.[140]

Using this criterion, economic analysis is limited, as the costs of public and private enforcement are unknown and could vary among different countries. As a general argument, legislators should examine whether criminal enforcement of copyright is costlier than civil enforcement of copyright, to determine which is the optimal law enforcement mechanism.

*

To conclude, criminal law can advance the state interest in protecting copyright, at least to some extent. An *ex-ante* evaluation of economic analysis of crime reveals that

---

[134] SVATIKOVA, *supra* note 64, at 76.
[135] Mitchell A. Polinsky, *Private Versus Public Enforcement of Fines*, 9 J. LEGAL STUD. 105, 114 (1980); SVATIKOVA, *supra* note 64, at 76.
[136] However, note that in some cases public enforcement costs are sufficiently small, close to private enforcement costs, meaning that public enforcement is more efficient. *See* Polinsky, *supra* note 135, at 120; SVATIKOVA, *supra* note 64, at 76–77.
[137] SVATIKOVA, *supra* note 64, at 83.
[138] *Id.*
[139] *See* Wechsler, *supra* note 65, at 144–45.
[140] SVATIKOVA, *supra* note 64, at 83.

rational utility maximizers and risk-neutral entities, will base their decision on the net benefit, weighting the benefits of an act against the probability and magnitude of punishment, and only complying with the law when the benefits of compliance outweigh their costs. Thus, increasing the magnitude of a sanction by criminal law could shape possible infringers future actions, and therefore, criminal copyright can create deterrence and advance the state interest. However, under an *ex-ante* evaluation of efficiency, criminal law is not necessarily the optimal enforcement scheme, as other mechanisms exist, and should be used only as a last resort. The efficiency criterion is further analyzed through an *ex-post* evaluation of non-criminal measures applied in practice.

Ex-Post Evaluation. Criminal copyright, with some exceptions, was many times legislated after a perceived failure to respond to copyright infringements through non-criminal measures.[141] As discussed in Chapter 5, rights holders responded to copyright infringements *via* the law, the market, social norms, and architectural design (code).[142] Non-legislative measures included filing lawsuits against various players, private ordering, technological protection measures, and education. As a non-criminal legislative measure, rights holders strengthen their copyright protection through legislation that increases their potential revenues from their rights, legally protects technological measures that aid their copyright protection, and expands the potential damages of infringements (by civil or administrative legislation).[143]

Whether non-criminal measures have decreased copyright infringement is debatable, especially when civil and criminal measures have usually been combined in an attempt to reduce copyright infringements, and have thus been inseparable. There is little doubt however that non-criminal measures have not solved copyright infringement's perceived problem, for this phenomenon has not yet ceased. Thus, a narrow review of the *ex-post* evaluation is that criminal copyright law is needed, since other measures have failed to address the perceived problem of copyright infringements. A broader view is required. Determining whether criminal law is effectively the last resort to reduce or eliminate copyright infringements requires reviewing two main elements: first, the question as to whether other non-criminal measures been exhausted; and second, the question as to whether criminal law is an effective measure to regulate infringement thus far.

Exhaustion of Non-Criminal Measures. Response to copyright infringements took various forms. Despite the many efforts to eliminate or at least substantively reduce copyright infringement, thus far, these efforts have not achieved their purpose. Copyright infringements still occur at a relatively high rate. Non-criminal

[141] For further information on the various reasons that led to copyright criminalization, see Chapters 5–6.
[142] *See* LAWRENCE LESSIG, CODE: VERSION 2.0 120–37 (2006); LAWRENCE LESSIG, FREE CULTURE 116–73 (2004).
[143] *Id.*

measures probably do not possess the same deterring effect as criminal sanctions, at least for some infringers.[144] Nevertheless, the fact that current methods have not achieved their purpose does not necessarily imply that they have been implemented to their fullest extent, or more precisely, that they have been implemented correctly. Under this argument, rights holders can continue their civil litigation against infringers; they could use better technological measures to protect their copyright; they could create more efficient educational campaigns; and they could try new business models or methods of regulation, such as implementing a non-commercial-use levy,[145] creating a balanced public enforcement process that is mostly civil in nature,[146] voluntary collective licensing systems,[147] or a government-run rewards system,[148] as suggested by the literature on copyright. After conducting an economic analysis of criminal copyright infringement, Jonathan Masur and Christopher Buccafusco argued that, for copyright infringement, civil sanctions should be sufficient to deter nearly all types of harmful conduct, while noting that imposing criminal sanctions for copyright infringement is only efficient for massive reproduction and sales of commercially valuable works.[149]

Moreover, the legislative review of both United Kingdom and United States in Chapters 2 and 3, revealed that legislators did not always resort to criminal sanctions after other measures failed. The United States for example, introduced both civil and criminal sanctions for the same activities under the DMCA.[150] Without first evaluating whether civil law sufficiently regulates infringement, the DMCA

---

[144] Masur & Buccafusco, *supra* note 14, at 277.

[145] WILLIAM W. FISHER III, PROMISES TO KEEP: TECHNOLOGY, LAW AND THE FUTURE OF ENTERTAINMENT (2004); Neil Netanel, *Impose a Noncommercial Use Levy to Allow Free Peer-to-Peer File Sharing*, 17 HARV. J.L. & TECH. 1 (2003).

[146] Peter Menell proposes a novel solution to deal with copyright infringement, through abandoning the "civil-criminal paradigm" and shifting to a private-public enforcement regime. Under this proposal, Menell argues that we should view government enforcement as a complement to private enforcement, i.e., that public enforcement will deal with the problems that cannot be handled effectively through private infringement actions. The U.S. government will combat infringing activities that require rapid response, while "enforcement procedures should be matched to the particularities of these problems," and while instituting a bonding mechanism to fund compensation for inappropriately targeted individuals. The process will at first be funded by the content industries, which will also receive the beneficiaries of the enforcement activities (received from the illegal operators). To assure objectivity in carrying out these activities, the process will be transparent and isolated from undue influence by interest groups. This process will operate under the civil law regime, except for serious criminal offenses. *See* Peter S. Menell, *This American Copyright Life: Reflections on Re-Equilibrating Copyright for the Internet Age*, 62 J. COPYRIGHT SOC'Y U.S.A. 201, 295–96 (2014); Peter S. Menell, *Governance of Intellectual Resources and the Disintegration of Intellectual Property in the Digital Age*, BERKELEY TECH. L.J. 1523, 1542–56 (2011).

[147] Lori A. Morea, *The Future of Music in a Digital Age: The Ongoing Conflict between Copyright Law and Peer-to-Peer Technology*, 28 CAMPBELL L. REV. 195, 236–39 (2006).

[148] *Id.* at 242–45.

[149] *See* Masur & Buccafusco, *supra* note 14, at 284–85.

[150] Digital Millennium Copyright Act (DMCA), Pub. L. No. 105–304, 112 Stat. 2860 (1998) (codified as amended at 17 U.S.C. §§ 512, 1201–05, 1301–32 & 28 U.S.C. § 4001 (2012)).

criminalized (para)-copyright.[151] This scheme is not optimal for criminalization, and imposition of criminal sanctions when other measures have not yet been employed should be de-criminalized.

The Success of Criminal Copyright. The discussion of criminal copyright in both the United Kingdom and United States remind us that the birth of criminal copyright occurred a relatively long time ago: criminal copyright has existed in the United Kingdom since 1862 and in the United States since 1897. Thus, a rough evaluation of its success in reducing copyright infringements is possible, at least to some extent.

A narrow analysis of criminal copyright's success posits that criminal law has failed to reduce infringements substantially. Under this narrow analysis, criminal copyright is an inadequate mechanism to regulate infringement – and has been unsuccessful in achieving the state interest. However, a broader analysis of criminal copyright posits that it is currently difficult to evaluate the success of criminal copyright, as one of the main reasons for its perceived failure resides in the scope of enforcement. By this argument, criminal copyright should only be examined when enforcement agencies take a more active role in enforcing criminal copyright infringements, and not otherwise, as enforcement is crucial for the success of criminal copyright. Moreover, as legislators have strengthened both civil and criminal copyright over the years, under the expansion paradigm, it is difficult to detect the impact of each strengthening method separately, for many times they have occurred simultaneously. The bottom line is that it is somewhat irrelevant as to which method succeeded more, as both seem to have failed in achieving their purpose. Thus, whether criminal law will succeed in responding to copyright infringement properly is highly doubted. Under this stage of the evaluation, the efficiency requirement of criminal copyright to achieve its purposes has not been fully met. Policymakers should generally refrain from criminalizing copyright law until all other measures have been exhausted and have failed to respond to infringements.

To conclude, under the examination of the third stage of the integrated criminalization approach, copyright criminalization can directly advance the substantial state interest to some extent, but it is not necessarily the only and the most effective mechanism to deal with copyright infringements. Copyright criminalization can advance the state interest through the deterring effect of criminal law on some infringers and because of other benefits of criminal enforcement. However, private and administrative law measures can also directly advance the substantial state interest, and the fact that these measures had not been fully employed supports the notion that under some approaches to criminal law, copyright criminalization was not always justified.

---

[151] *See* Moohr, *supra* note 17, at 752.

E Criminalization Fourth Stage: Consequences

Under the fourth and final stage of the integrated approach, justifying criminalization requires examining its consequences. Such an examination includes determining whether criminalizing copyright is socially desirable,[152] and it will be evaluated by a cost-benefit analysis, using insights from the *balancing* approach to criminalization. The balancing approach, which refers to the idea of weighing all the reasons in favor and against criminalizing an action (with the weightier set of reasons prevailing),[153] also considers the various normative level of each component. However, as each copyright theory might examine the benefits and drawbacks differently, this stage addresses different views of such cost-benefit analysis under each category. Legislators that do not consider the consequences of criminalization to be important, could disintegrate the theory and pass over this stage.

1 Criminal Copyright Benefits

Criminal copyright can be beneficial to rights holders, authors, end users, government, and society. The beneficial factor relies mostly on the assumption that criminal copyright achieves its purposes depending on the criminal and copyright theories held. To evaluate these benefits, I explore the positive explicit impact of criminal copyright on both copyright and criminal laws, and the implicit benefits for society under these categories.

Copyright Law Benefits. Criminal copyright can aid in protecting copyright and thus ensure copyright goals, whether they provide incentives, protect natural rights of authors, or protect the rights of users by maintaining a robust public domain.[154] The underlying goal of criminal copyright in this sense is to advance copyright goals, while benefiting rights holders and society. Stronger copyright protection could result in wider dissemination of ideas and the production of new works.[155] Due to various characteristics, criminal law can aid in advancing copyright goals: it expands copyright protection and means of enforcement; it could achieve higher levels of deterrence than other measures; and it could be more efficient than other measures. Throughout this book, I have discussed the benefits of criminal copyright from various perspectives. Chapter 1 located several advantages of criminal law in general. Chapter 5 analyzed the possible internal reasons for copyright criminalization,

---

[152] *See* Geraldine Szott Moohr, *Defining Overcriminalization through Cost-Benefit Analysis: The Example of Criminal Copyright Laws*, 54 AM. U. L. REV. 783, 785 (2005); EDWARD J. MISHAN, COST-BENEFIT ANALYSIS: AN INTRODUCTION 7 (1971).

[153] For this explanation of the balancing approach, see JONATHAN SCHONSHECK, ON CRIMINALIZATION 25 (1994); NINA PERŠAK, CRIMINALISING HARMFUL CONDUCT: THE HARM PRINCIPLE, ITS LIMITS AND CONTINENTAL COUNTERPARTS 10–11 (2007).

[154] Moohr, *supra* note 152, at 788–89, 791–96.

[155] *See* Lim Saw, *supra* note 10, at 104–05.

which included, inter alia, rights holders' and legislators' desire to enjoy various benefits. The current chapter questions whether criminal copyright could achieve the state interest in criminalizing copyright, and emphasizes the likely gains that criminalization could afford. To evaluate the cost-benefit analysis of copyright criminalization properly, the following part summarizes the various assets as described throughout this book, while addressing a few new components.

(1) **Expanding Copyright Protection and Enforcement Means.** Criminal copyright expands the given protection of copyright works for rights holders and grants them additional legal means to respond to copyright infringement. When other legal and non-legal measures have been found to be inadequate to eliminate, or at least substantially reduce unlawful infringement of copyrighted works, granting rights holders additional measures to respond to infringement can aid in reducing them. On a wider scale, it aids in preserving the incentive to create and invest. Primarily, criminal copyright adds another entity (enforcement agencies and the judiciary) to assist in protecting copyright goals. The entry of governmental agents could be beneficial for several reasons. First, it would expand the possibilities of lawsuits against infringers. Unlike civil copyright infringements, where the claimant must be the copyright owner, the addition of a criminal sanction expands the ability to file lawsuits to enforcement agencies.[156] Second, governmental resources and expertise could promote copyright protection, especially in those cases where rights holders lack sufficient knowledge, detection means,[157] funds, or expertise in filing civil lawsuits. Adding another prosecution entity could also aid in protecting orphan works – for which the copyright owner cannot be identified or located. Third, criminal copyright could increase the timeframe for filing suit – as sometimes the statute of limitations for a civil suit is shorter than that for criminal suits.[158] Fourth, criminal litigation would reduce the risk of counterclaims, i.e., defendants are less likely to sue the government than sue a rights holder.[159] Fifth, using governmental resources to file lawsuits could improve the industry's reputation. As the entertainment industry often suffers from bad publicity, due to civil lawsuits against alleged infringers, it fears alienating existing and potential customers.[160] Seventh, criminal copyright could solve the collective action problem, which arises from

---

[156] See Robin Fry, *Copyright Infringement and Collective Enforcement*, 24 E.I.P.R. 516, 522 (2002).

[157] See Hardy, *supra* note 6, at 312.

[158] See, e.g., in the United States, whereas initiating a civil copyright action can be submitted only within three years after the alleged infringement accrued, whereas a criminal copyright proceeding must be commenced within five years after the cause of action arose. 17 U.S.C. § 507; Brian T. Yeh, *Intellectual Property Rights Violations: Federal Civil Remedies and Criminal Penalties Related to Copyrights, Trademarks, and Patents*, CRS REPORT FOR CONGRESS 4 (2008).

[159] See Maggie Heim & Greg Geockner, *International Anti-Piracy and Market Entry*, 17 WHITTIER L. REV. 261, 267 (1995).

[160] See Moohr, *supra* note 152, at 799; Amy Harmon, *THE NAPSTER DECISION: THE REACTION; Napster Users Make Plans for the Day the Free Music Dies*, N.Y. TIMES (Feb. 13, 2001),

infringements that affect a wide swath of copyright owners.[161] Eighth, criminal copyright brings in the element of prosecutorial discretion, which does not exist in civil copyright.[162]

(2) **Deterrence.** Generally speaking, criminal sanctions serve as better deterrents than civil sanctions.[163] If criminal copyright achieves a higher level of deterrence for infringed copyright than civil proceedings,[164] it could result in fewer copyright infringements, and therefore, decrease the potential harm to rights holders. In that sense, criminal copyright could maintain the necessary incentive to create and invest in copyrighted materials, and protect businesses from potential bankruptcy.[165] Moreover, deterrence can aid foreign rights holders, who may not be aware of infringements or who may not have the ability to file civil lawsuits in that country.[166] In addition, society could benefit from stronger copyright protection. If some creators feel that their rights will be protected and enforced, they might create more works. Also, IP rights are significant to a nation's economy and could serve as an engine of growth,[167] adding new jobs, trade, and businesses.[168] Subsequently, non-monetary criminal sanctions may be necessary when the infringers are judgment proof, i.e., incapable of being deterred by civil damages or criminal fines.[169]

Take for example Kim "Dotcom" Schmitz, the founder of the file hosting service Megaupload. Being wealthy, monetary civil damages or criminal fines might not deter him from unlawful actions, as it may be economically advantageous to infringe, because having to pay damages or fines might be calculated as "the cost

---

www.nytimes.com/2001/02/13/business/napster-decision-reaction-napster-users-make-plans-for-day-free-music-dies.html?src=pm.

[161] Menell, *supra* note 146, at 295.

[162] *Id.*, at 294.

[163] Hardy, *supra* note 6, at 312.

[164] Fry, *supra* note 156, at 522.

[165] *See, e.g.*, Nadine Courmandias, *The Criminalisation of Copyright Infringement in Japan and What This Tells Us about Japan and the Japanese*, 17 ASIA PAC. L. REV. 167, 172 (2009).

[166] Fry, *supra* note 156, at 516.

[167] *See* H.R. REP. 110–617 at 21 (2008) ("[i]ncreasing intellectual property theft in the United States and globally threatens the future economic prosperity of our nation.").

[168] *See* U.S. DEP'T OF JUSTICE, PROSECUTING INTELLECTUAL PROPERTY CRIMES 1 (3d ed. 2006), *available at* www.justice.gov/criminal/cybercrime/docs/ipma2006.pdf ("[i]ntellectual property ("IP") is critical to the vitality of today's economy. IP is an engine of growth, accounting for an increasing share of jobs and trade. In 2002, the core copyright industries alone were estimated to account for 6% or more of U.S. GDP, and in 2005 the overall value of the "intellectual capital" of U.S. businesses – including copyrights, trademarks, patents, and related information assets – was estimated to account for a third of the value of U.S. companies, or about $5 trillion."). The DOJ relies on industries statistics reported in STEPHEN SIWEK, COPYRIGHT INDUSTRIES IN THE U.S. ECONOMY: THE 2004 REPORT 11 (Oct. 2004).

[169] *See* Lanier Saperstein, *Copyrights, Criminal Sanctions and Economic Rents: Applying the Rent Seeking Model to the Criminal Law Formulation Process*, 87 J. CRIM. L. & CRIMINOLOGY 1470, 1507–08 (1997); 143 CONG. REC. S12689, S12689 (daily ed. Nov. 13, 1997) (statement of Sen. Hatch) ("[f]or persons with few assets, civil liability is not an adequate deterrent."); Mehra, *supra* note 93, at 295.

of doing business." Impecunious infringers, who lack the ability to pay any fine, will likely not be deterred by civil damages or criminal fines, as they do not intend to pay them. In these cases, only nonmonetary criminal sanctions, and chiefly imprisonment, can create deterrence. Incapacitation could also be beneficial for another reason. It could physically disable wrongdoers from continuing their actions in those instances where monetary sanctions cannot.[170] Accordingly, monetary sanctions are insufficient in some cases to deter repeat infringers.[171] Finally, imprisonment has social costs. Many will be deterred by imprisonment due to its social consequences, such as barriers to reenter the labor market,[172] and by the stigmatization of the criminal legal system.

(3) **Efficiency/Economic Considerations.** Criminal copyright can be more efficient than other measures to respond to infringements. Criminal law reduces the expense of civil litigation and shifts the cost of enforcement to the criminal justice system and ultimately to taxpayers.[173] As many copyright owners lack the ability to investigate and file civil lawsuits against possible infringers,[174] criminal copyright can aid these rights holders. Thus, criminal copyright reduces enforcement and litigation costs, while shifting them to the criminal justice system and ultimately to taxpayers. Additionally, criminal copyright can reduce litigation time, as criminal cases are usually decided faster than state court dockets.[175]Finally, criminal copyright can be more efficient than civil copyright as it sometimes requires fewer formality requirements than civil copyright litigation, e.g., it does not require registration or preregistration of a work to be eligible for litigation.[176]

Criminal Law Benefits. Criminal copyright can advance criminal law's goals of protecting the public and third-party interests against harm, risks, and/or immorally wrong behavior.[177] If copyright infringement is perceived as immoral conduct, under a retributive approach to criminal law,[178] criminal liability should be imposed

---

[170] *See* Saperstein, *supra* note 169, at 1508.

[171] PARADISE, *supra* note 40, at 248.

[172] *See* Penney, *supra* note 32, at 74–75. POSNER, *supra* note 73, at 284.

[173] *See* Heim & Geockner, *supra* note 159, at 267; Moohr, *supra* note 152, at 798. Moreover, as civil litigation is expensive, rights holders which lack sufficient funds to sue are unable to civilly fight infringers, i.e., they require the help of the government in filing lawsuits.

[174] *See* Fry, *supra* note 156, at 516.

[175] Walker, *supra* note 116, at 688; Fry, *supra* note 156, at 522.

[176] 17 U.S.C. §§ 408–12 (2012).

[177] Bowles, Faure & Garoupa, *supra* note 51, at 391. Specifically, criminal copyright sanctions are usually "warranted to punish and deter the most egregious violators: repeat and large-scale offenders, organized crime groups, and those whose criminal conduct threatens public health and safety." *See* U.S. DEP'T OF JUSTICE, *supra* note 168, at 5–6. *See also* Kilpatrick-Lee, *supra* note 8, at 95.

[178] There are various forms of approaches to retributivism. For example, Oliver Wendell Holmes defined retribution as "vengeance in disguise" (OLIVER WENDELL HOLMES, THE COMMON LAW 45 (1923)). Thus, under this approach of retributivism, punishment is a form of revenge or

on these activities.[179] In addition, as some copyright infringement is often linked to organized crime and terrorist organization activities,[180] presuming that criminal copyright will achieve its purpose, it could reduce other criminal activities and therefore advance the general criminal law goal of reducing crime. Furthermore, criminalizing copyright could add to criminal law's expressive value, and thus fulfill its role (under some approaches).

In addition, criminal copyright can aid in shaping moral norms regarding copyright infringement, which is an unlawful conduct. As a portion of the public does not regard copyright infringement as a morally wrong behavior, and disregards its illegality,[181] using criminal law could aid in shaping the public perception regarding the wrongfulness of copyright infringement.[182] Finally, criminal law can assist the public in differentiating between legal and illegal activities, and some people will cease their actions because of this knowledge, while other people could also be deterred just by the legal prohibition.[183]

2 Criminal Copyright Drawbacks

Criminal copyright can negatively affect rights holders, authors, end users, the government and society. This part explores its possible negative explicit implications on copyright and criminal laws, while implicitly referring to the possible negative impact of criminal copyright on society.

Copyright Law Drawbacks. Inserting criminal provisions into copyright law could be undesirable for several reasons. The main possible drawback of criminal copyright is that it could undermine copyright law goals, by creating a chilling effect

---

retaliation (*lex talionis*). Another approach to retributivism relies on condemnation. Under this approach, punishment is an expression of society's condemnation of the offensive act. Others offer a deontological retributivism approach, noting that we punish because punishing is just, regardless of any other consequences (MARY MACKENZIE, PLATO ON PUNISHMENT 29 (1981)). Finally, retribution could be a necessary condition for legal punishment, albeit insufficient on its own (see ANDREW VON HIRSCH, DOING JUSTICE: THE CHOICE OF PUNISHMENTS 51 (1986)). For a general review of the approaches to retributivism, see MARK TUNICK, PUNISHMENT: THEORY AND PRACTICE 85–106 (1992).

[179] ANTONY DUFF, PUNISHMENT, COMMUNICATION AND COMMUNITY 17–30 (2001); Lloyd L. Weinreb, *Desert, Punishment, and Criminal Responsibility*, 49 L. & CONTEMP. PROBS. 47, 47 (1986).

[180] *See, e.g.*, Courmandias, *supra* note 165, at 173; Fry, *supra* note 156, at 516; PARADISE, *supra* note 40, at 21; Maureen Walterbach, *International Illicit Convergence: The Growing Problem of Transnational Organized Crime Groups' Involvement In Intellectual Property Rights Violations*, 34 FLA. ST. U. L. REV. 591, 592 (2007).

[181] *See, e.g.*, Fry, *supra* note 156, at 516.

[182] This educational benefit can also be categorized under benefits to copyright policies. *See* Moohr, *supra* note 152, at 796–98.

[183] As discussed in Chapter 7, some people comply with the law only as a measure of compliance, and therefore they will not infringe copyright, even though it could be considered as a socially acceptable moré that is not morally wrong.

on creating and using works, and jeopardizing the growth of learning and culture.[184] This is mainly owing to criminal law's deterrent effect, which could lead to an undesirably high level of deterrence. Authors might refrain from creating new works that could potentially infringe copyright, fearing prosecution. In addition, criminal sanctions could threaten many individuals who make permitted usage of copyrighted materials under their rights as users.[185] Thus, overprotection of copyright using criminal sanctions could be as harmful as under-protecting it,[186] and could lead to a chilling effect on the wide dissemination of new ideas and new forms of expression.[187] This chilling effect could also result in shrinking the public domain,[188] and could limit fundamental rights such as rights of free speech.[189]

Moreover, criminal copyright could also have a chilling effect on innovation.[190] Assuming that criminal copyright achieves its goal, and copyright infringements cease, humankind could be deprived of innovative technology, due to a de-incentivized effect to create. Imagine that in 1984, the U.S. Supreme Court would have held that the Betamax enabled people to infringe copyright (or more accurately, contributed to such infringement) and thus was illegal.[191] It is likely that many technologies that exist today would not exist if the Supreme Court had decided differently. Hence, if criminalization produces a deterrent effect, it could initially stop innovation, and negatively affect society.[192]

Criminal copyright could also have global implications. Copyright criminalization could increase pressure to criminalize copyright worldwide, due to international agreements or other forms of political pressure. This could pose a problematic and

---

[184] See note, *The Criminalization of Copyright Infringement in the Digital Era*, 112 HARV. L. REV. 1705, 1718 (1999); Moohr, *supra* note 152, at 800–02.

[185] See, e.g., Sang Jo Jong, *Criminalization of Netizens for Their Access to On-line Music*, 4 J. KOREAN L. 51, 65 (2004).

[186] See Keith Aoki, *How the World Dreams Itself to Be American: Reflections on the Relationship Between the Expanding Scope of Trademark Protection and Free Speech Norms*, 17 LOY. L.A. ENT. L. REV. 523, 532 (1997).

[187] See Lucille M. Ponte, *Coming Attractions: Opportunities and Challenges in Thwarting Global Movie Piracy*, 45 AM. BUS. L.J. 331, 335 (2008); Lindenberg-Woods, *supra* note 34, at 87.

[188] See this argument when linked the expansion of copyright protection: JAMES BOYLE, SHAMANS, SOFTWARE, AND SPLEENS: LAW AND THE CONSTRUCTION OF THE INFORMATION SOCIETY 18–20 (1996); Jessica Litman, *The Public Domain*, 39 EMORY L.J. 965 (1990); Birnhack, *Copyright Law and Free Speech After Eldred v. Ashcroft*, *supra* note 45, at 1280.

[189] See John Tehranian, *Whither Copyright? Transformative Use, Free Speech, and an Intermediate Liability Proposal*, 2005 BYU L. REV. 1201, 1216 (2005); Walterbach, *supra* note 180, at 594.

[190] See, e.g., Mehra, *supra* note 93, at 299.

[191] See Sony Corp. of America v. Universal City Studios Inc., 464 U.S. 417 (1984). The court held that the Betamax was legal, since it possesses substantial non-infringing uses, and that the recording act is considered as time shifting, and therefore a fair use under law. See Edward Lee, *The Ethics of Innovation: p2p Software Developers and Designing Substantial Noninfringing Uses under the Sony Doctrine*, 62 J. BUS. ETHICS 147 (2005); Gordon, *supra* note 27.

[192] See, e.g., *id.* at 299 (gives the example of Napster as a technology that may have cost the record industry a bundle but it and similar programs also demonstrated to many the positive uses of such technology).

high burden on less developed countries, which usually have limited resources to enforce rights, and could lead to the "withdrawal of resources from other competing, and at times more important, public needs."[193] Moreover, global criminalization will require allocating funds from other important investments, such as poverty, hunger, health, and education, and will reduce the ability to achieve those goals.[194]

Criminal copyright could also have negative economic ramifications. For example, in many instances, limitation on exclusive rights is more beneficial for rights holders than granting perpetual rights, i.e., criminalization could possibly cause financial harm to rights holders rather than aid them. In addition, criminal copyright could negatively affect foreign investments. As long as criminal copyright is not harmonized, i.e., the level of protection is higher in some countries than in others, foreign investors could avoid investing in that country.[195] Moreover, criminal copyright increases the usage of already limited governmental resources – costs largely incurred by the public – although these costs could be insignificant.[196] As governmental resources are limited, if criminal copyright results in increased enforcement, then enforcement agencies might be required to shift resources from other areas of law, while possibly neglecting them. Finally, on a procedural level, criminal intent, or "willfulness" as required in criminal copyright law, is higher than civil litigation, and could prove difficult to meet.[197]

Criminal Law Drawbacks. The underlying problem of copyright criminaliza-tion, when not fully justified, is that it negatively affects the role of criminal law.[198] This over-criminalization is a real problem. Over-criminalization produces too much punishment – which in turn is unjust.[199] It could therefore jeopardize the legal system, and especially, cause additional harm to individuals and society, while over-stigmatizing a wrongdoer to a greater extent than intended by law.[200] In addition, when not fully enforced, criminal copyright could negatively affect the

---

[193] Peter K. Yu analyzed the problematic outcome of global strengthening of IP enforcement, while listing as an example of resources withdrawal the following: purification of water, generation of power, improvement of public health, reduction of child mortality, provision of education, promotion of public security, building of basic infrastructure, reduction of violent crimes, relief of poverty, elimination of hunger, promotion of gender equality, protection of the environment and response to terrorism, illegal arms sales, human and drug trafficking, illegal immigration and corruption. *See* Peter K. Yu, *Enforcement, Economics and Estimates*, 2 W.I.P.O. J. 1, 3–4 (2010).

[194] *See id.* at 4.

[195] Yu, *supra* note 193, at 3.

[196] *See* The House Report, in the first draft of the NET Act (H.R. Rep. No. 105–339, at 6 (1997)):
Because DOJ may prosecute certain criminal cases that would not be tried under current law, enacting H.R. 2265 could result in additional costs for federal prosecutors and the federal court system, subject to the availability of appropriated funds. CBO, however, expects that any additional discretionary costs would not be significant.

[197] *See* Kilpatrick-Lee, *supra* note 8, at 116; Saperstein, *supra* note 169, at 1506–07.

[198] *See generally*, Moohr, *supra* note 152, at 802–03.

[199] Husak, *supra* note 41, at 2.

[200] *See* Kilpatrick-Lee, *supra* note 8, at 117.

deterrent values of criminal sanctions (as discussed in Chapter 4). Even if criminal law is deemed to be an appropriate measure to regulate copyright infringements, it must be practical in its usage to deter infringements and not overload the criminal system. Otherwise, despite the possible expressive value of criminal law, criminal sanctions should be removed. If criminal copyright is, to some extent, a dead letter, criminal copyright might not be perceived as criminal.

Moreover, the criminal system will be perceived as dysfunctional, causing social indifference and disregard for all criminal legislation.[201] In this sense, criminal law should be limited to specific offenses that are harmful and/or wrongful enough and characterized as the most heinous of violations, depending on the view of criminal law.[202] Overextending criminal law could result in degrading the perception of it. If more human conduct becomes criminal, the distinction between civil and criminal law could disappear over time, making the entire legal system criminal, and diluting the values of both civil and criminal laws.[203] In the criminal-copyright context, a norm-shaping attempt via criminal law could backfire and reduce deterrence, even if irrationally, from a narrow cost-benefit perspective, because individuals might feel that the law conflicts with preexisting notions of what is just and legitimate.[204] In other words, higher criminal sanctions could actually increase infringements.

Finally, criminal copyright possesses stronger ramifications for legal mistakes than civil copyright. Although criminal copyright is considered a more practical enforcement strategy than civil copyright, it could result in more mistakes.[205] The ramifications of mistaken arrests are more troublesome than mistakes in civil litigation.[206]

Evaluating the consequences, which derive from criminalization, is not necessarily easy. A cost-benefit analysis reveals that criminal copyright could be both beneficial, but also carry with it many undesired drawbacks. Since benefits and drawback are usually incompatible and sometimes are on a different normative level, I emphasize the most important elements under this analysis, which could support or not support criminalization.

The main benefit of criminal copyright is that it could provide stronger protection to copyright and aid in ensuring copyright goals. For this matter, the criminal deterrent is important to reduce copyright infringements, and therefore, decrease the potential harm for rights holders. This deterrent measure is particularly important when other measures are incapable of deterring such conduct. This main benefit

---

[201] Jareborg, *supra* note 90, at 526.

[202] *See* Kilpatrick-Lee, *supra* note 8, at 117–18; Francis A. Allen, *The Morality of Means: Three Problems in Criminal Sanctions*, 42 U. PITT. L. REV. 737, 738 (1981).

[203] Paul H. Robinson, *Moral Credibility and Crime*, ATL. MONTHLY, Mar. 1995, at 72, 77; Stuart P. Green, *Why It's a Crime to Tear the Tag Off a Mattress: Overcriminalization and the Moral Content of Regulatory Offenses*, 46 EMORY L.J. 1533, 1533 (1997).

[204] *See generally* Ben Depoorter & Sven Vanneste, *Norms and Enforcement: The Case against Copyright Litigation*, 84 OR. L. REV. 1127 (2005).

[205] *See* Mehra, *supra* note 93, at 295.

[206] *Id.*

should be weighed against the most dominant drawback of copyright criminalization. Mainly, criminal copyright could also negatively affect rights holders, creators, end users, the government, and society – as it could undermine copyright law goals, by creating a chilling effect on innovation to create and make use of works – and thus jeopardizes the growth of learning and culture for the public welfare. Therefore, locating the main benefits and drawbacks of criminal copyright leads us back to the relatively similar rivalry between copyright law theories. While natural-rights approaches place the author at the center, users' rights approaches place the importance on users. Applying the cost-benefit analysis under the incentive/utilitarian theory, reveals that criminalizing non-commercial infringements is not necessarily justified, as the potential drawbacks in deterring new creations and making permitted uses of copyright materials are vast. Thus, by the perceived consequences, the integrated approach does not support the criminalization of non-commercial gain infringements, whether they are done on a small or large scale.

CONCLUSION

The combination of current criminalization frameworks into the integrated approach of criminalization indicates that copyright infringement is not always justified. In the first stage of the integrated approach, it is sufficient to determine that commercial gain infringements are both harmful and wrongful and meet the first stage requirement. Non-commercial gain infringements should be dealt with differently. First, non-commercial gain infringements on a small scale should not be criminalized, as they do not pass the harm principle and the wrongfulness thresholds. Second, non-commercial gain infringements on a large scale do cause potential harm and wrongfulness, which could be sufficient to fulfill this stage's requirements, but nevertheless should not necessarily be criminalized as they could be over-inclusive to include conduct that is neither harmful nor wrongful. In the second stage of evaluation, copyright criminalization is justified as it protects the legitimate and substantial interest in creation and dissemination copyrighted works. The third stage indicates that criminal copyright is not always justified. Although criminal law can directly advance the substantial state interest, this stage argues that there are alternatives that could be equally effective and less extensive than criminalization. In other words, rights holders and legislators should first turn to other mechanisms for regulating behavior before turning to the criminal sanction, which should only be invoked as a last resort. The fourth and final stage of evaluation, which examines the consequences of criminalization, showed that mostly under utilitarian and users' rights approaches, criminalization is not always justified because it has negative consequences for copyright law goals.

Indeed, the outcomes of criminalization depend on both criminal and copyright law perspectives. As outlined in this chapter, legislators should adapt their view of criminal and copyright law, to disintegrate the integrated approach to best serve their views on copyright criminalization. Under a natural-right approach to copyright, criminalization will usually be supported, except when examining the third stage of efficiency. However, under the utilitarian/users' rights theories of copyright, all legislators, regardless of their views on the criminal system, should strive to abstain from criminalization for non-commercial gain infringements, even if on a commercial scale. This is evident from the harm/wrongfulness examination, which produced similar results. Nevertheless, by this approach, if legislators seek to fulfill the third and fourth stages of evaluation, then even criminalization for commercial gain infringements, on a commercial scale, are not necessarily justified. Thus, when following these approaches, policymakers should strive to abstain from criminalization of non-commercial gain infringements, even if they are on a commercial scale.

9

The Future of Criminal Copyright and How to Stop It

INTRODUCTION

Technology has changed the way people interact with the copyright system. Prior to the evolution of technologies that enabled distributing creative works, the ways to access copyrighted works were rather limited.[1] Films, television shows, recorded music and books, to name a few examples, required purchasing or renting the product, licensing by a service, or subscribing to it. There was no easy or cheap way for consumers to obtain these things without paying a fee. For consumers at that time, interacting with the copyright system was in practice hardly possible.[2]

As long as non-commercial infringement was implausible – or at least occurred at very low rates – most rights holders in the copyright industry had little to worry about.[3] A substantial change in the public's interaction with the copyright system only arose with the invention of devices that enabled affordable reproductions of works. Early examples include photocopiers in the 1950s[4], as well as home videotaping equipment in the 1970s.[5] Then many individuals suddenly found themselves able to make copies of protected works, even if their quality was below that of the originals. In the 1970s many people could record music, photocopy content, and videotape films.[6] That era probably marked the beginning of the so-called

---

[1] See Peter S. Menell, *This American Copyright Life: Reflections on Re-equilibrating Copyright for the Internet Age*, 61 J. COPYRIGHT SOC'Y U.S.A. 235, 241–44 (2013).

[2] *Id.*

[3] Peter Menell describes this evolution as part of copyright's public approval rating. *See id.*, at 248.

[4] In the early 1950s, photocopiers became available to the public, enabling for the first time the technological copying of copyrighted content without the direct control of the rights holders, and therefore free of charge to the rights holders. *See* Jessica Litman, *The Sony Paradox*, 55 CASE W. RES. L. REV. 917, 921 (2005).

[5] *Id.*

[6] PETER BALDWIN, THE COPYRIGHT WARS: THREE CENTURIES OF TRANS-ATLANTIC BATTLE 265 (2014).

"copyright wars" between various actors, namely the content industry, various intermediaries and consumers.[7]

That war had many battles. At first, when copies were imperfect and the marginal costs of reproduction were relatively high, the significance of the battles for the future of copyright was relatively modest. There was no imminent threat to the business models of rights holders. But even then many content owners fought to preserve their position in the market and reacted to almost any new form of technology that potentially threatened their business models. One renowned example is Sony's Betamax, which enabled recording content from television, and later copying content between videotapes, which in the United States resulted in a highly influential Supreme Court decision.[8] While Sony – and, as we learn from the development of technology that followed this decision, society – won this case, that battle merely marked the eruption of many more that followed. We came to witness copyright wars over, inter alia, CDs,[9] DVDs,[10] MP3 players,[11] DVRs,[12] file-sharing platforms[13] and streaming services, and devices.[14] We also witnessed power struggles among technology companies with substantial political power over controversial proposed legislation: an example is the proposed Stop Online Piracy Act (SOPA),[15] which was met with strong public opposition and blackouts by major online service providers.[16]

---

[7]   The term copyright wars could potentially refer to various types of battles within the realm of copyright protection. *See, e.g., id.*; WILLIAM F. PATRY, MORAL PANICS AND THE COPYRIGHT WARS (2009).

[8]   *See* Sony Corp. of America v. Universal City Studios Inc., 464 U.S. 417 (1984); Edward Lee, *The Ethics of Innovation: p2p Software Developers and Designing Substantial Noninfringing Uses Under the Sony Doctrine*, 62 J. OF BUSINESS ETHICS 147 (2005); Wendy J. Gordon, *Fair Use as Market Failure: A Structural and Economic Analysis of the 'Betamax' Case and Its Predecessors*, 82 COLUM. L. REV. 8 (1982).

[9]   *See, e.g.,* Cahn v. Sony Corp., 90 Civ. 4537 (S.D.N.Y. filed July 9, 1990).

[10] *See DVD-copying case heads to court,* CNET (May 15, 2003), www.cnet.com/news/dvd-copying-case-heads-to-court.

[11] *See* Recording Industry Ass'n of America v. Diamond Multimedia Systems, 180 F.3d 1072 (9th Cir. 1999).

[12] DVRs are Digital Video Recorder System. *See* Twentieth Century Fox Film Corp. v. Cablevision Sys. Corp., 478 F. Supp. 2d 607 (S.D.N.Y. 2007); Cartoon Network LP, LLLP v. CSC Holdings, Inc., 536 F.3d 121 (2d Cir. 2008).

[13] Examples of file sharing platforms are Napster, Grokster, Morpheus, KaZaA and Bittorrent. *See, e.g.,* A&M Records, Inc. v. Napster, Inc., 114 F. Supp. 2d 896 (Cal., 2000); A&M Records Inc. v. Napster Inc., 239 F. 3d 1004 (9th Cir. 2001); Aimster Copyright Litigation. Appeal of John Deep, 334 F.3d 643 (7th Cir. 2003); MGM, Inc. v. Grokster, Inc. 545 U.S. 913 (2005).

[14] *See, e.g., Sale of Kodi 'Fully-Loaded' Streaming Boxes Faces Legal Test,* BBC NEWS (Sept. 27, 2016), www.bbc.com/news/technology-37474595. For more on the copyright wars, see *supra* Chapter 5.

[15] H.R. 3261, 112th Cong. (2011).

[16] *See* Vlad Savov, *The SOPA Blackout: Wikipedia, Reddit, Mozilla, Google, and Many Others Protest Proposed Law,* THE VERGE (Jan. 18, 2012), www.theverge.com/2012/1/18/2715300/sopa-blackout-wikipedia-reddit-mozilla-google-protest.

These so-called copyright "wars" are far from over. Technological developments will likely keep evolving, enabling easier and cheaper access to high quality copyrighted works. But as these wars carry significant costs for all sides, it is important to discuss whether they can be mitigated to some extent, and what the optimal method is to protect copyright.

But first a caveat is due: solving the copyright puzzle is beyond this book's scope. It also clearly deserves much more than a single chapter. Hence, the intention of this chapter is rather modest. It strives to serve as an introduction to potential solutions to the copyright puzzle outside the criminal copyright realm. Essentially, as this chapter further argues, the future of copyright law should not rely on criminal law. Criminal copyright should be reserved for marginal activities that cannot be otherwise dealt with properly. If the future of copyright law lies in further criminalization, then something has gone wrong along the way. Stopping copyright law from becoming criminally-oriented will require, inter alia, better adaptation of consumer expectations to the market. Such a move, however, will not be easy without substantial shifts in the current dynamics of rights holders, intermediaries, and consumers.

I RESOLVING THE COPYRIGHT PUZZLE THROUGH PUBLIC ENFORCEMENT

In Chapter 8 I used a formulated criminalization theory to argue that criminal copyright is often unjust, and therefore should generally be reserved for limited forms of infringement. But arguing for limited use of criminal copyright serves only one aspect of the debate, namely how *not* to protect copyright. The other aspect relates to a far more complex and controversial question at hand: How may society optimally sustain the rationales behind copyright protection without adhering to criminal law? How can we achieve a proper balance between adequate incentives to create works and the public's ability to enjoy them? If copyright protection serves to satisfy its authors' fundamental human needs, how should the law best enable people to fulfill those needs while allowing the dissemination of knowledge? In other words, if criminal law is not the answer – as in most cases, then what is?

If the law is the optimal modality to regulate behavior – combined with other modalities or not, then the dichotomy between criminal law and civil law that policymakers usually use is not necessarily sufficient to fully attain the optimal legal regime to govern copyright. As this part will show, a firmer grasp of the future of criminal copyright might be gained by distinguishing public enforcement of copyright infringement from private enforcement, and suggesting that the former might sometimes be the best way, even if not criminal law.

Public enforcement is composed of criminal and administrative law. While this book argues that criminal copyright should only be used as an *ultima ratio* – a last resort – it still does not mean that the state should not play a role in the protection of copyrighted works. Public enforcement – the use of governmental agents to detect and to sanction violators of legal rules – could still partake in copyright protection in the digital age, even with the exclusion of criminal copyright.[17]

Adherence to public enforcement requires understanding the limits of private enforcement.[18] One of the main reasons to prefer public enforcement over private relates to the identity of infringers. Under this justification or challenge, public enforcement could be preferable when it is difficult for victims who have experienced harm to obtain knowledge of whomever injured them.[19] Without such ability, individuals are unable to initiate legal action and harness the information they have for purposes of law enforcement.[20]

Within the realm of copyright law, this *detection and attribution problem* arose in the 18th century in the United States, when unlicensed performances throughout the country were difficult to monitor.[21] As shown in Chapter 3, this concern eventually led to the birth of criminal copyright in the United States under the Musical Public Performance Act of 1897.[22] Technological changes clearly widened the detection and attribution problem. Given the technological ability to reproduce works, even with imperfect quality, it was difficult and implausible to detect what people were doing in the comfort of their homes, let alone, to prove that they infringed copyright. Moreover, with the globalization of copyrighted works and the emergence of the internet, it might be difficult for rights holders to file lawsuits when infringements occur in multiple jurisdictions and with overseas operators. At least theoretically, a potential solution to copyright infringements should be public enforcement.

As outlined in Chapter 5, one of the three interrelated reasons for the increase of copyright infringement is technological developments, mainly the invention of digital technology. In terms of the detection and attribution problem, while digital technology has provided better means of reproduction and has expanded the potential and actual scope of infringements, it has also potentially expanded the probability of detection and attribution. If legally permitted, digital technology has made it possible to detect what many users are doing, reveal their identity, and bring them to justice. Hence, the advance of technology in this instance might actually argue against public enforcement. It does, however, depend on a regime without

---

[17] See Menell, *supra* note 1, at 329.

[18] For a detailed explanation of public enforcement see, e.g., Gary S. Becker & George J. Stigler, *Law Enforcement, Malfeasance, and Compensation of Enforcers*, 3 J. LEGAL STUD. 1 (1974); A. Mitchell Polinsky, *Private versus Public Enforcement of Fines*, 9 J. LEGAL STUD. 105 (1980); A. Mitchell Polinsky & Steven Shavell, *The Theory of Public Enforcement of Law, in* 1 HANDBOOK OF LAW AND ECONOMICS 403 (2006).

[19] Polinsky & Shavell, *supra* note 18, at 406.

[20] *Id.*

[21] See Chapter 3.

[22] Musical Public Performance Right Act of Jan. 6, 1897, ch. 4, 29 Stat. 481 (1897).

legal or practical obstacles that might undermine the ability to detect and attribute copyright infringements to a specific infringer.

Nevertheless, some barriers to private enforcement in the digital age exist, which could jeopardize the effectiveness of this form of enforcement. The first is a collective action problem, posed mainly by large-scale, international piracy rings and platforms.[23] Under this argument, it would be rather difficult for small-scale rights holders to fight large-scale international operations that enable copyright infringement.[24] If copyright infringement is dealt with on the state level, this fight could become much easier and more efficient. As Chapter 8 showed, large-scale international operations that enable copyright infringement, especially those that operate in a for-profit mode, are generally supported by formulated criminalization theories, hence should be part of the criminal copyright regime.

Another possible barrier to private enforcement is its potentially low deterrent effect. Arguably, public enforcement – perhaps mostly criminal law – could better deter infringers.[25] Deterrence in general, as also argued throughout this book, is not easy to evaluate and many scholars generally contest it, at least in its purely economic form.[26] For instance, economic analysis of public enforcement would require taking into account various factors such as individuals' risk aversion, the probability of detection of the harmful act, and evaluation of social welfare.[27]

It is also difficult to evaluate whether criminal law serves as a greater deterrent for all infringers at all times. For example, some individuals might evaluate a high civil penalty as more aversive than a criminal sanction, even if it includes imprisonment. Statutory damages, which under American law could amount to $150,000 for each act of infringement, exemplify these potentially high civil fines that could serve as a strong deterrent to infringements.[28] The matter of deterrence in administrative law is also questionable. At least theoretically, deterrence of administrative law differs from deterrence of criminal law, mainly in the difference in the form of potential sanctions and the potential stigma of criminal conviction. But much like civil law's potential deterrence effect, administrative law could also deter potential infringers, especially if the state has the ability to place constraints on the individual's liberties. The example of graduated response mechanisms that, inter alia, could lead to suspending internet connectivity may well serve as a deterrent for individuals. But

---

[23] See Menell, supra note 1, at 329.

[24] Id.

[25] The trade-off between high sanctions and enforcement efforts were first identified by Gary S. Becker, Crime and Punishment: An Economic Approach, 76 J. POL. ECON. 169 (1968).

[26] See, e.g., Dan M. Kahan, The Theory of Value Dilemma: A Critique of the Economic Analysis of Criminal Law, 1 OHIO ST. J. CRIM. L. 643, 643–47 (2004).

[27] As defined by A. Mitchell Polinsky and Steven Shavell, social welfare relates to the benefits that individuals obtain from their behavior, less the costs that they incur to avoid causing harm, the harm that they do cause, the cost of catching violators, and the costs of imposing sanctions on them. See Polinsky & Shavell, supra note 18, at 406.

[28] 17 U.S.C. § 504.

as previously mentioned, reliance on deterrence in general should be treated with care. Overall, the potential deterrent of imprisonment does not act on all individuals equally – if at all, and it is highly doubtful that it serves as a higher deterrent than civil or administrative sanctions.

A final barrier to private enforcement is financial resources. Detection of infringers, even if possible, might require financial resources that small-scale rights holders might not possess. It also requires further funds to pursue legal action against infringers, whose outcome is unknown and could take a very long time to appear. Absent public enforcement, it would be extremely difficult for rights holders without sufficient financial resources to recoup their losses. This barrier, however, is not limited to private enforcement *per se,* and could equally be a barrier to public enforcement. As may be understood from the *criminal copyright gap,* discussed in Chapter 4, enforcement agencies might also lack financial resources, including manpower, to engage in infringement enforcement. Consequently, even when enforcement agencies have sufficient funds they might feel conflicted about the criminal nature or lack thereof of criminal copyright infringement, use prosecutorial discretion, and allow their personal feelings to override professionalism and "rule of law" norms.

All in all, both private and public enforcement has limits. If in some instances choosing public rather than private enforcement might be preferable – and scrutiny of the law under a formulized criminalization theory leads to the conclusion that criminal law is inadequate, then administrative law should be considered as a supplement. Administrative law is indeed no stranger to copyright enforcement. It has been chosen by various policymakers in recent years. In Italy, for instance, the Communication Authority (AGCOM) is now authorized to administratively police copyright infringement online. Under this administrative approach, rights holders are entitled to file complaints of online copyright infringement with AGCOM, which after proceedings could remove or block access to infringing materials.[29] Another leading example of administrative copyright is the so-called graduated response or three strikes policy, which has been legislated in several jurisdictions. France, for instance, decided to form an administrative body (HADOPI) that could authorize the termination of subscriptions and accounts of repeat infringers under the appropriate circumstances.[30] A final example is assets and domain-name

---

[29] See Giancarlo Frosio. *Italian Communication Authority Approves Administrative Enforcement of Online Copyright Infringement,* CIS (Dec. 17, 2013), https://cyberlaw.stanford.edu/blog/2013/12/italian-communication-authority-approves-administrative-enforcement-online-copyright.

[30] France (Projet de loi favorisant la diffusion et la protection de la création sur Internet [Bill supporting the diffusion and the protection of creation on Internet] (2009) (Fr.), *translated in* LA QUADRATURE DU NET, www.laquadrature.net/wiki/HADOPI_full_translation (2010). For more on this form of enforcement, see Peter K. Yu, *The Graduated Response,* 62 FLA. L. REV. 1373 (2010); Charn Wing Wan, *Three Strikes Law: A Least Cost Solution to Rampant Online Piracy,* 5 J. INTELL. PROP. L. & PRACT. 232 (2010); Olivier Bomsel & Heritiana Ranaivoson, *Decreasing Copyright Enforcement Costs: The Scope of a Graduated Response,* 6 REV. OF

seizures. In the United States, for instance, the PRO-IP Act 2008 provided, inter alia, for forfeiture of property used to commit or facilitate criminal copyright infringement.[31] Subsequently, under the codename *Operation in Our Sites*, governmental agencies seized the domain names of websites providing access to infringing content, "making it more difficult and more costly for infringers to harm U.S. rightholders."[32]

Nevertheless, it is still difficult to assess the efficiency of administrative law to properly regulate copyright infringements, as it has been used rather scantly by policymakers, hence its effectiveness must be evaluated over a longer time. Moreover, the use of administrative measures might carry negative ramifications for users and society. Take for instance the seizure of domain names of websites providing access to alleged infringing content. Beyond the practicalities, e.g., jurisdictional challenges, or operators of infringing websites easily bypassing these measures simply by reopening the site under a different domain, this measure could greatly harm users' access to knowledge and operators of legit websites, especially without proper transparency. It could affect constitutional rights such as due process and First Amendment rights, and generally lead to a chilling effect on investing time and effort in building and maintaining websites, especially for rational risk-averse actors.[33]

But even if we accept that public enforcement must be deployed in some cases, and even if we take into account their potential negative ramifications, I am not fully persuaded that the involvement of the state in protecting copyright holders will benefit them greatly. An optimal copyright regime in the digital age, in my view, necessitates a more wholesome use of the available modalities that regulate behavior other than the law, and perhaps most importantly requires of stakeholders to reinvent themselves and align with new ways of content consumption. I will further discuss this argument in the next part.

The future of copyright law also depends greatly on the role of intermediaries in copyright enforcement, which frequently expands due to legal obligations.[34]

ECON. RES. ON COPYRIGHT ISSUES 13 (2009); Annemarie Bridy, *Graduated Response and the Turn to Private Ordering in Online Copyright Enforcement*, 89 OR. L. REV. 81 (2010); Eldar Haber, *The French Revolution 2.0: Copyright and the Three Strikes Policy*, 2 HARV. J. SPORTS & ENT. L. 297 (2011).

[31] *See* 18 U.S.C. § 2323.

[32] U.S. INTELLECTUAL PROPERTY ENFORCEMENT COORDINATOR, 2010 U.S. INTELLECTUAL PROPERTY ENFORCEMENT COORDINATOR ANNUAL REPORT ON INTELLECTUAL PROPERTY ENFORCEMENT 4 (Feb. 2011), *available at* www.ice.gov/doclib/iprcenter/pdf/ipec-annual-report.pdf.

[33] For an analysis of this practice in the United States, see Karen Kopel, *Operation Seizing Our Sites: How the Federal Government is Taking Domain Names Without Prior Notice*, 28 BERKELEY TECH. L.J. 859 (2013); John Blevins, *Uncertainty as Enforcement Mechanism: The New Expansion of Secondary Copyright Liability to Internet Platforms*, 34 CARDOZO. L. REV. 1821, 1833 (2013).

[34] It should be noted that many times privatized copyright enforcement occurs without the direct intervention of policymakers, but rather by voluntary agreements. *See, e.g.*, Maryant Fernández

Policymakers may very well choose private enforcement by intermediaries to address copyright infringements. We have witnessed such moves in algorithmic enforcement under the Notice and Takedown procedure designed in the Digital Millennium Copyright Act (DMCA).[35] These moves toward the privatization of copyright enforcement – which must be carefully scrutinized due to their potentially chilling effect on innovation – might play a significant part in the future of copyright law, and should be further explored in future studies.

A final note on the future of copyright relates to the issue of "value neutral" or "dual use" technology. File-sharing services and cloud storage might play a more substantial role in the years to come. We have already witnessed a rise in the concept of criminalizing secondary (and perhaps mostly contributory) infringement in some jurisdictions. The most famous cases are Isamu Kaneko in Japan and The Pirate Bay in Sweden.[36] The step toward secondary criminal prosecution, however, might be perceived as too radical, as it places high burdens on intermediaries and could jeopardize innovation and damp down speech. For instance, under the current American approach to technological innovation, it would be most difficult to regulate "value neutral" or "dual use" technology, especially due to free speech.[37] But it would not be surprising if eventually courts relabeled contributory infringing to include mega-platforms, potentially like Megaupload, which greatly facilitate

---

Pérez, Portugal: Privatised copyright law enforcement agreement now public, EDRi (Sept. 9, 2015), https://edri.org/portugal-privatised-copyright-law-enforcement-agreement-now-public.

[35] Digital Millennium Copyright Act, 17 U.S.C. § 1201 (2012). For more on algorithmic enforcement in copyright law, see generally Maayan Perel & Niva Elkin-Koren, *Accountability in Algorithmic Enforcement*, 19 STAN. TECH. L. REV. 473 (2016); Maayan Perel & Niva Elkin-Koren, *BLACK BOX TINKERING: Beyond Transparency in Algorithmic Enforcement*, 69 FLA. L. REV. 181 (2017).

[36] Isamu Kaneko is a Tokyo University computer science department researcher that developed a decentralized P2P anonymous file-sharing program names "Winny." Mr. Kaneko was indicted for aiding in copyright infringement in Japan. While the Kyoto District Court found him guilty, the Osaka High Court overturned this decision and the Supreme Court eventually upheld the acquittal. The Pirate Bay was a BitTorrent index and tracker, which aided users to find torrent files, often directing downloaders to peers who possess infringing copies of popular content. Four individuals were charged in the Stockholm District Court, Sweden, for promoting copyright infringement and sentenced to serve one year in prison (which was shortened by the appeal court) and pay a fine. *See generally* Salil K. Mehra, *Keep America Exceptional! Against Adopting Japanese and European-Style Criminalization of Contributory Copyright Infringement*, 13 VAND. J. ENT. & TECH. L. 811 (2011); Michael Carrier, *The Pirate Bay, Grokster and Google*, 15 J. INTELL. PROP. RTS. 7, 7 (2010).

[37] In Sony's Betamax case, the Supreme Court ruled out contributory infringement when the technology was capable of "substantial non-infringing use." The following years of litigation against P2P software, and especially that of Grokster, the Court reinterpreted its Sony ruling and ruled that contributory infringement liability could not merely be based on a failure to take affirmative steps to prevent infringement, if the device otherwise was capable of substantial non-infringing uses. The Court also stressed that distributing a device to promoting its use to infringe copyright could be liable for the resulting acts of infringement by third parties.

copyright infringements and private enforcement is unable to challenge them.[38] It will be interesting to see courts' interpretation of "aiding and abetting" criminal infringement when new technology is involved. However, if not taken with extreme caution these steps could have dire consequences for innovation and free speech, therefore should be used carefully, if at all, especially if other measures exist.[39]

II RESHAPING THE FUTURE OF CRIMINAL COPYRIGHT: OPTIMISTIC SUGGESTIONS

It would be highly presumptuous to predict how copyright law will shape up in the future, even the near future.[40] The rapid evolution of technology in the twenty-first century will probably make almost any prediction attempt futile. What can be predicted is the high likelihood that as long as liberal democracies exist, technology will continue to develop. Consequently, individuals in modern society will most likely also continue to create works in the future, even if the copyright regime experiences dramatic changes. The future of criminal copyright, however, may be partially predicted from its past – which is outlined throughout this book. Without deciding which path should be taken by the state or by market players, policymakers may well learn some lessons from the past when contemplating criminalizing copyright law.

As discussed in Chapter 5, which outlined the internal reasons for criminal copyright, the law was not the sole modality used to regulate copyright infringements. Rights holders have attempted to use technological constraints such as Technological Protection Measures (TPMs) to prevent copyright infringement. They have applied encryption, watermarking, digital fingerprinting, and spoofing and interdicting, to name a few.[41] They have also attempted – and some still are attempting – to use the market and social norms to shape the copyright landscape. They have tried to raise public awareness through legal, social or moral education. But as we have come to learn, these modalities, at least as deployed thus far, proved somewhat too limited to make a substantial change in the copyright protection regime.

The future of criminal copyright largely depends on a combination of these modalities. If market players acknowledge the changes in consumers' expectations and the financial opportunities that new technologies could entail, then new

---

[38] For more on criminal contributory infringement, see Benton Martin & Jeremiah Newhall, *Criminal Copyright Enforcement Against Filesharing Services*, 15 N.C. J.L. & TECH. 101 (2013).

[39] For a critique on aiding and abetting in the IP criminal context, see Mark Bartholomew, *Cops, Robbers, and Search Engines: The Questionable Role of Criminal Law in Contributory Infringement Doctrine*, 4 BYU L. REV. 783 (2009).

[40] For an extensive analysis on the forces that will shape copyright law's future, see Peter S. Menell, *Envisioning Copyright Law's Digital Future*, 46 N.Y.L. SCH. L. REV. 63, 109 (2002).

[41] *See* Chapter 5.

business models could arise, as we have experienced with streaming services and digital shops. My optimistic view of the future of copyright law rests on several recommendations that greatly depend on a combination of Lessig's modalities. In my view, acting on these recommendations will most likely lead to an optimal regime that will adequately balance incentives to create and the public's enjoyment of protected works.

Prior to any recommendations, it must be further stressed that the future of copyright law – not just criminal copyright – is widely discussed in scholarship, therefore my contribution is rather modest. For instance, scholars have already suggested trying a different approach to the copyright infringement puzzle which would rely, inter alia, on compulsory licenses for file sharing.[42] Many policymakers have taken this way to tackle copyright infringements by establishing a royalty program on the sale of devices and blank recording media.[43] Other scholars such as Paul Goldstein have suggested the creation of a "celestial jukebox," whereby individuals have access to a library of music, literature, and video on a pay-per-use basis.[44] The list goes on and on.[45] To add to the general discussion on the future of copyright law, I now briefly describe my recommendations on how to stop the potential paradigm shift in copyright law from civil to criminal copyright, while also making a few more general recommendations on how the optimal balance of rights holders, intermediaries and the public should be set.

The first recommendation relates directly to copyright criminalization. For optimal balance, policymakers should first grasp that criminal copyright will probably not solve the copyright infringement problem. Even if policymakers could justify the use of criminal sanctions in copyright enforcement under a formulized criminalization theory, criminal copyright has many flaws that have been addressed extensively throughout this book. It is costly, largely non-pragmatic, and could have a dangerously chilling effect on lawful use of copyrighted works and lawful creation of new ones.

The criminal copyright movement must be stopped, or at least substantially slowed. It does little to advance the rationales of copyright protection and it carries many negative consequences for society. Naturally, these statements do not imply that copyright law should be only civil or administrative. In rare instances, when criminalization theories support them, copyright laws should contain criminal provisions. But these should be the exception rather than the rule for copyright

---

[42] *See generally* WILLIAM W. FISHER III, PROMISES TO KEEP: TECHNOLOGY, LAW AND THE FUTURE OF ENTERTAINMENT (2004); Neil Netanel, *Impose a Noncommercial Use Levy to Allow Free Peer-to-Peer File Sharing*, 17 HARV. J. L. & TECH. 1 (2003).

[43] *See* The Audio Home Recording Rights Act of 1992, Pub. L. No. 102–563, 106 Stat. 4237 (1992) (codified at 17 U.S.C. §§ 1001–10) (which, inter alia, imposed a three percent levy on the sales of blank digital audiotapes and a two percent levy on the sale of digital audiotape equipment).

[44] PAUL GOLDSTEIN, COPYRIGHT'S HIGHWAY: THE LAW AND LORE OF COPYRIGHT FROM GUTENBERG TO THE CELESTIAL JUKEBOX (1994).

[45] *See, e.g.,* WILLIAM PATRY, HOW TO FIX COPYRIGHT (2011).

protection. It is crucial that policymakers set a high threshold for legislating criminal copyright, and re-evaluate their current criminal copyright provisions in their legal systems.

The second recommendation is to embrace technology rather than fight it or use it to place constraints on the use of copyrighted works. As we witness in the 21st century, technological developments have changed the way many of us consume content. When mega platforms, like YouTube, enable listening to music free of direct charges, often with direct involvement of the rights holders, any legal battles regarding music-file sharing on P2P networks become redundant. The cat is out of the bag, and it would be presumptuous to assume that anyone could drag it back in. The use of technology, especially if combined with market forces, is crucial for the future of the copyright system. Rights holders should spend their efforts less on how to use technology to place constraints on media – a practice that has largely proven of not much use in advancing copyright's goals – and more on how to use it to reach bigger audiences.

In essence, this recommendation greatly depends on the market. Control as a business model cannot fully prevail in the digital age.[46] The reduction in costs of producing, marketing and distributing content nowadays should benefit both sides. Content industries should embrace new business models to obtain the appropriate revenue streams for their investments. Indeed, we witnessed such a shift in perception with Apple's iTunes Music Store in April 2003,[47] which was followed by many other services like Spotify and services other than music like Netflix and Hulu. As long as content providers can offer reasonably priced subscription plans and original content, this approach could be highly beneficial for all involved parties. Being adaptive to new forms of content consumption and distribution is essential for the future of creativity, hence for the future of criminal copyright.

Still, even this second recommendation will most likely not resolve the problem for all market players or for every market. Huge differences separate small, medium and large players and markets, which could affect the success of these mechanisms. Some authors might not be able to recoup their costs; some individuals might free-ride on the success of others and undergo a decline in their financial incentive to create; some markets could have high barriers to entry; some might be monopolistic or oligopolistic; etc. Essentially, potential market failures will also play a substantial part in the future of copyright. When market failures are present, supplementary measures must exist, and public enforcement could fulfill a role in such regulation. It would be wise, however, to further scrutinize existing market failures and seek appropriate tools to reduce them, prior to going for public enforcement.

---

[46] For more on control as corporate copyright owners' adoption of control as a main business model, see PATRY, *supra* note 7, at 26–30.

[47] *See* Menell, *supra* note 40, at 172–73.

The final recommendation in this context lies within the concept of deterrence. Policymakers and rights holders should generally abstain from threatening infringers. Deterrence, by civil, administrative or criminal law, has proven rather limited in the digital age.[48] The use of criminal law terminology to describe copyright infringements as theft or stealing, as outlined in Chapter 5, is generally misplaced and should be avoided. From a market perspective, it would also be wise for rights holders not to sue end users. Suing your customers is generally not a good idea, especially when some rights holders are perceived as greedy,[49] and the public generally contests such practice.[50] Otherwise stated, even if we accept deterrence theory it would be wise for stakeholders to reshape their relationship with consumers.

Apparently, rights holders have already embraced this final recommendation to some extent, at least in the United States: there, major lawsuits against more than 35,000 individuals were eventually abandoned by the market as a practice.[51] But not entirely. After some market players ceased their litigation against end users, others (sometimes called copyright trolls) began to embark on shakedown schemes.[52] Lawyers filed lawsuits against thousands of file sharers and threatened to disclose their identity unless they settled[53]; most suits related specifically to pornography.[54] Some simply sent threatening letters. It would not be surprising if these shakedown schemes are also linked to criminal copyright, through which actors could wave before end users the threat to approach state litigators. These schemes are not optimal for resolving the copyright puzzle in the digital age. Nor are they optimal for society.

*

The future of copyright – civil, administrative and criminal – depends greatly on new technologies. With the emergence of personal smart assistants like that of

---

[48] See Menell, *supra* note 1, at 298.

[49] For more on greed (by both industry and consumers), see Jane C. Ginsburg, *How Copyright Got a Bad Name for Itself*, 26 COLUM. J.L. & ARTS 61 (2002).

[50] See, e.g., Ben Depoorter, Alain Van Hiel & Sven Vanneste, *Copyright Backlash*, 84 S. CAL. L. REV. 1251, 1283–89 (2011); Menell, *supra* note 1, at 262.

[51] See Menell, *supra* note 1, at 360. While many scholars attempted to evaluate the deterrent effect of copyright litigation, it is fairly difficult to assess the scope of it. See, e.g., Stan J. Liebowitz, *File Sharing: Creative Destruction or Just Plain Destruction?*, 49 J.L. & ECON. 1 (2006); Cf. Peter DiCola, *Money from Music: Survey Evidence on Musicians' Revenue and Lessons for Copyright Incentives*, 55 ARIZ. L. REV. 301 (2013); Joel Waldfogel, *Copyright Protection, Technological Change, and the Quality of New Products: Evidence from Recorded Music Since Napster*, 55 J.L. & ECON. 715 (2012).

[52] See Menell, *supra* note 1, at 268.

[53] See Sarah Jacobsson Purewal, *Copyright Trolls: 200,000 BitTorrent Users Sued Since 2010*, PC WORLD (Aug. 9, 2011), https://www.pcworld.com/article/237593/copyright_trolls_200_000_bittorrent_users_sued_since_2010.html; Menell, *supra* note 1, at 268; Matthew Sag, *Piracy: Twelve Year-Olds, Grandmothers, and Other Good Targets for the Recording Industry's File Sharing Litigation*, 4 Nw. J. TECH. & INTELL. PROP. 133 (2006); For more on this practice, see generally Matthew Sag, *Copyright Trolling, An Empirical Study*, 100 IOWA L. REV. 1105 (2015).

[54] Matthew Sag, *Copyright Trolling, An Empirical Study*, 100 IOWA L. REV. 1105, 1108–09 (2015).

Amazon Echo or Google Home – capable among other things of playing music and reading books, the form of consuming content might change swiftly. When individuals are constantly surrounded by various technological devices that enable them to play almost any content they desire, at any given time, for a subscription fee (or for any other "currency" like advertisements or data), then consumers' willingness to pay could increase. If, for instance, people desire to use a technological device or service with embedded content consumption program, then many of them might pay the subscription fees regardless if they can also consume this content on other platforms.

CONCLUSION

It is extremely difficult, improbable, or impossible to forecast the future of copyright law. But if history has taught us anything in that regard it is that content owners will continue to pursue ways to maximize their profits, while many – if not most – end users will resist and find ways to consume their desired content. The fight will most likely go on. But simultaneously, market forces will play a significant part in reshaping this field. With the development of devices that enable individuals to consume media at their convenience, especially if these devices offer new and exciting ways of consumption, there will be little need to use the law.

Unfortunately, while technology could already enable this transition, reality seems to lag behind. As may be grasped from this book, criminal copyright still plays a rather large role in regulating conduct regarding copyright infringement. It should not. Criminal copyright should remain as an *ultima ratio* – a last resort – when all other means have failed. People should not go to prison or even simply fear criminal procedures for copyright infringement that is neither for a financial purpose nor financial gain. There are other more appropriate solutions that simultaneously preserve the rationale behind copyright protection and benefit the public. Legal intervention, in this instance, should be limited to the private realm. Public enforcement, which is not limited to the criminal realm, should be used only where appropriate, as Chapter 8 showed.

Even with such a transition the law will – perhaps rightly – still partake in protecting rights holders. In the realm of criminal copyright, the law must still grant the state the ability to hunt mega platforms that enable large-scale copyright infringement. Ultimately, these should be rare cases in which criminal law is invoked to protect rights holders, and the state should generally refrain from intervening otherwise. This would ensure a proper equilibrium between protection state and rights holders' interests and innovative technology that will enable change in the way we all consume content.

Conclusion

Copyright law is undergoing criminalization. Since the birth of *criminal copyright* in the nineteenth century, the copyright system has slowly blurred the distinction between civil and criminal infringements. Currently copyright law is over-criminalized and under-enforced, leaving a possible paradigm shift toward criminal copyright merely legislative, at least for the time being. Even with the gap in criminal copyright enforcement, over-criminalization of copyright law should not be disregarded. It has major ramifications for the legal system and for society, which greatly depends on the progress of knowledge and innovation.

Criminal Copyright has told the story of how a legal right in the private enforcement realm has become criminalized, by examining the movement of copyright criminalization from diverse angles. The story was first unfolded from an international perspective. As we came to learn, on the formal level criminal copyright is still mostly domestic in nature, while international agreements remain somewhat limited in their shaping criminal copyright domestically. Only in recent years have we witnessed some change of perception through ACTA and the TPP. The informal level, as represented through the Special U.S. 301 Reports, should not be overlooked and underestimated. These reports could greatly shape domestic criminal copyright legislation, therefore are crucial for the evaluation of criminal copyright worldwide.

From a domestic perspective, the story of criminal copyright has been told through an in-depth analysis of the criminalization process in the United Kingdom and the United States. The overview of copyright criminalization revealed that copyright law has not always contained criminal sanctions, and while some criminal provisions appeared in the nineteenth century, it was only in the 1970s in the United States, and in the 1980s in the United Kingdom, that criminal copyright became more substantial. However, even at that time copyright criminalization was rather limited in scope, and was applied only in cases of commercial infringement. Since the emergence of digital technology, chiefly the internet, copyright criminalization has grown to cover additional types of works, other categories of actions, and has increased monetary and nonmonetary sanctions.

Following the trajectory of criminal copyright, through a statistical analysis of enforcement and the use of the legislative increase of criminal copyright in both the United Kingdom and the United States in practice, I traced whether copyright was undergoing a paradigm shift toward a criminal-oriented law. Focusing on criminal copyright filings in the United States, I showed that the ongoing legislative process of copyright criminalization is not enforced in practice, or at least not to as large an extent as expected, causing a *criminal copyright gap* between the scope of criminal copyright liability and penalties and the infrequency of prosecution and punishment. I offered several possible explanations for the gap, revealing that the increase of criminal copyright legislation does not currently lead to a paradigm shift in copyright law.

For a better understanding of the process that could partially explain the possible *criminal copyright gap,* I searched for explanations, and examined different events that led to copyright criminalization. This book has examined internal and external reasons for copyright. Beginning with an internal analysis, I offered a taxonomy to understand criminal copyright, by conceptualizing the internal reasoning for copyright criminalization as an important part of a broader *framework of copyright expansion.* I argued that internal to copyright law, criminalization is another stage in an ongoing expansion of copyright holders' rights. This form of copyright expansion occurs in three dimensions: *first,* the negative impact on rights holders' business models, which is attributed mainly to the likely and actual increase of copyright infringements; *second,* the shift toward a pure property paradigm, i.e., the transformation of copyright law from a limited set of exclusive rights granted for purposes of a market regulation regime to a property regime; *third,* rights holders' increasing and successful political power over the legislature, which results in criminal legislation.

I continued exploring the criminalization of copyright law, and added external, non-copyright explanations to the picture. I located three main legal frameworks of criminal copyright: first, an *IP framework,* which locates copyright criminalization in a broader framework of Intellectual Property (IP) law; second, a *technological framework,* which views copyright criminalization as part of various legal fields that undergo criminalization due to similar technological developments; and third, a *legal framework,* which locates copyright criminalization in the wider context of the general criminalization of the law and covers both the IP and the technological frameworks. This part revealed that criminal copyright is part of other external frameworks – which sometimes affect each other as well and are all part of the general legal criminalization framework.

After establishing the various reasons for copyright criminalization, I moved on to examine the justifications and ramifications of criminal copyright, from the criminal and copyright law perspectives. By extracting the main elements of current principled approaches to criminalization to form an *integrated approach,* relevant to copyright criminalization, I continued with a normative evaluation of the process. This integrated approach, which provides a heuristic for policymakers under the various criminalization approaches, examines copyright criminalization through four consecutive measures of evaluation.

In the first measure, which determines whether the conduct is harmful, wrongful, or both, I argued that copyright infringement for commercial advantage or financial gain can meet the harm principle/wrongfulness requirements, while copyright infringement without commercial advantage or financial gain is not necessarily harmful and/or wrongful. On the second measure, which examines whether the state or society has a substantial interest in the statute's objective, I argued that criminal copyright generally satisfies this stage's requirements. Under the third measure, which audits whether criminal law will directly advance the substantial state interest and whether it is more efficient than other measures, I argued that under both *ex-ante* and *ex-post* evaluations criminal law can advance the state interest. Still, it is not necessarily the most optimal enforcement mechanism to handle all forms of infringement. Finally, on the fourth measure, which examines the consequences of criminalization, a cost-benefit analysis revealed that some types of activities support non-criminalization and as such criminal copyright is not always justified. Accordingly, this part of the book concluded that copyright criminalization should be carefully implemented, but only when the integrated approach supports it.

The book reveals that copyright law, at least in some jurisdictions, has become more criminally-oriented than ever before. Copyright law was initially a civil matter, providing only legal civil tools to respond to copyright infringements; the current reality is that criminal law plays an integral role in the copyright regime. However, the addition of criminal copyright is not always justified. The integrated approach to copyright criminalization acknowledges that criminal copyright is too broad and mostly not justified. And like criminalization processes in other legal fields, copyright law is unjustifiably over-criminalized.

The reasons behind the over-expansive nature of criminal copyright are embedded in the reasons behind the criminalization process generally. Using criminal copyright as an additional tool to respond to copyright infringement through the expansion of copyright protections is often misguided. As argued throughout this book, over-involvement and influence of the industry in shaping copyright law does not yield a well-crafted copyright policy and jeopardizes copyright law rationales. Legislating policies without attaching a structured examination could also prove dangerous for the criminal legal system. Thus, policymakers should take precautions against the over-involvement in the content industry's attempts to criminalize copyright law, as over-criminalization could critically threaten the existence of the copyright regime, as well as other fundamental rights.

The implications of such over-criminalization for the copyright regime are vast and potentially negatively affect rights holders, authors, end users, the government, and society. Mainly, it could undermine copyright law's goals by creating a chilling effect on the creation and use of works, while jeopardizing the growth of learning and culture designed for public welfare. It could stop people from creating new works; it could erode permitted usage of copyrighted materials; it could have a chilling effect on innovation; and it could cause rights holders actual harm due to negative economic ramifications. In other words, overprotection of copyright by means of criminal sanctions could be as harmful as underprotection, and could damp down dissemination of new ideas and forms of expression.

The normative claim behind *Criminal Copyright* is not meant to advocate copyright infringements. To achieve copyright goals, policymakers should respond to copyright infringements using available mechanisms. But not every mechanism is appropriate for every form of infringement, so only when a normative justification for this adaptation exists, namely through a formulated principled approach to criminalization, should policymakers carefully apply criminal sanctions to copyright law.

In considering criminalization of copyright law, policymakers should evaluate the consequences of criminal copyright for copyright and criminal law and for society. Moreover, they should implement criminal copyright only on the rare occasions when other methods are considered inappropriate or ineffective to meet the goal. Although rights holders have responded to copyright infringements in various non-criminal ways, it is hardly evident that these methods have been implemented to their full extent or even correctly. Accordingly, I urge rights holders to reconsider strategies against infringements, especially infringements without commercial gain, in the realization that the best solution to current, as well as future, legal battles to protect copyright could lie in the creation of new business models.

The future of criminal copyright is currently unknown and resides largely in the hands of the market. Copyright criminalization will most likely continue in the coming years, as copyright infringements are still relatively substantial and rights holders are still searching for methods to respond to them. If powerful market players invest more in innovative business models instead of lobbying for greater protection in the form of public enforcement, criminal copyright law could become a dead letter. Unfortunately, it is most likely that at least some rights holders will continue the copyright wars for greater means of control, and criminal copyright will most likely still play a substantial part in future battles. This situation is unfortunate, but remains to be further explored.

Index